Great Britain's Great War

JEREMY PAXMAN

PENGUIN BOOKS

PENGUIN BOOKS

Published by the Penguin Group
Penguin Books Ltd, 80 Strand, London WC2R ORL, England
Penguin Group (USA) Inc., 375 Hudson Street, New York, New York 10014, USA
Penguin Group (Canada), 90 Eglinton Avenue East, Suite 700, Toronto, Ontario, Canada M4P 2Y3
(a division of Pearson Penguin Canada Inc.)
Penguin Ireland, 25 St Stephen's Green, Dublin 2, Ireland (a division of Penguin Books Ltd)
Penguin Group (Australia), 707 Collins Street, Melbourne, Victoria 3008, Australia
(a division of Pearson Australia Group Pty Ltd)
Penguin Books India Pvt Ltd, 11 Community Centre, Panchsheel Park, New Delhi – 110 017, India
Penguin Group (NZ), 67 Apollo Drive, Rosedale, Auckland 0632, New Zealand
(a division of Pearson New Zealand Ltd)
Penguin Books (South Africa) (Pty) Ltd, Block D, Rosebank Office Park,
181 Jan Smuts Avenue, Parktown North, Gauteng 2193, South Africa

Penguin Books Ltd, Registered Offices: 80 Strand, London WC2R ORL, England

www.penguin.com

First published by Viking 2013
Published in Penguin Books 2014
001

Typeset by Jouve (UK), Milton Keynes
Printed in Great Britain by Clays Ltd, St Ives plc

ISBN: 978-0-670-91963-5

www.greenpenguin.co.uk

Let's not forget

Contents

List of Illustrations

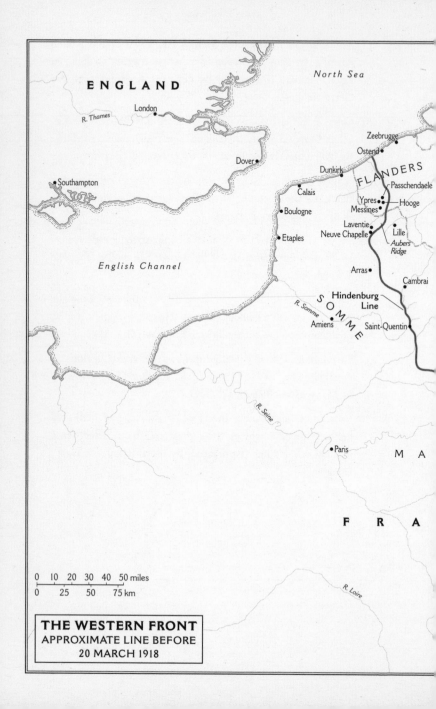

THE WESTERN FRONT
APPROXIMATE LINE BEFORE
20 MARCH 1918

Introduction

The Cigar Box

Uncle Charlie and his friends. They had no idea what modern war would be like.

There is a photo on the wall. It was taken, most probably, in the spring of 1915, and shows eight uniformed men in the jaunty confidence of youth, bedrolls slung over their shoulders. They stand, arms around each other's shoulders, caps askew, one with a cigarette in his mouth, another with a pipe. They smile cheerily. The bright spring sunshine leaves deep shadows on their foreheads. In the middle, arms folded, a young man with a heavy moustache leans on a roadsign: 'DANGEROUS! KEEP OFF THE TAR'. This is my great-uncle Charlie. He has a Red Cross badge on each shoulder and grins broadly.

In his entire military career Uncle Charlie won no medals for bravery, never advanced beyond the most junior rank in the army and almost certainly neither killed nor wounded a single German.

He had enlisted in the Royal Army Medical Corps and his job was to save lives, not to take them. The 1911 census records Charles Edmund Dickson as a twenty-year-old living in Shipley, working as a 'weaving overlooker' in one of west Yorkshire's numerous textile factories. Uncle Charlie looks a slightly unconvincing soldier, cutting none of the elegant dash of glamorous young officers like Rupert Brooke. He fills the uniform, for sure. In fact, he looks as if, with a bit of time, he could more than fill it.

On 7 August 1915 this bright young Yorkshireman, with his affable, cheery face, was killed in Turkey.

Uncle Charlie's is one of 21,000 names carved around the Helles Memorial, a great stone obelisk at the tip of the Gallipoli peninsula in Turkey, surrounded by fields of grain nodding in the breeze off the sea, and clearly visible to the boats that run up and down the coast from the Aegean to Istanbul. He was my mother's father's younger brother, dead well before she was born. Yet as children we were all familiar with him seventy or more years later – Uncle Charlie was a present absence. I often meant to ask my mother what she knew of how he had died, but I never did, and now she's dead I never will. Family legend had it that he signed up in the rush of naive, enthusiastic young recruits in 1914. Like most men of his background, he had almost certainly never been abroad before he travelled to his death on the far side of Europe.

How exactly he died may never be known, but the causes and circumstances of his death are easier to explain. His detachment of the Royal Army Medical Corps had been despatched to Gallipoli as part of First Lord of the Admiralty Winston Churchill's ill-conceived attack on the 'soft underbelly' of the enemy, its purpose being to relieve the stagnation of trench warfare in France and offer a decisive breakthrough. Clement Attlee, the 1945 Labour Prime Minister, once told Churchill that his Dardanelles adventure was 'the only imaginative conception' of the entire war. In truth, the scheme was one of the most wrong-headed, incompetently managed and murderous of the entire catastrophe. The idea had been for the Royal Navy to blast their way through the Dardanelles, the narrow strait that leads to Constantinople (as Istanbul was then called) and, by attacking Germany's ally, Turkey, to open a new front in the war. When the navy discovered that Turkish mines and well-positioned shore artillery made it impossible to force the strait, British generals compounded the disaster by putting tens of thousands of men ashore in an attempt to destroy the Turkish batteries and safeguard the sea passage from the land. They had underestimated both the difficulty of the terrain and the quality of the Turkish army: British and allied soldiers had to fight their way out of the sea and then scale cliffs and hillsides in the face of well-established Turkish machine-gun positions. After the best part of a year of misery British commanders admitted defeat. Captain Attlee was one of the officers in charge of the evacuation of the peninsula: the retreat from Gallipoli was the only successful part of the entire operation.

The family never learned precisely what killed Uncle Charlie. Was he machine-gunned to death? Was he one of the thousands who had been weakened by the dysentery and typhoid that quickly spread among the men, pinned down in disgusting conditions in the gullies below the enemy machine guns for days on end? The memory of some others who died there – bakers' sons from the Orkneys; gardeners and footmen from the royal estate at Sandringham; the almost 500 men of the Dublin Fusiliers; or the son of the vicar of Deal who won the Victoria Cross for repeatedly wading ashore under fire to rescue wounded men from the beaches – has been kept more conscientiously alive. The deaths of over 11,000 Australian and New Zealand soldiers at Gallipoli are venerated as a sacred part of their nations' histories.

All I know about Uncle Charlie is contained in an old, brown, broken-sided cigar box found among my mother's effects when she died in 2009. She never smoked cigars, so presumably it was passed to her complete with most of its contents. Inside, at the top of the small bundle of documents and effects, was the paper every family dreaded to receive: Army Form B 104-82.

Uncle Charlie must have made it clear when he signed up that his mother, Florina, was a widow, for the printed 'Sir', with which the form begins, has been scored out and replaced with a hand-written 'Madam'. The impersonal tone resumes with the printed sentence 'It is my painful duty to inform you that a report has this day been received from the War Office, notifying the death of —', and here the colonel in charge of Medical Corps administration at Aldershot has inserted into the blank spaces Charlie's name, rank and number, adding 'Number 34 Field Ambulance, of the Medi-terranean Expeditionary Force' in the space left blank for his unit. 'The cause of death was —', and here an entire line of the form is left empty, which the colonel has made no attempt to fill, just writing the single, unilluminating word 'wounds'. Personal effects, the form states, will be sent on later.

Lying underneath it in the cigar box is another form, apparently signed by the War Secretary, Lord Kitchener:

> The King commands me
> To assure you of the true sympathy
> Of His Majesty and The Queen
> In your sorrow.
>   Kitchener

Inside a cardboard tube is another mass-produced letter of condol-ence, a sheet of paper bearing the printed signature of the king, commemorating Private Charles Edmund Dickson for having joined those who had answered their country's call and 'passed out of the sight of men by the path of duty and self-sacrifice, giving up their own lives that others might live in freedom' and demanding that his name be not forgotten. A thick card envelope contains a 'Dead Man's Penny', a heavy bronze plaque about the size of a tea-saucer, decorated with a robed Britannia holding a trident in one hand and a garland in the other, with a growling lion at her feet. It is inscribed with Uncle Charlie's name and the words 'HE DIED FOR FREEDOM AND HONOUR.'

There is more in the box. Two days before Christmas 1920, Florina received another printed form, this time accompanying a medal – the 1914–15 Star – 'which would have been conferred upon Private C. Dickson had he lived'. In September 1921 – six years after her son's death, and almost three years after the signing of the Armistice – another official letter arrived, this time informing Uncle Charlie's mother that her dead son had been awarded the British War and Victory Medals. There were, apparently, some 6.5 million of these medals issued, sufficiently ubiquitous that, together with the earlier star, they were known as 'Pip, Squeak and Wilfred', after cartoon characters in the *Daily Mirror*. But the letter about Uncle Charlie's medals was treasured enough to be folded and tucked into the cigar box. Whoever gathered together these official documents had also included the residue of the state's intrusion into Florina's life: her 1917 sugar ration card, a copy of the certificate of Uncle Charlie's birth in 1891 in Shipley and that of her own death in 1924.

And that was almost all I knew about Uncle Charlie. A little research reveals that his was a very ordinary family: Florina's death certificate describes her as the widow of a 'Wholesale Grocers' Traveller'. Family legend had it that Charlie had faked his age when he signed up and that he was cut down by machine-gun fire as he waded ashore on his eighteenth birthday. The briefest glance at the papers in the box would have shown us that part of this was plainly untrue – that his twenty-fourth birthday had occurred almost six months before he was killed. But this imagined version of his death seems somehow to express a greater truth than the mere facts. How many other families in Britain have some similar ancestral story?

These stories fade by the year. My mother made the pilgrimage to seek out Uncle Charlie's name among the thousands etched into the wall of the Helles Memorial. Someone helped her find it, and it turned out to be so high above her head that when she posed for a photograph she could only point it out with the aid of a branch cut from a nearby tree. Then she plucked a few heads of lavender from a bush, recalled some words she had read of Mustafa Kemal

Atatürk – the father of modern Turkey and a veteran of the Gallipoli fighting – that all who had died there were now sons of
Turkey, picked three small pebbles from the ground, put them in
her handbag and climbed back on to the bus.

I doubt I shall ever go to see his memorial or that my children
will. In the one hundred years since it began, the First World War
has slipped from fact to family recollection to the dusty shelves of
history, too incomprehensible in its scale, too complicated in its
particulars, to be properly present in our minds. It is no longer our
fathers' or even our grandfathers' war but something that happened
to someone who might or might not have had our name, who possessed perhaps a recognizable nose or mouth, but who has nothing
really to do with us. The very last military survivors of 'the war to
end war' died in the early years of the twenty-first century, at which
point bloody experience gave way finally to print and theory, and
the whole thing is now as far distant from us as the battle of Waterloo was from Uncle Charlie when he died at Gallipoli in 1915.

In France, the killing fields of the Somme, where over a million men
shed blood, have long since returned to chalky grassland on which
local farmers grow wheat and barley, peas and sugar beet. Dozens of
roadside signs to this or that immaculately maintained cemetery testify that something awful once happened here. There are strange,
unnatural depressions in the ground, and if you kick the tilled earth
pieces of rusted metal, spent bullets and round grey shrapnel pellets
tell of another reality. Still, on a July afternoon, the sky is big, the
finches sing in the trees and the chalk-streams babble clear. The war is
long gone and, if not forgotten, it at least nestles comfortably among
a shared set of hazy assumptions: countless men mown down in the
mud, all victims of numbskulls in epaulettes, all slain for no purpose.

Even so, on a bone-chilling November afternoon at Tyne Cot
cemetery in Flanders, the war nourishes an emotional tourism,
where you might, as I have, come across half-a-dozen middle-aged
British visitors, all wearing poppies; twenty teenage German girls
in hired Australian army uniform (including puttees), which they
have matched with pink or purple bobble hats; and nine or ten

parties of Belgian primary schoolchildren. Some of these children are whooping and shouting as they scramble up the steps of the vast memorial cross, behaviour which would have scandalized the men who designed the cemeteries, but which is now encouraged by their teachers. A sullen Dutch teenage boy in another school party spits on a grave. There are poppies laid at individual plots and wreaths at the memorials, most of them bearing the name of a British school and adorned with a poem written by a student, in all of which the central message is the same: what a futile waste. Even the headstone of one Second Lieutenant Arthur Conway Young reads, 'Sacrificed to the Fallacy that War Can End War', for indeed this 'war to end war' did not do so. So what was it for? As the craters in the tilled ground near by attest to a more murderous life in the fields, the present lies as a palimpsest on the events of a century ago. Familiarity has not bred contempt so much as indifference.

The First World War has settled into our solid, unexamined prejudices, its causes and consequences submerged in sentiment, an episode of history that is more felt than thought about. If it is recalled at all, it is in black-and-white or sepia tones, grainy, dim and distant in a high-definition world, an impression which seems to confirm our belief that it was the product of (as well as an end to) our long-lost innocence, an express journey from naive enthusiasm to bitter disillusion.

Perhaps Uncle Charlie and his friends really did march off to war singing 'It's a Long Way to Tipperary'. Certainly, Julian Grenfell, eldest son of the sporting Lord Desborough and his society hostess wife, actually talked about it being 'like a picnic when you don't know where you're going to'. In November 1914 he wrote that 'It is all *the* best fun. One loves one's fellow man so much more when one is bent on killing him.' Six months later he was dead. In the generations since, we have all come to see the war through the eyes of Wilfred Owen in 1917:

> What passing-bells for these who die as cattle?
> Only the monstrous anger of the guns.

When Owen used the phrase 'Dulce et decorum est pro patria mori' ('It is sweet and right to die for one's fatherland') as the ironic title for another of his poems, he could assume his readers would get the bitter reference to Horace, whose original was meant in earnest. Google the Latin phrase now and the first 600 listings thrown up by the algorithm are all drawn from Owen's poem. It is fine verse – probably the best anti-war poem ever written – but was there really nothing more to the conflict that convulsed a continent than the 'old Lie'?

The First World War was as consequential as the Fall of Rome, the French Revolution, the invention of the nuclear bomb or the Al Qaeda attack on the New York World Trade Center. The immediate political repercussions were obvious: if so many young British, French and Russian citizens (to say nothing of Canadians, Australians, Indians, Irish, New Zealanders, Belgians and many others) had not lost their lives, a militaristic Germany would likely have built a European superpower. The thwarting of German ambition, however, created the conditions for the rise of fascism in Europe, as in Russia it set off the revolution that brought in seven decades of totalitarian rule, and thus the Cold War. The war finished the Ottoman empire and transformed Turkey from an Islamic sultanate to a constitutionally secular republic. It consigned the great aristocratic dynasties of the time, the Romanovs, the Habsburgs and the Hohenzollerns, to history.

In strictly numerical terms, the British did not suffer as badly as some other countries. But the war was the mechanism by which Britain became recognizably its modern self. Victorian time-travellers transported from 1880 to the spring of 1914 would have found themselves pretty much at home. If they had travelled on a further four years, they would have been baffled by what they saw.

There were over 700,000 British participants in this change who never lived to see the new society, so if the eight friends in Uncle Charlie's picture suffered at the same rate as the rest of the army, by 1918 four of them were dead, wounded or missing. There were so many copies of the miserable Army Form B 104-82 to be delivered that postmen resigned their jobs rather than face the sight of yet another family in tears on the doorstep.

The only way we can grasp the sheer scale of this loss is to simplify it, resulting in the received version of these vast and complicated events – the common man ordered to advance into machine-gun fire by upper-class twits sitting in comfortable headquarters miles away – a version that has sustained so many of us for generations. It is such an easy caricature. In 1936, David Lloyd George, who had been Prime Minister during the war, was talking of how 'the distance between the [generals'] chateaux and the dug-outs was as great as that from the fixed stars to the caverns of the earth', as if they *preferred* to be miles away from the action, when the truth was that in an age before radios, with communication by runner, messenger dog or carrier pigeon, the closer a commander was to the action, the fewer men he could control. The attitudes of many of today's grandparents were shaped by the 1960s musical *Oh! What a Lovely War* with the British commander, General Haig, manning a turnstile to charge visitors to watch the carnage, while staff officers played a game of leapfrog. A generation later and the same point of view underpinned the 1989 comedy series *Blackadder Goes Forth*. When General Melchett tells Captain Blackadder that he will be 'right behind him' in the charge over the top, Blackadder mutters, 'Yes, about thirty-five miles behind.' *Blackadder* was comedy – and rather a good one – yet it is now played to school classes by history teachers. It seems to have become much easier to laugh at – or cry about – the First World War than to understand it.

There is something unsatisfactory about all this received wisdom. Can British generals really have been as indifferent to the fate of their men as the image of 'lions led by donkeys' suggests? Siegfried Sassoon expressed it powerfully in his poem 'The General':

'Good morning; good morning!' the General said
When we met him last week on our way to the line.
Now the soldiers he smiled at are most of 'em dead,
And we're cursing his staff for incompetent swine.
'He's a cheery old card,' grunted Harry to Jack
As they slogged up to Arras with rifle and pack.

* * *

But he did for them both with his plan of attack.

The accusation of bluff stupidity and callous unconcern is as powerful now as when the poem was published in 1918. Let Uncle Charlie and his friends stand for all of the victims of military incompetence: the Gallipoli fiasco was distinguished by lamentable intelligence, poor planning, serious misjudgement and, in many cases, appalling leadership at the highest level. But is this adequate as a reading of the entire war? The most dim-witted high command would surely not have consciously planned to throw away soldiers' lives, and so make defeat more likely? Of course they blundered. But in the end the donkeys and the lions won. As for the poisonous legacy of war and the unrealized promises of peace, these surely were not the fault of the generals. Yet we are stuck with the default conviction that the First World War was an exercise in purposelessness.

That was not the prevailing view at the time. Wilfred Owen's 'Dulce et Decorum Est' was not published until after his death, when the war was well over, and the great harvest of anti-war memoirs and novels did not appear until ten years after the Armistice. It is simply nonsense to suggest there was generalized opposition to the war at the time it was being fought. On the contrary, Lord Kitchener's appeal for volunteers in the early days of the war had been so successful that lines at recruitment offices snaked for blocks down city streets. When he had predicted in August 1914 that the fighting could drag on for several years and would be won by what he called 'the last million men', his gloomy prediction was beyond the imagination of most of the cabinet and much of the military high command. Yet the unimaginable happened. Throughout it all, the resolve of the British people did not weaken. Charles Edmund Dickson and his cheery pals standing around the newly resurfaced road had joined up to embark upon an adventure. In that, they were naive. Yet, while there were serious mutinies in the German, French and Russian armies, there was nothing on a comparable scale among British soldiers. Why did men continue to fight if the thing was so obviously merely cruel, callous and futile? But continue to fight they did, and their families continued to support them and to suffer the separation, the anxiety, the rationing and the rest of the privations of wartime. They endured to victory. To understand how this was possible we need to get beyond the trite observation that the deaths of Uncle Charlie and his comrades were no more than a tragic waste. What aggravates our ignorance is the false assumption that we *do* understand the First World War. We need to cast ourselves back into the minds of these men and their families, and of their leaders, to try to inhabit the assumptions of their society rather than to replace them with our own.

I began this book after hearing a secondary schoolteacher set a homework essay in which her pupils were to answer the question 'How Does Wilfred Owen Show the Futility of War?' The question displays the easy, shared assumption on which so many of us approach the subject: the conviction not merely that this particular war was pointless but that *all* war is pointless. Yet most of us do not share the same prejudice about the Second World War – even if four times as many people conscientiously objected to it than to military service in the First World War. It seems to have become much easier to understand the 'Great War for Civilization' as poetry rather than history, and as anti-war poetry at that. How, one wonders, would the teacher explain to her students that after writing his celebrated denunciations of battle, Wilfred Owen returned to the Western Front to continue fighting, and, furthermore, described himself in his last letter to his mother as 'serene'? It was, he said, 'a great life'. The greatest of all war poets, Owen was killed before he ever had to explain it himself. His death confirmed his poetry's status, and that of the First World War, as the Urtext of the conviction that *all* war is futility.

It won't do. The first step towards a true understanding of the First World War is to recognize why so many people at the time believed it to be not only unavoidable but even necessary.

1. Tears and Cheers

Not the perfect read for the beach.

The deadline was midnight, Central European Time – eleven o'clock in London. A handful of the most senior members of the government sat together in the cabinet room at 10 Downing Street awaiting a message from Berlin. The room was poorly lit. No one spoke much. The eyes of the men flicked from the clock in the room to the door and back again, as the Chancellor of the Exchequer later recalled, hoping against hope for a knock that would announce the arrival of a telegram. A single telegraph cable remained open between Berlin and London, where an operator waited to receive a message from Germany that its government had acceded to the British demand that the Kaiser withdraw his troops from Belgium. Finally, the ministers heard Big Ben strike eleven. As they had expected and dreaded, the German government had simply not replied to the ultimatum.

The Chancellor, David Lloyd George – never a man to use one word where he might employ half a dozen – thought the chimes of the most famous clock in the world rang 'Doom! Doom! Doom! . . . Britain's most fateful hour since she arose out of the deep.' That, at least, was his recollection, twenty years later, of the fateful moment that Britain found itself at war. At the Admiralty, Winston Churchill, not yet forty and in political charge of the most powerful navy in the world, despatched the signal to all ships: 'Commence hostilities against Germany.'

The mood on the streets was very strange indeed. Obeying some tribal instinct to gather outside the chief's hut at times of crisis, a crowd had assembled at the gates of Buckingham Palace. Their precise feelings are hard to gauge. They were certainly not baying for German blood (just as well, since the royal family itself was German). When the last chime sounded they burst into 'God Save the King'. A reporter from *The Times* watched as they began running home shouting 'War! War! War!' They were excited. But about what?

At government communication headquarters, the telegraph operator sent the signing-off signal *GN*, meaning *Good Night*, to Berlin. It was almost midnight on 4 August 1914. The following morning orders were given for commandeered vessels to drag the seabed and cut all telegraph cables to Germany. Direct communication between the two countries would not be restored for four long years.

At dusk the previous evening the Foreign Secretary, Sir Edward Grey, had finally given up his attempts to prevent the conflict. A clever, solitary man who loved birds and fly-fishing – eccentricities which baffled the metropolitan elite – Grey was gaunt and exhausted after what had been the diplomatic equivalent of three-dimensional chess. There was now not a gambit, not an idea, not a hope left. Conflict had come to seem inevitable since 2 August, when the Germans had given Belgium the choice of surrender or invasion.

The British had presented their ultimatum to Germany as a matter of obligation: over seventy years previously a British government had signed the 1839 Treaty of London, guaranteeing Belgium's neutrality. The Belgian king had now appealed frantically for British protection, and by a large majority the British cabinet had decided that they would have to commit troops unless the Germans backed down. On the evening of 3 August, Sir Edward Grey looked out of the window of his office on a lamplighter illuminating the gas lights in a courtyard below and delivered himself of the plangent comment that 'The lamps are going out all over Europe. We shall not see them lit again in our lifetime.'

How on earth had it happened? It was not as if Britain had any ambitions in Europe. For the best part of a century, its main objective there had been merely to ensure a balance of anxiety among other European states so that none was sufficiently powerful to menace Britain's overseas empire. To protect its worldwide interests, which were what really mattered, Britain had the biggest navy in the world, but the smallest army of all the big powers in Europe. By chance, at the height of the finest summer in recent memory, much of the British fleet had been practising mobilization drills off the coast of Portsmouth. Watching events in Europe, Winston Churchill cautiously decided to keep the warships marshalled, just in case – it had been obvious for well over a decade that Germany had great-power ambitions, of which the Kaiser's determination to build a naval fleet to rival that of the British was the most telling evidence. Moreover, he had just opened the newly widened Kiel canal, 60 miles long and large enough to allow German battleships to slip from the Baltic into the North Sea – a sea that the British considered to be 'theirs'.

Britain in 1914 was, after all, an immensely self-confident country whose power had grown and grown for a century: the British people were accustomed to senior status in international affairs and were used to military victories large and small. The country commanded the biggest empire in history and dominated world trade: the empire-builder Cecil Rhodes declared that to be born

English was to win first prize in the lottery of life. For the chosen people, continental Europe was a distraction. Several newspapers had loftily reassured their readers that there was no need for Britain to get involved in continental squabbles involving arthritic powers like Austria-Hungary or parvenus like Germany. Besides, the British government had more urgent troubles to deal with closer to home: Ireland looked to be on the brink of civil war between nationalists, who considered the British presence there an act of colonialism, and northern unionists desperate to preserve rule from London. The British ambassador to France, a self-important little man who nonetheless grasped the threat from Germany, had met Grey a few weeks earlier to report the menacing storm brewing on the continent and found that all the Foreign Secretary wished to discuss was 'cricket, football and fishing', or so the ambassador claimed.

In fact, Grey had been worrying himself sick about events in Europe ever since, on a sunny day in late June, the heir to the throne of Austria-Hungary and his wife had been murdered in Sarajevo, capital of the recently annexed province of Bosnia-Herzegovina. There were hopes that this might perhaps turn out to be just another event in a part of the world that was already too full of events, and indeed not a single senior political figure from elsewhere in Europe had bothered to cancel their holiday plans to attend the funeral (not even, for that matter, the elderly Austro-Hungarian emperor). Perhaps, it was thought, cool heads would prevail again.

But what had begun in an obscure, squabbling corner of Europe could not be contained there. A month later, on the evening of 23 July, Austria-Hungary delivered an ultimatum to Serbia, which it held responsible for the assassination. The Austro-Hungarian empire was rather like a cross old man – a foot-stamping palsied version of its grand former self, outraged and angry and therefore dangerous. It demanded, among other things, that Serbia allow imperial officials to investigate the conspiracy. In London, the Austrian ambassador called on Sir Edward Grey to attempt to enlist British sympathy – after all, the British empire was in the habit of issuing threats to uncooperative peoples elsewhere in the world, and enforcing them by bombardment. But Grey told him that Britain was worried about the dangers of setting off a full-scale war in Europe. He feared – rightly – that Russia would certainly intervene in support of Serbia, which would mean that both France (bound to Russia in alliance) and Germany (bound to Austria-Hungary) would come in to help their respective sides. When the Foreign Secretary recounted the Austrian demands of Serbia to the rest of the cabinet, Winston Churchill had concluded that it seemed 'absolutely impossible that any State in the world could accept it, or that any acceptance, however abject, would satisfy the aggressor'. As he remembered it later, 'The parishes of Fermanagh and Tyrone faded back into the mists and squalls of Ireland, and a strange light began immediately, but by perceptible graduations, to fall upon and grow upon the map of Europe.'

The Liberal Prime Minister, Herbert Henry Asquith, had come to a similarly gloomy conclusion – the situation in Europe was 'about as bad as it can possibly be'. Yet he clung desperately to the hope that Britain might be able to stay out of it, writing to the object of his devotions, Venetia Stanley, on 24 July that 'we are within measurable distance of a real Armageddon which would dwarf the Ulster and nationalist volunteers to their true proportion. Happily there seems to be no reason why we should be anything more than spectators.' Sir Edward Grey fumbled towards a possible plan for Britain to join with France, Italy and Germany in a plea to the Russians to hold back. It got nowhere.

The confrontation with Germany which seems so inevitable from the perspective of history – and indeed which had been frequently discussed at senior levels of government and the military – did not seem inevitable to everyone. All manner of opinions were represented around the cabinet table. Senior figures in the Liberal government were vehemently against any thought of intervention and much of the cabinet was determinedly against the possibility of war, with five members, including David Lloyd George, looking ready to resign if Britain were to take any military action. Asquith's friend the Quaker MP Joseph Pease lay awake at night worrying about what course to steer (and later tried to persuade his son not to join the army). Sir Edward Grey thought that there was a real danger of the government imploding.

Winston Churchill was another case altogether, telling his wife that 'Everything tends towards catastrophe and collapse. I am interested, geared up and happy. Is it not horrible to be built like that?' Churchill had spent Sunday 26 July playing with his children on the beach at Cromer in Norfolk, and by the time he returned to London the Admiralty had implemented his advice for the fleet not to disperse after their manoeuvres. Yet even at this point there were fervent hopes that it might all come to nothing. How on earth could some obscure flash of Balkan nationalism imperil an entire continent? Anxiety, hope and gloom contended against each other. There was very little enthusiasm for war in Britain.

Elsewhere in Europe, though, blood was up. Faced with the anger of its powerful neighbour, Serbia had accepted most of the Austrian ultimatum. But it was not enough. In Vienna, a mob tried to storm the Serbian legation, while the Austrians obtained a German promise of support for massive retaliation. Asquith observed that the Austrians – 'quite the stupidest people in Europe (as the Italians are the most perfidious)' – were behaving like bullies. Russia, meanwhile, self-anointed protector of the Slavs, remained outraged on behalf of Serbia, and Asquith could not see how France could stand aside if Russia were drawn into the confrontation, given the alliance between the two countries. Winston Churchill ordered troops to seize two almost finished battleships being built in Britain that were intended to be the glory of the Ottoman navy.

The cabinet had been meeting every day, sometimes twice a day. Grey was assured by the German ambassador, Prince Lichnowsky, that his country did not want war. Nor, he said, did Austria. Lichnowsky begged Britain to remain neutral in any coming confrontation. But Grey was in a bind. Ten years earlier Britain and France, once described by an eighteenth-century British ambassador to Paris as 'natural and necessary enemies', had signed an Entente Cordiale, or 'friendly understanding'. It had been accompanied by the grandest diplomatic hoop-la, with reciprocal state visits and much doffing of unusual hats, but in essence it had been an attempt to divide up contested areas of the world between two competing empires. Under the terms of the deal the French would not challenge British rule in Egypt if they were allowed to swagger about in Morocco. France would give up fishery rights in Newfoundland and in exchange the British would leave the country free to build colonies in west Africa, and the two nations chopped up south-east Asia between them. Lord Grey had assured the British people that 'there are no unpublished agreements which would restrict or hamper the freedom of the Government or of Parliament to decide whether or not Great Britain should participate in a war', but in reality this assurance was not at all what it appeared. As long ago as 1906, he had disclosed to the cabinet that British protestations of affection 'have created in France a belief that we should help her in war . . . All the French officers take this for granted . . . If the expectation is disappointed, France will never forgive us.' Not to come to the aid of the French would wreck Britain's position in the world. The empire had struck back: what had seemed a civilized – though, as it turned out, hubristic – means of carving up the world had become a snare.

The sense of obligation was not universally shared, however, and it certainly did not amount to a formal commitment in the shape of a treaty to be used as public justification. Whatever the French may have felt, the Entente Cordiale was an imperialist arrangement. Could the right to trawl for Newfoundland cod really be a reason to send British citizens to risk their lives in a place they had done their best to avoid for a century? The British cabinet was deeply split. Influential voices argued that reluctance to join a confrontation which was spreading from Sarajevo to Vienna, Berlin, Moscow and Paris was not a sign of weakness but a way of buying time: uncertainty about what Britain might do could perhaps stay Germany's hand against France, while if Britain were to appear too supportive of Russia it might embolden the government there to attack Austria. Others argued, though, that the agonizing in cabinet was counter-productive. At least one of the men who sat at the cabinet table later claimed that war might have been averted altogether if only they had been united and given Grey the support he needed to tell Germany exactly what would happen if it persisted with plans for military domination of the continent.

The most irrelevant figure in all this had been the German ambassador in London, Prince Lichnowsky, a sophisticated, conscientious man who had been recalled from retirement on his country estate to take the ambassadorial post. He rather admired Grey, liked England and recognized how high the stakes had become. As the crisis deepened he had sent a series of cables to Berlin, begging his government to accept British suggestions of mediation. He had never believed in the Triple Alliance of Germany, Austria-Hungary and Italy, which was the cornerstone of German foreign policy, and privately felt he was being asked to defend a heresy and commit 'a sin against the Holy Ghost'. He was unable to understand what Germany gained from its guarantee to Austria-Hungary, yet could see clearly the damage that war would do to his country and to the rest of the continent. Lichnowsky was well liked by much of the British establishment, but unfortunately he was out of touch with his country and out of his depth. His recently united country was quite clearly the coming power in Europe and increasingly resentful that it did not have the imperial possessions which hung about Britain and France, or even around decaying edifices like Russia and Austria-Hungary.

Germany had, then, been waiting for an opportunity. It also had a plan, long in preparation. Now it required ruthless execution. The country had the great geographical advantage of sitting at the heart of Europe, and had been preparing for war for years: railway lines, for example, had been laid to the borders of

Luxembourg, Belgium and Holland, where they terminated in stations for which there was no conceivable commercial need. German ambitions were personified in 'The All Highest War Lord', the Kaiser, with his dressing-up box full of military uniforms and his passion for a German empire to justify them. The biggest military obstacle for the Germans looked to be Russia, with its enormous standing army of 1.4 million men. The Russian army was known to be badly trained and equipped and the country so backward that weeks would pass before it was ready to fight. German war plans therefore required an attack first on France, which was bound by treaty to aid Russia and was assumed to be able to mobilize much more quickly. This in turn required the marching of the German army through neutral Belgium, which had paltry defences. In Berlin, the case for swift action was unanswerable.

In Britain, however, the prospect of a European war had provoked noisy opposition. 'We must not have our Western civilisation submerged in a sea of blood to wash out a Servian conspiracy,' thundered the Liberal *Daily News* using the then current spelling. 'TO HELL WITH SERVIA!' screamed the posters on the sides of buses promoting Horatio Bottomley's nationalistic rag *John Bull*. To many educated Britons, while Germany was undoubtedly a militarized society, it was also the closest kindred spirit of all the nations of Europe. Quite apart from the royal family, products in every British home – Persil washing powder, Nivea face-cream, the wonder drug aspirin, all manner of toys and cameras – were German inventions. The Kaiser even hummed along to Gilbert and Sullivan.

Yet by the end of July the British had put the army and navy on precautionary alert and warned reservists not to be out of touch.

On Saturday 1 August, France had mobilized its army and Germany had declared war on Russia. Early the following morning, aware that it would take weeks before the Russians could assemble their forces properly, Germany had invaded Luxembourg. Since the main function of Luxembourg's armed forces was to provide a ceremonial guard for the Grand Duke, the occupation required no more than a few car-loads of troops. When a local gendarme protested that the soldiers were on neutral soil, he was told, 'We know that. Shut up or you'll be arrested.' The fate of this little principality was of no great concern to Britain, but if German forces were to cross into Belgium, intending to knock out France before it could come to the aid of Russia, everything might change. At this point, said Asquith – who admired his Foreign Secretary's principles and had decided that he would stick by him, come what may – Grey became 'violently pro-French'. Hoping for the best was no longer an option.

But that Sunday – 2 August – when the cabinet met from 11 to 2, some members still believed that Britain might yet be able to remain neutral. Lord Morley, for example, considered that if Britain stayed out of the war it might play a decisively helpful role in rebuilding the continent, instead of stoking a hatred that would last for at least a generation between 'two great communities better fitted to understand one another than any other pair in Europe'. Some ministers argued that Britain should state that it would stay out of the war unless it was attacked. But Grey was insistent that Britain would have no alternative but to enter the war if Belgium was invaded. He had a meeting with the French ambassador planned for 2.30. At previous encounters the ambassador had told him that France had deliberately kept its north-eastern coast undefended because it had been relying on the British. Sometimes at these encounters the ambassador broke down and wept when he heard the Foreign Secretary say that Britain had not yet decided whether it would come to France's aid. Grey informed the cabinet that he might feel obliged to resign if he could not reassure the ambassador.

This threat certainly persuaded some of the waverers around the table, and the cabinet agreed on the line of least resistance: if the German fleet came into the Channel or North Sea to attack France, the Royal Navy would give the country all the protection in its power. It looked like a triumph of stop-gap solution over the sort of long-term strategic thinking advocated by people like Lord Morley, one of the last of the great nineteenth-century Liberals. But Morley's judgement was warped by his own pro-German, anti-Russian feelings and a long-standing tendency to avoid hard choices by threatening resignation. It is very difficult to see how the aggressors' particular combination of pig-headedness and ambition – of Austria for asserting the pretence of authority, of Germany for the perks of power – could have been avoided indefinitely. And as the British ambassador in Berlin had already told Grey, Germany had Austria-Hungary under its thumb. Both countries, moreover, were deaf to offers of mediation.

It was no longer a question of honouring treaties or offering reassurance to countries more directly menaced. German ships in the waters around the British Isles might be able to impose a blockade and were certainly a threat to national security. If Britain wished to remain domestically secure and the pre-eminent world power, there was really no alternative to an ultimatum.

In the wake of such a momentous decision, political resignations were unavoidable. Despite frantic attempts by Asquith to persuade him to stay, John Burns, the first working man to achieve cabinet office, resigned, correctly pointing out that there was no military alliance with France, and that to threaten the Germans at sea must lead to a declaration of war on land. Burns believed he had an 'especial duty' to dissociate himself and the working class 'from such a universal crime as the contemplated war will be'. He was weeping as he told his friends of his decision: the ambitions of continental politicians stood to destroy a government which had believed its role was not international war but domestic social reform. Anxious that a weak and defeated Germany could lead to a rampaging Russia, a distressed Lord Morley also resigned, but because he was seventy-five and had a record of conscience-gestures this was taken as less of a political blow. Later there was more salt-water when two other cabinet ministers threatened to quit and Asquith tearfully, and successfully, begged them to stay their hands. On the afternoon of Sunday 2 August the Foreign Secretary did what he often did when he was anxious – he took himself off to London Zoo, to spend an hour in the aviary.* It hardly seemed to help – a friend who watched him at the Zoo a week later saw a man 'very distraught & full of preoccupations'.

At this point Grey had received an apparent assurance from Germany that if Britain were to stay out of the war, there would be no attack on the French coast. He declined the offer, which led Lord Morley to ask himself 'why?' It was a good question, to which the only answer was that by this stage no one was willing to believe a word coming out of Berlin. Yet what, Morley mused to himself, would be gained by war? If others wished to fight, then so be it: once the smoke of the battlefields had cleared from the skies of Europe 'England might have exerted an influence not to be gained by a hundred of her little Expeditionary Forces.' At the very least, it was a better prospect than the loss of a generation. Lord Morley may have been old and emotional, but his question deserves to be taken seriously. Was there a choice? It remains one of the great what-ifs of our history. Since the Entente Cordiale was not a formal mutual defence treaty with France, it might have been possible for London to ignore the desperate cries from Paris. Yet to have abandoned France to its fate would likely have left most of Europe under German control, and domination of continental Europe by a single power had been a nightmare the British had fought and schemed against for over 300 years. Once the Germans held both France and Belgium, they would have controlled the Channel ports from Ostend and Zeebrugge to Brest, which could have been used as bases for the German navy. As to Lord Morley's suggestion that, if it remained aloof, Britain might play a more effective role in constructing the world that would emerge after the fighting, it is worth noting that the United States had a similar choice in 1917: President Wilson concluded that if the

* 'It opens a door through which self-consciousness escapes and leaves him free for a time from moral doubts and strivings.' Sir Edward Grey, *The Charm of Birds* (London, 2001; first pub. 1927), p. 259.

country wanted to have a part in shaping the post-war world, it would first have to be part of the war. Had Britain been a Switzerland, ready merely to feast on the folly of others, perhaps indifference would have been a possibility. But the British political class, most of the country's newspapers, its business elite and many of its people had come to the conclusion that their small archipelago in the north Atlantic had a special destiny in the world, which Rudyard Kipling had defined as the white man's burden, or moral mission, to be pursued, if necessary, at the point of a gun. Kipling had been trying to justify imperialism in the developing world. A distorted echo of that conviction now underpinned the loyalty which Asquith and Grey felt for their fellow white men in France.

At the start of that weekend, Asquith had believed that perhaps a majority of his MPs were against war. But by the Sunday the leader of the Conservative opposition – which had won only two fewer seats at the last general election – declared his party's wholehearted support for British intervention. Asquith and Grey had the support they needed to act.

Matters came to a head on Monday 3 August, when the Belgian king appealed to George V for Britain to defend his country. Unlike the arguments about precisely what duty was owed to France, this was an urgent question which demanded an urgent answer, for Belgian neutrality had been guaranteed by Britain seventy-five years earlier. That afternoon Grey stood up in the House of Commons and told parliament what he feared was about to happen. The place was packed, the central aisle crammed with extra chairs. Grey's speech matched the gravity of the moment. The king of the Belgians had begged Britain for 'diplomatic intervention . . . to safeguard the integrity of Belgium'. But, Grey asked, 'What can diplomatic intervention do now?' To loud cheers, he declared that Britain had a vital interest in the independence of Belgium. The Foreign Secretary spoke for about an hour, a bleak message, delivered slowly, thoughtfully and persuasively. In theory it might have been possible for Britain to ignore a treaty signed before Asquith, Grey and most of the House of Commons had

been born – after all, Germany (more precisely Prussia) had also
been a signatory. But, Grey claimed, the country had a duty to
Belgium. The speech was striking for the way it mixed notions of
national honour with national self-interest. A full-scale European
war was inevitable, he explained, and 'we are going to suffer, I am
afraid, terribly in this war whether we are in it or whether we
stand aside. Foreign trade is going to stop, not because the trade
routes are closed, but because there is no trade at the other end.'
Moreover, if Britain were to stand aside from the war, the country
would be powerless to undo any changes to the European balance
of power at the end of it. And, this being the judgement of a government with a unique ethical responsibility, said Grey, 'I am quite
sure that our moral position would be such as to have lost us all
respect.' It was on the evening after this speech that Grey looked
out from the Foreign Office and delivered his mournful sentence
about the lights going out all over Europe.

A decent man had failed. Yet much of the crisis of 'national
honour' was of his own making: there were few other figures in
public life so enthusiastic about the relationship with France that
was now to cost so many British lives. Sir Edward lasted a couple
more years in cabinet until, his eyesight failing fast, he left the
world of politics to spend more time on the riverbank and contemplating the life of birds. He had always seemed a patrician,
nineteenth-century figure, yet it is hard to believe that a politician
with a keener ambition and sharper elbows – a Winston Churchill
or a David Lloyd George – would necessarily have done any better
in avoiding war. Rather the reverse. The Chancellor of the
Exchequer, Lloyd George – who laid aside his misgivings and
threats of resignation, and two years later became wartime Prime
Minister – reflected later that 'the nations slithered over the brink
into the boiling cauldron of war without any trace of apprehension or dismay.'

Asquith worried that the reluctance to go to war of some of the
cabinet did not seem to be shared by large sections of the public,
who were swept up in the excitement. He complained that 'we are

now always surrounded and escorted by cheering crowds of loafers and holidaymakers.' A British Neutrality Committee, dedicated to keeping Britain out of the looming conflict, held its first meeting on 4 August, and its last on 5 August.

Political discussion in government was now not about what to do but how to do it. Activity became frenetic – so many telegrams were despatched from Whitehall that there were clerks working thirty-six hours at a stretch. At lunchtime on 4 August confirmation came of the German invasion of Belgium. In one last vain gesture, the British ambassador in Berlin was instructed to repeat the now redundant request for assurances that Germany would respect Belgian neutrality. If he did not receive such an undertaking, Britain's diplomatic staff were to collect their papers and prepare to leave the country.

That evening – a couple of hours before the deadline expired – a news agency despatch claimed that Germany had declared war on Britain. A Foreign Office official was immediately sent to the German embassy in London with a reciprocal British declaration of war. An hour later, it turned out that the news report was wrong. Another official was sent to retrieve the document, in order that a rewritten declaration could be sent along when the deadline expired.

The German ambassador, Prince Lichnowsky, suffered an emotional collapse. When the American ambassador visited him on 5 August the prince received him in his pyjamas: it was three o'clock in the afternoon. The American described him to President Wilson as 'a crazy man'. Asquith felt genuinely sorry for 'the poor Lichnowskys: they are broken-hearted, and she spends her days in tears'. She was not the only one. When Grey explained the terms of the British ultimatum to the US ambassador, he too was crying.

Unfortunately, the cabinet's decision to go to war came too late for the humorous magazine *Punch*, which was already at the printers. On the morning of 5 August, it carried an article by the man who would later create *Winnie-the-Pooh*, A. A. Milne, claiming that the 'war in Eastern Europe' was no business of ours. There was also a piece of doggerel by the magazine's editor, beginning:

> Well, if I must, I shall have to fight
> For the love of a bounding Balkanite;
> But O what a tactless choice of time,
> When the bathing season is at its prime!
> And how I should hate to miss my chance
> Of wallowing off the coast of France.

This sort of tone would soon come to be seen as distastefully inappropriate. But *Punch* was not alone in its failure to recognize what was about to happen. Even the Germans could not really believe that Britain would fight for the sake of Belgium – according to the British ambassador the German Chancellor claimed that his country had been stabbed in the back for the sake of a 'scrap of paper'. It was, however, much easier for the masters of British public opinion, both politicians and press, to embrace what looked like a high-minded crusade than a political obligation or defensive necessity. And this was to be a war in which the mass media would be noisier and more influential than ever before. The *Daily News* suddenly stopped talking of Serbia going to hell and spoke instead of a war that had to be won to save European civilization. Not even *John Bull* screamed 'TO HELL WITH BELGIUM!', for it was the fate of Belgium that gave expression to moral purpose. Lloyd George, the great speechifier of the age, saw the cause as some sort of moral purgative, asserting that 'the great flood of luxury and sloth which had submerged the land is receding.' Even Utopian cyclists like H. G. Wells were seduced, writing in *The War That Will End War*: 'We began to fight because our honour and our pledge obliged us, but . . . we have to destroy or be destroyed.' Wells claimed to see the war not as a conflict between nations but as an enterprise on behalf of humankind, a war 'to exorcise a world-madness and end an age'. This would be 'the last war', 'a war for peace', at the end of which there would be no more Kaisers and no more Krupps, the great German arms manufacturer. Wells' vision was as intoxicating as much of his science fiction, and about as plausible. As Asquith put it on 6 August, Britain was fighting 'not for aggression, not for the maintenance even of its own selfish interest . . . but in defence of principles the maintenance of which is vital to the civilization of the world'. It is this tone of moral righteousness, so familiar to us from much smaller, more recent conflicts, which makes the enormous disaster that follows so especially poignant.

By the time of Asquith's declaration, the killing had already begun. On the night of 4 August, while the British government sat awaiting the German response to their ultimatum, Berlin had despatched a passenger ferry, the *Königin Luise*, into the North Sea. Normally the vessel carried tourists from Hamburg to the Heligoland islands off Germany's North Sea coast. She had now been repainted in the black, brown and yellow colours of the British Great Eastern Railway ferry service, which ran between Harwich and the Hook of Holland. The skipper of a British fishing trawler noticed that the crew of this ferry appeared to be dropping strange objects over her side. He reported his worries to the commander of HMS *Amphion*, a light cruiser leading a flotilla of warships off the east coast of England. Under the 1907 Hague Convention's attempt to civilize the conduct of war, any merchant vessels commandeered for military purposes were to be obviously marked as belonging to a combatant navy, yet the ferry was clearly laying mines. The Royal Navy ships gave chase and the *Königin Luise* fled, throwing more mines over the side as she went.

The British held decided views about what constituted 'proper' warfare. The submarine, for example, had been described by the editor of the *Naval and Military Record* as 'not an honest weapon. It suggests the footpad, the garrotte and the treacherous knife dug in the opponent's back when he is off guard.' Mines were also despised as 'cowardly'. Asquith considered them 'a hellish device which every civilised nation except the Germans wanted to abolish at the Hague years ago'. The *Königin Luise* had laid 180 of them.* The British warships chasing her opened fire, and by lunchtime on 5 August, the first day of British involvement in the war, the German ferry was lying on her side, sinking. *Amphion* retrieved the survivors – some of whom had been shot by their own officers as they leapt into the sea – and locked them into a secure compartment in the cruiser's bow. The British force then turned for home.

At this point the hapless German ambassador, Prince Lichnowsky, re-enters the story. The time for diplomacy being over, the British government had provided the poor man with a special train to carry him from London to Harwich, where they had laid on a guard of honour of British soldiers. The prince then boarded a *genuine* Great Eastern Railway company ferry to carry him to Holland, for his onward journey back to Berlin. As a mark of courtesy, the captain of the ferry ordered the German flag to be flown. 'I was treated like a departing Sovereign,' the prince fondly recalled later. But soon afterwards the ferry was spotted by lookouts from the cruiser HMS *Amphion*, still making her way home after her recent brush with the disguised *Königin Luise*. The cruiser fired a warning shot. Fortunately for the ambassador, the ferry captain swiftly hauled down the German flag and ran up the Red Ensign, the colours of the British merchant marine. The ambassador was spared to return to the country he had so fruitlessly represented and there he was put out to grass. His mission had been wrecked, he told his friends on returning to Germany, 'not by the wiles of the British but by the wiles of our policy'.

At 6.30 the following morning, with *Amphion* approaching the Thames estuary and most of the crew at breakfast, she struck one of the mines laid by the *Königin Luise*. An intense fire broke out on board and the ship quickly became uncontrollable. Surviving crew members – as well as those captive seamen from the *Königin Luise* who had not been killed by the mine they had laid – took to life-

* All told, the Germans would lay 43,000 mines during the war, most of them off British coasts.

boats and were rescued by other British vessels, from where they watched as *Amphion* drifted on, struck another mine and sank. Over 130 of her crew became the first British casualties of the war, along with nineteen of the German crew which had laid the mines.

Unlike continental states, which were accustomed to the possibility of armed incursion across borders, the English had not experienced a foreign invasion for almost a thousand years. That August there was something of an overreaction to the danger the country now faced. Residents of England's south coast were advised to be prepared to flee to the countryside, to follow the directions of special constables at crossroads, and then to 'take to the fields when necessary'. Miles of useless trenches were dug. Barbed wire was unrolled on beaches. Instructions warned the people of Folkestone that if the army had no use for any animals they could not evacuate, they were to be 'rendered useless to the enemy'. Envisaging the horrific possibilities of a marriage between powered flight and modern high explosives, notices appeared at east coast police stations instructing householders to burn as few lights as possible at night. Buildings were commandeered to be turned into temporary hospitals. To ensure no moral infiltration, meanwhile, German and Austrian music was removed from the programme of Promenade concerts later in the month, Wagner night being replaced by an evening of music composed in Russia and France.

Meanwhile, rumours quickly spread of atrocities committed on the continent by the invading German army: English convents, for example, were said to be sheltering Belgian girls who had had their hands lopped off; there had been much rape. Plans were made proposing that, if the Germans were to land on English soil, the contents of wine cellars would be poured away to prevent the invaders getting drunk and behaving similarly. Special constables were instructed to draw up lists of foreigners living in their area. American tourists rushed home, some of them so desperate to leave that they actually clubbed together to buy a ship, the *Viking*, in which to travel. There was frenzied activity in grocery shops as customers arrived with suitcases and dustbins to carry off panic-bought provisions, and queues at banks as some of the rich withdrew their gold. Workers in East End sweatshops found themselves laid off until their employers could work out the effect of war on the fashion trade. Boy Scouts began guarding tunnels and bridges. In schools, girls learned to practise bandaging on pretend victims. Sock-knitting spread like an epidemic among civilians, until the War Office declared that the soldiers of Britain's comparatively small army had enough socks, thank you. The headmaster of Marlborough House prep school in Kent was said to have received an unexpected parcel from India. He unwrapped it to discover a letter from the father of two of his pupils. It also contained a loaded pistol. If the Germans landed in Britain, the father begged, would the headmaster please use the gun to shoot them?

In the absence of any real evidence of what a European war would be like, there was a very strange – and dangerous – quality to this anticipation, a mixture of anxiety and eagerness. On the one hand there was fear of the unknown, on the other certainty of conviction. This confidence meant that the greater their fears were, the more just their cause, leading to a self-perpetuating cycle of paranoia and passion. Witnesses described crowds of tens of thousands on the streets of London, singing the national anthem. On the evening of Sir Edward Grey's 3 August speech to parliament about the awful implications of war the philosopher Bertrand Russell walked about Trafalgar Square horrified, discovering 'to my amazement that average men and women were delighted at the prospect of war . . . the anticipation of carnage was delightful to something like ninety per cent of the population. I had to revise my views on human nature.'

Though he remained steadfast in his opposition to war with Germany, Russell was no pacifist. But was he right about the delighted 'anticipation of carnage'? It was true that diplomats had been usurped by demagogues, and that politicians' anti-German menaces were greeted with cheering. There was certainly a mood of excitement on the streets of central London on 3 and 4 August. No doubt this eagerness went hand in hand with profound apprehension. But in truth no one really knew what lay in store. And nor was naivety an exclusively British affair, for across Europe reservists and volunteers were flocking to join up. 'This war is fine and just,' said the French author Henri Alain-Fournier. The German writer Thomas Mann believed that 'the German soul will emerge stronger, prouder, freer, happier from it.' So much enthusiasm, so little awareness.

2. Contemptibly Small

Goodbye Piccadilly.

The logic of the British government's decision to enter the war demanded that a military force be despatched at once to the continent. But the crisis was also going to demand a new kind of leadership. By odd chance, Britain had no Secretary of State for War, the previous occupant, Jack Seely, having been forced to resign that spring, after mishandling the 'Curragh Mutiny', a loyalty crisis among army officers stationed in Ireland. At the start of August 1914 his duties were being discharged by the Prime Minister. Clearly, the country was going to need a new, full-time War Secretary. There was only one man for the job.

The British have a weakness for military commanders – like Marlborough, Nelson or Wellington – who win famous victories. Field Marshal Horatio Herbert Kitchener – Lord Kitchener of

Khartoum – suppressor of the Boers in South Africa, commander of the Indian army, governor of Egypt, slayer of rebels in Sudan, had a look of imperial invincibility about him. It was true that he had several times said that he would rather sweep the streets than have a job in the War Office. But the press wanted him, so Kitchener of Khartoum it would be.

By chance, the great man had just been in Britain having an earldom conferred upon him for outstanding service to the empire and busying himself decorating the country house he had bought and on whose walls he had had his monogram 'K. K.' inscribed. On 3 August, he had driven to Dover to catch the Channel ferry on the first leg of his journey back to the Middle East, and was striding up and down the deck spluttering, 'Tell the captain to start.' It was being explained to him that it was normal for the ferry to wait for the arrival of the boat train bringing lesser beings from London when a messenger from Asquith reached the port. Kitchener was called off the ferry to be made War Secretary and to take his place around the cabinet table alongside the politicians he rather despised. Autocratic, taciturn, generally unsmiling and often morose, he became the first serving soldier to sit in cabinet since the middle of the seventeenth century. When he delivered his maiden speech in the House of Lords, to explain that 'as a soldier, I have no politics', he initially attempted to do so from the bench normally occupied by bishops of the Church of England, much to the knowing amusement of those whose oath of allegiance was to their own political advancement. Kitchener's unblinking eyes and bristling imperial moustache would shortly become the most familiar in the history of advertising.

The British people laboured – then as now – under many illusions about their army, not the least of them being that it was superior to all others. But one can see why, when mobilization took place, they felt jaunty. The armies of the continent were largely made up of conscripts, while the British army was a volunteer force, whose members had *chosen* to serve. For this reason, and because it was a much smaller force than those elsewhere in Europe, it was better trained. It tended to be drawn from the two opposite ends of the social spectrum. Its officers were not all aristocrats – far from it. But the prevailing atmosphere among them was landed: the posher regiments expected their officers to lead a way of life that could not be funded by mere military pay and required a private income. In contrast, many ordinary soldiers still fitted the Duke of Wellington's condescending description of their predecessors almost a century earlier: 'scum of the earth – mere scum'. The army offered a home and a purpose to those who otherwise often had neither. By the early years of the twentieth century this force was highly experienced: during Queen Victoria's sixty-year reign it had taken part in more than seventy wars, expeditionary campaigns and punitive raids all over the world. And it was accustomed to winning them.

This was the force that would now confront the Kaiser. Two months previously, in June 1914, Charles Carrington, a teenage boy from Warwickshire, had been taken to Aldershot to watch the cream of the army parade in honour of the king's birthday. Carrington would soon find his world changed utterly when Kitchener called for volunteers and he enlisted – going on to win a Military Cross. But for now he was an admiring spectator of the force that had spread imperial pink all over the map of the world. That summer's day on the Aldershot parade ground there were four brigades of infantry and one brigade of cavalry, attended by batteries of field artillery, horse artillery and engineers – in total, about 15,000 men. Most of the infantry wore scarlet tunics, the riflemen dark green, with cavalrymen in cherry-coloured breeches, and Highland regiments in kilts and bonnets. There were 2,000 horses on display. He found it a magnificent, heart-stirring spectacle. But there was not a single motorized vehicle to be seen.

Because the British Expeditionary Force (BEF) despatched to save Belgium was small by comparison with the conscript armies of continental Europe, the Kaiser is said to have referred to it as a 'contemptible little army', and in truth the total number of soldiers Britain could field was hardly bigger than the army of Serbia.

In the west, France and Germany could each deploy almost 2 million. An additional anxiety was that the reserves which could theoretically be called up to augment the British army might not even be as numerous as they appeared on paper: because a bounty was paid to each man who signed on, some reservists had become soldiers with several different battalions. The reasons for the relatively small size of the British army were deeply rooted in a combination of geographical good fortune (the defensive advantage of being an island), a seafaring history and the guaranteed security of the biggest navy in the world – as well as the customary reluctance of governments to spend money, and an aversion to the political dangers posed by standing armies (how do you stop military commanders using them for political power?). The new War Secretary immediately realized that if the Germans were ever to be defeated, the army would have to be hugely expanded. But turning volunteers into soldiers takes time, and for now the regular army was the only force that could be sent to the continent to confront the Germans.

On 5 August the newly formed government War Council met and authorized its despatch. The possibility of war in Europe had encouraged a previous War Secretary, Richard Haldane, to reorganize the army, and it mobilized with remarkable speed. There were six divisions available, but Kitchener was worried about security at home, and the following day he declared that only four of them – plus one cavalry division – would go to France. Following plans laid out in painstaking detail in a secret War Book, reservists were summoned by telegrams distributed through Post Offices instructed to stay open twenty-four hours a day, transported by railway – in five days an extra 1,800 trains were laid on to Southampton alone – issued with advance pay, examined by doctors, sorted by NCOs and supplied with uniforms and rifles. As required by mobilization regulations, the officer corps sent their swords off to be sharpened. Tens of thousands of horses were requisitioned from riding schools, hunts and stables. Three days later the force began embarking on ships sailing from ports all over the country, Southampton to Liverpool, Newhaven in

Sussex to Queenstown in County Cork. The ships set out to sea to the sound of horns blowing in the dockyards and loud cheering from the soldiers on board. By 17 August, over 80,000 men, 30,000 horses and more than 300 field guns had been transported. Arriving on the continent they sauntered down the gangways to the sound of excited men, women and children cheering them to the echo and begging for souvenirs of their expedition: many of the soldiers cheerfully parted with cap-badges and shoulder-tags and were given flowers, food and wine in return.

The British *Official History* of the war claimed later that the force sent across the Channel made up 'the best trained, best organised and best equipped British Army that ever went forth to war'. Perhaps. It was true that British soldiers could shoot more rapidly and more accurately than the conscripts of the big European armies. (This was not a claim which could be made by the latter stages of the war, when significant numbers of the British army could hardly hit a barn door.) And imperial warfare had taught them that scarlet tunics were best reserved for the parade ground at Aldershot: the British soldiers now rattling away from the coast towards the advancing Germans in stuffy, overcrowded troop trains wore khaki (an empire word, from the Hindustani for 'dust-coloured'). French soldiers, by contrast, were still wearing red pantaloons, blue serge kepi and greatcoat, and their officers were advancing into battle in white gloves, clutching swords. But in vital areas the British Expeditionary Force was terribly ill equipped for a modern war. Each battalion might have a couple of machine guns, but even the *Official History* conceded that 'in heavy guns and howitzers, high explosive shell, trench mortars, hand grenades and much of the subsidiary material required for siege and trench warfare it was almost wholly deficient.' It also knew next to nothing about the conditions in which it would be facing the Germans.

From the distance of one hundred years, accustomed as we are to seeing a First World War battlefield as a place of muddy, murderous stalemate, it is almost impossible to recognize the sort of campaign the British generals expected to fight. What were they thinking? Imperial wars, which had generally been fought in the tropics or in hotter, drier climates, had generally been a triumph of superior technology over more primitive weaponry. By the early twentieth century the army had used the invention of rapid-fire rifles and improved ammunition to refine tactics in which soldiers attacked while under covering fire from another part of the formation, until sufficient forces could be gathered in one area to mount an overwhelming assault. The importance of continual 'fire and movement' was well understood. As he looked back on it, Sir John French, the womanizing, debt-strapped commander of the BEF, was frank: 'All my thoughts, all my prospective plans, all my possible alternatives of action, were concentrated upon a war of movement and manoeuvre.' This approach would come to grief in Flanders.

But this lay in the unforeseen future. German forces had swept through Belgium and into France at ferocious pace and were pressing south. Unless they were checked, Paris would be encircled. As the British soldiers advanced north from the Channel ports to face them they were met in town after town by jubilant crowds, with food and drink forced on them and payment often refused. By the third week of August the BEF had reached the Belgian town of Mons, where the French commander asked them to protect his flank from German attack by digging in along the banks of a canal. When the Germans attempted to cross the canal, the well-trained British soldiers unleashed such a ferocious storm of fire that the Germans were later said to have believed they were facing massed machine guns. But over the hours the sheer weight of the German assault forced the British back. By nightfall they had had to form a new defensive line south of the city, but by this time their French allies had collapsed, and the Germans forced a further retreat across the border into France. Finally, some three days later, near the little town of Le Cateau, although hugely outnumbered, General Horace Smith-Dorrien, in command of II Corps, tried to stand and fight, to prevent the retreat becoming a rout. On the morning of 26 August, the British and their French allies managed to stem the German advance for several hours. But the British suffered almost 8,000 casualties before being forced to continue stumbling back in retreat once more. It was a valiant but inauspicious start.

The British involvement in the war had always been as part of an alliance: the very first sentence of the letter sent by Kitchener to every soldier – to be kept with his pay-book – read: 'You are ordered abroad as a soldier of the King to help our French comrades against the invasion of a common enemy.' But it had not taken long for the commander of British forces, the confusingly named Sir John French, to lose confidence in his allied counterparts. Kitchener's instructions to Sir John had been slightly ambiguous, anyway: he was to co-operate with the allied generals, but not to incur heavy British losses. By late August his army was already so knocked about that General French decided it could be saved only by a wholesale retreat and regrouping.

The British Expeditionary Force in France was now about 100,000 strong. On Friday 28 August Sir John French calculated that he had lost over 15,000 men in the previous five days. Even so, when he managed to intercept various columns of retreating soldiers, he found that 'these glorious British soldiers listened to the few words I was able to say to them with the spirit of heroes and the confidence of children,' evidence, he thought, of 'the wonderful instinctive sympathy which has always existed between the British soldier and his officer . . . they trusted them and were ready to follow them anywhere.' He clearly did not feel the same way about the relationship between his soldiers and the French commanders who were overseeing the struggle in which they were engaged. He resented his French allies for doing so little to shelter British forces, and wrote to Kitchener to tell him so. In keeping with the instruction he had been given to protect his force as much as possible, he was taking them out of the fighting to regroup.

The French generals were appalled – a British withdrawal would leave a gaping hole in the front line, exposing their flank to German attack. Kitchener understood their worry at once and sent a telegram instructing Sir John to do as the French commander, General Joffre, asked. To no effect. 'I think you had better trust me to watch the situation and act according to circumstances' was the British commander's reply. This defiant message reached London by midnight, 31 August. It was too much for Kitchener: if Sir John persisted with his plan to withdraw behind the protection of the River Seine, the French would collapse and the German army would pour through. Kitchener rushed to 10 Downing Street, where, to his irritated disbelief, he found the Prime Minister in the middle of a late-night game of bridge. The new War Secretary explained, to the handful of cabinet ministers who could be roused, what Sir John French was planning. An appeal from the President of France was read out to them. Asquith, who had so recently believed that Britain might manage to remain aloof from war, was appalled. National honour, so powerful in the decision to join the war, was at stake. If Sir John persisted with his plan, he told the weary-eyed handful of ministers, 'Paris will fall, the French Army will be cut off and we shall never be able to hold our heads up in the world again. Better that the British Army should perish than that this shame should fall on us.' Kitchener must go to France at once, to tell the British high command to change their minds and, Asquith said, to 'put the fear of God into them'. At 2.30 that morning, Kitchener left London on a special train, to rendezvous with a fast cruiser waiting at Dover.

Sir John, meanwhile, had been summoned by telegram and resentfully travelled to Paris to meet the War Secretary on the morning of 1 September. Although the two men had served together in South Africa during the Boer War, they were hardly kindred spirits. French was moody and insecure, and never did a man carry so inappropriate a surname: several years previously, when he had attempted to read a speech in the French language, his accent was so dreadful that his audience thought he was speaking English. When in London he enjoyed a distinctly unmonkish life, sharing a house with George Moore, a louche American millionaire. Kitchener, by contrast, was cold, hard, ambitious and ruthless, a tall, imposing man who preferred micromanagement to delegation. It was not a happy encounter.

When the two men met at the British embassy, French saw that Kitchener had not come to talk to him as any ordinary cabinet minister might do. For the War Secretary was dressed in the uniform of a field marshal. Sir John was furious. According to a (hardly unbiased) French general who was present at the meeting, 'the one, Kitchener, calm, balanced, reflective, master of himself, conscious of the great and patriotic task he had come to perform; the other, sour, impetuous, with congested face, sullen and ill-tempered in expression'. Sir John's resentment at being summoned from his headquarters had given him the look of an angry, spoiled brat. When he suggested to Kitchener that command in the field be left to commanders in the field, the War Secretary drew him into a private room, where he evidently fulfilled Asquith's request to put the fear of God into the general, for afterwards he telegraphed the cabinet to report that 'French's troops are now engaged in the fighting line where he will remain conforming to the movements of the French Army.' For all Sir John's continued irritation ('Kitchener *knows nothing* about European Warfare,' he told Churchill afterwards. 'Of course he's a fine organiser but never was and never will be a commander in the field'), there is a strong case for saying that without the War Secretary's intervention the Germans might well have taken Paris.

For the German invasion had been fast and ruthless, covering 150 miles, and reaching within 25 miles of the French capital before frantic resistance by French and Belgian troops, aided once more by the British, forced them to retreat to defensive positions behind the River Aisne. Here, the Germans seized the high ground, a move that would provide them with a major strategic advantage until spring 1918, and stood firm, protected by the colossal power of their artillery. In late October, though, having detected what they believed to be a weak point in the allied line around the Belgian town of Ypres, about 30 miles east of Dunkirk, the Germans attacked again. This battle, a series of intensely bloody encounters in October and November 1914, would define the role of the original British Expeditionary Force in the war.

Sitting across roads, railway lines and canals, Ypres was the only substantial Belgian town not to have fallen to the invaders. Symbolism apart, though, there was a more pressing worry for the British. If the Germans took Ypres – 'Wipers' as it became to the British soldiers – they stood poised to reach the North Sea coast. As the cabinet had heard in August, once the Channel ports were in German hands Britain would be in immediate danger. 'The stakes for which we were playing at the great Battle of Ypres', said Sir John French later, 'were nothing less than the safety, indeed, the very existence of the British Empire.' But French had catastrophically underestimated German determination. He ignored intelligence being provided by Belgian farmers and captured German soldiers, who reported that the Germans had brought in reinforcements. 'I thought the danger was past,' he admitted later. 'I believed that the enemy had exhausted his strength in the great bid he had made to smash our armies on the Marne and capture Paris . . . in my heart I did not expect I should have to fight a great defensive battle.'

The scene of this battle, Ypres, was a beautiful old town of cobbled streets that had grown rich on its textile industry, particularly the manufacture of delicate Valenciennes lace and elaborate ribbons. By the middle of the thirteenth century, the town had been accounted the wealthiest place in Flanders, and its Gothic cloth-workers' hall, completed in 1304, was one of the grandest monuments to commerce in Europe. The façade of Ypres' town hall was covered in elaborate decoration and the town was spattered with bell-towers, built over the centuries to summon residents if an enemy threatened. 'Every lover of art will find much to interest him in Ypres,' said the 1910 Baedeker guidebook, praising it as one of the most interesting towns in Belgium and

recommending a visit in the height of summer, because 'in spring
the weather is apt to be raw and unsettled, and autumn is windy
and often rainy.' It was now October 1914, and there were fewer
than 20,000 people living in the town. Over the next four years,
many times that number would die to gain or hold possession of
the place, and the town would be more or less flattened.

When British soldiers got down from their troop trains and
horse-drawn buses just outside Ypres they faced a torrent of refugees fleeing in the opposite direction. Behind the terrified civilians,
the soldiers saw houses on fire and deserted farms, with abandoned
cows and pigs wandering the roads. 'It is as if a plague has passed
over the land,' recorded a BEF colonel. When one of the horses in
his transport section broke its leg and had to be shot, the soldiers
watched, astonished, as local people surrounded the animal's
corpse with plates, knives and forks. In the fields around the town,
stolid Flemish farmers had been growing root vegetables in flat,
low-lying soil, which the relentless impact of high-explosive shells
and the movement of vehicles, horses and mules soon turned into
a swamp. In these conditions, the British doctrine of 'fire and
manoeuvre' became if not impossible then certainly slow, intensely
laborious and highly dangerous.

On the evening of 21 October 1914, French gave the order that
his troops should dig in. Each side was essentially engaged in an
attempt to outflank the other, in what became known as 'the race
to the sea', with the Germans attempting to reach the Channel
coast and the allies trying to extend the existing front line north-
wards to thwart them: the trenches being dug at Ypres were soon
incorporated into an allied line, populated by British, Belgian,
French and empire soldiers, that twisted all the way to the borders
of Switzerland, some 450 miles away. The trench idea wasn't
new – they had often been used in previous wars to provide shelter
from enemy fire. But they had always been intended as temporary
positions. In the sodden Flemish lowlands, under incessant fire,
the trenches became miserably permanent. By the time the troops
had dug down a couple of feet, they generally struck the water

table. They awaited their fate with their feet and much of their legs under cold, stagnant water. Then it started to snow.

A major in the Grenadier Guards noted in his diary that his men had made 'good dug-outs roofed with branches covered with earth' (they had yet to appreciate the destructive force of artillery), and that night, under a pale moon, the German infantry attacked through the woods. In a scene that might have been lifted from the seventeenth century, the German soldiers were accompanied by a drummer, 'who was beating his drum all the time, and not, like the others, taking cover behind trees'. The major never saw the drummer fall, from which he concluded that his men did not aim at him. The Grenadiers repulsed the attack with a mere seventeen casualties, which he called 'a quiet night'. (The following day 300 German bodies were counted in front of their trenches.) He ended his diary entry with the words 'Enemy heard digging all night.' The war was assuming the shape the world would forever remember.

On Wednesday of that week Major Lord Bernard Charles Gordon Lennox – the son of a duke and a direct descendant of Charles II – noted that even the newly dug trenches gave no protection against some modern weapons. A German reconnaissance aircraft passed overhead in the morning, and soon afterwards intense, accurate artillery fire engulfed them. It was Gordon Lennox's last diary entry – he was killed by an enemy shell. Under such a bombardment, the holes in the ground that gave protection from rifle fire became a prison. A direct hit on a trench meant instant death and injury, and a sustained barrage made it impossible to evacuate the wounded: survivors were condemned to cower in the bottom of the trench, often surrounded by the body-parts of their comrades. At times of intense terror the survivor might almost envy the dead. When the colonel of the Grenadiers learned of the fate of his friend Major Gordon Lennox, he wrote in a letter home, 'I think of him now at peace, away from all this noise and misery . . . he can rest at last. I can't bear seeing my friends go day after day.' In just over a fortnight at Ypres the colonel's battalion lost twelve officers and 466 men. It had been halved.

The intensity of the fighting at Ypres was quite unlike anything any soldiers had ever experienced before. British infantry were frequently outnumbered five or ten to one because the Germans had summoned great reserves of troops for the battle, some of whom had been dragged out and trained at such short notice that they arrived armed only with captured rifles and wearing Berlin police helmets – the only protective headgear available. Many of the British admired the courage of the poorly prepared enemy infantry, who advanced against their trenches in hordes, and died in vast numbers. 'They are brave enough, jolly brave, but at night it is too much like shooting a flock of sheep, poor things,' an English colonel wrote. 'They have discipline, and do what they are told, but their attacks at night in this wood developed into the poor devils wandering rather aimlessly about under our terrific rifle fire.'

Many of the British fought heroically, too, but their efforts were undermined by munitions problems. The German artillery was more plentiful and there was a critical shortage of shells for the British guns. Infantrymen had their problems, too: some discovered that the mud had jammed their rifles' firing mechanism, while others found that when the barrels of their rifles heated up – as they always do during heavy use – they couldn't reload because cartridges would stick in the breech. When an officer in the 2nd Battalion of the Yorkshire regiment the Green Howards saw what the fighting had done to his comrades, he lamented that 'what was as fine a Battalion as there was in the British Army, which had started the battle about 1000 strong, was now reduced to one captain, three second-lieutenants and less than 300 gallant men'. German shrapnel shells, which burst and sprayed small balls of metal in all directions, did terrible damage. An Irish lieutenant recalled how his platoon dug in under German machine-gun fire, before being relieved soon afterwards by an English regiment. The trenches then came under such intense shelling that the Irish were called back to the scene only hours later and found that 'most of the men we came to relieve were lying dead in the open and we took our places in the intervals between the corpses. These poor chaps, lying head on to the enemy, had all been shot in the backs by the raining shrapnel while fighting and trying to scrape holes for cover. Large numbers of black round bullets [shrapnel fired by German artillery] were scattered about.'

On Saturday 31 October, the Kaiser had arrived at the German lines, ready for a triumphal entry through the gates of Ypres. That afternoon Sir John French had found General Douglas Haig, commander of I Corps, white-faced. 'They have broken us right in,' he said, 'and are pouring through the gap.' At lunchtime, there had been even worse news. Senior officers of the British Expeditionary Force 1st and 2nd Divisions were meeting inside a château near the village of Hooge, 3 miles east of Ypres. Châteaux near the front lines were very obvious targets for the artillery of either side, and the fact that senior staff officers' cars were parked on the sides of the road outside made Hooge especially inviting. At about 1.15 a shell fell in the garden outside the office of Sir Charles Monro, the general commanding the 2nd Division. Many of the officers rushed to see the damage, and were caught by the next incoming shell, which struck the window-frame. Monro survived, but General Samuel Lomax, the highly regarded commander of the 1st Division, was seriously injured, and almost every other staff officer was either killed outright or wounded, some of them mortally. The British Expeditionary Force was now very close to extinction.

The British were exhausted. The *Official History*, which generally talks of the war in pretty colourless prose, summarizes the situation thus: 'The line that stood between the British Empire and ruin was composed of tired, haggard and unshaven men, unwashed, plastered with mud, many in little more than rags.' Soon after his meeting with Haig, French explained the bleak situation to General Foch, the French commander. 'The only men I have left are the sentries at my gates. I will take them with me to where the line is broken and the last of the English will be killed fighting.' While he was delivering this apocalyptic judgement, the remnants of the 2nd Battalion of the Worcestershire Regiment staged a counter-attack at the village of Gheluvelt on the Menin road, where they charged with fixed bayonets across open ground, routing a much larger force of German infantry and rescuing the situation. As Field Marshal French remembered it, 'no more than one thin and straggling line of tired-out British soldiers stood between the Empire and its practical ruin as an independent first-class Power. I still look back in wonder on that thin line of defence, stretched, out of sheer necessity, far beyond its natural and normal power for defence . . . When all has been said, it was their courage and endurance which spoke the last word.'

It had been a very close-run thing, and in truth it had been an allied effort, involving Belgian, French and Indian forces as well as the British soldiers. The Germans had suffered heavily – the deaths of so many raw recruits giving the place the nickname the 'Kindermord zu Ypern' – the Massacre of the Innocents at Ypres. But the first few months of the war had demonstrated to the British government that this would be a conflict like no other ever fought. And it had shown that a comparatively small force of professional soldiers in an expeditionary force was nowhere near powerful enough for the job that had fallen to it.

The same small patch of ground would continue to be fought over for the next four years. The following April, the Germans attacked again, this time using poison gas for the first time on the Western Front. In July 1915 their weapons included flamethrowers. In the summer of 1917 the area was the scene for a series of assaults which culminated in the Canadian capture of the village of Passchendaele. In between and after these recognized 'battles' there was constant skirmishing, sniping and shelling. Apart perhaps from the appalling battle of attrition which the French suffered at Verdun, nowhere speaks more of the war's dreadful loss of life than Ypres. The British war memorial at the Menin Gate records the names of 54,389 soldiers with no known grave; the nearby Commonwealth War Graves Commission cemetery at Tyne Cot holds a further 12,000 who died in the war, and also lists 34,927 with no known grave. There are many other cemeteries. The total of men killed in Flanders in the course of the war is far, far greater than the number who had set forth for France in August of 1914.

The fight for the ancient town of Ypres in 1914 marked the end of the grand design with which the British had entered the war. The cost had been enormous, with tens of thousands killed, wounded, taken prisoner or missing in action. Entire battalions had been destroyed. The 1st Battalion of the Loyal North Lancashire Regiment, for example, had landed at Le Havre in mid-August with twenty-five officers and 900 men mostly recruited from the county's mill towns. After Ypres it had been reduced to five officers and 150 men. And 22nd Brigade – normally around 5,000 strong – could muster a mere three officers and 700 men – a casualty rate of 97 per cent among officers. As the military theorist and First World War veteran Basil Liddell Hart put it, 'Ypres saw the supreme vindication and the final sacrifice of the old Regular Army. After the battle was over, little survived, save the memory of its spirit.'

Before the BEF had left Britain, Kitchener had predicted that the war would require the creation of a massive new army. The catastrophic experience on the continent had proved him right, and at home there had already been a tremendous response to the call for volunteers. It would certainly not be 'all over by Christmas' – as some people had fervently hoped.

3. Willing for a Shilling

All shapes and sizes volunteered.

Already, across the country, boys were kissing their mothers goodbye and promising to bring back half of the Kaiser's moustache; gangs of young men were boarding trains and hanging home-made signs from the carriages saying 'NEXT STOP BERLIN'; country cottages, city tenements and suburban semis were display-ing notices in their windows proudly announcing, 'A man from this house is serving in the forces.' There was even a brief fashion among women for khaki dresses. Men who had been left behind because they were too puny for military service began to exercise with dumbbells, ready for their next visit to the recruitment office. Many felt that the need to join the army was urgent – the whole thing might be over in weeks or months and they didn't want to miss it. A similar thought comforted parents – with a little bit of luck, the war might be finished before their sons had even completed military training.

That was not how Kitchener saw things developing. Even though a soldier with a reputation for relentless thoroughness rather than innovative ideas, he did at least see that, far from being all over by Christmas, it could well go on for years to come. To win such a protracted war, Britain would need an enormous supply of men. In fact, two days after the declaration of war, parliament had passed a bill agreeing with this assessment and increasing the size of the army to 500,000 men. This turned out to be a hopeless underestimate, soon to be doubled and then increased again. As the disturbing reality of the allied retreat hit home, the response to appeals for men to serve became overwhelming – the equivalent of every man, woman and child living in a town the size of modern Oxford in a week. On a single day in early September 1914, some 33,000 men signed up – more than the entire annual enlistment in an average year before 1914. They came from all parts of the country and from all social classes – farmhands and clerks, butchers and hairdressers, teachers and labourers, fishermen, joiners, musicians and actors. By 10 August, 600 Anglican clergy had applied to serve as chaplains in a 'khaki crusade whose mission is to save civilization'. As the Bishop of London, Arthur Winnington-Ingram, put it in an Advent sermon the following year, it was the duty of all Britons to take German lives – 'to kill them not for the sake of killing, but to save the world'. By the end of the year, 1,186,000 men had volunteered, and an even larger number followed in 1915.

Those who came forward found it very simple to join an organization that was very difficult to leave. Just a matter of stating your age (or, often enough, making it up – the recruiting sergeant earned two shillings and sixpence* per infantryman attested and didn't inquire very closely), and passing a medical test (for which doctors were paid a similar bounty – in December orders were

---

* About £10 at today's values. In October 1914 the bounty would be reduced to one shilling per recruit.

issued that no doctor was to process more than eight men in one hour, or forty in a day). The medical hardly did more than require that new soldiers be over 5 feet 3 inches tall, able to expand their chest to 34 inches and be able to see beyond their nose.

Recruiting offices were besieged by men offering to serve, with queues stretching for hundreds of yards down the street. Often groups of volunteers were first summoned to an advertised meeting at a town hall, public square, theatre or church. They were then sent to gather hand-luggage and reassemble at the nearest mainline railway station to be packed off for basic training, during which they would be billeted with local people. But the massive influx of new men soon exhausted the available equipment. Arriving at training camps they frequently found no uniforms, no instructors, no cooks and no kitchens. The departure of the British Expeditionary Force had left the army an empty husk, so veterans of engagements on dusty imperial battlefields were recalled from tending their country gardens and instead of supervising meetings of the parochial church council were asked to relearn the business of military command. Other such 'dugouts' were welcomed back into uniform to give the new recruits some basic training in drill and physical exercise. In the absence of the real things, weapons drill was carried out with broom-handles, pieces of wood or lengths of piping. The men paraded in their own clothes, with some northern battalions wearing their cloth caps as part of a home-made uniform. When it rained there were lectures on map-reading – without any maps – and musketry – without any guns. But by Christmas many were able to swagger down the street wearing a dark-blue uniform. They called it 'Kitchener Blue', and it was said to be part of an over-order of cloth for postmen's uniforms. Since groups of young men tend to attract the attention of young women of varying degrees of availability, city worthies endorsed 'moral patrols' by self-appointed virtuous ladies on a mission to keep them apart.

The sudden creation of an enormous army gave rise to logistical problems all over the country. One afternoon in early September

1914, for example, 250 angry Welsh miners who had been sent to a training depot in Preston suddenly appeared at the station there carrying a banner reading 'No Food, no Shelter, no Money'. After two weeks away from home, the miners had had enough and demanded to be put on a train back to South Wales at once. They said they were accustomed to wages of at least £2 a week, that they had given up everything to answer the call, and yet had still not received their army pay (one shilling a day, with an additional allowance for subsistence). The mayor was summoned, to be told that thus far their service to the Crown had consisted of wandering about the streets in the rain, 'in old boots, down at the heel, and with no money in their pockets . . . They had given up everything to serve their country. They had left their wives at home and had no money to send to them.' The miners were eventually pacified by being invited into the town hall and given a decent meal.

The discontented Welsh miners in Preston reflected the character of many of the new military formations, made up of men from the same area or trade. The sprawling nineteenth-century conurbations offered ready-made pools of potential volunteers in businesses, local authority departments and voluntary organizations such as sports clubs, Boy Scouts and Boys' Brigades. This in turn made city authorities ideal recruiting sergeants, giving local mayors, councillors and Chambers of Commerce the opportunity to do their bit: they could get their officials to find recruits, while offering friends and workmates the chance to serve in the army together. These formations of neighbours and colleagues became known very quickly as the 'pals' battalions'.

As with so many successful ideas, several individuals claimed credit for inventing the concept, but it seems to have developed in several parts of the country at more or less the same time, and was quickly co-opted by the government. The city of Liverpool ran one of the earliest and most successful schemes, enlisting over 3,000 men within five days. A competitive civic pride took hold, and on 28 August a group of Manchester employers got together and offered to raise, clothe and equip a Manchester Clerks' and

Warehousemen's Battalion. On the same day the *Birmingham Daily Post* declared its belief that there were over 50,000 single young men in the city and preached that 'there can be no question that patriotism insists that the unmarried shall offer themselves without thought or hesitation.' By lunchtime that day, the paper's offices had been besieged by eager applicants. In the course of the war the paper claimed credit for raising 150 battalions.

The *Birmingham Daily Post*'s particular mission was the enlistment of lower-middle-class office workers. Elsewhere, there were battalions made up entirely of men who worked for the North Eastern Railway, and others of miners and cotton workers, foundrymen and bank clerks. There were five battalions comprised entirely of young men who had attended public school. In Hull, the local newspaper defended the creation of a 'black-coated battalion' of office workers by saying that 'just as the docker will feel more at home amongst his every day mates, so the wielders of the pen and drawing pencil will be better as friends together.'* A Mrs E. Cunliffe-Owen got permission from Lord Kitchener to assemble a Sportsmen's Battalion, which included several first-class cricketers alongside rowers, footballers and the English lightweight boxing champion. (It also included Charles Montague, an assistant editor of the liberal *Manchester Guardian*, aged forty-seven and married with seven children, who had dyed his grey hair black and joined as a 'mountaineer'.) In Yorkshire, Sir Mark Sykes raised an entire battalion from the workers on his estates. In one of the Birmingham suburbs a Captain Huxley said he had been contacted by motorcyclists from all over the country, wanting to form their own specialist unit. One of the very first pals' battalions – nicknamed the 'Stockbrokers' – was brought together in the City of London and included men who turned out on parade in top hats and morning coats. Glasgow offered three pals' battalions, one of them composed of drivers, conductors and workers on the city's

---

* The city also raised the 'Hull Commercials', the 'Hull Tradesmen', the 'Hull Sportsmen and Athletes' and a fourth battalion just known as 'T'others'.

tramway system. The provost of Edinburgh raised a battalion under the command of an elderly colonel who had survived the siege of Paris in 1870, and a former MP in the city led another whose core was players and supporters of the Heart of Midlothian football team. Lloyd George dreamed of welding the many volunteer battalions from Wales into an entirely Welsh army, but the idea foundered on Kitchener's belief that, while a Welsh division might be acceptable, an entire army would prove an unreliable ally, being 'wild and insubordinate'.

These pals' battalions have a special hold upon the memory of the First World War not because they made up the bulk of the army – most men joined through the normal recruiting mechanisms – but because they had one terrible flaw. They were invented to allow neighbours and kindred spirits to serve together, and they began with friends singing as they marched off to war. But when one of these units was sent into battle, the loss of life was fearsomely concentrated, sometimes even in the space of a few streets.

Between August 1914 and January 1916, something like 2 million British and Irish men volunteered to serve. What led such vast numbers of men to decide to join up? Even if everyone understood that the new war would be quite unlike any other, they did not know precisely *what* it would be like. They were told that God was on their side, and the more or less constant expansion of the British empire over the previous hundred years had made defeat almost unimaginable. Philip Gibbs, the best known of the British war correspondents, claimed that the mood of the volunteers was 'I hate the idea, but it's got to be done.' This idea of duty – today almost invisible in British society – doubtless drove many. And, partly thanks to the work of such war correspondents, accounts of the suffering of the BEF inspired further support – if anything, the worse things sounded, the more willingly men volunteered. But it does not quite explain the collective surge of enthusiasm for military service, that sense of actively *wanting* to fight.

It is striking that the business of joining up in the early days of the war was a public affair, a shared rush to the colours. 'How eager we were to get to the front,' wrote a Private Kemp, 'war was a wonderful thing and [we] were so keen to be doing something.' The 'we' is instructive – enlisting was so often a shared activity. But the comparatively few surviving accounts of what drove men to enlist suggest another element. The writer J. B. Priestley joined as a private soldier in the Duke of Wellington's West Riding Regiment in early September 1914. (He spent almost the entire war in the trenches, and was wounded twice.) He later testified that the fate of his generation was to be slaughtered 'not by hard necessity but by huge, murderous folly', and when he tried to understand this folly, he recalled 'a challenge that was almost like a conscription of the spirit, little to do really with King and Country and flag-waving and hip-hip-hurrah, a challenge to what we felt was our untested manhood. Other men, who had not lived as easily as we had, had drilled and marched and borne arms – couldn't we?' Priestley was surely right to focus on the masculine characteristics of the business of joining up: what young man wanted to be the one who held back while his workmates or schoolfriends surged forward to do what their civic and national leaders told them was their obligation? What man wanted to be asked by a girl, who might perhaps have a brother in uniform, why he wasn't enlisting?

'We don't want to lose you, but we think you ought to go,' sang the pretty little entertainer Phyllis Dane for the first time that September. Even feminist campaigners like Emmeline and Christabel Pankhurst banged the drum, because a German victory, they said, would wreck everything for which the suffragettes had been fighting. Posters challenged women to urge their young men into the army. 'If he does not think that you and your country are worth fighting for – do you think he is worthy *of you*?' asked one advertisement, before going on to plant the anxiety that 'If your young man neglects his duty to his King and Country, the time may come when he will neglect YOU.' Baroness Orczy, inventor of the great gentleman hero the Scarlet Pimpernel, created a Women of England's Active Service League, whose members would pledge never to be seen in public with a man who had refused to answer the call to arms.

Orczy also supported a more poisonous organization, the Order of the White Feather. This set out to impugn the manhood of total strangers wearing civilian clothes by presenting them with a white feather as a symbol of their alleged cowardice. In the days of organized cock-fighting, birds with white feathers in their tails were supposedly inferior in comparison with pure-bred cockerels. In late August 1914, a retired admiral arranged for a group of women in Folkestone to chase 'slackers' and 'loafers' down the street and present them with white feathers. The practice soon spread, and among other supporters of the movement was the popular novelist and prominent enemy of female suffrage Mrs Humphry Ward. You needed a thick skin to be able to resist such a slur on your manhood, although the pacifist Fenner Brockway boasted of having been given so many that he had enough white feathers to make a fan, and others joked that the whole thing was a racket to enable young women to jettison boyfriends of whom they had grown tired. The harpies of the Order of the White Feather became such a nuisance that the Home Office had to arrange for men employed in civilian war work to be issued with metal badges showing that they were serving 'king and country'.

At times it could seem easier to enlist than not to do so. In shop windows, at railway stations, on the sides of buses and trams, in schools and town halls, all over the base of Nelson's Column, the new War Secretary's face was soon glaring out from recruiting advertisements, his enormous forefinger pointing: he wanted YOU for the army. The original targets of this intense advertising campaign were young men between the ages of nineteen and thirty (although the upper limit was soon raised to thirty-five). Were you masculine enough to accept the invitation? The imposing image of Kitchener's face was the work of a cartoonist, Alfred Leete, best known for a series earlier in 1914 called 'Schmidt the Spy', and it had first appeared on the cover of the influential weekly magazine *London Opinion* in September. The Parliamentary Recruiting Committee established at the outbreak of war recognized the power of the likeness and had it turned into a poster, one of the earliest uses of modern advertising in the service of the state. ('A poor general but a wonderful poster', as the Prime Minister's wife, Margot Asquith, was supposed to have said of Kitchener.) The mythology surrounding Kitchener of Khartoum often mentioned his penetrating blue eyes, which were said to strike terror into subordinates: 'the Sphinx must look like that' was the way one witness described them. Leete exploited this in his cartoon, although the explanation for the frightening eyes, which seemed to follow you around the room, was simple: Lord Kitchener had a slight squint. Soon Germany, Hungary and Italy were all using their own versions of the pointing finger. In revolutionary Russia the face behind it was Trotsky; in the United States, Uncle Sam.

There were over a hundred other recruiting designs commissioned by the Parliamentary Committee, including posters showing defenceless women and babies cowering as soldiers in spiked Prussian helmets forced their way through the door, or a genial kilted soldier standing above a thatched English country cottage, with the slogan 'Isn't This Worth Fighting For?' (The campaign for Scottish Home Rule had been put on hold for the duration of the war.) Should any potential recruit from an industrial slum wonder what this bucolic idyll had to do with him, his subversive question was drowned out by the sheer volume of propaganda. Within little more than a year, the committee had issued 12 million posters and 34 million leaflets. 'Don't lag – Follow your flag' was the universal message.

And then there was Horatio Bottomley. Bottomley had been raised in an orphanage, an experience which did nothing to damage his self-confidence but which perhaps allowed him to see the vulnerability of British social convention. Through a series of swindles, often centred on journalistic schemes of one sort or other, by 1900 he had acquired the means to bet vast sums on horse races and soon had himself ensconced in a spacious apartment in Pall Mall and a country seat in Sussex, with his wife sequestered out of harm's way in a villa in Monte Carlo and various mistresses installed in flats in London. A seat in parliament was the obvious next step, and he duly acquired one in 1906 as the MP for Hackney South, until bankruptcy forced him to leave the Commons six years later. No matter, for he had by now established his own soapbox in the paper he had founded, *John Bull*. Here he was free to lambast any target he chose. In 1914 this included the entire German race, or 'Germ Huns' as he preferred to call them, who should be 'exterminated', with Germany 'wiped from the face of the map'. Any Germans living in Britain at the outbreak of war should have their property confiscated, and all naturalized Germans be compelled to wear an identifying badge, because 'you cannot naturalize an unnatural beast – a human abortion – a hellish fiend. But you *can* exterminate it.'

By now, in his fifties, Bottomley was a squat, fleshy man who required a valet when he wanted to remove his shoes: he had long ago lost sight of his feet when he stood upright. Even so, just weeks after the outbreak of war he had put himself on stage as the star turn (with Phyllis Dane) at a recruiting concert in Holborn. There, to an audience of 5,000 people (with thousands more on the streets outside, clamouring for a ticket), he explained that if the war was won 'we, the British Empire, as the chosen leaders of the world, shall travel along the road of human destiny and progress at the end of which we shall see the patient figure of the Prince of Peace, pointing to the Star of Bethlehem that leads us on to God.'* Hundreds of similar performances followed. A moment's thought ought to have convinced any member of Bottomley's audiences that the world is rarely as black and white as he painted it, and that the Germans too probably believed they had some divinely ordained destiny. But rationality had nothing to do with it, for these events were more like religious revival meetings than political hustings. The British people of the time were insular, monoglot, comparatively homogeneous. Most had never been abroad, many had never even left the village, town or city of their

* Bottomley's luck ran out when it was discovered that the 1919 *John Bull* Victory Bond Club was another of his rackets. A visitor who went to see him in Maidstone prison found him stitching mailbags. 'Sewing?' asked the visitor. 'No, reaping,' said Bottomley.

birth. Those who spoke a foreign language were privileged or eccentric. Just as today we *feel* the war more than we think about it, so, at this early stage, did they.

Even the most gilded were seduced by the prospect of fighting. 'It will be Hell to be in it,' the poet Rupert Brooke had told a friend on the eve of the outbreak of war, 'and Hell to be out of it.' Unable to find what he considered a suitable military position, this clean-limbed Englishman – privileged, clever, athletic, talented and, as admirers both male and female believed, impossibly handsome – came up with an assortment of unthought-through ideas about going to France, one of which involved impersonating a local peasant who had been called up to resist the German invasion. He wondered about becoming a war correspondent, but decided it was 'a rotten trade'. Instead, he joined the navy, on the grounds that it was somehow a 'more English' military formation than service in the army, and managed to get a commission in the Royal Naval Division, a formation of sailors who would fight on land.

The best-known poem of his '1914' sequence, 'The Soldier' (originally called 'The Recruit'), became for a while the most famous sonnet of the twentieth century. Its opening sets the tone:

> If I should die, think only this of me:
> That there's some corner of a foreign field
> That is for ever England.

The poem has been parodied and derided for decades, because it seems absurd to attempt to try to reconcile the supposed glory of personal sacrifice with the massed rows of graves which now provide the readiest symbol of that war. But Rupert Brooke was far from alone: less likely figures, too, were caught up in this sense of romance and obligation. In 1915 another poet, Edward Thomas, decided that he could no longer resist the pull of army service. At the time, Thomas was thirty-seven and (unhappily) married with three children. The motives that drove younger, single men – naive enthusiasm, lust for what seemed an adventure, peer-pressure,

ideas of manliness and the youthful conviction that you will live
for ever – meant much less to him. Horatio Bottomley's racism
and jingoism struck no chord. Nonetheless, Edward Thomas
found the urge to join up to be irresistible. He wrote to tell his fellow poet and friend Robert Frost of his decision. The American
replied, 'You are doing [it] for the self-same reason I shall hope to
do it for if my time ever comes and I am brave enough, namely,
because there seems nothing else for man to do.' It is tempting to
call this a sense of duty, which was certainly one of the casualties
of war. But there is something else at work, too.

In another, less remembered '1914' sonnet, 'Peace', Brooke
presents the war as a form of purification, thanking God for the
opportunity it offered and talking of young soldiers as:

> swimmers into cleanness leaping,
> Glad from a world grown old and cold and weary.

The odd thing about this poem, which seems the innocent product of ignorance of the realities of war, is that it was written *after*
Brooke had been caught up among the Belgian citizens fleeing the
German attack on Antwerp in October 1914.★ In fact even Siegfried Sassoon – later to compose his celebrated denunciation of the
war – was producing similar verse at the time:

> war has made us wise,
> And, fighting for our freedom, we are free.

★ 'Rivers and seas of flame leaping up hundreds of feet, crowned by black smoke
that covered the entire heavens. It lit up houses wrecked by shells, dead horses,
demolished railway stations, engines that had been taken up with their lines and
signals, and all twisted round and pulled out, as a bad child spoils a toy. And
there were joined the refugees, with all their goods on barrows and carts, in a
double line, moving forwards about a hundred yards an hour, white and drawn
and beyond emotion. The glare was like hell.' Letter to Cathleen Nesbitt,
17 October 1914, *The Letters of Rupert Brooke*, ed. Geoffrey Keynes (London,
1968), pp. 622–5.

The enthusiasm of some of the early war poets for combat is astonishing and the idea of fighting as something purifying simply irreconcilable with the bleak picture of the conflict left to us by later writers. The poems are a metaphysical counterpart to the cheery 'let's all join up together for this adventure' enthusiasm of the pals' battalions. There is something of the consolation of religion about them. As T. S. Eliot put it later, 'human kind cannot bear very much reality.'

For ordinary soldiers separated from loved ones – and for anxious or bereaved families – the sentiments of writers like Rupert Brooke offered comfort and purpose. Echoes occur time after time in the letters home which men in the trenches were encouraged to write before going into battle, and which were sealed with the instruction 'only to be opened in the event of my death'. On the eve of the Somme offensive, long after Brooke had died, Second Lieutenant John Engall of the London Territorials wrote to his 'dearest Mother and Dad' that 'the day has almost dawned when I shall really do my bit in the cause of civilization . . . I ask that you should look upon it as an honour that you have given a son for the sake of King and Country . . . Your devoted and happy son, Jack.' He was killed on the first day of the battle.

In 1915, Sub-Lieutenant Rupert Brooke joined his friend Winston Churchill's ill-fated adventure to the Dardanelles, trying to open a new front in the war. When he perished on the journey there Churchill wrote in *The Times* of a voice 'more true, more thrilling, more able to do justice to the nobility of our youth in arms engaged in this present war, than any other – more able to express their thoughts of self surrender, and with a power to carry comfort to those who watched them so intently from afar'. Brooke's body had by then been taken ashore to lie on a Greek island beneath a wooden cross among grey-green olive trees and flowering sage bushes.

While young men rushed to enlist, some of their families were encouraged to do their bit for the war effort by rooting out German fifth columnists. They were everywhere: German barbers planning to slit throats, German governesses with pistols hidden in their drawers, or a mysterious figure seen racing around on a motorbike, giving poisoned sweets to sentries. A man who claimed to be an employee of the Ordnance Survey caused great suspicion when he was seen making notes and sketches: the giveaway was that he was working on a Sunday, unimaginable in an employee of the state. In Edinburgh a seventy-four-year-old man was arrested for firing both barrels of a shotgun outside his tenement in the south-west of the city. He told the police who took him away that he had only been attempting to 'disable' a pigeon, which he was convinced was working for a German spy. In the same city the following year, the daughter of a bishop was arrested because she had been overheard on a train speaking in a foreign language. She had been practising her French for an imminent exam. Later, English soldiers stationed in Inverness arrested an old lady on similar suspicions: it turned out she had been speaking in Gaelic. In Essex, meanwhile, where there was a particular fear of German invasion, an elderly lace-seller was arrested and locked up by a local squire after rumours circulated that she'd been heard asking how many rooms there were inside various houses. An artist who had rented a cottage in the West Country was pulled in by the police after the local schoolmistress demanded to know 'If he's not a spy, why does he wear a hat like that?' By November, according to the Home Secretary, 120,000 cases of suspicious activity had been reported. By March the following year a grand total of one spy had been arrested.

Part of the reason for this manic anxiety about German spies was the heightened awareness that came from a glut of popular spy fiction before the war. Almost the only one of these scare stories familiar to modern readers – because it is the only one with any small literary merit – is Erskine Childers' 1903 *The Riddle of the Sands*. But in the early years of the twentieth century, while many in the upper classes admired German science, music and seriousness, much of the middle class thrilled to their skulduggery. Scary Germans sold cheap newspapers. In 1906, for example, the *Daily*

Mail serialized William Le Queux's thriller *The Invasion of 1910*. It told the story of a German force landing on the east coast of England and advancing on the capital, helped by acts of sabotage from cunning German spies – bakers and barbers, taxi-drivers and waiters – out to destroy noble, naive Englishmen. The author had taken £3,000 from Lord Northcliffe, the newspaper's proprietor, to help pay for his 'research'. When the newspaper baron read the manuscript he sought a return on his investment by insisting that the author rewrite the invasion route to include more of the towns where he hoped to increase the *Mail*'s readership. So in the serialized version the Germans marched through every decent-sized town between Chelmsford and Sheffield. On the eve of the first episode in the *Mail* Northcliffe dressed sandwich-board men in mock-Prussian uniforms and spiked helmets and marched them up and down Oxford Street to advertise the invasion. So effective was the book's marketing campaign that it eventually appeared in twenty-seven languages (including German) and sold a reputed million copies. At the outbreak of war, Le Queux was only one among literally dozens of hack authors making a living from worrying the citizens of the greatest imperial power in history as they ate their breakfasts.

Le Queux was a squat little snob who liked to sport pince-nez, and listed his recreation in *Who's Who* as 'revolver practice'. With characteristic immodesty, he claimed that the formation of the government's Secret Service Bureau in 1909 – which later became MI5 and MI6 – had been the consequence of his passing on intelligence he had collected. For a while – until he was forced to give it up after being declared bankrupt – he had been an honorary consul for San Marino, which gave him a uniform of which he was rather proud. But Le Queux's great discovery was of the British middle-class appetite for anxiety. In *Spies of the Kaiser: Plotting the Downfall of England*, a dashed-off thriller about the theft of plans of the naval dockyard at Rosyth, he claimed to know *for a fact* of 'over five thousand' German agents in place in Britain. When the tale was serialized in D. C. Thompson's *Weekly News*, swarms of anxious readers across the country tittle-tattled to him about suspicious Germans seen hanging around railway stations, military bases and telegraph lines. In a foreword to the book he warned as 'a patriotic Englishman' (he was the son of an immigrant French draper) that he had no wish to spread anxiety. But, even as he wrote, he had 'a file of amazing documents' on his desk, 'which plainly show the feverish activity with which this advance guard of our enemy is working to provide their employers with the most detailed information'. He claimed to have shown these papers to the Minister of War, who, shockingly, had merely returned them to him without comment.

The outbreak of war had seemed to justify Le Queux's fantasies, and in early 1915 the British people were treated to *German Spies in England*, which sold so fast that it went through six editions in three weeks. In his preface to *The German Spy System from Within* the same year, the fearless Le Queux claimed to have infiltrated 'various little foreign restaurants in the neighbourhood of Tottenham Court Road' and found seditious foreigners eagerly anticipating a German invasion. In *Britain's Deadly Peril* – yet another of his books published in 1915 – he claimed to have been out spy-hunting with naval counter-espionage officers and trapped a German waiter sending signals to passing Hun aircraft. Like so much in Le Queux's life, this was almost certainly fantasy. But you cannot fault his inventiveness. Nor his industry – in 1915 he knocked out ten books (not his record year, which was 1917, when he seems to have produced twelve).

If you were looking for spies, there was no shortage of suspects, for links between Britain and Germany were deep and complex, characterized, like relations between siblings, by mutual respect and intense rivalry. Of all the countries of Europe, it was Germany with which Britain considered it had most in common. The British admired German technology, universities and trades unions and applauded German efficiency. In 1914 the Kaiser himself was an honorary admiral of the Fleet in the Royal Navy, an honorary field marshal of the British army and Colonel in Chief of the 1st

Royal Dragoons. The Secretary of State for the Germany navy, Grand Admiral Alfred von Tirpitz, was fluent in English and had sent his daughters to Cheltenham Ladies' College. The 1911 census showed there were 53,324 Germans living in Britain: they had been one of the biggest immigrant groups in the latter years of the nineteenth century. At the outbreak of the war perhaps half the bakers in London were German (at least, that was the estimate given by an official of the master-bakers' society). There were in addition over 3,000 German waiters, nearly 4,000 German domestic servants and 2,000 German hairdressers. When the fighting began these people were terrified. The American ambassador described how some of them mobbed his embassy. 'Howling women come and say their innocent German husbands have been arrested as spies. English, Germans, Americans – everybody has daughters and wives and invalid grandmothers alone in Germany. In God's name, they ask, what can I do for them?'

Suddenly, there were German spies everywhere. The MP for West Essex, Colonel Amelius Lockwood, a man previously best known for his familiarity with the dining rooms of parliament and for the home-grown carnations he wore in his buttonholes, had already demanded to know what was to be done about the foreigners who had been snooping about Epping for the last two years, drawing sketches and taking photographs. The MP for Frome had wanted to pounce on the '66,000 trained German soldiers in England' and on the cellar 'within a quarter of a mile of Charing Cross' where there were '50,000 stands of Mauser rifles and 7½ millions of Mauser cartridges'. The minister had thanked him for this nonsense: it was an excellent example of the ludicrous stories believed by apparently sensible people. Had it not been for the pre-war reforms of the army by the then War Secretary, Richard Haldane, it is hard to imagine that the British Expeditionary Force could have left the country so efficiently. But even Haldane himself was suspect, for he spoke German, had attended a German university and was an intellectual. Any one of these qualities would have been enough to render him suspect in the eyes of much of the press. As a trinity they sealed his fate. Newspapers held forth on his unsuitability for high office, based on what *The Times* called his 'predilection for Germany', and hate mail began to arrive by the sack-load. When a coalition government was formed in 1915, Haldane was not in it.

An Aliens Registration Act, giving the government power to control the activities of foreigners in any way it chose, was passed within days of the declaration of war. (It defined as British anyone born within 'his Majesty's dominions and allegiance' worldwide.) Many Germans in Britain were instructed to leave the country forthwith (23,000 of them did so), and all others were to register themselves with the local police at once or risk a £100 fine or six months in prison. The Act also created 'prohibited areas', from which aliens were banned without a special police permit. In the next four years over 30,000 alien men would be interned. In London some were carried to the alien marshalling point in Olympia in buses bearing the slogan 'Your King and Country Need You'. At weekends, Londoners could drive out to Frith Hill Detention Camp near Camberley to look at the blond barbarians caged behind barbed-wire fences. Visitors' cars were parked in rows 'in a fashion reminiscent of Derby Day on the Downs'. *Tatler*'s motoring correspondent said that a visit was 'the very last word nowadays'. Osbert Sitwell, a young Guards officer assigned to a warehouse full of Germans in Edmonton, claimed to have encountered some oddly familiar faces. The reason became clear when one of them looked him in the eye and asked, 'Which table would you like tonight, sir?'

But all this was not enough to satisfy many loyal British. In October 1914, the *Evening News* wanted to know how it was that there were still '2,000 Germans' working in London hotels, and the *Daily Mail* was advising its readers to refuse to be served by them. German and Austrian waiters were soon losing their jobs, as organizations like the British Empire Union proclaimed the need for the 'Extirpation – Root and Branch and Seed – of German control and influence from the British Empire'. A reader wrote to tell the editor of the *Daily Mail* that he had recently visited a town on the east coast where he had seen 'a large establishment still labelled "Kindergarten". This surely ought to have been one of the first enemy words expelled from our language. It is an insult to the parents of murdered children that it should desecrate the lintel of any school door.' When Asquith refused to throw out of Downing Street the naturalized German maid of a relative, it merely bolstered dark rumours that he was a secret admirer of the Kaiser.

At the start of the war the chief British spy-catcher was a man named Basil Thomson, the senior plain-clothes detective at Scotland Yard. Thomson's father had been Archbishop of York, and Basil had spent his earlier career as a British empire official in the Pacific, until his wife's ill-health forced him to return to Britain and a job as a prison governor (where the witnessing of executions in prison yards did nothing to dim his faith in capital punishment). On the day war was declared, Thomson swooped on all the suspected German agents known to the police. There were twenty-one of them, only one of whom was ever brought to trial. But among the refugees pouring into Britain after the fall of Belgium was a man bearing an American passport in the name of Charles A. Inglis. In fact this was a genuine German spy, Karl Hans Lody, who spent the next few weeks cycling around the British countryside, sketching military installations (including, incidentally, plans of the naval base at Rosyth). Lody was captured, tried and sentenced to death in the Tower, a fate he met with courage and dignity.* ('I have had just judges, and I shall die as an officer – not as a spy,' he wrote to friends in Germany on the eve of his execution. 'Farewell. God bless you.') This was the sort of German the British could respect. 'He never flinched, he never cringed, but he died,'

---

* All told, eleven spies were executed in the Tower of London, mostly in the rifle range there. All were shot at dawn by detachments from the Guards.

Thomson noted approvingly, 'as one would wish all Englishmen to die – quietly and undramatically, supported by the proud consciousness of having done his duty.'

At the height of spy mania, some of Basil Thomson's investigations were farcical. In the early days of the war he received an excited telegram from police in Suffolk, with dramatic news that they had captured two German spies travelling in a car loaded with radio equipment. This was soon followed by a request from the War Office: two of their men, sent into East Anglia to track down a suspected German wireless transmitter, had been arrested – could he help? Thomson put two and two together, made four and sent the Suffolk Chief Constable a message telling him to set the men free, while at the same time advising the War Office that it might be a good idea if in future all counter-intelligence officers travelled in uniform. The following Monday a message came from another Chief Constable. His men had had a couple of German spies in the cells overnight, each speaking fluent English and disguised in British military uniform.

In this collective feverishness, astonishing rumours swept the country. Vast numbers of Russian troops were said to have clandestinely arrived in Britain to help the tiny British army fight the Hun. Transported by boat from Archangel to the east coast of Scotland, they were making their way by train to London. A Perthshire landowner testified that 125,000 Cossacks had crossed his estates, and Lady Baden-Powell, wife of the founder of the Boy Scouts, rushed down to the local railway station to see them pass through. In Edinburgh, porters had been seen sweeping out of railway carriages the snow which had fallen from the soldiers' coats. At Carlisle the Russians had demanded vodka from inside their shuttered train. In Durham they had been getting off their trains to jam roubles into station slot-machines. A marine engineer interviewed by a newspaper claimed to have travelled with the Russians all the way from Archangel and to have been in the 193rd train-load of troops to pass through York. Four Russians billeted on a landlady in Crewe had eaten her out of house and home. At Rugby they drank all the coffee the station could provide. By the time the Russians reached London – where Euston Station had been closed for a day and a half to allow them all to disembark – they were said to be tossing their now useless coins to East End children. Where, precisely, this rumour had come from was never properly established. But the official British Press Bureau did nothing to deny it until 15 September. By then, any still undiscovered German spy would have passed the alarming news back to Berlin.

4. Learning to Hate

Frohe Weihnachten!

On 8 January 1915 the front page of the *Daily Mirror* ('certified circulation larger than any other daily newspaper in the world') carried a photograph of a couple of dozen soldiers posing in the frozen cold of a Western Front morning. There was a sergeant at the front of the group, a lance-corporal alongside him. The men stood relaxed. One soldier had a cigarette in his mouth. There was the flicker of a smile on some of the faces staring at the camera. The remarkable thing about the picture – what had made it worthy of the front page – was the uniforms. For these were clearly men from *both* the British and German armies, proof that something remarkable – something that generals on both sides had feared – had actually happened.

Few events in the entire war are more resonant than the Christmas truce of 1914, and none has been more frequently co-opted into the service of ideological argument about the war. The decision to stop fighting, to allow time to collect and bury the dead, to sing together, to exchange presents, have a smoke, play football in no man's land even, seems a triumph of the human spirit over the brass-hats who thought of the soldiers not as individuals but as ranks of expendable automatons.

Although often presented as one of the myths of the war, like the angels which were said to have protected the retreating British Expeditionary Force at Mons, the spontaneous decision by pockets of men on both sides to lay down their arms over Christmas 1914 is completely true, and it much troubled the commanders. It did not, however, involve anywhere near the entire army on either side. By late December the British Expeditionary Force had been augmented by thousands of Territorial reservists, and many more soldiers from the empire: the total stood at well over a quarter of a million men. Only a minority of them were in the front line, and only a minority within that minority were involved in the extraordinary events of the Christmas truce. After five months of combat, the armies were stranded in their trenches wherever the last fighting had left them, often just a few dozen yards apart. It was assumed on both sides that there was little likelihood of a new offensive until the spring, and so an attitude of 'live and let live' had developed; in parts of the line an unwritten agreement had come about that neither side would shoot while the men ate their breakfast and visited the latrines in the morning. With no further advance expected within the next few weeks, and with Christmas approaching, senior commanders saw a real risk of these informal truces becoming more widespread. General Sir Horace Smith-Dorrien, the short-tempered commander of the British II Corps, issued an order banning 'unofficial armistices and the exchange of tobacco and other comforts, however tempting and occasionally amusing they may be'.

Senior officers knew that without an offensive spirit armies lose wars, and they had been relieved when a proposal from Pope

Benedict XV for a Christmas ceasefire ran into the ground as the Vatican reluctantly accepted that the festival fell on different dates in western Europe and Russia, and meant nothing much in Turkey (Germany's ally) or Japan (Britain's ally). Men in the trenches were, of course, well aware that it was Christmas. Letters, cards and parcels from home had been arriving in the trenches in great numbers. Some British officers even complained that the 350,000 embossed brass boxes sent as gifts in the name of the king's seventeen-year-old daughter Princess Mary – filled with tobacco, cigarettes or sweets (or writing paper and pencil for non-smokers) – caused such inconvenience to the supply chain that they disrupted the distribution of normal rations. Then, on 23 December, a sentry with the 2nd Battalion of the Cameronians looked out from his trench near Laventie on the Belgian border and saw unarmed Germans clambering out of the trenches opposite. They were making friendly gestures. In other sections of the line, British soldiers heard Germans shouting 'Happy Christmas!' That evening an order came from headquarters advising 'special vigilance', because 'it is thought possible the enemy may be contemplating an attack during Xmas or New Year.' But by the time the order had been delivered, front-line troops had already heard Christmas carols from the other side of no man's land. 'They sang "Silent Night" – "Stille Nacht",' remembered a private in the Queen's Regiment. 'I shall never forget it, it was one of the highlights of my life.' When the Germans in the trenches opposite the 2nd Battalion of the Bedfordshire Regiment gave out a tuneful version of 'O Tannenbaum', the English soldiers replied with a tribute to a music-hall impresario –

> We are Fred Karno's army, the ragtime infantry,
> We cannot fight, we cannot shoot, what bleeding use are we?

– to the tune of the popular hymn 'The Church's One Foundation'.

There seems to have been nothing particularly premeditated about the Christmas fraternization, and accounts of the time are so varied that they seem to support the idea that the truce arose spontaneously in different sectors of the line. Sometimes it began with soldiers in the British trenches listening spell-bound as they heard the men they had been trying to kill singing recognizable carols, at other times with home-made 'YOU NO FIGHT, WE NO FIGHT' placards hoisted above ground level. In some sections of the line British soldiers were perplexed by the sudden appearance of lights in the German trenches before realizing that their enemies had put up Christmas trees. Almost all accounts suggest it was a German initiative. In some parts of the front the truce was only possible because the German units contained men who had learned English while working in Britain as hairdressers, waiters* or taxi-drivers. Lieutenant Bruce Bairnsfather described how 'a voice in the darkness shouted in English, with a strong German accent, "Come over here!"' to be answered with a lot of laughter and then a sergeant suggesting the German might like to come over to the British trenches. The two individuals agreed to rendezvous half-way, from which meeting the sergeant returned with German cigars and cigarettes which he had swapped for a couple of tins of vegetable stew and some Capstan cigarettes. Similar exchanges took place in any number of places along the line – plum puddings for sauerkraut, biscuits for coffee, cigarettes for schnapps. Men who a day or so earlier would have liked nothing more than to put a bullet in the man beside them now stood showing off photographs of their families, girlfriends or children. In some sections of no man's land there were even shared Christmas dinners. It is often suggested that the friendliness did not involve officers, but there are several accounts of junior officers also climbing out into no man's land to shake hands and exchange gifts with their German opposite numbers.

The weather had changed on Christmas Eve, and on Christmas Day a sharp frost froze the mud and glazed the ground with white. The sky was clear and blue. 'It was just the sort of day for peace to be declared. It would have made such a good finale,' thought a

---

* British soldiers joked that if someone shouted 'Waiter!' 'a dozen German heads would appear in the trenches opposite answering "Yes sir!"'

lieutenant in the Warwickshire Regiment. 'I should have liked to have suddenly heard an immense siren blowing. Everybody to stop and say "What was that?" Siren blowing again: appearance of a small figure running across the frozen mud and waving something. He gets closer – a telegraph boy with a wire! He hands it to me. With trembling fingers I open it: "War off, return home – George, R. I." Cheers! But no, it was a nice, fine day, that was all.' Instead, they used the time to bury their dead, until, with a pre-arranged series of shots into the air or the firing of a signal flare, the peace ended and the killing resumed.

The truce in the trenches is one of the most poignant tableaux of the entire war. Back in Britain, Christmas 1914 was very different from usual, with menfolk missing and mothers, wives and sweethearts anxious. In recent years an estimated seven out of ten children's Christmas toys had been imported from Germany. In the current hostilities that clearly could not continue, so the December edition of the children's magazine *Little Folks* advised:

> Little girls and little boys
> Never suck your German toys
> German soldiers licked will make
> Darling Baby's tummy ache.
> Parents you should always try,
> Only British toys to buy,
> Though to pieces they be picked
> British soldiers can't be licked.

While parents were absorbing this advice, the unimaginable happened. At breakfast time on 16 December 1914, a group of German warships slipped through coastal defences and opened fire on England's east coast. Their targets were Scarborough, Whitby and the Hartlepools, none of which had had any warning of danger. The shells struck houses, churches and schools. A seven-year-old girl in Hartlepool recalled seeing panic-stricken families running past her front window, mothers carrying babies and fathers their larger children. In 2013, at the age of 105, she was still struck by the fact that some had grabbed the cakes they had baked for Christmas. All were trying to get as far inland – and out of the range of the German naval guns – as they could. But the shells fell randomly in the streets as well as on buildings, and many were killed by their hot shattering fragments. Forty-two of the 119 people killed were children, including a six-month-old girl. The victims also included the first British soldier to die on English soil for hundreds of years, a former head teacher and choirmaster who had signed up as a private with the Durham Light Infantry. From now on, while families in England worried about the dangers their menfolk faced on the continent, some of the menfolk worried about the dangers their families faced at home.

Then, on Christmas Eve itself, came Britain's first experience of aerial warfare, when a German plane dropped a small bomb near Dover Castle and a man gathering holly to decorate the church next day was blown out of a tree. Meanwhile, a newspaper reported that four escaped German prisoners of war had been arrested in Birmingham. They had been trying to get into a pantomime.

There is nothing at all normal about living in a hole in the ground and trying to kill your neighbours. The Christmas truce of 1914 had been proof of a more natural human instinct, and it pointed up the difficulty of attempting to maintain what the army called 'an offensive spirit'. It might not, perhaps, be strictly necessary to *hate* the enemy. But it would certainly help. How, then, to maintain a moral passion in the war, an instinctive sense of why there could be no wavering? Second only to Kitchener's commanding stare, the most reproduced poster of the war showed a British soldier standing guard as behind him a mother and child fled their burning home. The caption read 'REMEMBER BELGIUM'. The message was clear: fight the Germans or they will do in England what they have done in Belgium.

An estimated million Belgians had fled their country after the German invasion at the beginning of August 1914, about 100,000 of them to Britain. This was such an influx that at one point the Home Secretary thought he would have to build great camps to accommodate them, probably in the south of Ireland. In the short term, public buildings like Earls Court, Alexandra Palace and the Aldwych skating rink in London were turned into temporary refuges. Later, there was even an entire Belgian town for refugee munitions workers near Gateshead, named after the Queen of the Belgians – 'Elisabethville' – and patrolled by Belgian police. But most of the Belgian refugees were billeted in British towns and villages, where they were not necessarily very popular. 'Most people agree they are fat, lazy, greedy, amiable and inclined to take all the benefits heaped on them as a matter of course,' commented a vicar's daughter near Stroud, in Gloucestershire. But the fleeing Belgians had brought with them all manner of horror stories which bolstered Britain's moral cause to such an extent that some society ladies seem to have decided that a small collection of Belgian refugees was a positive adornment. 'How are your Belgian atrocities?' they asked one another.

Disentangling fact from fiction was not easy. Villages had been burned to the ground. Babies had been tossed on the points of bayonets. Women and girls had been raped. Children had had their hands cut off, women their breasts. German soldiers had played football with babies' heads. The accounts were more than sufficient for the *Daily Mail* to roar that the evidence was 'unanswerable', never to be forgotten or forgiven. All civilians suffer when their country is fought over. But the swift and ruthless German invasion did seem to include a policy of deliberately terrorizing non-combatants. The stories reaching Britain suggested the German military had decided that the subjection of Belgium involved exemplary destruction. The German term was *Schrecklichkeit* – 'frightfulness' – and it involved the murder of men, women and children, the burning of homes and, in the case of the medieval treasure-house of Louvain, the systematic destruction and looting of an entire city. Terrible brutality seemed to have been meted out to monks and priests in particular, some of whom were said to have been hung upside down inside massive church bells and used as clappers.

The effect of these atrocity stories on the British people among whom the Belgian refugees were now living was to invest the war with a clear moral purpose. Yet how many of them were completely true? If the stories could be authenticated and published abroad, would not other countries – notably the United States – also feel outraged and join the crusade? So in December 1914 the British government announced that it would establish firm facts by collecting proof, in preparation for a propaganda exercise that could be shown to be based on proper evidence. The man it invited to chair an official inquiry was James, Viscount Bryce, a distinguished lawyer who had once sat around the cabinet table with Gladstone. His snow-white hair, beard and eyebrows gave him an appearance described by a biographer as 'alarmingly like an energetic West Highland terrier'. A kinder comparison would be to say that his twinkling eyes and full beard gave him something of the look of an Old Testament prophet. Indeed, in 1876, he had climbed Mount Ararat, where he believed he had discovered one of the timbers from Noah's ark. There was nothing dramatic about his speaking powers, but his dull speeches and known devotion to the facts made him well suited to the job: what was required was credibility, not flashiness. Bryce's credentials were much enhanced by the fact that he had recently been British ambassador to the United States. If his report could swing American political opinion and persuade that country to join the cause it would certainly hasten an allied victory.

Yet Bryce's investigation laboured under a terrible handicap. Although it had teams of barristers at its disposal, it took no evidence itself, merely examining the 1,200 accounts collected from refugees and soldiers, augmented by diaries and letters taken from dead or captured German soldiers. Some of these letters freely admitted the execution of civilians and the looting of Belgian property. But entire sections of testimony from refugees were impossible to verify – one of the English barristers noted that they had been given six separate addresses where Belgian children had been seen with their hands cut off, but that 'no such children have been seen or heard of at any of those addresses'. Still, the sheer volume of claims was overwhelming. Witness statements painted a consistent picture of grotesque abuses. German soldiers had used civilians as human shields. They had murdered children, old people, priests and the disabled. They had burned down villages. Women had been raped, children too. They had broken into houses, gathered all the food together, and then fouled it. Wounded prisoners had been shot and the Red Cross and white flag disregarded.

The refugees reported plenty of examples. 'A hair-dresser was murdered in his kitchen while he was sitting with a child on each knee. A paralytic was murdered in his garden,' said Bryce's report. 'The corpse of a man with his legs cut off, who was partly bound, was seen by another witness, who also saw a girl of seventeen dressed only in a chemise – and in great distress. She alleged that she had been one of a group of girls who had been dragged into a field, stripped naked and violated, and that some of them had been killed with the bayonet.' Dates and places were given for some of the outrages, but not for all. And while the attacks upon women and children made the most sensational reading, the majority of the victims of what would now be considered war crimes seem to have been able-bodied Belgian men. Bryce and his committee made sensible observations about excesses happening in many wars, and noted that what the Germans had done in Belgium did not justify reprisals against German civilians. But the effect of reading about German soldiers murdering children or sauntering about with babies hanging from the bayonets of rifles slung over shoulders can be imagined. 'These disclosures will not have been made in vain if they touch and rouse the conscience of mankind,' Bryce remarked. At its most legalistic level, the British decision to go to war had been about upholding international treaties – if nations were to start ignoring agreements freely entered into, the entire basis of civilization was at risk. The Bryce report into what had happened in Brave Little Belgium translated the war into a struggle altogether less philosophical. Will Crooks, one of the very first working-class Labour MPs (he had spent part of his childhood in an East End workhouse), signed up potential soldiers with the words 'Our homes are in danger, our wives and families are threatened . . . The brutal murders of innocent folk in Belgium show us what Germany would do.'

Every nation on earth was now at risk from enemy agents smoking Turkish cigarettes who were plotting, warned the thriller-writer William Le Queux, to repeat the 'same savagery and unbridled lust with which poor Belgium was swept from end to end'. The use of the word 'lust' is appropriate, for what had happened to Belgium was more than the breaking of an elderly treaty intended to guarantee an inherently implausible state. It was a national 'rape'. Bryce's report was published in the spring of 1915 and was a treat for the newly created War Propaganda Bureau established in Wellington House, near Buckingham Palace. Here, they fell on the gory details with relish, translated them into thirty languages and sent tens of thousands of English-language copies to the still neutral United States. The effort paid off: three years later, after the country had at last joined the war, the American government was still printing the words 'REMEMBER BELGIUM' above posters encouraging citizens to buy war bonds to fund the fighting. They were illustrated with a picture showing a long-haired girl being dragged away by a sour-faced German soldier in a pickelhaube helmet.

Days before the Bryce report was published in North America, Germany obliged the allies with a monumental new atrocity. On 7 May 1915 a German submarine torpedoed the transatlantic liner the *Lusitania*. This great four-funnelled vessel had been built with a subsidy from the British government, and been designed as a symbol of national prestige, one of the biggest and fastest ships crossing the Atlantic, the world's premium international shipping route. While the United States was neutral in the war, the *Lusitania*'s destination, Britain, was not, and just before the liner departed

New York for Liverpool on Saturday 1 May 1915, the German embassy in the United States had issued a formal warning, printed in fifty newspapers. It cautioned anyone intending to cross the Atlantic that 'a state of war exists between Germany and her allies and Great Britain and her allies' and that any vessel flying the British flag was 'liable to destruction'. It provoked a few passengers to cancel their journeys, but most shrugged off the warning and boarded the *Lusitania* as planned. On 7 May the liner was just off the coast of south-west Ireland. Here, a German submarine, the *U-20*, lay in wait.

The danger posed by German submarines was well understood. In the first weeks of the war, the Royal Navy had deployed three ageing cruisers in the North Sea, nicknamed the 'live-bait squadron'. All three had been destroyed by torpedoes from a single U-boat (*Unterseeboot*), with the loss of almost 1,500 lives. In the days between the *Lusitania* leaving New York and arriving off the Irish coast, German submarines had sunk twenty-three merchant ships in the area. On the morning of Friday 7 May a messenger from the *Lusitania*'s telegraph room brought Captain Turner an encrypted message from the British Admiralty warning him that U-boats were known to be operating off the Irish coast. As a precaution, the captain ordered a blackout on board, posted extra lookouts and readied the lifeboats. When the liner came in sight of the Old Head of Kinsale lighthouse in County Cork he decided to hug the Irish coast. It was lunchtime on a lovely spring day – bright and clear – and passengers gathered on deck, ready to admire the wild Irish coastline.

Unknown to everyone on the *Lusitania*, when the captain altered course he had presented Kapitänleutnant Walther Schweiger on the *U-20*, watching through his periscope 700 yards away, with a perfect broadside target. The ship was too big, too defenceless, too perfectly positioned, to escape when one of the liner's lookouts spotted a torpedo burrowing through the water towards it 'like an invisible hand with a piece of a chalk on a blackboard'. At about ten past two in the afternoon, the torpedo struck the *Lusitania* 10 feet below the waterline. The great ship heeled over in the water, making it almost impossible to launch many of the lifeboats, and then plunged bow first into the sea, her stern rising to lift the enormous propellers of her four engines clear of the water – one of them slicing off the leg of a man hanging by a rope over the stern. The surface of the sea was alive, one survivor recalled, with 'waving hands and arms belonging to men and frantic women and children in agonizing efforts to stay afloat'. Within eighteen minutes of the attack, the *Lusitania* had vanished. Most of those still aboard – well over a thousand – were now dead or dying. Over a hundred of them were American.

Now there was no longer any need to remind people of the outrages the Germans were said to have perpetrated in Belgium. A new recruitment poster quickly appeared, shrieking 'REMEMBER THE LUSITANIA'. There was no picture, just 300 words of text describing how a mother had been pitched into the sea with her three children and tried desperately to hold them above the waves until, on being hauled into a lifeboat, she realized they were all dead. 'With her hair streaming down her back and her form shaking with sorrow, she took hold of each little one from the rescuers and reverently placed it into the water again, and the people of the boat wept with her as she murmured a little sobbing prayer to the great God above. ENLIST TODAY.'

Lord Northcliffe, proprietor of the *Daily Mail*, was a man convinced that the British people like nothing so much 'as a good hate',* and his newspaper displayed a horrifying photograph of dead children under the headline 'BRITISH AND AMERICAN BABIES MURDERED BY THE KAISER'. Even the Kaiser seemed to acknowledge that the sinking of the *Lusitania* had been a mistake, claiming that he would never have authorized the attack had he known in advance there were so many women and children

---

* He could never be accused of saying one thing and doing another. He died after the war convinced the Germans had poisoned his ice-cream.

aboard. This was casuistry, for the Kaiser's government attempted to justify the sinking on the grounds that the vessel had been carrying soldiers and munitions: to be certain of that they would have had to examine the passenger list. (As to the munitions on board, a manifest submitted after the liner had left New York showed that, in addition to quantities of meat, leather, confectionery and automobile parts, there were over 4 million Remington rifle cartridges, 1,250 cases of shrapnel shells, eighteen cases of fuses, a great quantity of aluminium and fifty cases of bronze powder.)

Hostility towards German immigrants remaining in Britain now became very ugly. There were plenty of them living in the *Lusitania*'s home port of Liverpool (even the two birds on the city's emblematic Liver Building had been designed by an immigrant German woodcarver), and German-owned businesses, notably pork butchers, were trashed or burned out. In east London there were more violent riots. A new Anti-German League set out to recruit a million members. Lord Derby proposed raising a 'Lusitania Battalion' in Liverpool (it never happened). On 12 May, the *Daily Sketch* demanded mass internment of the remaining Germans in Britain, under the headline 'Lock Them All Up!' For their own safety as much as anything else, Prime Minister Asquith made an effort to do so, with foreigners despatched to hulks anchored off the English coast, confined in disused factories or interned in camps. Conditions in these internment camps varied hugely. Near Wakefield the internees were accommodated at a holiday camp. At Newbury racecourse they were kept in horseboxes. The biggest group – which included the unfortunate designer of the Liver Birds – was sent to the Isle of Man. Here, almost 3,000 wealthier families lived in some comfort at holiday homes. The less well-off were held in wooden huts at Knockaloe on the west of the island, which grew to the size of a small town, complete with hospitals, theatres and recreation grounds, all presided over by a colonel newly returned from administering Bechuanaland, a British protectorate in southern

Africa. The 23,000 inmates included many who felt their loyalty to their new country gave the authorities no right to lock them up. 'I ain't no bloomin' 'Un, I came from The Smoke,' an apparent Cockney protested to a visiting reporter from the *Manchester Guardian*. The camp authorities provided the reporter with a leaflet suggesting inmates had a balanced diet, but internees claimed food supplies were sometimes so poor that they were reduced to eating dogs, seagulls and Manx cats.

The Swiss consul in London, who was looking after German interests during the war, visited the camps and coined the expression 'barbed-wire disease' for the restless, bad-tempered psychological condition that he claimed afflicted everyone who spent six months or longer interned. They 'cannot stand the slightest opposition and readily fly into a passion . . . They find intense difficulty concentrating on one particular object; their mode of life becomes unstable, and there is restlessness in all their actions.' People lost their memories and found it difficult to get a decent night's sleep. The pervading sense of gloom meant that one internee's piece of bad news – a son lost in the war, for example – could make the whole community dejected. In single-sex internment camps, like the men-only one in Wakefield, the loss of peace and quiet and privacy aggravated the deprivation caused by the absence of women and children. As the Swiss consul pointed out, an imprisoned criminal could tick off the days to the date of his release. Internees had no idea how long they were in for. When the war finally ended there were still 24,255 aliens held in internment camps. Some of them had sons serving with the British army.

The declaration of war had been presented as the honouring of an international duty. Early recruitment had been the product of romantic exuberance and patriotic duty. Now, the fighting had become a humanitarian cause, to save the world from barbarism. By late 1915 the war had already lasted for longer than many had thought possible when it began. But there was good reason to believe that the longer it continued, the more appetite there would be for it to be brought to a definitive resolution. Hatreds had been set, and, with skilful manipulation of information, could be maintained. In 1915 there was no Christmas truce in the trenches. 'People remembered the *Lusitania* a bit,' wrote a captain in the Queen's Westminster Rifles. 'The Huns shouted across and wished us a merry Xmas, but all they got from us was two hours of 9.2 howitzer in their front parapet.'

5. Drunken Swabs

Even Methuselah, London Zoo's tortoise, apparently understood the shell shortage.

Six months before the catastrophe of the *Lusitania*, another British ship had been sunk by the German navy, but news of this event was handled in an entirely different fashion. On the morning of 27 October 1914, HMS *Audacious*, one of the prized state-of-the-art battleships of the Royal Navy, had emerged from Lough Swilly on the northern Irish coast for gunnery practice. *Audacious* had been in service for only a year and had yet to engage the enemy. Shortly before nine, as the enormous ship prepared for her firing exercise off the coast of Donegal – 'being as their [the German] fleet wouldn't come out we had to fire at something,' remarked a crew member – there was a low thud. Officers on the bridge thought nothing of it, and a Sub-Lieutenant Spragge, who was in his bath at the time, assumed it was perhaps a start to the target practice.

The bugle call 'Close watertight doors' disabused everyone, and the cause of the thud became abundantly clear when the captain attempted to alter course. The ship had been holed, just below the port engine room, and was almost unmanoeuvrable. Fear of submarines had already caused the entire Grand Fleet to be relocated from the great natural anchorage in Scapa Flow in the Orkneys to Lough Swilly, and the captain's first instinct was that his ship had been torpedoed. He hoisted a flag to warn other warships and watched as they followed safety rules and fled the scene as quickly as possible. In fact, *Audacious* had struck a mine, almost certainly laid by a commandeered German passenger liner, the *Berlin*, which had just passed through the area.

The captain of *Audacious* attempted to head back to Lough Swilly where he hoped he might beach his ship, but after a couple of hours, with the engine rooms flooded, the ship was all but immovable. As the day wore on and the ship settled further and further in the water, the crew was gradually evacuated and attempts made by one ship after another to tow *Audacious* back to the naval base. At this point another luxurious, four-funnelled liner, the RMS *Olympic*, came on the scene, nearing the end of a crossing from New York to Britain. Because of the war in Europe the ship had been repainted in grey and carried only 153 passengers – the smallest number in her history. The *Olympic* offered shelter to much of the *Audacious* crew and attempted to give a tow to the stricken warship. Three attempts were made, and three times the rope broke. It was now clear that the pride of the Royal Navy would have to be left to sink, and the few of the crew who had volunteered to stay aboard evacuated. At about nine that evening the passengers on the *Olympic* and the rescued crew members of the *Audacious* heard a tremendous explosion on the wallowing warship. Either her magazine had exploded or her boilers had burst. The great battleship sank beneath the waves.

Almost every one of the crew had been saved, many of them later disembarking from the generous refuge of the *Olympic*, dressed in the dry clothing they had been given – everything from dancing slippers to top hats. But the loss of one of the navy's most modern ships was a calamity which the Admiralty was determined to keep from the Germans. To do this it attempted an extraordinary cover-up. The *Olympic* was detained in Lough Swilly for almost a week, the passengers refused permission to leave the ship, her radio silenced and all other communication with the shore heavily censored by a Royal Navy officer sent aboard the liner. The only person allowed to leave the ship was the American steel magnate Charles Schwab, who, after giving a promise of silence, was permitted to continue his journey to London in pursuit of a contract to supply munitions for the Royal Navy. Since the loss of *Audacious* had been witnessed by everyone aboard the passenger liner, a moment's thought might have suggested that the decision to try to hush everything up was, in the words of a navy doctor on board the nearby HMS *Marlborough*, 'obvious balls', as 'a whole liner full of women etc. can't be kept quiet.' Talkativeness may not be the exclusive prerogative of either sex, but an attempt to silence an entire deck crammed with spectators, many of whom were equipped with cameras, was never likely to succeed.

Nonetheless, in cabinet Churchill argued forcefully in favour of the strategy, and Lloyd George and Asquith agreed, albeit with major misgivings. Lord Kitchener's view was simple: he couldn't see why the public was ever given *any* bad military news. When the *Olympic* was finally allowed to continue on her way and docked in Belfast, sixty of the British passport holders who disembarked immediately volunteered for the army. 'We had a splendid passage,' one of them told a reporter, 'what more could you want to know?' But when the ship's orchestra was returned to New York, American reporters had a much easier time of gleaning the story and published detailed accounts of the sinking in the newspapers. The British Admiralty, however, remained blithely indifferent, distributing the *Audacious* crew around other vessels of the fleet, and keeping her name on the official list of ships serving in the Royal Navy until the war was over. It was not until Thursday

14 November 1918 that the British government disclosed that their prize battleship had spent almost all of the fighting at the bottom of the sea.

So how much were the British people entitled to be told about the epic struggle in which they were engaged? Not very much, if the War Secretary, Lord Kitchener, got his way. During his 1898 mission up the Nile to avenge the death of General Gordon at Khartoum he had once been besieged in his tent by journalists anxious to know how he saw the campaign progressing. He strode through them with the words 'Out of my way, you drunken swabs!' As War Secretary he was no warmer to the Fourth Estate. His attitude at least had the virtue of being clear: since it was often so difficult to distinguish between pieces of information that might be useful to the enemy and those that were harmless, 'whenever there is any doubt, we do not hesitate to prevent publication.' Asquith felt that the imperial hero's disregard for the role of journalism was attributable to an 'undisguised contempt for the "public" in all its moods and manifestations'. But then Asquith was a politician, another species for whom Kitchener of Khartoum felt nothing but disdain.

The reason why the government could even consider a cover-up on the scale of the *Audacious* was that within days of the outbreak of war it had pushed a Defence of the Realm Act through parliament. This was a remarkable, catch-all piece of legislation, allowing the government to commandeer land and businesses and making it illegal for civilians to buy binoculars, fly kites, ring church bells or give bread to animals. Subsequent provisions of the law cut the opening hours of pubs, allowed for beer to be watered down and introduced British Summer Time. One of its more straightforward effects, though, was to make it an offence to discuss military matters in public or to spread military rumours. To Kitchener's pleasure, it also allowed the government to censor newspapers: under section 27, for example, it was an offence for a newspaper to report anything that might 'prejudice recruiting', 'prejudice relations with foreign powers' or 'cause disaffection to His Majesty'. It didn't leave much room for dissenting comment on how the war was being managed.

At the outbreak of war the government had sent for Winston Churchill's friend the clever Conservative lawyer F. E. Smith, and asked him to take command of an official Press Bureau, with a specific brief to stop newspapers publishing anything that might help the enemy or undermine public morale. (Journalists quickly named it 'the Suppress Bureau'.) F. E. Smith was arrogant, a master of the insouciant one-liner and one of the very few men in Britain with an ambition as great as Churchill's. But he did at least understand that fighting the sort of war that Britain was now embarked upon would require a slightly more sophisticated approach than Kitchener's. ('Kitchener cannot understand that he is working in a democratic country,' he said. 'He rather thinks he is in Egypt where the press is represented by a dozen mangy newspaper correspondents whom he can throw in the Nile if they object to the way they are treated.')

The sinking of a single warship at sea – with almost no loss of life – was an easier thing to try to keep secret than the fate of most of the British army in continental Europe. In the early stages of the war, since they were being told little or nothing by officialdom, the newspapers had had to manage as best they could, by printing extracts from soldiers' letters home, usually sent on by the men's families. Indeed, throughout the war it is fair to say that the regional press, which was able to avoid much government censorship, published remarkably accurate accounts of battlefield combat, and a number of reporters did manage to get themselves to France, despite a notable lack of official help. But they did not find life easy. When, for example, Kitchener discovered that Philip Gibbs of the *Daily Chronicle* was covering the advance of the British Expeditionary Force, he ordered his arrest, with a warning that if he was caught again he would be put up against a wall and shot.

Yet within a month of the outbreak of war, on 30 August 1914, under the headline 'BROKEN BRITISH REGIMENTS BATTLING AGAINST ODDS', a special Sunday edition of

The Times had brought terrifying news to the breakfast table. The newspaper's reporter Arthur Moore described how the unthinkable had happened: the British Expeditionary Force at Mons was in full retreat before the German onslaught, 'forced backwards and ever backwards by the sheer unconquerable mass of numbers'. Kitchener thought this precisely the sort of pessimistic gibbering that he had wanted to prevent. There was more: 'Our losses are very great,' the report continued, 'I have seen the broken bits of many regiments . . . To sum up, the first great German effort has succeeded. We have to face the fact that the B. E. F., which bore the great weight of the blow, has suffered terrible losses and requires immediate and immense reinforcement.' Nothing could have more given the lie to the confident forecasts of quick victory. A similar report in the *Weekly Dispatch* – 'GERMAN TIDAL WAVE – OUR SOLDIERS OVERWHELMED BY NUMBERS' – told the same unhappy story. Both newspapers were the property of Lord Northcliffe.

Since journalists were banned from the BEF, the reporters had gathered their information from retreating soldiers they had met on the roads. What was more, their story was accurate. Having missed the opportunity to do so literally, the first reaction of the military authorities was to try to shoot the messenger metaphorically. In Westminster, politicians demanded to know what was going to happen to the perpetrators of this defeatist nonsense, to which a third member of Northcliffe's newspaper organization, the *Daily Mail*, responded by pointing out that *The Times* article which so distressed them had been passed for publication by the government's own Press Bureau under F. E. Smith. To the astonishment of the paper's editors, Smith had not only authorized the report but added at the end, 'The British Expeditionary Force has won indeed imperishable glory, but it needs men, men and yet more men. We want reinforcements and we want them now.' The *Daily Mail* noisily disclosed that the offending articles bore Smith's fingerprints. The chief censor attempted to defend himself in the House of Commons by saying that he had been doing his best to ginger up recruiting. Winston Churchill wrote to Lord North-cliffe to object that 'I never saw such panic-stricken stuff written by any war correspondent before.' But, though it cost him his job at the Bureau, it turned out that Smith had calculated correctly: in the week following publication of the reports, 175,000 men volunteered for military service, 33,204 of them on a single day.

In the wake of this debacle, Kitchener began to realize that the thirst for information had somehow to be quenched, especially if he wished to fill the ranks of the new army he was trying to build. It was one thing to be fighting a distant war in Sudan or South Africa, with a regular army of professional soldiers. It was quite another to be staring out from posters telling civilians 'Your Country Needs You' for battles only a few dozen miles from the English coast. His distaste for the drunken swabs did not lessen. He merely found what he thought to be a way around them. Kitchener appointed a Royal Engineer major, Ernest Swinton, to be the only official war correspondent. As Swinton's instructions specifically prohibited him from giving any indication that he had seen anything at all with his own eyes, his by-line – 'Eyewitness' – was something of a misnomer. Among ordinary soldiers he was soon known as 'Eyewash'. In early 1915, the British War Office finally gave in to pressure and accredited five correspondents, albeit on the condition that anything they wrote had to be approved by the censor's office before publication. They included the enterprising Philip Gibbs.

By this time, the Press Bureau had come to recognize the danger of incessantly gung-ho portrayals of the fighting. The language – 'heroic resistance' instead of 'retreats' – was one thing. But as the army grew bigger there were thousands more individual witnesses to the war, for in their letters home and in conversations on leave soldiers were giving their families a much more realistic portrayal. There was an additional danger in coverage that was too upbeat. The Press Bureau told newspaper proprietors that if the papers continually claimed that Germany was within measurable distance of starvation, bankruptcy and revolution, 'the public can have no true appreciation of the facts or of the gigantic task and heavy sacrifices before them.' If the British people were to endure the long road ahead of them, they needed to be prepared and informed.

The proprietor who claimed (with some justice) to understand the instincts of the British people best was the man whose papers had broken the news of the smashing of the British Expeditionary Force, Alfred Charles William Harmsworth, first Baron Northcliffe of the Isle of Thanet. While there have been occasional newspaper proprietors who are neither mad nor bad, they are unusual. Northcliffe was bombastic, bullying and brilliant, and by the end of his life he was also most certainly mad. His paper the *Daily Mail* was a glittering success – modestly priced, simply written, noisy, conservative, scaremongering, sporty, full of human interest and medical quackery, larded with competitions and stridently imperial in tone: 'We know that the advance of the Union Jack means protection for weaker races, justice for the oppressed, liberty for the down-trodden,' declared an editorial on the paper's fourth birthday in 1900. Its correspondence columns bubbled with anxious inquiries from alleged readers on such topics as 'Should the Clergy Dance?' (a debate which ran for a fortnight). It was, naturally, thoroughly Germanophobic.

'A newspaper run by office boys for office boys' had been the Tory Prime Minister Lord Salisbury's majestic turn-of-the-century put-down of the *Mail*, exactly the sort of remark one might expect from a member of the traditional ruling class uneasily watching the growth of mass democracy. The *Mail* was a perfect product for the new age of wider literacy brought about by Victorian educational reforms. By the time war broke out it was selling nearly a million copies a day, and its proprietor controlled four out of every ten morning newspapers, including *The Times*, then the noticeboard of the establishment. Asquith claimed that he knew of 'few men in this world who are responsible for more mischief, and deserve a longer punishment in the next'. But Northcliffe was a startlingly intuitive newspaperman – perhaps the greatest that ever was – and the sheer noise he created could not be ignored. Despite having allegedly sneered that when he wanted a peerage he would 'buy it, like an honest man', Alfred Harmsworth acquired it in the usual British fashion, as a reward for commercial success and in recognition of his growing political influence. As Lord Northcliffe – the youngest peer ever created – he enjoyed a country estate in Kent, affected a Napoleonic curl on his forehead, signed himself 'N' and kept a string of doctors in business with various ailments, many of which were entirely imaginary.

The *Mail* greeted the outbreak of war with an 'it gives me no pleasure to say this, but . . .' editorial, claiming that the whole thing could have been avoided if only the world had taken seriously the cheap fiction it had published earlier, and listened to its advice about the need to distrust the Germans, buy more guns, build more warships and introduce compulsory military training. Northcliffe initially claimed that not a single soldier need leave Britain, because the Royal Navy could comfortably protect the nation. But consistency is not among the requirements of being a proprietor and he was soon thoroughly in favour of sending millions of young men to fight on the continent. The outbreak of war had confirmed for Northcliffe that he spoke for the vast numbers who bought his newspapers. In their name he was willing to make or break ministries.

At the start of hostilities he optimistically despatched reporters across western Europe, each equipped with £200 in gold to cover expenses. But when they were denied proper access to the British army the *Mail* had to content itself with official news releases, making sulphurous utterances about the German shelling of English east-coast towns, atrocity stories from Belgium and scaremongering about the menace from airships and alien spies. To his credit – and in contrast to those optimistically waffling that it might all be over by Christmas – Northcliffe sensed that the war would last for years, and he also saw that it would require conscription to keep sufficient numbers of soldiers in the field. In the spring of 1915 came his chance to assume the military role to which, as the self-styled Napoleon of Fleet Street, he felt entitled.

From the outset, the big-calibre guns of the British Expeditionary Force artillery had been outweighed by those of the opposing Germans. The problem was compounded by repeated demands that officers economize on the number of shells they fired. By the end of 1914, however, the British commander, Sir John French, had come to the conclusion that, if artillery fire was sufficiently concentrated, his men could smash their way through the German front line. The plan to try to use artillery in a new fashion seemed a significant refinement of battle-planning (although it took the Germans very little time to adjust their tactics), and on 10 March 1915 Sir John French launched an attack on German positions around the village of Neuve Chapelle. This time, before the infantry attacked, there was a massive artillery bombardment: in thirty-five minutes the British fired more shells than they had done during the entirety of the Boer War. There was plenty wrong with French's approach – the longer and more sustained your artillery barrage, for example, the greater the warning you gave the enemy that an attack was imminent and the Germans became better and better at preparing their defences. It also meant that, since the attacking infantry were confined to the one area of the front in which the barrage was supposed to have blown a hole in the defences opposite, they had little room for individual initiative. On 10 March there were also insufficient reserves of fresh troops to consolidate the gains made by the exhausted first wave. But for a while it seemed the attack might succeed, as British soldiers poured through nearly 2,000 yards of German front line. In the end, though, the assault failed. Sir John French reported to the War Office that it was all because he had not been supplied with sufficient artillery shells. This very neatly shifted the blame on to Kitchener and his staff in London.

The question of whether British soldiers were dying because commanders had been given the wrong shells became the sort of campaign that Northcliffe adored, since it offered a patriotic cause, an opportunity to pose as a defender of the ordinary citizen, and powerful people to blame. It was all – obviously – the government's fault. Privately, the Prime Minister claimed not to care a 'twopenny damn' what 'Northcliffe and his obscene crew' said about his government. But on 20 April Asquith was irritated enough to use a public speech to declare there was 'not a word of truth' in claims of a shell shortage. Northcliffe wrote to French soon afterwards suggesting that 'a short and very vigorous statement from you to a private correspondent (the usual way of making things public in England) would, I believe, render the government's position impossible.'

On 9 May 1915, Sir John French launched another British attack, this time at Aubers Ridge. The assault was an unmitigated disaster, at the cost of 9,500 British casualties on the first day alone. There were many reasons for this failure, not the least of them being defective intelligence and lack of surprise. But Sir John himself again blamed a shortage of ordnance – even though less than a month previously he had told Kitchener that he had all the shells he needed. Soon after his unsuccessful attack at Aubers Ridge, Sir John received an order from the War Office that he was to send 20,000 shells – a fifth of his entire reserve – to Marseilles for use in a planned attack on the Dardanelles. French now boiled over with anger, ordering that Lieutenant Colonel Charles à Court Repington, the military correspondent of Northcliffe's *Times*, be told that the battle had been a failure because of artillery weaknesses.

Repington's despatch was heavily censored, but he nonetheless managed to inform his readers that, despite fighting heroically, the British infantry had been met with devastating German fire because the artillery bombardment that preceded their attack had failed to destroy German machine-gun positions, barbed-wire entanglements and trench fortifications. The explanation he gave was that 'the want of an unlimited supply of high explosive was a fatal bar to our success.' These were almost exactly the words French had himself used to explain the failure of the attack.

The origins of the problem lay in British military doctrine which decreed that artillery shells were designed to support the infantry in their pre-war tactics of fire and movement: a large proportion of shells were filled with shrapnel – the small metal balls designed to kill or wound the enemy like a hail of bullets. But shrapnel shells were more or less useless at destroying well-built defences in the soggy stalemate of the Western Front. In an editorial five days later, *The Times* groaned that British soldiers had 'died in heaps on Aubers Ridge' because Kitchener's supplies of shrapnel shells had been about as effective against the German defences as 'sprinkling them with a watering can'. Sir John had already given the *Daily Mail* an interview in which he lamented his shortage of men and munitions, and had received a promise from Lord Northcliffe that his papers would continue to urge that more soldiers be sent to French's army. The *Mail* printed a chart it had lifted from *Le Matin* which showed that France was responsible for over 543 miles of trenches and the British 'an ignoble' 31¾ miles.

But Northcliffe's ambitions did not stop with adding the role of field marshal to his many other accomplishments, for he was coming to the conclusion that an entirely new government was needed. The first requirement was a new minister of munitions. After the publication of Colonel Repington's despatch in *The Times* Northcliffe used the *Daily Mail* – now carrying beneath its masthead the slogan 'THE PAPER THAT PERSISTENTLY FORE-WARNED THE PUBLIC ABOUT THE WAR' – to take his message to the general public. On 21 May, in that grand tone of voice so beloved of newspaper proprietors who believe they are shaping the destiny of nations, the paper declared that it had been all for Lord Kitchener as a recruiting sergeant, but 'it has never been pretended that Lord Kitchener is a soldier in the sense that Sir John French is a soldier,' and that he had made a very grave error in ordering the wrong kind of shell, a decision which had killed thousands of British soldiers. By the end of the month a new coalition government had been formed, with David Lloyd George appointed Minister of Munitions. The new *Daily Mail* slogan was

'THE PAPER THAT REVEALED THE SHELL TRAGEDY'.
Northcliffe seemed now to be a maker and breaker of governments. It would have been unimaginable before the outbreak
of war.

This self-made son of an alcoholic not only understood the
spirit of the age, he expressed it. The traditional baubles – the
peerage, the country house – he acquired through appreciating, in
a way that the traditional ruling class had failed to grasp, that by
the early twentieth century Britain was a very different country to
the one it had been. Traditionalists like Lord Kitchener were happy
enough to bask in the adulation of the newspapers, but had failed
to see that the massive circulations becoming commonplace in
journalism revealed a shift in the national power structure. The
authority figures of peacetime did not understand that the new
sort of war being fought, with mass mobilization and control of
the population, demanded a new, recognizably modern, relationship between the press and power.

Acute politicians like David Lloyd George understood that men
like Northcliffe could flourish by exploiting distrust between government and the readers of his papers. There grew up between
these two men a guarded mutual respect, grounded in the fact that
both were parvenus who saw how Britain had changed. To be
sure, the growing power of the mass media offended some. Alfred
Gardner, for example, a journalist of impeccable liberal credentials, characterized the tension as between 'democracy, whose
bulwark is parliament' and 'mobocracy, whose dictator is Lord
Northcliffe'. But the mass media were not going away. Where the
previous generation of politicians had been outraged and alarmed
by Northcliffe, Lloyd George sought to manage a noisy dema-
gogue. In 1917, he sent him on a mission to the United States to
'find an occupation for his superfluous energies', and rewarded
him with a viscountcy. In February 1918, Northcliffe was appointed
director of propaganda in enemy countries. There was no thought
any longer of trying to hush up events which could not be hushed

up: the ambition was to manage them by manipulation of the mass media.

All of this fed Northcliffe's vanity, of course, and at the end of the war he considered himself entitled personally to approve any government formed after the elections. He also wanted a seat at the Versailles peace conference. But he had not recognized that, with the war over, Lloyd George didn't much need him any longer. In April 1919, the Prime Minister stood up in the House of Commons and denounced Northcliffe's 'diseased vanity'. He tapped his head as he spoke. Everyone knew what he meant.

6. What Happened to Uncle Charlie

A beach to die for.

'I don't know what's to be done . . . this isn't war,' wailed the War Secretary, Lord Kitchener. Within four months of the beginning of hostilities, Great Britain's great war was at a standstill. Conventional British military tactics were redundant, with both sides stuck in a series of trenches that ran from the North Sea to the borders of Switzerland, and neither side holding the initiative. But Sir John French, commanding British troops on the Western Front, remained adamant (as, naturally, were the French commanders) that it was only on the Western Front that a decisive victory might be won: any reduction of the pressure would give the impression that Britain considered Germany unbeatable there. But a third man thought he had a way to break the deadlock.

In the Admiralty, Winston Churchill, with his sensitive political nose, believed there was an opportunity to attack Germany 'through the back door'. He demanded a plan from the admiral in command of the East Mediterranean Fleet, who reluctantly provided one, which he then presented to the War Council in the middle of January 1915. The idea was seductive, if complicated. Suppose an allied force could break through from the Aegean to the Sea of Marmara, the inland sea on which sat Constantinople, the capital of Germany's ally, Turkey. Menacing the Turkish capital would oblige Germany to divert troops to defend it – troops that might otherwise be facing Britain and France on the Western Front. Should its capital fall, Turkey would be forced out of the war and Britain and France would then be able to open a supply route north through the Black Sea to their ally Russia. Churchill anticipated that a successful attack on Turkey would also ensure the safety of British-controlled Egypt and encourage irritatingly neutral Balkan states to get off the fence in the war. At the very least, it was an alternative to the stagnation on the Western Front, and no one seemed to have any better idea.

The difficulty was that this bold enterprise hung upon forcing a passage through the Dardanelles, the narrow strip of water that runs for 40 miles or so between the Aegean and the Sea of Marmara. It was well known that the Turks had built a series of forts to protect the channel, and a feasibility study had already shown that attempting to take the straits would be a hugely dangerous enterprise. Churchill talked blithely of risking only a few out-of-date warships, but, infuriatingly, the most significant dissenter was the most senior officer in the Royal Navy, the well-respected seventy-three-year-old Admiral 'Jackie' Fisher, who grew increasingly hostile to the whole plan – even storming out of the room at one point when it was being discussed. Despite this, most of the rest of the War Council were upbeat and excited. By mid-February, the idea of a purely naval mission had been modified – Kitchener agreed that ground troops would also be sent, to complete the occupation of the Turkish forts after the naval bombardment of the coastline of the Dardanelles.

It was another disaster. On 19 February a large force of British and French battleships, cruisers, destroyers, submarines and associated vessels began the attack. Everyone knew about the Turkish forts, but there was a general assumption that the Turkish armed forces weren't up to much and there was great confidence in the power of the Royal Navy guns. This turned out to be very misplaced – apart from anything else, the Royal Navy had not had enough practice in firing at shore targets. In the event, the naval force ran into a thicket of mines laid across the straits. No one had suspected the minefield's existence, and allied minesweepers were incapable of clearing the mines while under fire from the Turkish shore batteries. To the great embarrassment of Britain's naval commanders, three of the expedition's biggest warships were sunk and another three disabled. Now, what in prospect had seemed a relatively cheap and cheerful naval mission risked becoming a military catastrophe. There was a swift retreat.

Sir Ian Hamilton, the general appointed to command the land operations, was a veteran of imperial wars from Afghanistan to South Africa. He was a brave, decent, cultured man with a taste for poetry, but had been rather baffled to have been given the mission. As he later admitted: 'my knowledge of the Dardanelles was nil; of the Turk nil; of the strength of our own forces next to nil.' The only research material he could find to prepare himself was a guidebook and a collection of 'travellers' tales'. But the British government was desperate and Sir John French's strategy of slugging away on the Western Front was going nowhere.

Sir Ian concluded that the naval disaster meant the only thing to do was to send soldiers ashore to destroy the Turkish gun emplacements. In other words, he wanted to turn the original plan – a naval bombardment followed by a land operation – on its head. Unfortunately for him, the naval calamity meant that any element of surprise had been lost, and the Turks used the break in hostilities which followed it to prepare their defences. They were blessed with a skilled German commander, General Otto Liman von Sanders, who came to admire and promote a brilliant young Turkish officer, Mustafa Kemal, later to become the founder of modern Turkey. Tens of thousands of reinforcements of men and guns were brought into the Gallipoli peninsula alongside the Dardanelles and positioned high on the cliffs. The British planning of the ground assault, by contrast, was confused and indecisive, not that that was apparent to many of the young men involved. Rupert Brooke, the beautiful boy of his age, had turned down an offer to join General Hamilton's staff and was among those eagerly looking forward to splashing ashore. 'Oh God! I've never been so happy in my life,' he exclaimed. 'I suddenly realise that the ambition of my life has been – since I was two – to go on a military expedition against Constantinople.' He did not achieve his dream because he died of blood poisoning on the way to the invasion, almost certainly from an infected mosquito bite on his lip. It was an unheroic death, 'as though Sir Lancelot had been diagnosed with terminal dandruff', as one historian put it.

Sir Ian Hamilton eventually assembled about 75,000 troops – roughly 18,000 from the 29th Division (a regular army unit made up of soldiers gathered from garrisons in the empire), some 30,000 Australian and New Zealand (Anzac) soldiers, 10,000 from the Royal Naval Division and a French contingent of some 17,000 troops. He had very few high-explosive shells and not much of a clue about the enemy he faced. He also made a significant mistake, for instead of a single overwhelming attack, there were to be several separate landings, all of them against an enemy ensconced on high ground above the beaches, perfectly positioned to pour terrible fire down on the incoming troops.

Even so, on 25 April two beachheads were established, one at Helles, at the tip of the Gallipoli peninsula, where British troops ran into feebler resistance than had been feared, and another further up the coast. This one was soon renamed Anzac Cove, in honour of the loss there of Australian and New Zealand soldiers pitched ashore at night, with little idea of the lie of the land and under murderous fire from well-placed Turkish positions. Over the next few weeks, further landings were attempted, but with no critical mass they were repeatedly repulsed by the increasingly effective Turkish soldiers. Now, even the new battle plan was failing. Hamilton sent a message to Kitchener: 'Our troops have done all that flesh and blood can do against semi-permanent works and they are not able to carry them. More and more munitions will be needed to do so. I fear that this is a very unpalatable conclusion, but I can see no way out of it.'

On the Western Front, meanwhile, in the new battle raging around Ypres the Germans launched the first gas attack, a horrifying development that transfixed military and civilians alike. Contrary to predictions, gas did not turn out to be the wonder weapon to break the deadlock in Europe, since its destructive power was literally thrown to the wind. But its use was a reminder of the fact that it was in France and Belgium that the outcome of the war would be determined. If so, the Dardanelles campaign was an irrelevance, and this might have been the moment to call time on the whole mission. Fisher resigned from the post of First Sea Lord. But yet again national 'honour' was used to justify fighting – Kitchener believed that to abandon the attack would be catastrophic for Britain's standing in the world. There must be another attempt to take the peninsula. It would cost many more lives. One of them would be Uncle Charlie's.

The form sent by the military to his mother records Uncle Charlie's place of death as '34 Field Ambulance'. If so, he died in his place of work. Field ambulances were front-line medical units usually made up of ten officers and a couple of hundred stretcher-bearers and medical orderlies, their job being to carry the wounded and erect tented hospitals on the battlefield (vehicles were then called ambulance 'wagons'). The records show that 34th Field Ambulance was attached to the 11th (Northern) Division, which had been raised in the early days of the war when Kitchener appealed for volunteers. Sir Ivor Maxse, who became the army's Inspector General of Training, damned it with faint praise when he later described it as showing 'what may be called "Yorkshire" characteristics: steadiness – amenability to discipline – rather than enthusiasm; slow in thought and movement rather than the mental alertness which is seen, say, in the Irish or London regiments'.

These comments come from 1917. At the time the division was despatched to Gallipoli in 1915, the volunteers had enormous gaps in their training and were inexpertly officered. Many travelled to the Dardanelles on board two requisitioned transatlantic liners, the *Aquitania* and the *Empress of Britain*, chosen because – unless they were very unlucky, like the *Lusitania* – they could outrun any U-boat. By early August, over three months after the ground campaign had been launched, the division was on the island of Imbros, off the mouth of the Dardanelles. It was accompanied by two other divisions, also comprised of men who had joined up in response to Kitchener's 1914 appeal for volunteers: the Irish of the 10th Division and the West Country men of the 13th. Of the three divisions, the War Office considered the 11th the most impressive, but with what turned out to be a key proviso: that much would depend upon the personality of its commander.

Kitchener was under incessant pressure from Sir John French at this time not to deprive him of his more able officers, but even so the commanders he decided to send to Gallipoli were an odd choice to bring off an operation that he had previously decreed to be vital to the success of the war. The original officer commanding the 13th Division, a hero of the Boer War, killed himself with a shot to the head soon after the outbreak of hostilities. He was replaced by the mountainous figure of Major General Frederick Shaw, who weighed the best part of 20 stone. The 10th Division, meanwhile, was under the command of Sir Bryan Mahon, a rather over-the-hill cavalry officer who had been part of the relief of the siege of Mafeking during the Boer War and whose favourite recreations were riding steeplechases, hunting and pig-sticking. As for the commander of the 11th, Major General Frederick

Hammersley, Kitchener appointed him to the mission with the ominous caveat that 'he will have to be watched to see that the strain of trench warfare is not too much for him.'

Hammersley was another magisterially moustached veteran, who had fought at the battle of Khartoum and been seriously wounded fighting the Boers in South Africa. But the reason for Kitchener's concern was that a few years before the war with Germany had broken out, he had suffered some kind of mental collapse. Hammersley later brushed it off as a minor nervous breakdown, but according to the tittle-tattle it had been a much more serious affair, during the treatment for which he had had to be held down while being medicated. Together these three divisions (approximately 25,000 men) came under the command of Sir Frederick Stopford, an easy-going old fellow who had retired in 1909 and at the outbreak of war had been Lieutenant of the Tower of London, where his main duty had been the wearing of fancy dress. He chose to command the landings from his sloop, the *Jonquil*, moored offshore. Here he slept through much of the assault.

The vast majority of young men under the command of these near-extinct volcanoes had never heard a shot fired in anger, for this was to be the very first attack by soldiers in Kitchener's so-called 'New Army'. Nor did they arrive in great shape, as the August temperatures climbed to over 30 degrees Centigrade during the day. Many of them had contracted diarrhoea or dysentery en route. These inexperienced men were landing on an exposed beach directly beneath enemy guns. It struck such terror in some that they lay paralysed with fear in the bottoms of the 'beetles' – the early landing craft taking them to the shore. Soldiers stepping off into the water discovered it was so deep that they were lucky not to be drowned by the weight of their own equipment. Others were taken to the wrong beaches, and because senior officers had expected much of the landing to be stealthy and unopposed, some had even been ordered not to load their rifles, denying them the minor satisfaction of shooting back at invisible Turkish snipers. Yet more found their rifles jammed by the effects of seawater and sand. Somewhere in this mass of frightened men was Uncle Charlie.

For Charlie and other men of 34th Field Ambulance there was an additional problem: almost all their equipment had been left behind on the dockside in England. For the duration of the attack they were ordered to join up with the 35th Field Ambulance which was wading ashore at Suvla Bay at 2.30 in the morning of 7 August. By 8 a.m. they had established a substantial dressing station. That day and the next it treated over 700 wounded men.

Conditions on the beach were hellish, for it was intensely hot during the day and very cold after dark. There was virtually no shade and very little water. With the heat, the dust and the smell of cordite parching their throats, the more inexperienced soldiers soon finished the meagre allowance of water they had brought with them when they landed. Without portable radios and with Turkish snipers picking off anyone who tried to lay a telephone line, officers could give direct orders only to those within earshot. Stretcher-bearers ferried wounded men to the medical posts, but there was hardly any more safety there: however often the first-aid posts were moved about the beaches, shrapnel from Turkish artillery still tore through them.

A sergeant in one of the field hospitals described trying to provide medical care on the beach as 'a task to make angels weep . . . we have accommodation for about 150, our usual number of patients is about 280 . . . we are never out of the zone of fire, both artillery and rifle. Hardly a night passes without a patient or someone being hit.' The official war diary of the 35th Field Ambulance records of 7 August that 'during the greater part of this day the Bearer Division and Dressing Station were working under shrapnel fire & there were some casualties among the personnel of the 34th Field Ambulance who were attached (3 killed – six wounded).' Assuming the information provided to his family is correct, Uncle Charlie must have been one of these men, although whether he was killed at the medical facility or while carrying a stretcher on the battlefield will never be known.

Uncle Charlie did not go to Gallipoli to fight, but the whole invasion force was singularly ineffective. Perhaps a more battle-hardened force would have done better, although it is hard to imagine any head-on assault making spectacular gains. The problem was leadership. When General Hamilton demanded to know what had gone wrong with the 11th Division he concluded that the problem was less with the men of Kitchener's New Army than with the generals of the old army: they seemed to have no offensive spirit. The Germans agreed: Major Wilhelm Willmer, the Bavarian cavalry officer commanding the Turkish defence, delightedly reported to Sanders that 'No energetic attacks on the enemy's part have taken place. On the contrary, the enemy is advancing timidly.' It mattered not whether men died bravely or cravenly, full of belief in their cause or simply terrified, because their senior officers had led them so badly.

For all the blood shed, yet again, the attempt to break out from the beachhead failed. Kitchener decided that Freddy Stopford must be sacked, cabling Hamilton that 'this is a young man's war, and we must have commanding officers that will take full advantage of opportunities which occur but seldom.' It was Kitchener, of course, who had appointed the old men – summoning Stopford from the Tower of London because he didn't want to take anyone better from among the generals on the Western Front. Sir Frederick Hammersley, meanwhile, commanding the 11th Division upon which the attack had hinged, was evacuated – not, as had been feared, because of a mental breakdown but, as General Hamilton reported it, because he was said to have a blood clot in his leg, and 'he has to lie perfectly prostrate and still . . . as the least movement might set it loose and it would then kill him.' On 17 August, ten days after the landing, General Hamilton was cabling Kitchener with the familiar refrain: 'Unfortunately the Turks have temporarily gained the moral ascendancy over some of our new troops.' If there was to be any chance of success, he needed 'large reinforcements' immediately, because 'it has become a question of who can slog longest and hardest.' The brilliant initiative to break the stalemate of the Western Front had become a stalemate itself.

Had the British people known in detail what a shambles the Gallipoli misadventure had been, perhaps it would have been called off earlier. But they were never given the full picture. In the early days of the campaign it had seemed as exotic as Kitchener's merciless march up the Nile to Omdurman in 1898 to wreak revenge on the rebels who had dared to defy the British empire. The press coverage did little to put them right. In April the *Daily Telegraph* had hailed the start of the campaign with the headlines 'Great attack on the Dardanelles. Fleet and armies. Allied troops land in Gallipoli. Success of Operations. Large Forces Advance.' This had been followed by a fantastical claim two days later that troops had fought their way 20 miles inland.

The campaign was a censor's dream – soldiers on the Western Front might return home on leave or for medical treatment, but Turkey was thousands of sea-miles away. It was easy to control the flow of information. The one national newspaper reporter whom Kitchener had allowed to travel officially with the expedition was in trouble from the start. For some reason Ellis Ashmead-Bartlett landed at Anzac Cove wearing an old pale-green felt hat, which somehow convinced Australian soldiers that he was a spy. He was saved from summary execution only when a Royal Navy sailor recognized him from the journey out. Ashmead-Bartlett, an arrogant young man with a taste for high living that could not be sustained by his income, did not make things easy for himself: on the voyage out he had been noted for appearing in the mornings in a yellow silk robe and shouting for his breakfast 'as though the Carlton [Club] were still his corporeal home'. For all this, though, he recognized at the start that the Gallipoli campaign was bound to fail, even if the rules meant that any report he sent home could only be transmitted long after the commander's official anodyne communiqué.

At first, Ashmead-Bartlett did his best to play the patriotic game, describing the Australian landings at Anzac Cove in heroic terms, and including the observation that 'the first Ottoman Turk since the last crusade received an Anglo-Saxon bayonet in him at five minutes after five a.m. on April 25.' At home the War Secretary's assessment told the House of Lords that the landings at Gallipoli had been 'a masterpiece of organisation, ingenuity and courage', and that 'though the enemy is being constantly reinforced, the news from this front is thoroughly satisfactory.' Newspaper commentators offered further comfort. On 29 May, Archibald Hurd assured readers of the *Manchester Guardian* that despite the sinkings of naval ships, and the possibility of more losses to come, 'There is no occasion for alarm.'

But the public was growing sceptical of official cheerleaders – the campaign was taking a great deal longer than had been expected. Increasingly, the casualty roll-calls in the newspapers included men who had been hit in the fighting at Gallipoli. Letters were printed that described the condition of the wounded who were lucky enough to make it to the military hospitals in Mudros and Cairo (albeit couched in terms of praise for their good treatment there). Even the newspaper despatches allowed through by the censor were much less positive than the jolly presentations coming from officialdom.

In the squalid conditions at Gallipoli itself, disease was rampant and perhaps half of the men were unfit for duties. Ashmead-Bartlett concluded that the attack had been amateurish in style and under-prepared in execution. The mission, he decided, was well-nigh impossible. In September – a month after Uncle Charlie's death – Ashmead-Bartlett decided he'd put up with it for long enough. He had already taken the opportunity during a visit home to call on Asquith and had informed the Prime Minister that official accounts of the campaign gave a very misleading impression. Things were not going well at all. In early September, after returning to the theatre of operations and being begged by disillusioned officers to tell the truth, he persuaded a visiting Australian reporter, Keith Murdoch (father of Rupert), who was travelling to London, to smuggle a letter to Asquith. Apologizing for disturbing the

Prime Minister, Ashmead-Bartlett described the latest British offensive as 'the most ghastly and costly fiasco in our history since the Battle of Bannockburn'. Lives were being squandered, morale was appalling and the commanders despised. Unfortunately his whistle-blowing plan did not remain secret. Years later Ashmead-Bartlett discovered that his conversation with Murdoch had been over-heard by another correspondent, Henry Nevinson, who informed General Hamilton. When Keith Murdoch landed in Marseilles on his way to London he was promptly arrested and the letter seized.

Murdoch now sat down and wrote his own letter, this time to the Prime Minister of Australia, Andrew Fisher. His account of the situation in Gallipoli made Ashmead-Bartlett's seem inhibited. The generals were inept, conceited and complacent. The staff were bunglers. The volunteers of Kitchener's army were miserable specimens, physically and mentally inferior not merely to Australians but to the average Turk: at Suvla Bay British officers had been ordered to shoot their own men to prevent formations dithering. Now, after weeks of achieving almost nothing, the soldiers were utterly demoralized and feeble. 'You would refuse to believe that these men were really British soldiers,' said Murdoch; 'they show an atrophy of mind and body that is appalling.' Morale was dreadful. 'Sedition is talked round every tin of bully beef on the peninsula.'

Some of this was rubbish – there had, for example, been no order to officers to shoot their own men. But there was enough truth in it not merely to rock the boat but to sink it. Somehow Murdoch's explosive document found its way into the hands of Lloyd George, who didn't care for Kitchener, and had decided the campaign was a foolish irrelevance. This presented Kitchener with a real dilemma. He was already attempting to root out every available soldier for a new offensive on the Western Front. He could see French commitment to the Dardanelles campaign waning by the week, and it was abundantly clear that the much sought-for break-through had failed to occur. And yet he had ordered that, once embarked upon, there could be no letting up until victory. An honest appraisal would have led him to the conclusion that he had never given the campaign the resources or backing it needed to succeed. Instead, Kitchener decided to change the commanding general.

In October he sacked Hamilton. The closest the general would get to active service again would be when he was appointed to Sir Frederick Stopford's old job as Lieutenant of the Tower of London in 1918. Hamilton's replacement was General Sir Charles Monro, who had disliked the Dardanelles 'sideshow' from the start and needed only a three-day visit to the British toeholds in Turkey to conclude that their inadequate trenches, exposure to enemy shellfire and hopeless artillery positions comprised 'a line possessing every possible military defect' – the only thing to do was to abandon the whole mission and get out as soon as possible. Churchill, who had been such a forceful advocate of the Dardanelles operation, commented tartly that 'He came, he saw, he capitulated.' Kitchener could still mesmerize the public, but he was now looking a liability to many of the politicians in the cabinet. He resisted attempts to remove him from the War Office, but agreed to travel to the Dardanelles to judge for himself. Seeing the situation with his own eyes finally convinced the War Secretary that Monro was right: there was nothing for it but to cut allied losses and evacuate.

As soon as he returned to London Kitchener tried to tender his resignation as War Secretary, but Asquith talked him out of it. There was worse to come for the poor soldiers at Gallipoli. At the end of November, a winter storm struck, and in addition to hunger and dysentery and Turkish fire, the soldiers lived in the midst of snow and ice. Finally, in early December – a full five weeks after General Monro's recommendation – the cabinet reached a decision to abandon the whole operation. On 18 December, the British began a remarkably successful evacuation in which over 80,000 men were spirited away to sea with virtually no casualties. Nothing so became the invasion of Turkey as the leaving of it. All told, the Gallipoli adventure had cost the lives of over 29,000 British soldiers, nearly 10,000 French, over 11,000 Australians and New Zealanders, and almost 2,000 Indians.

Over twenty years later, when the American army attempted to house-train the future Second World War commander George 'Old Blood and Guts' Patton by sending him to staff college, he was asked to write a dissertation on the Gallipoli campaign. He made a number of practical points, among them the observation that it was not particularly sensible during a night operation to try to protect your soldiers from friendly fire by making them wear white patches on their uniforms, since it made them immediately identifiable to enemy snipers. But his most devastating criticism was reserved for the British commanders. 'It was not the Turkish Army which defeated the British – it was von Sanders, Kemal Pasha, and Major Willmer who defeated Hamilton, Stopford, Hammersley . . . Had the two sets of commanders changed sides it is believed that the landing would have been as great a success as it was a dismal failure.'[23]

It is a characteristically aggressive analysis: better leadership might have won the day. There is something in it, although the truth is probably that the more experienced Turks outclassed the allies at every level. But Kitchener could only use the generals he had available, and the plain fact was they weren't up to the job. The levels of incompetence displayed make it hard to consider the entire venture as anything other than a misguided, irrelevant and costly sideshow which wasted scarce resources and undermined morale. The Dardanelles campaign demonstrated the chasm between the young men who had volunteered to fight the war and the old men who directed it. Its failure meant that the British were now more than ever committed to the trenches of the Western Front and to a victory of attrition. If, indeed, the war could be won at all.

7. Mud

A Lancashire sergeant wishes he had webbed feet.

The afternoon of 22 April 1915 was warm and sunny, but at the promise of dusk a light wind blew up. It came from the direction of the German trenches and fanned the faces of the allied soldiers near the village of Langemarck, near Ypres. At five o'clock three red rockets shot into the sky, signalling the start of a terrifying barrage of artillery fire on the French trenches.

Then the French soldiers, many of whom were in fact Algerian, saw something they had never witnessed before. Two greeny-yellow clouds drifted across no man's land from the direction of the German trenches. The clouds spread and merged to form a single fog, about 5 feet high, which rolled on the wind. It was now a light, bluish-white colour, and looked, said one of the soldiers later, like the mist you sometimes see above watermeadows at night.

This cloud had been produced when German soldiers opened the nozzles on 6,000 canisters of liquid chlorine, which had been smuggled into their lines over the previous few days. Once released the chlorine vaporized to form a low-hanging cloud of gas. Within a minute, the cloud had rolled into the allied trenches, where the effect on the soldiers was terrible. The chlorine stripped the lining of the bronchial tubes and lungs, and the consequent immediate inflammation produced enormous quantities of liquid within the body. Soldiers gasped and choked as their faces turned blue from the effort of trying to breathe. Panic spread instantly, as men tried to run from the cloud. The effort merely made things worse. Soldiers tried to bury their faces in the earth, others lay gasping and retching, sometimes having ruptured their lungs. As a later casualty report put it, each man was 'being drowned in his own exudation'.

Thirty-six hours later, the Germans released more gas – this time the victims were Canadian. Shortly before three o'clock on the morning of 24 April a Captain Bertram observed a green-tinged smoke rising from the German lines. It soon formed a cloud about 7 feet high, which drifted towards the Canadian trenches at a speed of about 8 miles an hour. Before he collapsed with vomiting and diarrhoea, Bertram watched as two dozen of his men fell to gasping deaths. The German soldiers who advanced behind these clouds wore rudimentary protection that made them look like deep-sea divers – large hoods with a single eyepiece set in the front. The Canadians could only urinate on their handkerchiefs or towels and stuff them into their mouths to try to protect themselves.

There was no excuse for the unpreparedness of the allies, for the French had captured a German soldier carrying a gas mask over a week before the first attack and he had described the cylinders being readied in the German trenches. Those warnings had been passed on to the British high command, but had been ignored. Then, later on 24 April, came another, bigger gas attack, this time upon British soldiers. Thousands were poisoned. As British newspapers gave their readers vivid accounts of what this terrible substance did to the human body, and the *Daily Mail* appealed to the women of Britain to run up home-made respirators,* the military had decided to retaliate with gas attacks of their own. For the rest of the war, research scientists tested compound after compound – 150,000 of them all told – to try to find chemicals that would be even more destructive. Five months after the first German gas attack, the British unleashed their first use of what was coyly referred to as 'the accessory'. Chlorine gas was followed by phosgene, and then by mustard gas, which covered the body in big yellow blisters. By 1918, between one-fifth and one-third of all shells being fired on the Western Front contained gas. The masks issued to troops offered greater protection from gas as the war went on, but even so, official figures – which took no account of prisoners or those whose deaths had not been recorded – showed that the total of British soldiers gassed during the war was 181,000.

This new weapon – like the flamethrowers, warplanes, tanks and new forms of artillery developed during the war – was a desperate attempt to turn the conflict from stagnation to movement. For the consequence of industrial warfare had been to force men to live in holes in the ground. It was as if technology had reversed the course of evolution and returned humankind to the primeval mud from which it had emerged millions of years before. Humankind looked to technology again to extricate it. 'When all is said and done,' said Siegfried Sassoon as he looked back after years of fighting, 'the war was mainly a matter of holes and ditches.' The trenches of the Western Front were a paradox: a series of primitive defences which had originally been intended to make attack easier: the deeper you dug, the greater the protection you might achieve. But the deeper you dug the more evident it was that you were going nowhere. There were places on the front line where men were still using trenches in 1917 that had been excavated three years earlier. Anything that seemed to offer a way of gaining the

* A million were produced in a single day, virtually all of which turned out to be useless.

initiative seemed attractive – even digging deeper still. Both sides, for example, recruited miners to tunnel beneath no man's land and lay explosives below the enemy trenches. Bent double in the often soaking tunnels the men hacked away with the tips of their bayonets, often directly parallel to German miners engaged in exactly the same toil: they listened to each other through doctors' stethoscopes pressed to the walls of their tunnels.

The trenches had been dug to give protection from bullets. But the awful destructive force that dominated trench life was the artillery shell. As we have seen, in previous conflicts heavy field guns had been used to support an infantry attack. But when men were sheltering in trenches, these guns became the primary weapon: it was easier to kill one's enemy with an artillery shell fired high into the sky from a great distance than with bullets. A conventional shell sounded, one lieutenant thought, 'just like a boat going through water as it goes over your head and in the ordinary way you get about two seconds advice of its arrival'. But the much faster 'whizzbangs' were terrifying – they came at such speed you got virtually no warning at all. A direct hit meant red-hot metal, rocks, earth, brick, wood and body-parts flying everywhere. At the first impact, those who hadn't been hit looked at each other in wild panic. Which way to run, for you might scuttle to a position directly under the next shell? Or might there – God willing – be no more to come? Edmund Blunden, a lieutenant in the Royal Sussex Regiment (and a fine poet), described how a shell fell behind him as he made his way along the trench. He turned back, and 'its butting impression was black and stinking in the parados [the side of the trench furthest from the enemy] where minutes ago the lance-corporal's mess-tin was bubbling over a little flame. For him now, could the gobbets of blackening flesh, the earth-wall sotted with blood, with flesh, the eye under the duckboard, the pulpy bone be the only answer?' At this point the lance-corporal's brother came around the corner of the trench and saw what had happened: 'he was sent to company headquarters in a kind of catalepsy.'

If whether you lived or died depended not on the outcome of a fight with an enemy soldier you could see but on the decision of someone commanding an enormous weapon out of sight over the horizon, it produced a new kind of fear: totally incapable of retaliation or self-preservation as the shells rained down, the men were reduced from warriors to victims, and their response – perhaps the only response available to them – was a widespread fatalism. When there was no attack taking place, though, there was just endless sniper fire, watching and waiting for the next brew of tea. Life was a ghastly combination of tedium, discomfort and danger. But when you weren't bored, you were terrified.

The soldiers who disembarked in France in 1915 would learn the particular stoicism this environment required. First they endured the bullying of training instructors in the 'bullrings' of the British base on the coast at Etaples ('Eat-apples' as it was generally known)* before sitting crammed into French railway carriages for a tedious onward journey to some place whose name most could not pronounce. After a march along crumbling roads to their promised billets, they sometimes met with the discovery that there were none, and that the French citizens on whose behalf they were fighting had padlocked the local well to ensure they wouldn't steal a bucket of water.

The closer they got to the front line, the worse things became. First came the trudge up through a series of communication trenches – 'avenues', 'lanes' or 'alleys' – to the reserve and second-line trenches. They had been told what a front-line trench was supposed to look like – the firing step, the dugouts and so on. But it rarely prepared them for the reality when they arrived. Practice trenches on the well-drained soil of Salisbury Plain might be nothing like the ditches awaiting them. 'At length we reached what looked like an open drain full of mud,' said a private in one of the

---

* Before the war, this small fishing port had a population of around 5,000. By 1918, there were 12,000 people lying in the British military cemetery alone.

Birmingham battalions. 'This, we were informed, was the front line ... The situation was very different from what we had imagined. We seemed to have reached the depth of misery.' It was a cold, wet night, but at least he was spared the experience of comrades in other sections of the line, who found that the wet weather had so eroded the front line that bits of decaying Frenchmen had emerged from their trench walls.

Despite stretching all the way from the North Sea coast to the borders of Switzerland, the trenches of the Western Front were not entirely continuous, did not run in straight lines and were often broken by shell craters or other obstacles. Some were deep and fortified with reinforced concrete, but others were little more than scrapes in the ground. They ran through fields – which in spring and summer might be scattered with blue cornflowers, yellow buttercups and red poppies – across roads, through farm buildings and around factories, some of which still displayed their pre-war warning signs reading 'DANGER DE MORT'. Some trenches enjoyed the protection of geography and were invisible to enemy gunners, while others, at bulges in the line, could come under artillery fire from three sides. There were good trenches and bad ones – the best were deep and dry and well established, the worst, shallow or waterlogged. You might be lucky enough to be in the chalk hills of Picardy or you could be sent further north to Flanders, where the high water table and the broken drainage ditches meant trenches filled with water soon after the first spade blows. Duckboards jammed into position at the bottom of the trench might give some protection from the water and mud below, but men who slipped and fell could drown, their bodies sinking into the water only to be discovered when someone later walked on them. Shorter men had a harder time of it in the water than tall men, for obvious reasons. Thinner men fared better than heavier ones.

Every section of British trench was numbered, in approximately 300-yard sections, but, famously, many also had informal names – 'Piccadilly', 'Oxford Street', or intersections nicknamed 'Hyde Park Corner' or 'Marble Arch'. The soldiers painted these names on home-made wooden signs in an attempt to make this troglodyte metropolis homely. Several hundred yards behind the front line was a support trench, and several hundred yards further back, a reserve line. The three were linked by communication trenches, which ran from the comparative safety of towns, bases and marshalling centres through the rear trenches to the front line. From there, shallower ditches, or 'saps', ran out into no man's land. Men crawled out into these at night to lie spying, sniping or throwing grenades.

All in all, the trenches were a mighty labour, running in squiggles over a distance of more than 450 miles, and – since each side had several trenches running parallel to one another, and further trenches running up, between and beyond them into no man's land – the total length of these extended holes on the allied side alone was thousands of miles. Add a similar length on the enemy side and you get ditches estimated by some to be long enough to encircle the earth.

A well-ordered firing trench was 6 or 8 feet deep. Layers of sandbags protruded a couple of feet above ground at its front, offering further protection. From the fire step, you might look into no man's land through periscopes or armoured observation or sniping slits. Along the back of the trench ran the parados, also built up with sandbags. Good trenches did not run in a straight line, but zig-zagged. This was so that the blast of any incoming shell might be relatively contained, and meant that if enemy soldiers got into the trench they would be unable to shoot straight down it. A tangle of barbed wire in front of the trench gave some protection against such attacks (but had to be cut before there could be any attack of your own). 'Funk holes' in the walls of the trenches might provide a little protection in a barrage. 'Most of our time is spent digging holes in bits of France to fill other holes in other bits of France' was the pawky comment of a Sergeant-Major Ness in a letter to his family in Edinburgh. 'Much of the country is now contained in sandbags. The rest is in our boots, our pockets, our rifles and clarted thick all over our uniforms.'

It was said that men digging a trench in Flanders would occasionally discover a musket from the Waterloo campaign, or even from one of the soldiers led by the Duke of Marlborough against the French a hundred years before that. But that had been an entirely different sort of warfare. In May 1916 the future Prime Minister Harold Macmillan wrote to his mother that in between artillery bombardments 'One can look for miles and see no human being. But in those miles of country lurk (like moles or rats, it seems) thousands, even hundreds of thousands of men, planning against each other perpetually some new device of death . . . The glamour of red coats – the martial tunes of flag and drum – aide-de-camps scurrying hither and thither on splendid chargers – lances glittering and swords flashing – how different the old wars must have been!'

Knowing what was happening beyond your personal swamp was a luxury restricted to the men hanging in baskets beneath vast balloons tethered to the ground by steel cables, and to the daredevils of the Royal Flying Corps, an organization which attracted more than its share of reckless young men and teenagers who drove too fast and drank too much. Military aviators were conscious of being an elite who, as they climbed and swooped at speeds of up to 200 miles an hour, lived in a permanent intensely exhilarating present. 'Sometimes, jokingly, as one discusses winning the Derby Sweep, we would plan our lives "after the war". But it made no substantial difference. It was a dream, conjecturable as heaven, resembling no life we knew. We were trained with one object – to kill. We had one hope – to live,' one of them recalled. In 1916 the life expectancy of a combat pilot could be three weeks. On the other hand at the end of their patrols they returned not to a sodden dugout but to an airfield with beds and baths and decent food. The glamorous, rakish lives of these young men careering about the sky could not have been in greater contrast to the dank terror of trench warfare, where gains, if they came at all, were measured in yards. From the air, the pilots could see the endless expanse the infantry still had to cover, if only they could ever escape from their trenches.

Aircraft offered intelligence – photographs of enemy positions and activity, taken with a camera inside a big mahogany box clamped to the outside of the fuselage – and an alternative to the unreliable communication between headquarters and front line by the more common methods of runner or pigeon or messenger dog. In good conditions and with a bit of luck, aircraft could tell senior officers precisely where front-line troops were. A method was developed in which pilots would sound a horn, to be answered by a flare fired from infantry positions below. The observer in the aircraft would then scribble down the map co-ordinates of the position from which the flare had been fired and later drop the piece of paper over battalion headquarters in a specially weighted bag. Headquarters might even send a signal back to the aircraft with an enormous sheet configured like a Venetian blind, trans-mitting messages in Morse code. (One of the many flaws in this cumbersome system was an understandable reluctance on the part of the infantry to fire a flare that would immediately give their position away to German machine-gunners.) Men in the trenches envied the flyers their freedom. There was nothing about life in the front line that the pilots envied.

Allied trenches may have formed a single front line, but they were far from identical. When a British commander visited a sec-tion of Portuguese trench due to be taken over by his men, he found the sentries asleep, the Lewis guns jammed and the entire place covered in 'filth'. When he asked to speak to the command-ing officer, he was told he was away being treated for venereal disease. By contrast, a British private who was part of a detach-ment inheriting a section of French trenches in 1916 was flabbergasted to discover they had plundered nearby houses so effectively that 'We have here beds, stoves, tables, chairs, mirrors, pots and pans, and dishes. Even some clocks and other orna-ments.' By and large, the longer the stalemate continued, the more trouble soldiers took to try to make their trenches comfortable.

British trenches were, by (theoretical) definition, temporary, and their inhabitants were often astonished to discover the comfort and apparent permanence of some German trenches. The positions to which the Germans withdrew in the spring of 1917 on the northern part of the Western Front – the Hindenburg Line, named after Field Marshal Paul von Hindenburg – were particularly strong and well appointed. But even before that line had been completed, British soldiers had discovered a German officers' underground bunker at Beaumont-Hamel in 1916 where the walls were hung with tapestries. Since they had got there first the Germans had the advantage of being able to choose the ground on which they dug: they might decide to construct their fortifications on any convenient geographical feature they had already taken. The German trenches signified a job half done. To the French and Belgians they were a reproach, a reminder of failure. Early in the war, the British army had been under orders when building their trenches not to make them too comfortable, to prevent soldiers thinking of anything other than attack.

For many men, whatever their nationality, the abiding memory of the trenches was the awful smell. In front of the trenches lay no man's land, grass burned away, trees shattered, the ground macerated, potted with shell craters and often grotesque with the decomposing bodies of men from either side and farm and pack animals. In addition, very large numbers of men concentrated in very small spaces created predictable sanitary problems. Medical officers were supposed to ensure that official guidelines for temporary trench latrines were adhered to, and regulations even decreed the number of lavatory seats to be provided for more permanent installations (two per hundred men). The contents of the men's bowels were to be collected in old biscuit tins with wire handles and carried away at night. Each company had its designated 'shit wallahs', responsible for such duties. Since none of them appears to have written his memoirs it is hard to be sure how effectively the system worked.

In practice, standards of hygiene varied from one unit to another. To their displeasure, the men of the Royal Naval Division had found themselves under army command on the Western

Front – despite their beards and other defiantly held nautical habits, such as asking to 'go ashore' when requesting leave from the trenches. When the unpopular Major General Cameron Shute visited their trenches in 1916 he was appalled by the naval sanitary arrangements, provoking the Naval Division's Sub-Lieutenant A. P. Herbert, a sadly rather less fêted poet than Rupert Brooke, to write:

> The general inspecting the trenches
> Exclaimed with a horrified shout,
> 'I refuse to command a division
> Which leaves its excreta about.'
> But nobody took any notice,
> No one was prepared to refute
> That the presence of shit was congenial
> Compared to the presence of Shute.
>
> And certain responsible critics
> Made haste to reply to his words,
> Observing that his staff advisers
> Consisted entirely of turds
> For shit may be shot at odd corners
> And paper supplied there to suit
> But a shit would be shot without mourners
> If somebody shot that shit Shute.

Latrine problems were unpleasant. But they could at least be sorted out relatively quickly. What to do with dead bodies was something else. Where and when they could, soldiers tried to bury their dead comrades and erected wooden crosses as soon as it was safe to do so. But frequently it was too dangerous – and what would be gained by it? – to venture into no man's land to recover corpses. Their time in the trenches was the most intense experience of these young men's lives, and it is no overstatement to say that relationships between those living in these dreadful conditions were at times loving: they ate together, slept together, fought together and tried to control their fear together. At night they snuggled up to each other to keep warm. What must it have been like not only to lose a friend, but then to have to watch him decompose?

There was no reliable estimate, but there must have been millions of rats living on the battlefields, feeding off the soldiers' rations, their waste and the bodies of the dead. It was not at all uncommon for the uniforms of the dead in no man's land to be constantly moving as rats burrowed inside. The soldiers hated the rats, not only because they knew that they had grown fat (and many became enormous) by feasting on the bodies of fallen comrades, but also because of their habit of running over or biting the living while they were trying to sleep. A soldier reading by candle in a dugout might find the light catching ten or twelve pairs of watching eyes. A lance-corporal in the 1st Somerset Light Infantry recalled how he slept in his boots and puttees and with his greatcoat over his face for protection. 'They crawl over you at night,' he said, 'and we give the thing a biff from under the coat and send him squealing in the air, there is a short silence, then a thump as he reaches the ground, a scuffle and he is gone. If you walk along the track near the reserve trenches with a torch at night you can kick a rat every two paces.' The men attempted to control the plague of rats by bayoneting them, clubbing or kicking them to death, or shooting them. The only consolation in a gas attack was the spectacle of rats staggering about woozily in their final minutes.

Not only was life in the trenches subterranean, it was often also nocturnal, for it was too dangerous to do much in daylight. After dark, intelligence officers slipped over the parapet and lay in no man's land, listening to the conversations of German sentries, trying to discover which unit was occupying the facing trenches. Soldiers went out in wiring parties, whispering to one another as they tried to knit together barbed-wire entanglements that would hold up an enemy advance. In good conditions, when the front lines were far apart, a night patrol in no man's land might almost be like a Boy Scout exercise, reading the stars to work out in which direction to crawl or scramble to find their way back home. But, however benign the conditions, anyone trapped by enemy fire in a forward observation post knew their hopes of survival or rescue could hang – literally – upon a carrier pigeon. Before being taken out with the men to observation posts in no man's land, the birds would be starved to make them more eager to return to their lofts at headquarters once released with a message. Trapped men might later discover that the birds had become so waterlogged they could not get airborne with a message, or so terrified by shellfire that they would not leave at all.

If the enemy front line was only a few dozen yards away – when the sentries on either side could hear each other clearing their throats – patrols into no man's land were terrifying. Soldiers inched along on their bellies, moving only one limb at a time, lying absolutely still among the craters and corpses, listening, listening, always listening, for the breaths and whispers of enemy sentries, knowing that if they fired a shot or used the grenade in their pocket it would bring down a devastating storm of bullets. Afterwards they crawled back as quickly as they dared to the British trenches, praying that a nervous sentry would remember to whisper the challenge for a password and not shoot them in panic.

Several reminiscences of life in the trenches claim that ghost stories were very uncommon – real life was scary enough. But a myth did grow up that somewhere out among the craters and tunnels of no man's land there was another army, made up of filthy, unshaven soldiers – English, Australians, Germans, Frenchmen and Canadians – who had deserted their units to live together between the lines. These feral men sheltered in abandoned dugouts and the cellars of shell-shattered houses during the day, emerging under cover of night to forage for food and to rob the dead and dying. A strange 'memoir' published after the war described 'inhuman cries and rifle shots coming from that awful wilderness, as though the bestial denizens were fighting amongst themselves'. Once, the soldiers who heard these noises put a basket out in no man's land, filled with food, tobacco and a bottle of whisky. But the following morning they found the bait untouched, and a note in the basket: 'Nothing doing!'

'War is the normal occupation of man,' Winston Churchill once remarked, and then added, 'war – and gardening.' And, indeed, some soldiers did cultivate gardens among the tangles of barbed wire. They must have been mainly in the support trenches, and seem to have been particularly common in some of the marshalling centres. There men of all ranks tended allotments. One letter from a soldier to his mother, written in 1915, thrilled in the 'profusion of old-fashioned flowers, marsh marigold, mignonette, snapdragon, convolvulus, nasturtium, all flourishing right under the parapet' and jealously protected from any clumsy footfall. 'My daffodils and hyacinths are topping,' exclaimed a proud Captain Crouch in a letter home requesting his family to post him some spring-flower seeds. 'Will you please send as soon as possible two packets of candytuft and two packets of nasturtium seeds,' a captain in the Oxfordshire and Buckinghamshire Light Infantry asked his family. 'The pansies and forget-me-nots are growing well,' wrote a lieutenant in the 2nd Argyll and Sutherland Highlanders happily, adding that he had been thrilled recently to find a sparrows' nest and had discovered an enormous water beetle. In the midst of apparently interminable brutality, flower gardens gave a chance to imagine a different sort of future, and promised hope or home. Vegetable plots, meanwhile, offered the prospect of a supplement to the dreary army rations of stale biscuits, tins of bully beef or 'Maconochie', a meagre stew of potatoes, turnips and carrots. There were even gardening jokes about the apparent endlessness of the war, like the encounter between two subalterns, one of whom remarks that his men are planting daffodil bulbs on the parapet to give some extra cover. The second replies that *his* men are planting acorns.

There were few creature comforts – the occasional hot meal (most of the food was stone cold by the time it had been carried up the communication trenches from battalion kitchens), cigarettes, parcels from home, the daily rum ration (supposed to be drunk in front of an officer, so that no one could hoard enough to go on a binge). Summer offered welcome relief from the cold and the wet, but terrible thirst was a common problem in the heat, as the only drinking water was generally tainted by the taste of petrol, since it had been carried to the line in fuel cans. But, like the comfort the occasional glimpse of the horizon can give to a prisoner, the passing of the seasons could also bring unlooked-for delights: daisies, poppies and buttercups; birds nesting in hedgerows and blasted trees, oblivious to the shellfire. After a quiet time in the summer of 1915, a corporal of the 9th Highland Light Infantry wrote home rhapsodically of 'ripping weather, a decent dugout for two, and sentry duty for only one hour in seventeen . . . our camp fire with the Dixie on for tea, and we ourselves, stretched out on the grass near the fire, yarning [and] smoking to keep the mosquitoes from getting busy. There *is* romance in our life out here. Don't believe anyone who tells you otherwise.' The freedom of the birds was especially enchanting to men for whom one false move could mean a sniper's bullet through the head. 'They don't seem to care a button for all the shells that are flying about and keep on singing merrily all the time,' an officer in a highland regiment wrote to his 'dear Nancy'.

The counterpart to the birdsong, though, was the cries of the wounded at night in no man's land, and the flies, brought on by the summer heat, which hung and hummed in enormous clouds, laying their eggs in corpses and settling on any food left uncovered. Familiarity never lessened the revulsion at discovering a maggoty corpse. More irritating to the living were the body lice, which sucked the men's blood as they tried to rest. In the filthy conditions of the trenches, where men slept in their clothes, crammed against each other, lice spread easily. There was minor pleasure to be had from the satisfying crack and the release of stolen blood when you managed to crush one of the wretched things between your fingernails, but the discovery of louse eggs in the seams of your clothing promised more misery. They were almost impossible to eliminate and everyone was constantly scratching.

The lice also transmitted Trench Fever, with its debilitating headaches, fever, shooting pains in the shins and discomfort in the eyes. Between one-fifth and one-third of all troops reporting ill in Flanders in the middle years of the war had succumbed to the sickness. Although the fever characteristically lasted only a few days, it could take a man out of the line for weeks. Then there were the 74,711 men admitted to military hospitals with trench foot or frostbite. Virtually no part of a military uniform was waterproof. In wet weather, an already heavy military greatcoat would just absorb the rain and could end up weighing dozens of pounds. Boots and puttees soon let in water. Trench foot was very rarely fatal, but in extreme cases it could turn the foot gangrenous and meant the amputation of toes. The only way to prevent it was to keep the feet dry, and from late 1915 soldiers were supposed to carry three pairs of socks with them and to change them at least once a day. A whale-oil grease was issued to battalions to be used as a barrier between the skin and the water – an average battalion could use 10 gallons of the stuff each day. In many of the well-managed units there was a package deal: you had to oil your feet in order to get the daily tot of rum, which came up to the front in earthenware jars stamped 'SRD' for Special Rations Department – universally known as 'Seldom Reaches Destination' or 'Soon Runs Dry'.

No one could stand these sorts of conditions for very long. Quite apart from the terror of death or dismemberment, men dreamed of finding somewhere warm to sleep, even a proper lavatory. The French had invented the practice of *roulement* – the constant replacement of one unit by another – which was soon adopted by all the armies involved. As one veteran described it, 'the Corps Commander stood firm and fought the battle, while divisions were rolled through his hands in succession, brought into action, bled white, and then taken way for a blood transfusion in some other more healthy corps area.' If circumstances allowed, the idea was for a unit to spend up to a week in the front line, followed by a similar length of time in a support trench, before being withdrawn to a reserve trench, and then enjoying a week behind the lines. Here were shabby little cafés – *estaminets* – where soldiers might buy an omelette and a glass of rough wine or rum. Officers and NCOs organized concerts and pantomimes, sports competitions and occasional parties. There were brothels and bars, too, of course, but the most striking characteristic of so many of these men was their innocence.

The city of Ypres continued to be fought over for most of the war, but the small town of Poperinghe near by was generally untroubled by German shells, and it was here that men on their way to and from the Flanders front line took what pleasure they could find. The place had been abandoned for the most part by its original inhabitants, who were replaced by very large numbers of soldiers and a few refugees who had opened tatty shops with rabbit-wire windows, from which they sold rosaries, brightly coloured sweets and what they claimed to be 'real Ypres lace'. Chinese labourers, recruited for non-combatant work in the British Chinese Labour Corps, scurried across the cobbles carrying pots of stew slung from bamboo poles on their shoulders.★ There was an officers' café of dubious repute named after Skindles, the Maidenhead hotel of choice for adulterers. Apart from the countless indifferent bars and cafés and prostitutes of varying degrees of professionalism, the only entertainment for the aimless soldiers was provided by 'The Fancies', an improvised music-hall show celebrated for the performances of two Belgian women known by the men as Lanoline and Vaseline. A Church of England army chaplain noted they 'could neither sing nor dance, but at least added a touch of femininity'.

The author of this assessment was the Reverend Philip Clayton, known to all as 'Tubby' – a deep-voiced, plump-waisted, absent-minded, bristle-mopped, pipe-smoking twenty-nine-year-old,

★ These 'coolies' were paid a pittance, and by 1918 there were 96,000 of them in the British Chinese Labour Corps. Nearly a thousand are buried or commemorated in a Commonwealth War Graves Commission cemetery at Noyelles-sur-Mer in Picardy.

although his sense of humour suggested he was hardly more than a teenager. 'I was cut out to be a genius,' he boasted. 'Unfortunately somebody forgot to put the pieces together.' Yet bad jokes turned out to be a rather more effective way of making a connection with the men he was supposed to be tending than bishops blathering on about 'the Great Adventure'. The war challenged the whole notion of belief. What room was there for it when those made in God's image were being blown to pieces all around? How could hell be any worse than what they were living through? As for the wages of sin, one soldier recalled a conversation with a battalion padre: 'why a judgement on these young men, almost boys, too young to have really sinned? Perhaps they had masturbated, had fornicated, had committed some adultery. The whole concept of a God so concerned with bedrooms and sex seemed to me slightly blasphemous, even rather ridiculous.'

Tubby Clayton had arrived in Poperinghe in 1915. Apart from a canteen supplying warm food in the little town square, run by a Methodist minister, there was something of a shortage of wholesome leisure activities. So, at the suggestion of another military chaplain, Neville Talbot, he rented an abandoned house. Once renovated, the building was named Talbot House, in honour of Neville's brother Gilbert who had been shot dead a few weeks previously; the name was soon abbreviated to the signallers' 'Toc H' – 'Toc' being a predecessor of 'Tango' in the signalling alphabet. Beneath the sign hanging outside was painted 'Everyman's Club', and above the door to Clayton's room were inscribed the words 'Abandon rank all ye who enter here.' The rules of this egalitarian haven tell something of the nature of the soldiers who went there. By overwhelming vote, billiards were banned on Sundays. The attic was turned into a chapel ('The foundations are in the roof,' said Clayton), and on other floors were games rooms, classrooms, a 'dry' canteen and a library with 2,000 books. (The chaplain ensured the books were returned by requiring those borrowing them to leave behind their cap, knowing that turning up on parade without one was a disciplinary offence.) There was a garden out back with the invitation 'COME INTO THE GARDEN AND FORGET THE WAR.' It was easier said than done.

Tubby Clayton was offering an illusion of 'home', which all men dreamed about. Yet the most extraordinary thing was that – in terms of miles at least – the soldiers' real homes were so very close. Most of the wars of the nineteenth century – like those of the twenty-first – were fought thousands of miles away. But the guns of the Western Front could be heard in Sussex, in Kent, in Surrey, even sometimes on Wimbledon Common. The novelist Arnold Bennett claimed that in 1917 he knew of an officer who had eaten his breakfast in the trenches and his dinner that evening at his London club. Lord Northcliffe listened to the artillery from his country house near Broadstairs in Kent, while soldiers in Flanders were buying his newspapers as they trudged up from the marshalling points to the front line. Letters from home arrived within a couple of days or so, so parcels could be sent with newly baked cakes or freshly cut flowers from the garden. When Wilfred Owen left a couple of towels at home while on leave, he just had them posted back to him at the front. Anything from binoculars to portable gramophones could be posted to men at the front. Soon smart department stores like Fortnum and Mason's had a comfortable business supplying hampers for the trenches. They were delivered even in the midst of artillery bombardments.

While they relied on such contact with home to help them cope, this geographical closeness only emphasized the bottomless cavern between those doing the fighting and their families at home doing the worrying. The difference of perspective was sometimes bitterly ironic, with newspapers informing their readers of strategic intentions that were utterly unknown to the poor men who were supposed to be making them reality. As one subaltern, who survived two years in front-line trenches, noticed, 'what the infantryman in France knew about the war as a whole was seldom worth knowing.' His worries were more immediate, and words seemed inadequate when it came to explaining your life in the mud to your well-meaning family – they might as well be living on a different planet.

So while soldiers longed for leave, dreamed about it, and often dreaded getting the notification that it was imminent (because it triggered superstitions that they might not live to enjoy it), the reality of home-visits could be unendurable. When men returned on leave, wives, mothers, sisters and girlfriends often found their men were uneasy amid home comforts, sometimes able to offer the occasional pleasantry or laboured joke, but mentally absent. Homely preoccupations – who was stepping out with whom, what was for dinner, all the banal excitements of workaday life – were intolerably trivial. And soldiers often wanted to spare their families' feelings, too. 'I spoke with caution of the fighting, and withheld most of the horrors,' said a corporal. 'Anyway, I wanted to forget them, in this heavenly change to home life, so soft, so easy, so peaceful. Gardens, flowers, regular habits, good food, books, papers, armchairs, talk, and drinks were riches rediscovered.' But even so, he found that after months of army rations, the rich food of home upset his stomach, and he secretly bedded down on his bedroom floor because he was unable any longer to sleep in a comfortable bed.

And then, at the end of the interlude, came the inevitable return, the goodbye at the garden gate or the front door or amid the hundreds weeping at the railway station, each with the same thought: will we ever see each other again?

Why did the soldiers put up with it all? Exhausted, terrified, distressed by the death or disfigurement of their friends, ignorant of any overarching plan and with no end in sight for years on end: the greatest question of all is why men continued to fight. For what did they endure the separation, the squalor, the terror, the cold, the mud, the sleeplessness, the deafening noise of outgoing artillery barrages and the loss of friends to incoming fire? There were mutinies in the German, Russian and French armies, but not, on any significant scale, in the British army. Why?

Part of the reason might be that the British simply did not have to endure as much as their allies or enemies, because they did not

suffer similar levels of casualties until the summer of 1916, a full
eighteen months into the war. But our incomprehension is owing
to the hundred years that separate us from them. The latter half of
the twentieth century was characterized by an ever-increasing
obsession with individualism. From Iceland to Albania, Cork to
Tbilisi, citizens can now theoretically claim the protection of the
European Convention on Human Rights. This idea – the promotion of an individual's rights above all else – would have been
extremely difficult for many adults of 1914 to imagine. The incomprehension is mutual: the concept of duty, as understood then – the
disregarding of individual concerns for a greater good – has been a
notable casualty of the campaign for individual rights.

Even after years of fighting, some romantic notions of a noble
cause – that love for the idea of 'country' that had stirred Siegfried
Sassoon and Rupert Brooke – survived. If anything, the contrast
between sordid trench life and the dream of a blossom-drowsy,
bee-humming English idyll might make it even more powerful. A
few months before he was mortally wounded in the summer of
1917, Lieutenant Christian Creswell Carver of the Royal Field
Artillery wrote that 'I always feel that I am fighting for England,
English fields, lanes, trees, English atmospheres, and good days in
England – and all that is synonymous for liberty.' This pastoral
dream must have been a solace in the squalor. But the English countryside also seemed to express a set of political values. As the poet
John Masefield explained it when he went to the United States the
same year to explain Britain's war effort, 'the England for which
men are dying . . . is in the little villages of the land, in the old
homes, in the churches, in countless carvings, in bridges, in old
tunes, and in the old acts of the English, a shy, gentle, humorous and
most manly soul, that stood up for the poor and cared for beauty.'

Yet Masefield must have known that the England of green val-
leys, rolling grasslands, verdant forests, thatched cottages, country
churches and clear chalkstreams was not the England that most
British soldiers came from (many of whom weren't 'English' anyway): only perhaps a fifth of the population lived in Masefield's

semi-feudal paradise, with the rich man in his castle and the poor man at his gate and the vicar dispensing the comfortable platitudes of the Church of England. Perhaps, then, they were being forced to fight? Military law was harsh and unbending, and there were certainly occasions when officers on the Western Front found themselves having to draw their revolvers on British soldiers running away. Brigadier Frank Crozier, a portly little Irishman who showed great courage in combat, held it as an axiom that 'Men will not, as a rule, risk their lives unnecessarily unless they know that they will be shot down by their own officers if they fail to do so or if they waver.' Crozier boasted of shooting at least one of his own soldiers during a battle and of ordering his men to machine-gun allied Portuguese troops who were running away. Could it have been, simply, that death in combat was marginally less certain than the execution that awaited a soldier if he refused to enter into it?

The 1914 edition of the red-bound *Manual of Military Law* was 3 inches thick and carefully listed most conceivable offences and their punishments, from trying to sell or pawn military kit through to mutiny and sedition. The notorious Field Punishment No. 1 for serious offences was clearly intended as a very public spectacle and warning to others. Tied with both arms outstretched to the wheel of a cart or a field gun, the prisoner looked like Christ crucified. When his face was covered in flies the spectacle was particularly loathsome. Though it was frequently commuted, the punishment was handed out over 60,000 times during the war. As to formal executions, while over 3,000 death sentences were passed by courts martial – the great majority on captured deserters – only just over one-tenth of them were carried out. Some were certainly intended to have an impact upon other soldiers. The very first such execution was of Private Patrick Downey of the Leinster Regiment, a man with a string of previous offences who was described in court as being of 'very bad character'. He was nineteen years old. The court papers were sent to the Commander in Chief for confirmation of sentence in December 1915, accompanied by the observation that an 'exemplary punishment' was 'highly desirable'.

The few surviving accounts of these executions make plain that they were every bit as horrifying as might be imagined – the condemned man tied to a post with a white cloth pinned to his tunic above his heart; the men of the firing squad weeping, vomiting or shaking so violently that death was often brought about only when the officer in charge put his revolver to the chest or temple of the struggling, wounded prisoner. Crozier's form of compassion was to leave a good quantity of alcohol in the condemned man's cell: with any luck, by the time he was dragged to the stake he might scarcely be able to walk. Although some were in favour of the firing squads, the ordinary soldiers required actually to participate in them sometimes never forgave the army for what it had forced them to do, and respected the man tied to the post much more than they did those who had dodged military service altogether. But nor can they have forgotten how the army could deal with disobedience. Private Downey's crime had been to refuse repeated orders to put on his filthy cap.

The lucky prisoners were comforted by compassionate army chaplains, like Julian Bickersteth. At Christmas 1917 he found himself called to attend a teenager about to face a firing squad. The boy gave the padre his wallet, a few photographs, his lucky farthing and a letter to his best friend in the regiment, wishing them all a happy new year and saying he was sorry he hadn't made good. Bickersteth wrote home after the event that 'As they bound him, I held his arm tight to reassure him – words are useless at such a moment – and then he turned his blindfolded face up to mine and said in a voice which wrung my heart, "Kiss me sir, kiss me," and with my kiss on his lips and "God has you in his keeping," whispered in his ear, he passed into the Great Unseen. God accept him; Christ receive him. I do not think he died in vain.'

But while it is true that the British army had 'battle police', who maintained a network of 'straggler posts' and 'battle stops' behind the front line, and whose job was to direct genuine stragglers towards the gunfire and to apprehend those trying to go as fast as they could in the opposite direction, most soldiers seem actually to have needed little pushing out of the trenches when the whistles blew. And if they survived the crossing of no man's land, soldiers had every opportunity to ignore the orders from headquarters: telephones required cables, which were frequently cut by artillery fire, carrier pigeons got lost, were killed or refused to fly, and soldiers sent as runners with messages on scraps of paper could be killed at any moment. There was simply no way that a senior officer could exercise close control once an attack had begun. Yet, again and again, the British soldier clambered out of his trench into a hail of bullets. Fear of punishment will not do as a complete explanation.

Armies may seem from the outside to be organizations in which some people give the orders and others simply obey them. In reality, the business of command depends upon everyone being complicit in the chain of command – those being ordered as much as those doing the ordering. It is a deal. In some ways, British soldiers were better provided for than those in many other armies, including their French, Russian and Italian allies. But much of the readiness to continue must have been due to leadership. The British frequently had more officers for each battalion than the Germans had, and the burden of expectation laid on these young men was enormous: in an attack they were required to lead their men from the front rather than pushing them from behind. This inevitably meant that the most dangerous role in the British army was that of the junior officer and, for all the caricature, most of them did what was expected of them. Many of these subalterns had had dinned into them at their public schools the question asked by Alfred Austin, a bad poet with the resonant message, 'Who would not die for England?' Even in 1917 Paul Jones, a myopic young man who had failed his initial army medical after leaving Dulwich College but had somehow worked his way into the Tank Corps, finished a letter home reflecting that 'I rejoice that war has come my way. It has made me realize what a petty thing life is . . . I have never in all my life experienced such wild exhilaration as on the commencement of a big stunt . . . The only thing that compares with it are the few minutes before the start of a big school match. Well, cheer-oh!' He was killed on 31 July that year. It is very hard to believe that this stiff-upper-lip cheeriness was the universal reaction to the prospect of battle, but the generally steady leadership of junior officers must have had an inspirational effect.

Even so, the discipline – or biddability – of the British soldier is remarkable, given the unique circumstances of trench combat. Even when you were close enough to peer through the eyeholes of your gas mask and make out the human beings trying to kill you, smoke and confusion could make it impossible to work out what on earth was happening. Death and hurt arrived from nowhere. As H. W. Yoxall wrote to his mother, 'When you have seen a shell fall into the midst of six men and packed three of them away in a sandbag . . . one wonders whether anything matters.'

It is too easy to use the Christmas truce of 1914 as evidence that, were it not for inept politicians and heartless, incompetent generals, the soldiers of both armies would have laid down their guns and made peace, but it is true that there were numerous other informal arrangements between enemy soldiers along the great length of front line – stagnant corners where the poor bloody infantry in one lot of trenches shouted out to the poor bloody infantry on the other side and agreed informal ceasefires so that they could collect their wounded and bury their dead; where enemy patrols in no man's land took care to avoid bumping into one another or where hostilities stopped for tea. No wonder the generals worried about preserving the 'offensive spirit'. But they were constantly reassured. The more the soldiers had seen of combat, the greater the number of friends they had seen suffer or die, the harder their hearts could become. 'Leave to shoot the prisoners, sir?' a sergeant in the Scots Guards asked his officer, before avenging his brother's death by doing so. It cannot have been a unique event.

It was said that the Kaiser once told recruits that they had 'surrendered your souls and bodies to me' and should be ready to do unquestioningly whatever he commanded, even shooting their own parents. Sense of duty, love of country, fear of punishment, valiant leadership, thirst for revenge: if all else failed there was, in the end, this total abstention of one's own self. But the British army did not work like that. Something else had been inculcated that was infinitely superior to any of these motivations. When Charles Carrington, who served on both the Western and Italian fronts, looked back, he recalled that it 'was one thing to make jokes about "swinging the lead" [shirking duty], or "working your ticket" [getting your discharge papers] and quite another thing to avoid a dangerous task which someone else must do if you did not'. Those who acquired a reputation as shirkers could only lose it by an outstanding act of bravery, for 'the assumption in a service battalion was that every man could be trusted to behave like a soldier on the day.' Of course, no one *wanted* to be living in a hole in the ground, but the feeling among the soldiers that they existed in a parallel universe so frightening, so perverse, so repellent that no one else could comprehend it, gave these men a sense of brotherhood that few felt able easily to cast aside. 'We looked at each other wondering how long we should be together,' recalled one veteran. 'Rough, often foul-mouthed and blasphemous, we were tied by the string of our experiences past, present and future.' The few yards of trench were their world, and each stayed there and fought there for the simple reason that his comrades were staying there and fighting there, too.

The important loyalty was less to flags, anthems and kings than to each other. 'A Corporal and six men in a trench were like shipwrecked sailors on a raft,' Charles Carrington felt, each aware of the others' strengths and vulnerabilities, for their survival depended upon their pals. The infantry section was 'we'; everyone else – from the Germans to British staff officers, to other British regiments, to the French peasants on whose behalf the war was being fought – was to some degree 'they'. When J. R. R. Tolkien sat down to write *Lord of the Rings* long after the war he created Sam Gamgee, Frodo's steadfast companion, as tribute to the private soldiers he had served with on the Western Front, and whom he 'recognized as so far superior to myself'.

In their sheer dogged readiness to endure fear and personal suffering for the sake of one another, there is something enormously admirable about them.

8. The Hand that Rocks the Cradle Wrecks the World

Old enough to marry, but not to vote.

By late 1915, with the trenches in France and Belgium looking deeper and more enduring than ever, the war had acquired an awful appearance of permanence. It was also forcing profound change at home, overturning ideas that had once been thought rather key to British life.

That winter, churches in eastern parts of England cancelled evening services, fearful that the light from their windows might provide a guide to German aircraft intent on bombing Britain. The following spring, there was much debate about whether to succumb to the proposal of moving the clocks forward an hour, to give more daylight during working hours. This practical plan had been around for almost a decade, but had got nowhere. In 1916, some of that political hostility remained. For Sir Frederick

Banbury, a frock-coated Conservative MP of the 'any change is a change for the worse' variety, the fact that the Germans had done something similar a few weeks beforehand was enough to condemn the idea as worthless. In the House of Lords, a member of the aristocracy raised the worry of a mother giving birth to twins as the clocks changed back in the autumn: she might find that her second child was older than her first-born, which would pose enormous problems for aristocratic families where inheritances really mattered. But there were more immediate worries. Working in darkness required artificial lighting, which demanded precious coal that could be better used to power the shipyards and munitions factories. The clocks changed.

Anything that could be taxed would be taxed, yet the revenue still failed to keep pace with the enormous cost of the war – the national debt, which had been just over £700 million in 1914, was to grow to almost £8,000 million by 1920, despite income tax quintupling in the course of the war. All sorts of other freedoms had already been swept away as well. The Defence of the Realm Act, passed by parliament without debate in the first days of the war, was barely more than a paragraph long and intentionally vague, banning the citizenry from doing anything that might be considered to impede the war effort. The Act would now be used to try to tackle the historic British folly with alcohol, since hangovers were having such a bad effect on industrial production – as Lloyd George put it: 'men who drink at home are murdering the men in the trenches.' Beer was watered down and made more expensive, and new laws restricted the opening hours of pubs. 'Treating', or buying drinks for friends, was made an offence, the *Morning Post* reporting in March 1916 that a Southampton court had fined a Robert Andrew Smith £1 for buying his wife a glass of wine in a local pub. He claimed that she had given him sixpence to pay for the drink, but the court was unconvinced, fined her an additional £1 and the barmaid £5 (the equivalent in economic power of over £500 now) for serving them.

The war was now no longer an entirely male business. The

struggle for a woman's right to vote, which had so transfixed the nation before the war, had been suspended for the duration by many of the suffragette leaders. Shortly before the outbreak of war they had bombed the country house being built for Lloyd George near Walton Heath golf course in Surrey: police discovered hat-pins at the scene, along with unexploded black powder. 'We have blown up the Chancellor of the Exchequer's house . . . to wake him up,' Emmeline Pankhurst had boasted, before being carted off to gaol. In July 1915, accompanied by numerous bands, Mrs Pankhurst led a march of tens of thousands of women through the heart of London, demanding the 'right to serve' by war work at home. A newsreel report of the demonstration carried the headline: 'The British Lion is Awake, so is the Lioness.' The march had been funded by Lloyd George's Ministry of Munitions.

The under-employment of women in the early days of the war had been little short of a scandal, caused by a feeling among many (male) trades unionists that they would much prefer the lioness to stay asleep. The danger from allowing too many women into the workplace was 'dilution': women would work for lower pay and disregard laboriously negotiated restrictive practices. But the void caused by so many men having volunteered for military service had to be filled somehow. Soon there were women working as tram-drivers, bus conductors, bakers and butchers, welders, even blacksmiths. In 1916 Lord Northcliffe felt moved to patronizing praise for the 'nice girls' from 'dreary manless suburbs' who had entered the workforce. Even if the war was 'delaying the marriage to which every patriotic woman looks forward, they have the great satisfaction of knowing that, whether they be women doctors, women dentists, women clerks, women ticket collectors, or engaged in any other profession, they are helping the great cause of freedom'.

By 1918 it was reckoned that there were 1.5 million women working in jobs previously done by men. An estimated 400,000 women left domestic service never to return. The young feminist writer Rebecca West was only one of the women campaigning for the right to vote who believed that without the suffragist campaign this army of labour would never have been mobilized. She might equally well later have observed that without the war the suffragist campaign would have taken longer to achieve its goal. 'I'd never known what it was to be a free woman before,' said a working-class woman trapped in a miserable marriage. You could see the effect of this new-found freedom in the very appearance of the young women of Britain. War work would have been almost impossible in the long dresses and petticoats of pre-war fashion. Now, while the colours might still be subdued, the skirts were shorter, hair was cut in a bob, and the bra was replacing the corset.

Most famously, there was a great force of 'munitionettes' engaged in the dangerous business of assembling and packing shells for the Western Front. By the end of 1915 there were three times as many women working in munitions as there were men. 'Tell the boys', a munitionette instructed one of Lord Northcliffe's reporters, 'not to be downhearted, but to stick to it, and us girls will do our bit and stick to our machines, so that they won't be hung up for shells.' Quite large numbers of these women become 'canary girls' when the trinitrotoluene fumes in the factories caused their hair to fall out and turned their skin a ghastly shade of yellow. In 1916 over fifty of them died of jaundice. At the front 'Woodbine Willie' – the army padre Geoffrey Studdert Kennedy, who acquired his nickname by recognizing that the average soldier cared much more for nicotine than for the Nicene Creed* – exulted of an offensive: 'By George it's a glorious barrage, and English girls made 'em. We're all in it, sweethearts, mothers and wives. The hand that rocks the cradle wrecks the world. There are no non-combatants.'

And yet there *were* non-combatants – and a great number of men who were happy to stay that way. No one could assume the

---

* An army chaplain, he said, should have 'a box of fags in your haversack, and a great deal of love in your heart'.

supply of soldiers was infinite. The question was, could the country rely indefinitely upon men volunteering to fight?

Not forcing men into uniform had been a cause of national pride before the war. Occasionally a few voices on the Conservative backbenches in parliament argued that more would be done for the health of the poor by spending money sticking them in the army than by pulling down their slums, but the campaign for compulsory military service, endorsed by the *Daily Mail*, foundered on the deeply held conviction that a volunteer, professional army was one of the things that distinguished Britain from its tyrannical European neighbours. At any rate, there had been such a prodigious rush of volunteers in the early days of the war that conscription had been unnecessary.

These early volunteers may have had hugely diverse social backgrounds, but they had in common the fact that they had answered Kitchener's call. For some people, however, this raised an altogether different question about the constitution of the army: why should nobler men risk life and limb to protect those who would not volunteer? For others, it even led to anxieties about the very future of the race. Leonard Darwin, youngest son of the father of the theory of natural selection, spoke for many when he said that those being killed were the very people who 'should produce the stock of the future'. Fellow eugenicists proposed ways of counteracting the damage, among them the idea of offering badly wounded soldiers 'eugenic stripes' to wear on their uniforms, to make them more attractive to potential brides who might otherwise shudder at their damaged bodies.

By late 1915, though, it was clear that the country could not rely for much longer on a supply of willing volunteers. The minimum height required for the army had already been reduced, with special 'Bantam' battalions formed of short men, some of whom were hardly taller than a rifle. Yet it was reckoned that there might be 5 million men of military age who were still not serving with the forces. Many were doubtless doing work of national importance. But at a guess that still left nearly 2 million who could have

answered the call and had failed to do so. In parliament one politician after another pronounced on how to increase the size of the
army: surely the rich ought to be sending their chauffeurs to join
up? What about encouraging individuals to go to Africa and
raise private armies in, say, Basutoland, asked another? The idea of
compulsion at home was gaining ground, too. Raymond Asquith,
son of the Prime Minister, had considered it a matter of honour to
join the army when the war began – even at the age of thirty-six.
In April 1915 he wrote to his wife and remarked acidly of Lady
Sybil Grant,★ a minor writer and army officer's wife and now one
of a growing number of people who had been converted to conscription, that 'The idea that they have at the back of their minds
seems to be that if their lovers are being killed, it is only fair that
their footmen should be killed too.' For most people, fairness was
at the heart of it. Why should young men risk their lives in the
trenches, so that some of their contemporaries could snuggle
under the blankets at home? The cheery appeals for volunteers
developed a more menacing undertone. Those who did not answer
the call would be seen as cowards and shirkers. They would eventually be compelled to join up, anyway, and then, as one recruiting
major wrote in a letter to young men in his area, 'you will be
mightily sorry.'

The calls to enlist became increasingly frantic. '*The Huns* are
fighting to enslave the world!' read one. '[They] believe in cruci-
fying women, in raping young girls to death, in hacking off babies'
limbs, and impaling them on their lances . . . in inoculating disease
into the blood of POWs, in pouring oil over old men and women
and setting them on fire, in raping mothers in the presence of their
children, and daughters in the presence of their mothers, and
innumerable horrors too filthy to publish!' There were plenty of
senior officers who knew that most of these atrocity stories were

---

★ Lady Sybil was an eccentric egalitarian, spending much of her later life (by
which time she had dyed her hair orange) living in a caravan or up a tree, from
whence, reputedly, she gave instructions to her butler by megaphone.

rubbish but who were willing to nod at them benignly if they offered the prospect of more men in uniform, not least because there had been genuine atrocities which had a profound effect on British public opinion, even before the exaggerations and lies. The execution in October 1915 in occupied Belgium of a British nurse, Edith Cavell, did at least provide one such genuine example of German brutality. She had been caring for allied prisoners, and had undoubtedly been helping some to escape home. Her execution was alleged to have been a rather botched affair, with the German officer in charge having to step forward and administer the *coup de grâce* with his revolver. The Bishop of London, Arthur Winnington-Ingram, exclaimed that 'this will settle the matter, once for all, about recruiting in Great Britain . . . there will be no need now of compulsion,' and in Edith Cavell's native village in Norfolk every single eligible young man is said to have joined up the next day.

But even with all these horror stories ringing in their ears it did not look as if sufficient numbers of the young men of Britain would enlist. To avoid compulsion, there was to be one last heave. In late 1915 the seventeenth Earl of Derby, the prodigiously wealthy Lancashire landowner appointed Kitchener's director of recruiting, concocted a scheme in which all men between the ages of eighteen and forty-one would be *invited* to join up, or to attest to their willingness to fight. Crucially, he promised married men that they would not be required actually to serve until the supply of single men had been exhausted. The result was a fiasco. Married men lined up patiently to declare their readiness, safe under Lord Derby's guarantee, but the number of unmarried men attesting reached a final total of only 343,000. If the burden of military service was to be spread fairly, there now appeared to be no other option than compulsion.

Political opposition to this idea remained strong to the last. The Trades Union Congress was set against it, as was the Labour party, and the idea was anathema to most of the Irish MPs at Westminster. Many English politicians considered the introduction of conscription an admission of moral bankruptcy. It would also produce a worse army, because, as the *Nation* remarked, 'The genuine conscript . . . marches in the ranks precisely as the requisitioned horse trots in the commissariat train.' But the mood of the nation had changed from one of enthusiasm for enlistment to resentment against those who had not done so. Lord Northcliffe used his bully pulpit in the *Daily Mail* to support the idea of an armband worn to distinguish those who wanted to fight but could not do so from those who could but lacked the requisite moral fibre to sign up. It would, he said, prevent 'the gross injustice that is inflicted on such people as . . . my chauffeur, Pine, who is an ex-soldier, lamed for life . . . [by] a cannon ball', but who had suffered the indignity of being 'loudly abused by a company of soldiers' for not having joined up. As public attitudes hardened, so political positions altered with them: perhaps it was time to lay aside opposition to conscription temporarily, to preserve British freedoms in the long term.

When the matter came before parliament late in 1915 it was clear from the debate that the appalling casualty rates were swinging opinion in favour of compulsion. Only a couple of months beforehand, Prime Minister Asquith had worried that conscription might threaten 'the maintenance of national unity'. Now he argued that the national interest demanded the military burden be properly shared. A suggestion by a prominent opponent of conscription in the Labour party that, as the war was the creation of old men, it should be the elderly who were forced to put on uniform before anyone else, got nowhere, and nor did it strike much of a chord with the public. When the vote came there was an overwhelming majority of MPs in favour of conscription, with a mere thirty-six voting against the proposed law. In January 1916 the Military Service Act introduced compulsory military service for all single men aged eighteen to forty-one, apart from those doing work of national importance, the disabled, those able to show they were the sole means of support for their dependants, and conscientious objectors. The social reformer Beatrice Webb lamented to her diary that, coming after the Defence of the Realm Act, the

Munitions Act, the curtailment of labour rights and censorship of the press, conscription marked the arrival of the 'servile state'.

Her anxiety was understandable, for Britain was now a very different country to the one it had been before August 1914. As Sir John Simon, the Liberal Home Secretary, asked in the parliamentary debate, 'Does anyone really suppose that once the principle of conscription is conceded you are going to stop there?' He had identified something critical, for in removing the decision about who was to fight from the individual and giving it to the government, conscription had opened a door that would never be closed. 'The real issue', he told parliament presciently, 'is whether we are to begin an immense change in the fundamental nature of our society.' They were. By the end of the war the state was involved in determining not merely who wore uniform, but what people ate and drank, where they worked, how much they were paid and who was entitled to a pension.

A carefully constructed list was published, showing the order in which citizens would be obliged to join up. The task of deciding who might have a valid excuse for not doing so was to be assigned to local committees, or tribunals, across the country. Until conscription was extended to include married men four months later, these committees would generally be sitting in judgement not on householders, who were the only people allowed to vote, but on unmarried young men living with their parents. 'The maxim that the task of defending the homes of the country should fall primarily upon those who had no homes to defend was accepted without demur,' said the mayor of Preston, who sat on a Lancashire tribunal. Many older married homeowners thought that if conscription ever marched them off to the army the country would almost certainly be in such a terrible state that there would be hardly anything left to fight for.

But the war was consuming men at an unimagined rate. The early categories were soon exhausted and married men were summoned to join the forces. The panels required to distinguish between those who should be obliged to do their bit and those who might be allowed to stay at home were now meeting several times each week. These gatherings of between five and twenty-five local worthies – magistrates, councillors, vicars and local tradesmen – were making what might literally be life-and-death decisions in a matter of ten or fifteen minutes per man. Although the panels were encouraged to have local trades union officials and members of the Labour party sitting with them, they seem to have been selected mainly on the basis of an old-boy network. They therefore represented the largely middle class passing judgement on the largely working class, the middle-aged and elderly determining the fate of the young. Sometimes members invited their wives or friends to sit on the panel with them. Occasionally – as happened in Huntingdon, when a nurseryman sitting on the panel stepped down to argue his own case for being exempted from military service in front of his colleagues (successfully) – they decided their own fate.

Compulsion was not as draconian as elsewhere in Europe, and those who considered the panel's decision unfair could appeal. But local panels were usually attended by a retired army officer, who was also entitled to appeal if he believed a man had been treated too leniently. These army men took a bluff approach. Confronted by a religiously inspired pacifist at a tribunal in Oxford, one of them asked whether Jesus hadn't advised 'an eye for an eye and a tooth for a tooth'. When Tolstoy's name was mentioned, the army man wondered where it was. In Manchester, one whiskery old soldier asked how the meek could inherit the earth if there was no one to fight for them. A young pacifist who appeared before a tribunal in the Home Counties and began to explain the meaning of a passage in his Greek Bible was interrupted by the chairman blustering, 'Greek? You don't mean to tell me Jesus spoke Greek? He was British to the backbone!'

Ignorance apart, it was a well-intentioned system, albeit one that had its weaknesses. Because the panels were designed as local institutions, the judgements across the country varied hugely. The men working for the Atherstone Hunt in the Midlands were exempted from military service because maintaining the quality of horses was in the national interest; a group of attendants at sea-side bathing huts escaped the khaki because their work was said to promote public good health. Temporary exemptions were often granted to give an employer enough time to find a replacement hairdresser, wheelwright or shop assistant to stand in for the man summoned for duty. The tribunals were frequently more consid-erate than mass public opinion might have been, but in the end the system worked efficiently because the court of last resort was the mob. When others saw their sons and husbands, brothers and uncles packed off to the war, they were more than ready to help the panels to identify scrimshankers. In this context, the barefaced cheek of some of the applicants was astonishing: a man in Leeds, for example, requested his freedom so that he could complete a course of hair restoration. Much more common were businessmen appearing before tribunals to plead that an employee be granted exemption, but the appeal that 'Ladies must have hats' was generally met by the military representative's 'The Army must have men.'

What, then, constituted vital work which might entitle a man to escape wearing khaki? All manner of businessmen – even rag-and-bone men – tried it on. On several occasions in Lanca-shire, black-pudding-making and tripe-dressing were described as essential, with plenty of detail given about the unsuitability of women for the grisly business of scraping out the contents of a beast's stomach or mixing blood and oatmeal. Surviving records from the West Country show numerous attempts to get exemp-tions for farm labourers on similar grounds (that the work was too heavy for women to undertake). Experience soon taught these tri-bunals various ways of determining whether the country would indeed cease to function if a particular individual was co-opted into the army. When an employer arrived to argue that a clerk was indispensable to his business and irreplaceable, the chairman might ask how much this vital man was paid. If the employer answered the query with anything less than generous wages, the clerk could find himself packed off to the army.

The tribunals allowed a shaft of light to fall on the interior of

British society. There were teenagers supporting entire families of orphan siblings, others who held down not one or two but perhaps three or four jobs. Parents testified that they already had two or three or even more sons serving in the army or navy – could not one be spared? In Croydon, a widow argued for her eleventh son's exemption from military service – of her ten elder boys, five had already been wounded, two were prisoners of war in Germany and one a prisoner in Turkey. The tribunal was compassionate.*

Most men did not need to be dragged before a tribunal. But, for the canny, it was a waiting game. Tribunals might grant exemptions for three months, which could possibly be extended. If a decision went against you, there might be an appeal – the process could keep you out of the ranks for a year. Those most likely to be successful at appeal seem to have been the self-employed and those for whom military service would mean members of their close family going hungry. At other times, however, anonymous letters were sent to the tribunal panel pointing the finger at young men who the writer believed ought to have been sent off to France but were still at large. Sometimes even wives expressed their outrage that their man had *not* been called up. 'You have never seen him yet; there isn't a stronger or healthier man in town,' a woman wrote to the tribunal in Preston. 'Come for him now, it will learn him to make a better man of him, and do not send him back . . . Fetch him now; he might be the missing link.'

It was one thing to decide whether a man was fit and able to fight, and generally not too hard to rule on whether his work really was of national importance. But deciding matters of belief was altogether more tricky. For the British system of compulsory military service was much more accommodating to personal convictions than arrangements elsewhere in Europe: in France, for example, those who objected to military service on grounds of

---

* 'I don't think his Majesty would ask for more than three sons out of four. I think it's a fair share,' the chairman of a tribunal in Newton Abbot told an applicant in February 1916, and the colonel present agreed.

conscience were treated as deserters. When introducing the necessary legislation in the House of Commons, Asquith had explained that there was a long British tradition of permitting ethical exemption from military service – Prime Minister William Pitt, for example, had allowed Quakers to exercise their conscience by not fighting against Napoleon. There was opposition to the idea, of course. In the House of Lords, Lord Willoughby de Broke said he believed that 'A man who conscientiously objected to fighting for himself or his wife and family, but who was willing that others should be persuaded to lay down their lives for him and his possessions displayed a selfishness, an hypocrisy and an arrogance which was difficult to forgive.'

There were plenty of clergy who took a similar view. The chaplain to the Speaker of the House of Commons, Archdeacon Basil Wilberforce, proclaimed that 'to kill Germans is a divine service in the fullest acceptance of the word.' At the same time, conscription legislation exempted clergymen of all Churches from military service – a case of exemption on grounds of conscience if ever there was one – while their French equivalents were required to serve. Principled objections to a war that was killing untold numbers of fellow human beings invited insults from those who obeyed the call, and there are numerous accounts of men who had chosen not to wear uniform being attacked, abused or sneered at. When confronted with a troublesome 'conchie' (and were there any others?), the tribunals examining men summoned for military service liked to ask what the dissident would do if his mother or sister was about to be sexually assaulted by a Hun. It was a question that required a sophisticated answer to do with the difference between crime and politics, but the most celebrated and entertaining of these duels took place when the sexually ambiguous writer Lytton Strachey was asked this question by the Hampstead tribunal in 1916. His sisters had come to support him at the hearing, and now he looked at each of them. Then he turned to the panel and answered: 'I should try and interpose my own body.' Strachey was declared unfit for military service on medical rather than moral grounds.

When objectors appeared before tribunals they could find the mob packing the public benches to see that those with exquisitely principled beliefs suffered the same fate as their own menfolk. The solitary pacifist confronting a well-upholstered panel of worthies required genuine courage of conviction. The men who objected to being called up on religious or ethical grounds were exceptional – most of those seeking exemption claimed that their work was vital to the well-being of their families or that they had skills or trades which could not be replaced by others – but they were tricky to handle. Statements of religious or humanitarian belief lay well beyond the imagination of many a panel chairman boasting noisily that he would allow no 'shirkers' to escape. Presented with a young man who argued that 'thou shalt not kill', a thick-set local butcher might bluster about Deuteronomy's instruction to put enemies to the sword, but it was generally wiser to remain silent. Near Oldham, a tribunal member facing a conchie ranted that he was 'a deliberate and rank blasphemer, a coward and a cad, and nothing but a shivering mass of unwholesome fat'. God had already been conscripted. By all sides.

In total there were about 16,000 conscientious objectors who refused to serve, from a vast array of occupations, with schoolteachers prominent among them. It was a very tiny proportion of the population indeed. The No-Conscription Fellowship might boast of having the world-renowned philosopher Bertrand Russell among its leading supporters, but it never commanded majority endorsement, never escaped its reputation for rope-soled eccentricity and was periodically raided by the police. When Russell addressed a gathering of about 2,000 members in London in April 1916 the crowd outside was so menacing that his audience were asked to express their feelings silently, for fear of inciting attack. They did so by waving their white handkerchiefs. 'Earnest of face and tense of spirit,' a Quaker remembered, 'they met with the knowledge that the world held them in contempt and that persecution hung over them.'

Resisting the herd required courage, and many of those who refused to serve on grounds of conscience suffered for their beliefs.

Over a third of them spent some time in prison, where they could expect solitary confinement with just a Bible for company, a couple of blankets, a washing bowl and chamberpot, and an uncomfortable sense that there was someone watching through the spyhole in the door. Some spent years in gaol and ten are said to have died there. Attempts to bend them to the will of government ranged from the brutal to the boneheaded. In May 1916 several dozen resisters were taken under military guard to France and ritually humiliated in front of a battalion of soldiers. Others even faced the death penalty, later commuted to penal servitude. The Home Office came up with projects for 'work of national importance' like forestry or farming for many of them. Some objectors found their consciences allowed them to serve in the Royal Army Medical Corps, but Seventh Day Adventists might refuse even to work in a military bakery. Yet although the Society of Friends – Quakers – believed that war was against the will of God they still sent more than a thousand men to serve with the Friends' Ambulance Unit, whose members – often wearing shorts in the middle of the coldest winter – came to be regarded by the soldiers as cranks with courage. Nine of them were killed, ninety-six awarded the Croix de Guerre or other honours. Corder Catchpool, who was one of the first to arrive in France, found caring for the wounded of both sides the most uplifting experience of his life: 'Thank God from the bottom of my heart for the inestimable privilege of being allowed to try and patch up the results of this ghastly mistake. But oh! the infinitesimal effect of the patching . . . I was chatting to a lad in the wards this afternoon; both arms amputated, and he was trying to compose a letter to his fiancée about it.'

Perhaps 3,000 objectors agreed to serve in a Non-Combatant Corps – the most despised unit in the army, nicknamed the 'No Courage Corps'. A sergeant-major serving in France suggested that their stark 'NCC' cap badge be augmented with a formal coat of arms showing 'three maggots recumbent proper, baby's bottle rampant, down pillow; supports are two tame rabbits rampant and above this "We Don't Want To Fight" and below " 'Tis Conscience doth make cowards of us all"'. A correspondent for *The Times* who visited a detachment of the Corps working on a section of railway 'amid very pleasant surroundings, some distance from the front' in France reported that 'their conduct is exemplary, an unusually large percentage of them being total abstainers as well as non-smokers.'

Testimony from the resisters themselves is often generous-spirited, giving examples of soldiers who had told them that, while they didn't share the conchies' ideas, they admired their determination. But the strain imposed on the families of objectors was great. When others in town endured the absence of young men who were doing their patriotic duty, the wives and children of objectors had to live with the accusation that their menfolk were 'merely' in prison.* Even after the war was over, the troubles of conscientious objectors continued. When the inevitable final question came in a job interview – 'And what did you do in the war?' – the CO abandoned hope. To save time when hiring teachers, advertisements in *The Times Educational Supplement* often carried the line 'No CO need apply.'

It is important to remember how few people objected to military service on moral grounds, not because it makes the conscientious objection any less courageous (indeed, rather the opposite). But it ought to give us further reason to doubt the idea that the whole war was coerced sacrifice: it cannot have been seen like that at the time. By comparison with the approximately 16,000 who declined to fight, a 1916 letter to the right-wing *Morning Post*, purporting to have been written by 'A Little Mother' and offering her children for the army, was reprinted in pamphlet form and sold 75,000 copies within one week. The letter would not have embarrassed one of Northcliffe's sub-editors, claiming that 'we women will tolerate no such cry as "Peace! Peace!" . . . We women pass on the human

---

* A popular story told of a man waiting outside a prison to visit a friend: 'I'm going to see a conscientious objector,' he explained to a woman in the queue. 'Thank God my man's not one of them,' she replied. 'He's in for forgery.'

ammunition of "only sons" to fill up the gaps, so that when the common soldier looks back before going "over the top" he may see the women of the British race at his heels, reliable, dependent, uncomplaining.' The *Morning Post* boasted that Queen Mary had been 'deeply touched' by the letter. 'A Bereaved Mother' who read it was said to have been so overcome that she would 'now gladly give' the two sons she had lost in the war 'twice over'.

But in the end conscription could not feed the military machine with the men it needed, even though the physical standards required of recruits plunged and the upper age limit was raised to include any man who was not yet fifty-one. In December 1917 a cabinet committee was told that the army would soon be missing over half a million men, and domestic industry short by 100,000. By then many aliens resident in Britain had also been deemed liable for military service or deportation, and the tribunals were instructed that there were to be fewer exemptions. The cabinet committee could only lamely recommend that the generals find a way of fighting the war that did not cause so many casualties.

In September 1915 a notice appeared in the personal columns of *The Times*: 'Lady, *fiancé* killed, will gladly marry officer totally blinded or incapacitated by the War.' Has a more poignant lonely-heart appeal ever been printed? The one man in the world replaced by someone unknown. The dashed hopes, the calculation that since now all men are the same, why not hope to do something useful?

Although in Russia several thousand women served as combatants in the Women's Battalion of Death, the British would not contemplate meeting the shortage of warriors in the same way. Instead, an early recruiting poster showed a mother and her children looking out from the window of a rather grand house as a group of soldiers marched by outside. There was a proud set to the mother's mouth and a caption: 'WOMEN OF BRITAIN SAY "GO!"' For the man capable of resisting such family pressure, a music-hall song suggested that taking the King's Shilling might lead on to all sorts of delights:

On Sunday I walk out with a soldier,
On Monday, I'm taken by a tar,
On Tuesday I'm out
With a baby Boy Scout,
On Wednesday with a hussar,
On Thursday I gang oot with a Kiltie,
On Friday, the captain of the crew.
But on Saturday I'm willing,
If you'll only take a shilling,
To make a man of any man of you.

But once very large numbers of young men had enlisted and been taken away from the social constraints of homes, families and local communities, another question began to trouble the authorities. In the early days of the war a group of bishops' wives worried about young women succumbing to 'khaki fever'. 'Don't let your excitement make you silly and lead you to wander aimlessly about,' they warned. 'Remember that war is a very solemn thing.' Just in case admonitions about 'wandering about' were not enough, a philanthropist and mountaineer called Margaret Damer Dawson had founded what was soon named the Women's Police Service. A veteran of the campaign against the 'white slave trade' (prostitution), she had begun voluntarily patrolling the streets of London to offer help to bewildered Belgian refugee women, after discovering British men at railway stations attempting to lure them into prostitution. She had soon assembled a few dozen other middle-class women to act as a voluntary force of policewomen, despite the opposition of the Metropolitan Police Commissioner, who felt that patrols of educated females would make his constables feel stupid. In 1915, when the population of the Lincolnshire town of Grantham was doubled by the opening of an enormous army camp near by to train machine-gunners, a Mrs Edith Smith emerged to confront the predictable collection of amateur and professional doxies who began to hang around. The redoubtable Mrs Smith, a fearsome-looking sub-postmistress who boasted that 'my presence in the streets is sufficient to bring about order among girls,' patrolled the parks and streets at night and created a black list of individuals whom she banned from the local theatre and cinemas. She became the first woman to hold a police warrant card and in 1916 recorded that she had cautioned or acted against eighty prostitutes, kept twenty suspected 'disorderly houses' under observation and warned off a hundred 'wayward girls'. That year, a new provision of the Defence of the Realm Act made it an offence for any woman convicted of prostitution to be found anywhere near a military camp.

Central London had long been notorious for the prevalence of prostitution. Now the capital teemed with men in uniform on their way to or from the front, and after dark it could seem that the whole city was on the prowl for sex. The great traveller and Arabist Freya Stark recalled emerging into the Strand one winter evening, suffering from a cold. Each time she coughed, 'two or three huge Australians came looming out of the night like the hulls of ships.' She scurried home, frantically sucking lozenges. Stuart Cloete, who had been commissioned in the Yorkshire Light Infantry, recalled being accosted sixteen times one evening as he walked between Piccadilly and Knightsbridge. He fobbed the women off and described how a particularly persistent importuner 'kicked my shins, saying: "You're too fucking particular!" She was right though I did not say so. Fortunately I was in uniform and wearing puttees.' Another female police officer, Mary Allen – Margaret Dawson's friend and probably her lover – thought that at night the Strand was 'a veritable Devil's playground. White slavers crowded there. Drugs were bought and sold with the freedom of confectionery. Scenes of indescribable disorder prevailed.'

The drugs accusation was something of an exaggeration. At the start of the war there had been no restrictions on the possession and use of what are now illegal drugs. Indeed, in 1914 the army supplies department had been ordered to have stocks of 'Indian treacle' (opium) available for colonial troops, while Harrods was soon offering its customers 'A Welcome Present for Friends at the

Front', containing cocaine, heroin and syringes for families to send to their loved ones. It does not appear to have been a particularly popular gift, and there is little evidence that the British army had a drug problem. But in February 1916 *The Times* reported the trial of a man and woman caught selling drugs to Canadian troops at a camp in Folkestone, where about forty soldiers were claimed to have become what the paper's medical correspondent called 'cocainomaniacs'. In May, the newspaper reported the collapse of the trial of a porter caught selling cocaine to soldiers via prostitutes in Leicester Square: the magistrate loudly complained that there was an urgent need for a new law to deal with 'a serious social evil'. The drug, it was often pointed out, had first been refined and marketed in Britain by the Germans, while 'Heroin' was a German-derived trade name, because workers at the Bayer factory where it was synthesized claimed that samples they had taken made them feel 'heroic'. The Defence of the Realm Act was wheeled out again, with a new provision banning the sale of psychoactive drugs to soldiers without a prescription.

When death at the front seemed to be so imminent, pre-war sexual inhibitions came under immense strain. Officers returning on leave found that at home 'respectability' had often survived, which made the transition even more difficult than it might have been. 'I found myself leading a double life,' one of them discovered. 'The quiet respectability of my family with its unaltered moral standards could in no way be related to the all-male society of the regiment, with its acceptance of death and bloodshed as commonplace events, and its uninhibited approach to women.' Kindly men, aware of how randomly death could strike, might refrain from sex with their fiancées at home in the hope that a preserved virginity might make it easier for them to marry someone else, should they not return. But 'abroad' could be another proposition altogether. 'We were not monks, but fighting soldiers and extraordinarily fit . . . full of beans and bull-juice' was the way one soldier recalled it. 'I suppose that subconsciously we wanted as much out of life as we could get while we still had life.' Young men away from home – and very large numbers had never left their county before, let alone their country – have always sought out young women. Once they had been in battle and understood how capricious were the chances of their living or dying, soldiers seized pleasures where they could. They lived for the present. 'Men and women do not "love" in war,' a young officer in the Royal Flying Corps noted. 'They desire, they demand, they take. The conventions, the morals, the obligations go.'

Lord Kitchener's message to the troops, a copy of which all soldiers were instructed to keep in their pay-book, had anticipated such an effect on their behaviour and explained that they were being sent to the continent to 'help our French comrades against the invasion of a common enemy'. It asked them to be always courteous, kind and considerate, and ended with the pious warning that 'In this new experience you may find temptations both in wine and women. You must entirely resist both temptations, and, while treating all women with perfect courtesy, you should avoid any intimacy.' This turned out to be beyond many of the men, if the new unofficial chorus to 'It's a Long Way to Tipperary' is any indication:

> Hooray pour Les Français
> Farewell Angleterre.
> We didn't know how to tickle Mary,
> But we learnt how over there.

In the imaginations of many of these sexually innocent young men, France was one enormous brothel, where women wore nothing but georgette underwear and long silk stockings. The reality was a great deal more sordid, but if you found yourself in the right place, sex was almost as ubiquitous as in some of the soldiers' imaginations, for the French military had a very different attitude to that of Lord Kitchener – they preferred to manage temptation rather than to resist it, with plentiful brothels behind the lines – blue lamps indicating those for officers and red lamps those for other ranks. In the sectors they controlled, the British military authorities might do all they could to suppress prostitution, but a sign in a window saying 'Washing Done Here for Soldiers' told another story.

The brothels were dismal places, from the few accounts that survive, with men standing around in the street outside, like a football crowd waiting for the turnstiles to open. George Coppard, who had enlisted in August 1914, had his first experience of a Maison Tolérée in Béthune. At the bottom of an alleyway 'there were well over a hundred and fifty men waiting for opening time, singing "Mademoiselle from Armanteers" and other lusty songs,' he recalled. 'Right on the dot of 6pm a red lamp over the doorway of the brothel was switched on. A roar went up from the troops as they lunged forward towards the entrance.' Inside, the 'jaded and worn-out' prostitutes, some of them old enough to be grandmothers, stood on the spiral stairs, as a couple of bouncers sorted the men into groups. 'Madame-in-charge, a big black-haired woman with a massive bosom, stood at the foot of the stairway, palm outstretched, demanding tribute of two francs from each candidate: one franc for madame, one franc for the dame.' Sex here was a very perfunctory business, especially since it was a new experience for many of the young men. Sergeant Alfred West of the Monmouthshire Regiment recalled that he'd 'seen up to twenty men waiting in one room, and there were probably others upstairs. Afterwards these women used to sit on the end of the bed, open their legs and flick this brownish stuff around their private parts, ready for the next man.'

Whatever 'this brownish stuff' was, it was not up to the job, for the inevitable consequence of all this activity was the spread of venereal disease, notably syphilis. Between the outbreak of war and the signing of the Armistice the British military dealt with 400,000 cases of VD: there were times when it was said to have taken more soldiers out of action than the Germans did. By comparison with the regular army, Kitchener's volunteers were a relatively chaste and innocent bunch. Nonetheless, the vast influx of new recruits meant a large increase in the total number of young men suffering from sexually transmitted diseases (even if the number of cases per thousand fell by about one-third). The army coped as best it could: men suffering from venereal disease were not allowed home until all symptoms had disappeared; an infected soldier who was discovered trying to conceal the fact that he had contracted a dose would be court-martialled and faced up to two years in prison with hard labour; a man who reported his condition was sent to hospital and lost all pay while he was there, including the separation allowance paid to his wife at home. The soldiers much enjoyed the trench myth that there was a VD hospital in Le Havre reserved for the exclusive treatment of army chaplains.

A few years earlier, syphilis had been almost untreatable. But by the outbreak of war scientists had refined Compound 606, an injectable form of chemotherapy, marketed as Salvarsan, and soon supplied to military hospitals in bulk. It was a German invention.

9. Lost at Sea

Lord Kitchener's Last Afternoon Alive

'Now we've lost the war!'

It did not matter whether you were in uniform or civvies, rich or poor, male or female, chaste or promiscuous, there was now no escape from the war. There may have been non-combatants, but there were no non-participants. What had begun as a macabre novelty was now a fact of life in Britain, one that had already demanded huge changes, many of which would last for decades. And it was all about to get worse.

Nineteen-sixteen was a very bad year.

In one part of the kingdom, however, the war offered an opportunity. The British had been in military control of Ireland for the best part of 700 years, and since 1801 had been trying to merge Irish and British political identities by making the smaller of the two islands part of the 'United Kingdom', living under London-made laws. Irish nationalists chafed at their powerful neighbour and occasionally burst into open revolt, but their patriotic sentiment generally expressed itself in sullen resentment. The question of how to satisfy demands for Home Rule had been a repeated irritant to British governments throughout the last years of the nineteenth century, and sooner or later it would have to be resolved. But when Germany invaded Belgium in 1914, the issue was elbowed aside by more pressing matters, and the Liberal government decided to place the debate over Ireland's destiny in cold storage until the fighting was over. For the next year or so, the cabinet took virtually no interest in Irish politics. As the Chief Secretary for Ireland remarked of his role, 'a jackdaw or a magpie could do just as well by crying out "Ireland, Ireland, Ireland!" ' at cabinet meetings.

The squawking was loud enough to ensure, at least, that the law introducing conscription did not apply in Ireland. The war was felt differently in John Bull's Other Island – there had been widespread sympathy in Ireland for the Belgians, but the anti-German fervour which had swept Britain did not take quite the same hold there. Nonetheless, in the first year of the war about 75,000 Irishmen came forward to join the army, large numbers of them from among the Protestant community 'planted' in Ulster, and by the end of 1915 seventeen Irish soldiers had won the Victoria Cross. In total, 200,000 Irishmen served in the British forces during the conflict, as many as 49,000 of whom were killed, the overwhelming majority volunteers or pre-war regulars. But after the initial surge to enlist, interest in the British cause fell away. Among advanced nationalists, anyway, only an independent, sovereign Ireland was entitled to make war. It was not their quarrel.

The maxim that 'England's difficulty is Ireland's opportunity' had been a guiding light of those opposing the British colonists for decades, and prolonged war with Germany more than merited the description of 'difficulty'. In early 1916 the leaders of the Irish Republican Brotherhood saw their chance. It was time to settle the question of Ireland's political destiny by force of arms.

The Easter Rising, the most symbolically important event in

the political history of what became the Republic of Ireland, took place in April. It turned out to be a weird mixture of valour, idealism, folly, cruelty and comic opera. On the principle that 'my enemy's enemy is my friend' the nationalist conspirators had recognized how useful Germany could be to their cause early in the war. Sir Roger Casement, an emotionally unsteady former British diplomat who had become convinced by the Irish separatist cause, conspired tirelessly to persuade the Germans to provide the rebels with military aid. A plan for a German landing on the west coast of Ireland was devised, partly modelled on the French invasion supporting the rebellion of 1798. Easter was set as the time for the Rising to take place. Paramilitary volunteers would seize control of Dublin and declare an Irish republic, while a German ship would land weapons on the coast of Kerry.

It turned out to be a shambles. The date of the rebellion was changed and changed again. The revolutionaries also altered the date for the landing of the guns, but for some reason this information did not reach the captain of the German freighter carrying the arms shipment. The vessel had in any case been tracked by British intelligence and was captured off the coast. Casement had persuaded the Germans to smuggle him to Ireland in a submarine, but was promptly arrested when he landed. In tones more suited to a tiff in a gentlemen's club in St James's than to treason Casement despaired, asking himself why he had ever trusted the Germans: 'They have no sense of honour, chivalry, generosity . . . They are Cads . . . That is why they are hated by the world and England will surely beat them.' In Dublin, the conspirators did not even stage a proper attempt to seize Dublin Castle, the heart of British rule in Ireland.

Despite the missing guns, the Rising went ahead anyway, the future of British rule in Ireland now depending upon the 400 British soldiers and 200 policemen on duty that Easter Monday. There were at least 1,500 rebels, and perhaps as many as 1,800 by the end of the week: noticeable enough, you might think, but the army subsequently flannelled that they hadn't been observed because many had been mistaken for Bank Holiday visitors. The biggest group of revolutionaries, eventually about 400 strong, seized the General Post Office in the heart of Dublin, turning the place into a makeshift fortress. It was here that Patrick Pearse, a former lawyer, read out the rebels' proclamation of an Irish republic. The text, declaring 'the right of the people of Ireland to the ownership of Ireland and to the unfettered control of Irish destinies', is the most resonant in Irish political history. Pearse clearly saw it as a document to be understood by posterity, but did not expect to survive the Rising himself. In that he was correct – he was dead within ten days.

At Dublin Castle the revolutionaries shot dead the only guard at the gate, an unarmed policeman, but then retreated. On St Stephen's Green, Countess Markievicz, an Anglo-Irish former debutante born Constance Gore-Booth, strutted about in view of the wealthy guests at the Shelbourne Hotel, wearing the dark-green uniform of the Irish Citizen Army, with a rifle on her shoulder and issuing occasional commands to a group of revolutionaries: the head porter considered 'the Countess took unfair advantage of her sex.' Her squad of insurgents was soon outmanoeuvred by British soldiers and forced to withdraw. Some Dubliners responded to the call for national freedom by embarking on a spree of looting. According to the Lord Lieutenant's private secretary, at his mansion in Phoenix Park Viscount Wimborne 'simply *swilled* brandy the whole time' and 'insisted on his poor secretaries using the most melodramatically grandiloquent language down the telephone – standing over them to enforce his dictation: "It is His Excellency's command . . ."' One of these commands was to impose martial law. When Francis Sheehy-Skeffington, a pacifist and feminist instantly recognizable all over Dublin because of his great dark beard and voluminous knickerbockers, took to the streets to try to prevent lawlessness, he was seized by an army patrol, taken off and summarily executed. A later court martial sent the officer responsible to Broadmoor Lunatic Asylum. He, too, was Irish.

By Wednesday morning, substantial numbers of British reinforcements, in the form of the Nottinghamshire and Derbyshire

Regiment, or 'Sherwood Foresters', had been shipped across the Irish Sea and were arriving in Dublin. They were mainly Midlands boys, many of whom had hardly finished their basic training. Some had never even fired a rifle, while others were under the impression they were disembarking in France. Up against determined rebels they initially took heavy casualties, and in a firefight at Mount Street Bridge lost 234 men killed or wounded, for the lives of five of the Irishmen. But the resources of the British army – which included not only machine guns but artillery – inevitably ground down the rebel outposts, and while the buildings the revolutionaries had seized initially offered protection, once they had been set on fire the Irishmen faced a choice of incineration, being shot by the soldiers outside or surrendering. By Sunday the commanding British general believed that the revolution had been 'practically crushed'.

The Rising had been a military failure, even if it assuredly raised support for the republican cause and made it impossible for the British to ignore the calls for independence as soon as the war finished. But it had been a huge embarrassment, too: a country waging a total war against an imperial bully had been unable even to command allegiance in what was supposed to be an integral part of its kingdom. In political terms, now was a moment for magnanimity, and indeed of the eighty-eight men sentenced to death by the courts martial that began within a couple of days of the end of the Rising the great majority found their sentences commuted to penal servitude by the commanding British general. Some of the younger rebels who had surrendered were released with no more than a lecture about their naivety. But Patrick Pearse and thirteen other rebel leaders were shot by a firing squad composed of men of the Sherwood Foresters in a courtyard of Kilmainham prison. The last of them to die, James Connolly, had been wounded during the fighting and was executed sitting on a chair. A fifteenth, Thomas Kent, was executed in Cork a week later. Irish nationalism now had a fresh set of martyrs, 'the men of 1916', which also included Sir Roger Casement, who was tried by a judge and jury and hanged inside Pentonville prison in London the following August.

The Easter Rising, a great event in Irish history that helped pave the way to independence, was an irritating sideshow for the British government of the time. Meeting the demands of the nationalists would have involved dismembering the British state, and at a time when it was engaged in what looked increasingly like a struggle for national survival. So finding an answer to the Irish Question would have to wait. But the Rising had sent an unmistakable message. Those with eyes to see might reflect that if British rule was rejected so close to home, it could soon become untenable in much further-flung parts of the empire.

In terms of the war effort, Ireland was already being treated differently from the rest of the country: conscription, which had been introduced at the start of the year, was not applied there. Now it received further special treatment. When Asquith travelled to Ireland in the middle of May, he made a point of visiting some of the captive rebels and ordered that their food should be as good as possible, 'regardless of expense'. (The soldiers guarding them, who had to make do with standard army rations, did not find this particularly amusing.) Countess Markievicz continued to 'take unfair advantage of her sex', finding her death sentence commuted on grounds of her gender and serving just over a year in Aylesbury gaol, before being released in a general amnesty in the middle of 1917. The following year she became the first woman to be elected to the British parliament, in order that she could fail to attend it in person. Naturally.

That same spring, the very institution that had made Britain's overseas empire possible in the first place was also brought to the test. Afterwards, no one could rightly judge what had happened.

The British army had been small at the start of the war because the British navy was big. Massive sums had been spent ensuring that the Royal Navy remained the biggest and most powerful in the world, the safeguard of the empire and the defence of the nation. When, before the war, it became clear that Germany coveted a naval force of comparable power, British naval engineers came up with HMS *Dreadnought*, the most heavily armed vessel in history. The *Dreadnought* had more big guns, with a more accurate range, than any vessel afloat. Ten of her guns could fire shells that were 1 foot in diameter for a distance of up to 10 miles. The ship was clad in thick armour-plating and was additionally equipped with torpedo tubes. Her four steam-powered turbines meant she could outrun or hunt down any other battleship, and the *Dreadnought* instantly made all other battleships obsolete. Although Germany lost no time in creating its own Dreadnoughts, by August 1914 the Royal Navy had twenty of these leviathans on the water and possessed comfortably the most destructive force ever to take to sea. But the maritime fighting did not follow the course the military planners had imagined.

In the early days, it had been a desultory affair. The biggest shock had been the one in December 1914, when a small force of German cruisers had crossed the North Sea and shelled the coastal towns of Scarborough, Whitby and the Hartlepools. It was not just the guests at their kippers in the dining room of the Grand Hotel in Scarborough who had been outraged – most of the British people had believed the Admiralty's confident assertion that the Royal Navy could keep the country safe. A month later the Germans embarked on another sudden assault, but were themselves surprised by British ships at the Dogger Bank shallows in the North Sea, about 60 miles off the English coast. This time, the Germans lost one heavy cruiser, the *Blücher*, and might have suffered further damage had British communications been better. For a year after that, the Kaiserliche Marine hardly ventured out of its coastal waters.

But in the spring of 1916 frustration overcame Reinhard Scheer, commander of the German High Seas Fleet. He had an enormous, unused force at his disposal and was determined to take command of the seas by luring part of the British fleet into a trap. He was unaware, however, that the same British code-breakers in the Admiralty's top-secret Room 40 who had intercepted messages to the German arms ship en route to Ireland were also reading his orders. Forewarned, British senior officers prepared themselves for the assault. At the end of May the two navies clashed off the coast of the Danish peninsula of Jutland. While Scheer had planned to achieve superiority by taking on only part of the British navy, advance warning had enabled the British to alter the odds by sending Admiral Jellicoe's Grand Fleet out from its base in the Orkneys to support Scheer's target, the more southerly-based battlecruiser fleet commanded by Admiral Sir David Beatty. All told, 250 warships were at sea. The British force included twenty-eight Dreadnought battleships, whereas Germany had only sixteen of their equivalent ships and six of the older, slower model; in addition there were nine British battlecruisers compared to Germany's five; eight British armoured cruisers and twenty-six light cruisers, more than twice as many as Germany, which sent out only eleven; and nearly eighty destroyers, substantially outnumbering Germany's sixty. The British also boasted a seaplane carrier. Both sides were supported by submarines, hoping to be able to fire an opportunistic torpedo. It looked like being the biggest naval battle in history.

Since a single lucky shot could sink an enormous capital ship, naval warfare was a very high-stakes game that depended upon surprise, dash and initiative. Although Admiral Beatty found the outlying German ships before they found him, he was suckered into chasing them towards the main German fleet, at which point he was forced to turn tail as the German battleships pursued *him* north. But then the Germans came within range of Admiral Jellicoe's fleet, which they had believed was still in Scapa Flow. Now it was Scheer's turn to try to run. At each stage, intense fire was exchanged between the warships, with Beatty at one stage exclaiming – as a second of his cruisers exploded – 'there seems to be something wrong with our bloody ships today.' The remark became one of the most famous of the entire war. The battle culminated in fierce fighting in the dark, as the German fleet turned for home. But who had won?

In Jellicoe's report after the battle he was gracious about the enemy's 'gallantry', and judged his own officers and men 'cool and determined, with a cheeriness that would have carried them through anything. The heroism of the wounded was the admiration of all.' He was unable adequately to express his 'pride in the spirit of the Fleet'. But the Royal Navy had not covered itself in glory. On the eve of battle two British cruisers had collided with one another, and a battleship had run into a merchant vessel. And, in the end, Admiral Jellicoe's Grand Fleet – the greatest force afloat – had failed to destroy the German menace. The Germans named the battle the 'Victory of the Skaggerak' (after the strait connecting the North Sea with the Baltic), despite having lost one battlecruiser, one pre-Dreadnought battleship, four light cruisers and five destroyers. The British emerged from the fog of battle minus three battlecruisers, three armoured cruisers and eight destroyers, while thousands of sailors had been blown to pieces, incinerated or drowned. In terms of military accountancy, Jutland was a German victory – the Royal Navy had lost a greater quantity of shipping. British communications had been shown to be not up to the job, and plenty of British shells had proved to be defective.

The one figure the nation took to its heart was Jack Cornwell, an Essex delivery lad and Boy Scout who had been at sea for only a month. He was serving with the naval rank of Boy in one of the gun turrets when his ship, the cruiser HMS *Chester*, was pursued by four German warships. The official history of the battle described the cruiser 'dodging the salvoes like a snipe' as she fled. Seventeen shells hit the *Chester* within three minutes, wrecking all but one of her guns. When the ship reached sufficient safety for an inspection to be carried out, Boy Cornwell was discovered standing in his gun turret awaiting orders, with a shard of metal protruding from his chest. The rest of the crew were dead. Jack Cornwell died of his injuries two days later and was buried in a common grave when his ship limped into Grimsby. Faithful unto death: here was a much easier story to comprehend than the complicated, contentious audit of who, precisely, had won the battle of Jutland. Two months later Boy Cornwell's body was exhumed, to allow him to be given a state funeral. Then they gave him a posthumous VC.

The outcome – or lack of outcome – of the battle of Jutland was to raise the stakes in the land war, and to turn both London and Berlin to considerations of how quickly they might bring the enemy down by starving their people into submission. The Royal Navy's renewed command of the North Sea and the German navy's commitment to submarine warfare both had the same intent. There was some comfort for the British Admiralty, for the battle had shown the Germans they could not risk their fleet at sea, which may explain why there was no other battle on a comparable scale during the war. But it was a very odd engagement that could set off decades of argument about who, precisely, had won. And they were strange weapons, these great navies that were so valuable they were too important to use.

What had once been called the 'wooden walls' of the Royal Navy had been the ornament and defence of the nation for centuries. At the outbreak of war, the endless lines of smoke-belching grey hulls had seemed the very embodiment of British self-confidence. Now, while still formidable, the navy no longer looked the force of legend. And then, in early June 1916, something unthinkable happened.

The last sight ordinary Londoners had of Lord Kitchener, the man who was going to win the war for them, was on the evening of Sunday 4 June, when he had been seen stalking up and down one of the platforms at King's Cross railway station. The most famous soldier in the world was easy enough to recognize, wore no disguise and had a total entourage of fewer than a dozen men, including staff officers, servants, policeman and driver. There was no private waiting room organized for his benefit. People who saw him there claimed he had seemed 'abnormally agitated and anxious'. After every mysterious event there are always some people who claim to have had premonitions, but Kitchener had reason to be irritated: the Foreign Office cipher clerk who was supposed to be travelling with him had not turned up. The War Secretary boarded the 8 p.m. train to Edinburgh and travelled on to Thurso on the far north coast of Scotland. From there he was to begin a secret journey to Russia, for a meeting to co-ordinate strategy on the Western and Eastern fronts. After the near-700-mile train journey to Thurso, on the morning of 5 June Kitchener crossed by navy ship to Scapa Flow, the great deep-water sanctuary in the Orkneys where the British Grand Fleet had its northern base.

From the point of view of the rest of the cabinet the Russian mission was an ideal occupation for K: it had the great merit of keeping him out of the way. His endless waverings, notably over the campaign to take the Dardanelles, had depressed and worried them, and did not sit at all well with his insufferable self-confidence. 'K.'s position at present is untenable' was the view of the king's private secretary at the end of 1915. 'He is discredited with all his 21 colleagues in the Cabinet. Even his colleagues on the War Committee think he is a positive danger.' The press baron Lord Northcliffe – inevitably – thought he personally could prosecute the struggle more effectively than the War Secretary, and a few days before Kitchener's train journey there had even been a motion in the House of Commons to reduce his salary by £100. Since Kitchener was paid £6,140 – about £450,000 at today's values – the issue was not really about money but about his handling of the war effort, which, everyone could see, was not achieving great results. In the debate he was depicted as incompetent, obstinate and 'absolutely lacking in brains'. Though his political enemies cloaked their demand with predictably insincere protestations that it was nothing to do with personality, it was abundantly clear that the 'iron grasp of one personality' on the management of the war was precisely what bothered them.

Sensing that an apparent attack on the War Secretary could have the effect of undermining the entire government, the Prime Minister, Asquith, made a generous and high-minded defence of K: perhaps he had made mistakes (haven't we all?) but there was no one else in the land – in the entire British empire – who could have created such a vast new army. Military men in the House of Commons – there were plenty of colonels in attendance that day – spoke up for the War Secretary. 'Do play the game,' one of them begged. Kitchener himself later agreed to appear before a gathering of MPs where, resplendent in his field marshal's uniform and pleading that he wasn't used to political speeches, he so disarmed his critics that a vote of thanks was seconded by the very MP who had begun the censure motion. And whatever reservations politicians might have felt, Kitchener of Khartoum continued to bask in celebrity status among the general public: he was the face of the war effort and much the most important passenger on the fast cruiser, HMS *Hampshire*, which was to take him to Russia.

Conspiracy theorists have had a field day with the fate of the *Hampshire*. It was claimed that she had previously been attacked in the Mediterranean, and that a spy on board had been caught signalling to a German submarine, for which he was executed. Both stories were nonsense. The ship was eleven years old, 450 feet long, weighed 11,000 tons and was more lightly armoured than some of the navy's latest vessels. But her four tall funnels and scooped bow testified to her power: she could surely outrun any German submarine, and at the battle of Jutland she had indeed rammed and sunk a U-boat – the standard method of attack before the use of depth charges.

By the time Lord Kitchener boarded the ship a storm was raging across northern Scotland. To avoid the heaviest seas – and to allow the escorting destroyers to have a better chance of keeping up – it was decided that the *Hampshire* would sail up the western side of Orkney: since the gale was blowing from the north-east, the seas would be calmer there. These waters were swept for mines much less frequently than those off the eastern coast, but naval commanders believed the weather had been too bad for any recent German mine-laying; at the height of summer in the Orkneys there were anyway only a few of hours of real darkness when this might take place. It was true that a German submarine had been seen at the entrance to Scapa Flow only a few days beforehand and had somehow eluded the British warships sent in pursuit. But Kitchener was an impatient man and in no mood to wait for the weather to improve. By late afternoon on 5 June, the *Hampshire*, with

Kitchener on board, was moving. She was soon joined by two destroyers, *Unity* and *Victor*, which were to provide an escort, and the three vessels set off into the teeth of the fierce gale. As heavy green seas crashed over their bows, the different capabilities of the three ships became alarmingly apparent. Despite the poor conditions, the *Hampshire* could manage a speed of 18 knots. The two destroyers laboured to keep up, their captains eventually signalling to the cruiser that the maximum speed they could get up was around 10 knots. As they fell further and further astern, the captain of the *Hampshire* looked back through binoculars and, catching only occasional glimpses of his escorts between the mountainous seas, signalled, 'Destroyers return to base.' With a flashed 'Good luck' message, the two escort vessels made for the shelter of Scapa Flow.

At about 7.45 that evening the pitching cruiser shuddered. It was 'as though an express train crashed into us', remembered a stoker who survived. The *Hampshire* had struck a mine, which had blown an enormous hole in her side. It was quickly obvious that the ship was going down and her commander, Captain Herbert Savill, gave the order to abandon ship. Most of the lifeboats depended upon a now ruined electrical supply and could not be launched. The last picture we have of the man the British public believed would lead them to victory comes from one of the handful of sailors to survive the disaster, who described Kitchener watching the calamity from the starboard side of the quarterdeck, talking to two of his officers. Soon afterwards the bows of the ship were under water and the vessel listing at a terrifying angle. Then the *Hampshire*'s propellers were out of the water – still turning, according to one witness – and men were leaping into the sea or sliding down the vessel's sides. Suddenly the great ship turned turtle. Within fifteen minutes of striking the mine, she had sunk.

What followed – or rather the rescue operation that did *not* follow – this disaster was a scandalous example of red tape and lack of initiative. Unsurprisingly, because the weather had driven most people indoors, there were few eyewitnesses on the very sparsely populated islands near by. But the struggling *Hampshire* was seen from the shore, and the sub-postmistress at the tiny community at Birsay sent a telegraph message to the military authorities to tell them what seemed to have happened. Yet it was ten that night before four destroyers – including *Unity* and *Victor* – were despatched to search for survivors, and not until 3.30 the following morning that five other ships were sent to help them. None of these ships rescued a single survivor. It was also later claimed the Admiralty had even prevented the local lifeboat from being launched. A total of twelve men from the *Hampshire* lived to tell the tale and Lord Kitchener was not among them. He had become the highest-ranking British soldier to perish in the war.

Hands trembled as people read of his death in the early editions of the newspapers – the *Daily Mirror* distributed 1.5 million copies on the day it printed the news. For years afterwards people could remember where they had been on the day they learned that Kitchener had drowned. Shops closed. George V ordered army officers to wear black armbands for a week. A Yorkshire coroner recorded that the news had caused a man to take his own life. Clergy preached sermons openly wondering why more had not been done to protect a figure of such national importance. So-called 'relics' of the *Hampshire*, from shards of wood to pieces of life-raft, were treasured for years afterwards, like the alleged bones of saints. Within one year of Kitchener's death, publishers had rushed out five biographies. Kitchener of Khartoum had embodied so much of Britain that his disappearance took some of the heart out of the war effort. 'Now we've lost the war. Now we've lost the war,' a platoon sergeant who had just received the news had been heard muttering to himself as he rocked back and forth in his trench. There was certainly something especially plangent about the manner of the field marshal's death. Like hundreds of thousands of others, he had become one of the 'missing', whose absence from families across the land had no definitive explanation. The great majority of this tribe had been blown to pieces. Kitchener was, as one panegyric put it, 'drown'd in waters which no line can plumb'.

The absence of a body and the fact of his almost religious celebrity made for a popular refusal to believe that Kitchener could have succumbed to anything as banal as a mine floating in the sea. *John Bull* – ever on the lookout for official incompetence and enemy fifth columnists – blamed 'the sneaky, slimy Hun, who pollutes our atmosphere by his presence and defiles our streets by his very footsteps'. Conspiracy stories proliferated. Kitchener had been murdered with a time-bomb planted by his enemies in British intelligence. A German spy posing as a Russian duke had accompanied Kitchener on the *Hampshire* and signalled to a waiting German submarine to fire a torpedo. There had been a Jewish conspiracy. The *Hampshire* had been sunk by a bomb hidden on board by Irish republicans. Sailors who made it to the shore had been shot as they staggered up the beaches. Lord Kitchener had survived the sinking and then been murdered as he clung to a rock in the Orkneys. A field marshal's epaulette had been discovered in a Norwegian fisherman's hut. Kitchener had not been drowned at all, but had blown his brains out in his cabin, after a senior officer delivered him a revolver and asked him to do the decent thing. The fact that one of Kitchener's sisters had failed to make contact with him through a spiritualist was proof that he was still alive somewhere or other. He was in Russia, commanding the Tsar's army. He was a prisoner of the Germans. He had been spirited away by submarine and was on a secret mission somewhere in the Middle East. He had been spotted disguised as a Chinese potentate. He had not been on the *Hampshire* at all because he had been spotted after the disaster striding about Whitehall. In 1917, an Orkney crofter's wife claimed to have seen Kitchener living in a cave and waving to her. Variants of this story had him promising to emerge in the hour of England's need, like King Arthur or Sir Francis Drake. In 1922, the field marshal appeared to a spiritualist and dictated a long story, replete with implausible details, of how he had come to drown. He would materialize again 'to a noble English family', he promised.

In the space of a few weeks there had been an attempted revolution at home, the Royal Navy had been found wanting and now the country's most famous army commander and face of the war effort had been drowned. There is no appropriate modern comparison (who can even name a single serving general today?). With all its public displays of grief and crackpot conspiracy theories, the reaction to Kitchener's disappearance had about it some of the characteristics of the death of Princess Diana. Kitchener – tall, tough, cold-hearted – was a hero for a different age, the man the politicians had sent for when war was inevitable, and many people found it impossible to imagine winning the war without him. Coming on top of the failure of the Gallipoli campaign, the navy's failure in the North Sea left many wondering where on earth salvation was to come from. Options were now very narrow indeed: there would have to be a breakthrough on the Western Front.

Not everyone was downcast, though. When a journalist broke the news of Kitchener's death to Lord Northcliffe, he replied, 'Now we can at last get down to winning the war.' If only.

10. The Great European Cup Final

Whistles blow and the dying begins.

The worst day in the history of the British army dawned bright and clear. Many of the men who mustered early on the morning of Saturday 1 July 1916 in the gentle downland around the River Somme were filled with eager anticipation, having been told they would be taking part in the decisive battle of the war. This would be the battle to end all battles, in the war to end all wars. Douglas Haig, who had replaced Sir John French as Commander in Chief of the British Expeditionary Force in December 1915 after French had succumbed to intense pressure to resign, had gone to bed the previous evening having confided to his diary that 'preparations were never so thorough, nor troops better trained. Wire very well cut, and ammunition adequate . . . The weather report is favourable for tomorrow. With God's help, I feel hopeful.' The attack had been prophesied by deafening artillery barrages – which had lasted for days on end, louder and more prolonged than anything the soldiers had ever heard before – in which British guns had poured shell after shell on to the opposing German positions. Many felt sorry for the poor devils hoping to survive the bombardment. Come to that, it was almost unimaginable that flesh and blood could endure such a thing.

What followed was the most sickening calamity in British military history. There were a number reasons for its failure. For a start, while soldiers returning to Britain on leave before the planned Somme offensive had been told not to talk about it, it was not much of a secret. 'Everybody at home seemed to know that the long-planned offensive was due to "kick off" at the end of June,' recalled Siegfried Sassoon later, 'even Aunt Evelyn was aware of the impending onslaught.' Secondly, although the Allies had agreed months beforehand to co-ordinate attacks on the Germans in 1916, the timing and location had been altered by frantic appeals from the French for a new offensive to relieve the pressure on the emotionally important city of Verdun, more than 100 miles to the west. Here, the German commander, Erich von Falkenhayn, had promised to 'bleed France white' by luring in reserves and then destroying them with artillery fire. This 'meat grinder' battle – the most sanguinary in history – severely reduced the number of troops France was willing to commit to the Somme attack. Thirdly, the original British Expeditionary Force having now been more or less wiped out, most of the British forces at the Somme were untested volunteers from Kitchener's army. Fourthly, British intelligence had underestimated the strength of the German trenches, some of which were up to 30 feet deep. Fifthly, General Haig persistently deluded himself about the state of the German army, even maintaining after the catastrophe of the first day of battle that it was on the point of collapse. Sixthly, while the accumulated reserves of shells at the start of the battle were bigger than anyone had ever seen before, too many of them were either duds or of the wrong type. Seventh, the bombardment was too widely spread to be effective, and the generals were absurdly overconfident about the damage it would do to the German barbed-wire entanglements (General Aylmer Hunter-Weston predicted beforehand that 'the troops could walk in'). Eighth, the British detonation of mines minutes before the attack gave time for enemy machine-gunners to scuttle out of their dugouts, so that by the time British soldiers began their advance there were places where the ground before them was already being kicked up by a hail of incoming bullets.

The battle of the Somme justifies the cliché about 'lambs to the slaughter'. Famously, Captain Wilfred 'Billie' Nevill, commanding a company of the East Surrey Regiment, had provided footballs for his four platoons to chase across no man's land as they attacked. On one of them he had written:

> The Great European Cup-tie Final
> East Surreys vs Bavarians
> Kick-off at zero.

Poor Captain Nevill, who was a fortnight off his twenty-second birthday, has been ridiculed ever since for supposedly treating war as a game. But that was not how it was seen at the time, with the *Daily Mail*'s resident poet inspired to summon the spirit of the imperial panegyrist Henry 'Play up! Play up! And play the game' Newbolt:

> The fear of death before them
> Is but an empty name.
> True to the land that bore them
> The Surreys played the game.

In many respects Nevill embodied the public school ideal – not overly intellectual, he had been head boy of Dover College, a minor institution which, like many similar places, cultivated what it presumed to be the beliefs of grander schools. He played rugby in the first fifteen, cricket and hockey in the first elevens, and attended chapel ardently. An idea had been taking shape in his head that when he finished his time at Cambridge (much more sport) he would become a schoolmaster himself. Nevill's muscular Christianity, with its confidence in activity, institutions and national destiny, meshed easily with army life. He volunteered and was commissioned in November 1914. One hundred and seventy-seven former pupils of Dover College were killed in the war, including one who won a VC. But it was Nevill with his footballs who became the best known, scoffed at for treating slaughter as sport. This is unfair. Nevill may not have been especially deep-thinking, but nor was his football idea entirely stupid – he had had the empathy to recognize how terrified his men might become as they advanced into a storm of machine-gun bullets, and had outlined his notion to his commanding officer before the attack. He never had the chance to explain his thinking to later generations because he was shot in the head and died on the battlefield.

Other soldiers at the Somme dealt with the fear as best they could. Some tried to sing as they advanced. Some struggled forward mumbling the Lord's Prayer to themselves, but found they could not recall the words, and instead kept repeating 'Our Father' over and over again. And there were scenes of remarkable courage. Young officers scrambled out of the trenches, urging on the men behind them, and died in great numbers. But machine-gun fire did not discriminate between the ranks. A lance-sergeant in the 'Heart of Midlothian' pals' battalion of the Royal Scots saw his company sergeant-major fall to the ground in front of him. 'Even on his knees, he looked to the direction of his men. "Be brave, my boys," he cried before he fell. I looked back as I passed over him, and he did not stir.'

Mostly, the British came on at walking pace, as if expecting to find nothing alive when they reached the German trenches. 'It was', said a German, 'an amazing spectacle of unexampled gallantry, courage and bull-dog determination on both sides.' When they reached the German front line and discovered that the British shells had left most of the barbed wire intact, the infantry took what cover they could, then made for any gaps in the wire they could find. This inevitably bunched them into unmissable targets for the Germans. Meanwhile, the artillery barrage kept to its schedule, assuming the wire had been cut and that the infantry would be advancing behind its protection. The wall of ordnance which was supposed to open the enemy trenches to them crept on into the distance, leaving them utterly exposed.

Why, later generations have wanted to know, why on earth didn't the generals stop the attack at the Somme the moment they knew that the artillery had not done its job, that so much of the barbed wire was uncut, that so many of the machine-gun posts were largely intact, that so much of the British army was facing annihilation? The initial answer is that they did not know – or they did not know soon enough. The generals are castigated for not bleeding and dying like the men they commanded (although seventy-eight generals were killed in the war). But had they been in the front-line trenches they could have directed only a tiny proportion of the army at their disposal, for the simple reason that they could not have communicated with anyone else. Could they have managed things differently that day? Certainly. But they would have had to have known what was going on.

Radio ('wireless') sets were unsophisticated, big and cumbersome and required enormous masts, not suitable for the battlefield. They were largely confined to great installations and ships. In fixed positions like trenches there might be telephone lines (indeed, by 1918 it was claimed there were more phones in the allied trenches than in the whole of France, Britain or the United States), but the standard army instruction that cables should be buried at least a foot and a half underground was simply impossible to achieve in the heat of combat. In theory, there were all sorts of other means of communication available – lamps, heliographs, black-and-white signal discs, semaphore flags and carrier pigeons among them. But, once an attack had begun, the only communication possible between the men and their commanders might be by writing a message on a piece of paper and giving it to a runner, who would have to scramble back to headquarters as best he might. There was no certainty that he would survive the journey.

The problem of communication also meant that, once the attack had begun, it could not easily be called off. The more serious question is why the commanders – specifically why Douglas Haig – continued to send more and more men to death and mutilation at the same place for months to come. For despite the initial catastrophe, the battle of the Somme did indeed continue for months, as summer gave way to autumn and then to the rains of winter. Yet Haig kept faith with the offensive. In military – as opposed to humanitarian – terms, it is hard to see this as a crime: wars cannot be won if energy flags. Since the cavalryman's natural instincts for dashing strikes and unexpected flanking attacks could not be followed in the stagnation of trench warfare, all that was left to him was a philosophy of grinding attrition. The fault was not his alone. Kitchener's plan to create a vast new army was based on the same thinking, and Haig's intelligence chief, Sir John Charteris, believed the war would be won only by 'wearing out' the Germans. The great sin was Haig's lack of imagination. But against that has to be set the failure of the Dardanelles attack – which was certainly imaginative – and the fact that it was now clear that the war was not going to be won by the Royal Navy destroying the German fleet. General Haig really had little choice and had to believe in what he was doing. The day after the bloodletting of the initial assault he visited a couple of Casualty Clearing Stations, and seemed genuinely to believe that 'the wounded were in wonderful good spirits. The AG [Adjutant General] reported today that the total casualties are estimated at over 40,000 to date. This cannot be considered severe in view of the numbers engaged, and the length of the front attacked . . . At night situation much more favourable than when we started today!' The cheery exclamation mark is typical of the diaries, for Haig retained his faith in the campaign. One week after the attack began he wrote to his wife that 'the battle is developing slowly but steadily in our favour,' adding that with God's help in another fortnight 'some decisive results may be obtained. In the meantime we must be patient and determined.' By mid-July, he was talking of victories in which miles of German second-line trenches had been taken. Events had proved that 'the British troops are capable of beating the best German troops. They are fully confident, and so am I, that they can continue to do so, provided we are kept supplied with men, guns and munitions.' The posthumous reputation of Douglas Haig has never really recovered from his readiness to believe that in the end the battle would be won. But what use is a general unwilling to prosecute an action to which he has committed others? The battles at Gallipoli had already answered that.

Blind though he may have seemed to the possibility of failure, Haig was aware that the war was being fought in an entirely new context, in which the late Lord Kitchener's 'drunken swabs' played a rather vital role. He could not be confident that all reporters would be as helpful as William Beach Thomas, the *Daily Mail*'s resident drum-banger, whose report of the slaughter on the first day of the Somme made it seem like some combination of children's game and strange religious ritual. 'The very attitudes of the dead, fallen eagerly forwards, have a look of expectant hope. You would say that they died with the light of victory in their eyes.' By late July there was a constant stream of journalists and politicians at Haig's door demanding interviews, many of whose requests he granted, even Colonel Charles Repington's, representing *The Times*. 'I hated seeing such a dishonest individual,' he reflected, 'but I felt it was my duty to the army to do so – otherwise he might have been an unfriendly critic of its actions.' Unlike Kitchener, Haig had recognized that a war being fought by an enormous army of volunteers required that some attention be paid to the mass media. Lord Northcliffe got an invitation to stay the night. But the biggest public relations exercise came through the new medium of film. Cameramen working for 'the poor man's theatre' had been involved with the war effort since it began, with recruiting efforts like *England's Call* in 1914. At the Somme they at last succeeded in recording and showing the reality of war.

The Battle of the Somme, Geoffrey Malins' assembly of footage from War Office camera crews, was a sensation. An estimated 1 million people saw the film in its first week in the cinemas, and perhaps 20 million (getting on for half the total population at the time) within six weeks – in some towns the police had to be called to control the crowds trying to get in. The production of the documentary had been remarkably efficient. The cameras were bulky, hand-cranked and needed tripods, the film was highly inflammable and the end product had to be approved by official-dom, yet by 21 August British civilians were watching footage of their fellow citizens fighting, and in some cases dying, at the front. It was a risky thing to do, but the film came with the endorsement of the king himself. Lloyd George urged everyone to go to the cinema, to 'Herald the deeds of our brave men to the ends of the earth. This is your duty!' The *Daily Sketch* pronounced, 'It is war, grim, red war: the real thing.' It wasn't quite – various scenes had been recreated by soldiers who were rewarded with cigarettes and an extra tot of rum. But most of it was genuine enough, and when a scene of two stretcher-bearers was shown at the Electric Cinema in Droylsden, Lancashire, a woman leapt to her feet exclaiming, 'It's Jim. It's my husband.' She had just learned that he had died of his wounds, leaving her a widow with nine children.

Lloyd George's secretary and mistress, Frances Stevenson, who had lost her brother in the war, spoke for many when she decided that she was 'glad' she had gone to see the film, even with its shots of dead bodies and mortally wounded men. 'It reminded me of what Paul's last hours were: I have often tried to imagine to myself what he went through, but now I *know*: and I shall never forget. It was like going through a tragedy. I felt something of what the Greeks must have felt when they went in their crowds to witness those grand old plays – to be purged in their minds through pity and terror.' There were, doubtless, others who simply found the spectacle utterly distressing. But, overall, the decision to allow the film to be made and shown to the public had been vindicated. Asquith had likened the government's information policy to something from the Old Testament: 'For all the public know, they might as well be living in the days of the prophet Isaiah, whose idea of a battle was "confused noise and garments rolled in blood".' *The Battle of the Somme* had shown that the public could take a bit of reality. The film may not have been the unvarnished truth that it pretended to be (the final images of the ruins of German positions, crowds of enemy prisoners and cheery Tommies were calculated to leave the audience feeling the offensive had been not merely worthwhile but successful), but the decision to let the British public see the conditions in which so many of their menfolk were living and dying acknowledged that the war was everyone's business.

The entire bloody four months of the battle of the Somme exemplified the central challenge of the war. Trench warfare was an endurance contest: whoever could suffer the longest would triumph. As any marathon runner can attest, endurance is as much a matter of psychology as of physical strength.

But all endurance has a limit. Alongside the psychological battle at home, a race had begun to develop technology that might save life by the more effective taking of it. Movement was what was needed – at one point there had even been an ill-judged and quickly abandoned plan to mount Maxim guns on mules. Both Haig and Falkenhayn had come to believe that tunnelling beneath the enemy, or using ever more high-explosive artillery shells, or blowing gas or fire over them might shatter the immobility. But there had still been no great breakthrough. In September, Haig decided to use the Somme to deploy another weapon to try to break the deadlock.

Precisely who invented the tank, or 'landship', is, even now, a matter of argument. In the 1830s a father and son from Cornwall claimed to have devised a 'modern steam chariot', but before that the Dutch had made prototype 'landships', one of which was said, remarkably, to have been powered by a windmill. Winston Churchill certainly lost no opportunity to claim credit as the chief sponsor of the modern tank, while Colonel Ernest Swinton – the former 'Eyewitness' of the government press machine – was a tireless promoter of 'machine-gun destroyers' in the face of government indifference. Swinton raised recruits by, among other things, advertising in *Motor Cycle* magazine. At the Somme his idea got its first trial in combat. But a combination of lack of imagination, lack of energy and the incompetence of British manufacturing doomed its chances of success.

The basic idea of the tank – a mechanized weapon which also acted as a moving shield – was a simple one. When strategists now came to think about deploying them on the battlefield they realized that to achieve the long-wished-for breakthrough they would need to be used in groups and in large numbers. But the tanks had not arrived at the Somme in time to take part in the launch of the attack, and by September General Haig had only just over four dozen of them available. Although this was not an adequate number to fulfil the needs of a mass attack he decided it was better than having none at all. (Winston Churchill complained that 'My poor land battleships have been let off prematurely on a petty scale.') The tanks were a dismal advertisement for British industry: of the forty-nine at Haig's disposal, seventeen did not even reach the front line, and another fourteen broke down or were ditched during the offensive.

The combination of armour-plating, caterpillar tracks and mounted guns meant they were primitive, lumbering things, inside which the eight-man crews may have been protected from direct infantry fire, but were still alarmingly vulnerable to the splinters of metal that could fly around when bullets struck the armour – for which reason early crews were issued with chainmail visors to protect their faces. A direct hit from a shell could destroy a tank, but the real terror was fire: the fate of many tank crews was to be cremated alive. Even at the best of times, the men inside were choked by exhaust fumes and deafened by the sound of the engines: young tank commanders issued orders by gesticulating. Communication between tanks was by semaphore or by sticking a shovel out of the roof, with various angles signalling different messages. Baskets of yet more carrier pigeons loaded with canisters ready for scribbled messages were supposed to enable communication with base.

The symbolic and propaganda impact of these 'motor monsters' spouting fire was enormous. They had clanked straight out of the pages of science fiction. Geoffrey Malins, who had filmed *The Battle of the Somme*, could not believe his eyes when he saw one crashing down into shell craters and climbing out the other side. 'And all the time as it slowly advanced it belched forth tongues of flame, its nostrils seemed to breathe death and destruction, and the Huns, terrified by its appearance, were mown down like corn falling to the reaper's sickle.' The man from the *Daily Mail* talked of 'blind creatures emerging from primeval slime'. Watching in the half-light he thought of 'the Jabberwock with eyes of flame . . . Whales, Boojums, Dreadnoughts, slugs, snarks – never were creatures that so tempted the gift of nicknaming. They were said to live on trees and houses and jump like grass hoppers or kangaroos.' Other reporters described Germans bolting like startled rabbits when they saw the vehicles approaching. Fewer than a quarter of the machines broke through the German lines, but they boosted the spirits of the British infantry. One officer thought their only function had been to raise morale: 'Haig tried his forty tanks. Thirty six started; some were ditched; some broke down; some were shot up, eleven crossed the front line; and four or five made a useful contribution to the battle.' It would be another year before the British learned how to use them properly.

The battle of the Somme, which had begun on 1 July, continued until November. The attack had gained a few paltry miles of ground. They had been won at enormous cost.

The Prime Minister and his wife were entertaining a weekend party at their house in Oxfordshire on 17 September when the telephone rang. It was Sunday night and the Asquiths were playing bridge with their guests. The air was heavy with cigar smoke.

With a horrible sinking feeling, Margot Asquith took the phone. The news was every bit as bad as she had feared. Asquith's gilded son from his first marriage, Raymond – said to have been such a brilliant student at Oxford that his professor raised his hat to him when they passed in the street – had been shot dead on the Somme. She asked a servant to summon her husband, but the Prime Minister had already realized what the call was about. He would never recover from the blow. Raymond had been serving in France with the Grenadier Guards when he was killed. He had died a classic young officer's death: shot in the chest during an attack, having spurned his father's attempts to get him a safe staff job. To make light of his wounds, as he lay on the ground he nonchalantly lit a cigarette, dying soon afterwards on a stretcher. One of his soldiers wrote home that 'there is not one of us who would not have changed places with him . . . he did not know what fear was.' The Prime Minister wrote bleakly to a friend, 'I can honestly say that in my own life he was the thing of which I was truly proud, & in him and in his future I had invested all my stock of hope. This is all gone, & for the moment I feel bankrupt.' His cabinet colleague David Lloyd George judged that the loss had '*shattered his nerve*'. Even ten weeks after the telephone call, his wife was still finding Asquith sitting quietly, weeping.

The Prime Minister was far from alone in his grief. Of the 120,000 troops who took part on that first day, 57,000 were killed, captured, wounded or missing. There had been gains in the battle – even on that first day they had smashed a hole in the German line. But it had been a pyrrhic victory. The attack had revealed the risks of fighting in alliance: once the French had withdrawn the forces they had planned to use on the Somme, in order to protect Verdun, the offensive lacked critical mass. It did – as the French had hoped – relieve the pressure on Verdun. But that was the extent of its success: British, empire and dominion forces died in great numbers on behalf of the French. By the time the campaign petered out, the number of British and empire casualties had risen to more than 420,000. As well as Asquith's son, the British dead included two members of parliament, at least four county cricketers, a similar number of first-class soccer players, a couple of international rugby players and seven recipients of the Victoria Cross. Among the wounded was the future Prime Minister Harold Macmillan.

In the wake of the Somme, thousands of families across the country received the bleak Army Form B 104–82 with the printed message: 'It is my painful duty to inform you . . .' Sometimes their own letters to a son, father or husband were returned unopened along with the form, with the single word 'killed' stamped on the envelope. Often, they were also given the letters written by their loved ones shortly before climbing out to join the attack and to be sent only 'in the event of my death'. They are some of the most heartrending documents of the entire war. Five days before the attack began, Private John Scollen of the Northumberland Fusiliers, a Catholic miner from County Durham, sat in his trench and wrote to 'My dear wife and children':

> Do not grieve for me for God and his Blessed Mother will watch over you and my bonny little children and I have not the least doubt that my Country will help you for the sake of one of its soldiers that did his duty. Well Dear Wife Tina I would ask . . . [understandably, given the number of times it must have been read, parts of the letter are frayed and illegible] you have been a good wife and mother to look after my canny bairns and I'm sure they will be credit to both of us.
>
> Dearest Wife Christina accept this little souvenir of France a cross made from a French bullet which I enclose for you.
>
> My Joe, Jack, Tina and Aggie not forgetting my little bonny twins Nora and Hugh and my last flower baby whom I have only had the great pleasure of seeing [once] since he came into the world God bless them . . . I have put a X on top of this missive so you will know that I died in God's Holy Grace. Tell all my friends and yours also that I bid farewell. Now my dear wife and children I have not anything more to say only I wish you all God's Holy

Grace and Blessing, so Good bye, Good Luck and think of me in your prayers I know . . . hard words for you to receive but God's will be done.

From your faithful soldier Husband and Father

John Scollen B Coy, 27th SBNF

xxxxxxxxxxxxxxxxxxxxxxxxxxxxxxxxxxxxxxxxxxxxxxxxxx
xxxxxxxxxxxxxxxxxxxxxxxxxxxxxxxxxxxxxxxxxxxxxxxxxx
xxxxxxxxxxxxxxxxxxxxxxxxxxxxxxxxxxxxxxxxxxxxxxxxxx
xxxxxxxxxxxxxxxxxxxxxxxxxxxxxxxxxxxxxxxxxxxxxxxxxx
xxxxxxxxxxxxxxxxxxxxxxxxxxxxxxxxxxxxxxxxxxxxxxxxxx
xxxxxxxxxxx

Good Bye my loved ones Don't cry.

Five days later he was killed on the first day of Haig's attack at the Somme. His body was never found.

Fresh cannon fodder was constantly being marched up to the line, even before the bodies of the men they were replacing had been buried. As they trudged resolutely to their front-line positions the incoming units could see their future pass before them, as the glassy-eyed survivors stumbled down the communication trenches towards base. Many of their replacements decided that the only way to keep their sanity was not to look at them too closely. A lieutenant in the Warwickshire Regiment described how 'Day and night the road was one long line of ambulances and walking wounded and occasionally a battalion which had been relieved would march through with a total strength of about 150 instead of 600 or 700. Although we realised what losses these men had, it never seemed to occur to us that we might be the same.' Many of the victims of that apocalyptic first day lay on the battlefield for weeks – the stench was stomach-churning. A fortnight after the first attack, a young officer leading another attack found the ground in front of him 'strewn with bodies, like St James's Park on a fine afternoon, and [I] did not know that these carrion men that smelt upon the earth were my friends.'

Some of these exhausted men shuffling down from the front

were walking wounded. Others came away on stretchers. While the new warfare damaged the body in new ways – high explosive did not merely break bones, it pulverized them – and while some wounds – to the head, for example – were obviously more serious than others, one significant hazard was not new at all. Merely preventing infection on a muddy battlefield contaminated with the bodies of men and pack animals and all the attendant vermin and the shit of thousands was a great challenge. A wounded man prayed for a pair of stretcher-bearers to get him to a Regimental Aid Post in a reserve trench for initial treatment and then on to an Advanced Dressing Station with a luggage label tied to his body giving information about injuries ('shot in the face – blind in both eyes') and any drugs administered. Here casualties were laid in rows on the floor of a tent or barn or bunker, stretchers often so closely packed together that there was hardly room for a boot between them. In winter the wounded arrived chilled to the bone: it was essential to get some warmth back into them as soon as possible, so orderlies moved around the stretchers carrying metal buckets of warm water and soap. The army doctor had then to make a very quick judgement of the wounded man's survival chances: the most seriously injured sometimes got the least treatment. The wounded still wore the khaki in which they had been hit, often caked in blood and mud: if they were lucky the orderlies cut their woollen tunics and trousers from them, paying little attention to the instruction that they were to try to preserve the uniforms. Other times, it seemed the uniform was the only thing that kept the body together: when the bandages were removed from some head-wounds, portions of brain came away with them. The place might be littered with amputated limbs. But in the intense fighting of the first day of battle at the Somme, often all that doctors could do for those who might survive was to staunch their bleeding. Those who did not make it were buried outside.*

---

* There are three war-grave cemeteries in Flanders with the cod-Flemish nicknames given them by soldiers of Bandaghem, Dozinghem and Mendinghem.

Men needing urgent treatment were carried by train to base hospitals near the Channel, where many died. The symptoms of imminent death, a wounded man recalled, 'were an extra visit or two from the doctor, a consultation with the nurses and sisters, and a red screen put round the bed. In the morning the screen was gone and there was another man in his bed.' Once sufficiently stabilized for evacuation home, it was a hospital ship across the Channel and another rail journey, often to one of the great London termini teeming with crowds of quietly anxious parents and wives. By the end of the war, over 2 million wounded men had been treated, and those who had been repatriated were distributed around the country to hospitals or placed in nursing homes set up in requisitioned colleges, houses, stately homes and city office buildings, the streets outside strewn with straw to muffle the sound from horses' hooves. In spas and seaside towns and at the country houses where they were sent to convalesce, the spectacle of horribly maimed men pushing each other in wheelchairs, the partially sighted guiding the blinded, was an everyday occurrence. Those who recovered sufficiently might rejoin a military unit, wearing the newly instituted 'wound stripe' on the left sleeve of their uniform. By the latter stages of the war, there seemed to be entire battalions comprised of the damaged.

Nineteen-sixteen had been a truly terrible year. The succession of calamities – the Easter Rising, the failure at Jutland, the catastrophe of the Somme – was bound to have political consequences.

Asquith had been over sixty when the war began, and while age itself need not have been a bar to command (Winston Churchill, after all, was to sail past that age years before he became Prime Minister in 1940), the first modern war had laid bare his Edwardian languor – the afternoons sitting in his club reading a novel, the games of bridge in the evening, the too-many brandies. In the early stages of the conflict he had managed to maintain political unity (not least in his own party), but as the fighting dragged on, tensions were increasingly apparent. The cabinet was careworn and tired, and there was hardly a member of it who did not have a loved one who had died or another whose life was at risk. Lord Kitchener, the public idol as the face of the war effort, was dead. Every few months Lloyd George's mistress, Frances Stevenson, became convinced her lover was on the edge of a nervous breakdown.

And there was no end in sight. By late 1916 Asquith had been presiding over a coalition government for a year and a half – ever since the revered First Sea Lord, Admiral Jackie Fisher, resigned in a fit of pique at Churchill's management of the Dardanelles campaign* and he had been forced to accept that the exceptional circumstances of war demanded places at the cabinet table for the Conservative leader Andrew Bonar Law and some of his colleagues. This made a lot of political sense, but creation of a coalition had removed the most tactically useful weapon of any Prime Minister trying to control a cabinet: the argument that 'if we don't all hang together, we shall hang separately.' As time passed Conservative members of the government began to lose whatever confidence they had had in Asquith's leadership. To win the war would take magic. And David Lloyd George seemed to display all the showmanship necessary. The man had the flamboyant charlatanry of the circus conjuror. Later in the war a young officer home on leave went to watch him speak in the House of Commons. The impression was unforgettable: 'his mane of white hair, his mobile features, his eyes gleaming, first with fun and then with fury, his eloquent gestures and his words that carried us away . . . He dominated the House and by sheer force of personality. It was enchantment.' Afterwards, the officer could not recall a single word Lloyd George had said. This flashy figure had been

* He had become increasingly angry at the fact that his prize super-Dreadnought, *Queen Elizabeth* – the most modern warship in the world, capable of firing a 1-ton shell almost 20 miles – had been deployed in the operation and made potentially vulnerable to German submarines, another example of the odd philosophy of building warships which are too valuable to send into battle.

made Minister of Munitions after Northcliffe's campaign in 1915 to expose the inadequacy of the shells supplied to the army. Asquith claimed that Lloyd George had repeatedly assured him of his loyalty, on one occasion protesting, 'his eyes wet with tears', that 'he would rather (1) break stones (2) dig potatoes (3) be hanged and quartered . . . than do an act, say a word, or harbour a thought, that was disloyal to me.' Which he doubtless thought was true at the time he said it.

By late 1916, this modern Merlin had succeeded the drowned Kitchener as War Secretary, in a cabinet presided over by a man who often seemed miles away mentally. Asquith's managerial style was incurably haphazard, and during cabinet discussions he increasingly gave the impression of being a mere spectator. He had been Prime Minister for the best part of nine years, he was tired and grief-stricken, and the war which had taken his son seemed endless. As one minister described it, in cabinet meetings Asquith seemed 'content to preside without directing'. There would have to be a change.

In the middle of November Andrew Bonar Law told Asquith that the war required a new style of political management. A plan was produced for a new War Council, to be chaired by Lloyd George, with Asquith as 'president'. When Asquith rejected the proposal, Lloyd George came up with a scheme which excluded him altogether. Asquith replied that if he wasn't fit to manage the war, he wasn't fit to be Prime Minister. This was more or less precisely what Lloyd George felt, and the plotting became intense. Somehow the planned reorganization got into the newspapers. By early December they were full of stories that the new War Secretary was on the brink of quitting the government altogether – 'Lloyd George Packing Up' was the headline in Northcliffe's *Evening News*. The Conservatives then demanded that Asquith tender the government's resignation, backed by the threat that if he failed to do so, the coalition would implode. Soon the newspapers were printing details of how the government was to be reconfigured,

with the Prime Minister relegated to the sidelines of the management of the war. Again, Lloyd George wrote to Asquith, blithely
protesting his loyalty. 'Northcliffe frankly wants a smash,' he told
the Prime Minister, claiming that he could neither restrain him
nor influence him. He was partly right – ever since his victory in
the shells crisis Lord Northcliffe had become more and more like
the legendary man-eating tiger, which, once it had tasted human
flesh, would stalk the village night after night.

Asquith was now clinging by his fingernails to what remained
of his authority. But Lloyd George had won the support of the
Conservative leader, Bonar Law, and on 5 December he wrote a
formal letter of resignation to Asquith, talking of the 'supreme
need' for 'vigour and vision' in the war effort. Asquith had no
sooner written a letter accepting the resignation than he discovered
that senior Conservatives were also unwilling to serve under his
leadership. He had become a general without an army. Asquith
now felt that his own resignation was the only available option,
deciding that 'In the end there was nothing else to be done, though
it is hateful to give even the semblance of a score to our black-
guardly Press.' He believed – rightly – that his prime ministership
had been the victim of a very clever conspiracy. But his hour had
come and gone. He continued to protest that there had been nothing lacklustre about his war leadership. Yet he seemed to bow out
with relief. The day after quitting Downing Street in favour of
Lloyd George he wrote to a friend to say what a pleasure it was not
to be burdened with red boxes, cabinet meetings and tiresome colleagues. He concluded, 'I am glad you are reading the Book of
Job: I think I must refresh my memory of it.' The theme of the
tale is 'why do the righteous suffer?'

Northcliffe, who preferred more worldly reading matter, had
seen the *Morning Post* ask the question 'Who Killed Cock Robin?'
When he repeated the question to his younger brother, a Liberal
MP, his brother dutifully replied, 'You did.'

In truth, it was the war that did for Asquith's career. Herbert

Henry Asquith, the first representative of the professional middle class to occupy 10 Downing Street, had once been Gladstone's Home Secretary, and somewhere in the late nineteenth century was where he belonged. This was a conflict that did new and terrible things not only to the bodies of Britain's soldiers but to the minds of its people, too. New ways of thinking were required.

11. Upsetting the Country Altogether

'The men must take the swords, and we must take the ploughs.'

It was now 1917, two and a half years since the war began. Khaki was everywhere. Even small boys dressed up in it, often proudly wearing copies of their father's regimental insignia. Babies in English cities were being named after the towns in France and Flanders that were now familiar from letters sent by men at the front. Primary schoolchildren posted home-made blankets in the other direction, accompanied by notes promising they wouldn't eat any sweets until the war was over. Girl Guides earned merit badges by volunteering in hospitals or making socks and mittens for the army. Boy Scouts ran messages and acted as lookouts on public buildings. Family members of all ages were enlisted in collecting scrap and rags to be recycled for the war effort. Thousands of young women volunteered as nurses and ambulance-drivers with the Voluntary Aid Detachment (VAD) and the First Aid Nursing Yeomanry (FANY). And in January 1917 a huge barrier was overturned when plans were put in place for a Women's Auxiliary Army Corps, to serve in non-combatant roles on the continent. A Women's Royal Naval Service (WRNS) followed, and when the Royal Air Force was created the following year so too was a Women's Royal Air Force.

As well as bitter experience, rumours and lies continued to bolster support for the war effort. You could say what you liked about the Germans, and as the war continued there were more and more stories to make your flesh creep. In May 1915 it had been alleged that German soldiers had captured a Canadian sergeant and used their bayonets to crucify him on the side of a barn. As the story spread, the details became more confused, with two, three or even six Canadians crucified – on trees, on the walls of buildings or on barn doors – and with the popular British-Canadian poet Robert Service writing a twelve-verse poem on the subject, in which a French soldier was murdered on the orders of a blond, cruel-eyed Prussian. But the mother of all Hun horror stories appeared in the spring of 1917. In April, Lord Northcliffe's *Times* and *Daily Mail* claimed that hidden in a wood behind the German front line, less than a mile from the Belgian border, was an enormous, evil-smelling factory, where a succession of trains drew into secret sidings. Here, tied with wire into bundles of three or four, the bodies of German soldiers who had been killed in action were unloaded. The young men continued to serve their country by being boiled down inside the factory to provide the raw material for pig-feed, fertilizer and soap. Workers in oilskins at the German Offal Utilization Company Limited attached the bundles of bodies to big hooks on an endless chain that carried them 'into a digester or great cauldron', in which 'they remain from six to eight hours, and are treated by steam, which breaks them up while they are slowly stirred by machinery.'

Authorship of this sensational twaddle was later claimed by Frederic William Wile, a freelance reporter for the *Daily Mail*, together with 'my brilliant colleague of *The Times*, Mr. J. E. Mac-kenzie, who ... shares with me the responsibility of having brought to public notice the activities of the Hun body-boilers'. After the war there were plenty of others who boasted of invent-ing the horror story. At the time of publication, Northcliffe's two newspapers merely claimed to have plundered the story from a Belgian newspaper published in London, which in turn appeared to have gleaned it from another Belgian paper. Before that, some-one with not very good German had (mis)translated a report in a German newspaper. In fact, it seems the tale – or something quite like it – had been circulating as rumour for a couple of years. The permutations were endless: one claimed that German prisoners of war habitually referred to margarine as 'corpse fat', another that consignments of soap delivered to German troops at the front had been buried there with full military honours. An angry German government denied the whole story as fabrication (but they would, wouldn't they?). The British government provided no corroborat-ing evidence, but did nothing to deny it (but they wouldn't, would they?).

Although the German Corpse Factory was an excellent – too excellent – example of the behaviour of the Evil Hun, it was not officially disseminated by the government propaganda machine, which by now had learned a certain degree of caution. Yet the British propaganda forge, managed by Asquith's scruffy friend Charlie Masterman, never cooled. Within a year of Masterman's appointment in 1914 it had produced 2.5 million books, leaflets and pamphlets in seventeen languages, a large number with their true origin disguised. World-famous novelists, including H. G. Wells, John Galsworthy, Arnold Bennett and John Buchan, contributed tales and homilies.

Masterman tried to insist on factual accuracy wherever possible, but the longer the war continued the more strident were the calls for his operation to become as shrill and dishonest as the enemy's. In February 1917, Lloyd George installed John Buchan above Mas-terman to beef things up a bit. Buchan came to the same conclusion as Masterman about the importance of accuracy and allowing people to make their own judgements. By this stage of the war, though, the public were accustomed to a rich diet of hate: you could buy writing pads illustrated with war scenes, postcards showing U-boats being attacked, diaries commemorating British victories, and a German Crimes Calendar to hang on the wall, in case you needed reminding that Uncle Fred's birthday fell on the day they executed Nurse Edith Cavell.

Despite this, or perhaps because of it, the newspapers continued gleefully to report on the presence of subversives and the need to root them out. In March, Alice Wheeldon, a matronly fifty-two-year-old shopkeeper from Derby, and several members of her family were put on trial, charged with plotting to murder the Prime Minister, David Lloyd George, and the Labour cabinet minister Arthur Henderson, by firing poison-tipped darts into them while they were playing golf. It was a scheme worthy of a Victorian penny dreadful, but the Wheeldons' confection of beliefs – Marxism, atheism, suffragism, vegetarianism – made them excellent tabloid villains, and indeed Alice's son was a conscientious objector. Under the alias 'Alex Gordon' and pretending to be a kindred spirit, an undercover government agent had contacted the family at their secondhand-clothes shop (where they were already sheltering a conscientious objector on the run from conscription), gained their confidence and discovered that they were in the process of acquiring the South American poison curare. The family claimed they were merely planning to poison guard dogs at one of the camps where they had been told conscientious objectors were held. But in the face of a prosecution at the Old Bailey, led by the flashy Attorney General and former head of the War Office Press Bureau F. E. Smith himself, they failed to convince a jury made up of Londoners living in daily fear of German bombing. Alice Wheeldon was sentenced to ten years' penal servitude, a daughter and son-in-law to shorter terms. 'Alex Gordon' was never produced in court, which is probably just as well: a competent defence lawyer would almost certainly have disclosed to the world that he had previously been declared criminally insane and had served time in Broadmoor. By the time of the trial 'Gordon' had been given a one-way ticket to South Africa at the taxpayers' expense. This bizarre conspiracy had provided a satisfying cast of dissidents and much entertainment. It emphatically did not demonstrate that there had been any organized attempt to subvert the conflict with Germany, but it amply showed the British people's commitment to their cause. In this area, as in so many others, they were on the side of the war.

On 7 June 1917, according to Britain's national news agency, later the Press Association, the Prime Minister asked for an especially early wake-up call. He didn't want to miss the chance of hearing what he had been told would be the biggest man-made explosion in history. At ten past three in the morning the sound reached London as a dull roar. The site of the explosion was Messines in Flanders, which had been taken by the Germans in the fighting at Ypres in 1914. Beneath the ridge of ground where the Germans had dug their positions, the British had driven shafts which they had packed with explosives. When he pushed the plunger to detonate the bombs, the Royal Engineers officer sighed, 'There! That's avenged my brother.' The enormous explosion he had triggered blew the top off the hill. Nearly three years of fighting had not only embittered soldiers, but had also hugely improved British understanding of tactics, and the initial explosion was followed by a conspicuously successful attack. The assault was such a triumph that within a month the king had taken himself off to the area, to watch soldiers re-enact it in a safe area behind the lines, with drummers recreating the sound of gunfire.

The capture of the ridge at Messines was intended as the curtain-raiser for a battle the following month which would turn the war. An optimist might just about have been able to see a glass half full. But only just: the French army was in a terrible state and Russia at the point of ditching its imperial family, the Romanovs, and baling out of the war. On the other hand, General Haig now had large numbers of troops available to him, artillery tactics that had improved immensely, and he had amassed sufficient heavy guns to lay down an efficient rolling barrage, 100 yards in front of the advancing infantry. Haig genuinely believed he could make the long-awaited breakthrough.

It did not turn out that way. British artillery tactics had indeed improved enormously, but the battle of Passchendaele still took four months, cost 70,000 lives, with a further 205,000 wounded or missing, and gained a scrap of land that was lost back to the Germans soon afterwards in the space of three days. It was yet another disastrous bloodletting, in almost the very place where the original British Expeditionary Force had been broken, and it bore many of the marks of earlier failures. The objective was little different to the one in 1914: troops were to smash their way to the coast. Then there was the appalling timing, with weeks passing between the attack at Messines and the main assault, during which time British soldiers played much football and German engineers reinforced defences. And there was the familiar misery of the mud.

In fine weather, perhaps, the land would have dried out enough. It was not fine weather. In fact it was so bad that it was often impossible for spotter aircraft to locate the targets for artillery fire. Mud-caked ammunition could not be fired, and no one had guessed that the concrete German defences – fortified farmhouses, blockhouses, pillboxes – were as strong as they turned out to be. Meanwhile the British heavy guns sank into the ground, and when their shells exploded they churned the earth into a swamp: some soldiers thought that when they landed in water-filled shell craters it looked almost like a battle fought at sea. When a wind got up it proved almost impossible to use the technique of 'sound ranging'* to identify enemy artillery positions, and communications were a

---

* You located the position of enemy heavy guns by spotting them when they fired, taking a compass bearing and measuring how long it took between the launching of the shell and its arrival. If it worked – which it sometimes did – you could then pass details on to your own artillery for what was known as 'counter-battery' shelling.

nightmare. The wind was sometimes so strong that carrier pigeons were blown backwards.

At the appointed hour the infantry advanced across the sodden, churned-up ground, slithering, sliding, sinking and falling. The German machine-gun fire produced astonishing sights – six men struggling to bring a single stretcher through waist-deep mud or a kilted soldier sliced in half, his legs still moving forward, his torso lying on the ground. On other, drier battlefields, shell craters had offered the wounded some protection. Not here – a young officer in the Royal Warwickshire Regiment sheltering in a pillbox listened in distress as he heard 'sobbing moans of agony and despairing shrieks' in no man's land, realized they came from friends and realized too that they were drowning as the summer downpours – the worst for decades – filled the craters. From a tactical point of view, the worst discovery was that in several places the German front line was not the front line at all: the enemy had had plenty of time to withdraw before the attack, and now poured sustained fire on the attackers from well-hidden concrete bunkers in the ground beyond. But still the allied attack continued, week after week.

'Dante would never have condemned lost souls to wander in so terrible a purgatory,' wrote a colonel.

> Figure to yourself a desolate wilderness of water-filled shell craters . . . Here a shattered tree trunk, there a wrecked 'pill box' sole remaining evidence that this was once a human and inhabited land . . . Here a shattered wagon, there a gun mired to the muzzle in mud which grips like glue, even the birds and rats have forsaken so unnatural a spot. Mile after mile of the same unending dreariness, landmarks are gone, whole villages hardly a pile of bricks. You see it best under a leaden sky with a chill drizzle falling, each hour an eternity, each dragging step a nightmare. How weirdly it recalls some half formed horror of childish nightmare.

Haig kept his men in these dreadful conditions because he remained convinced that a German collapse was imminent. No one appears to have dissented. No one could think of anything else to do.

Lloyd George claimed never to have been particularly enthusiastic about the attack at Passchendaele. But now he seemed simply to be averting his gaze while men stumbled and staggered and got stuck in the mud, to be machine-gunned by the Germans.

Soon, Haig was also looking elsewhere, as he searched for the elusive breakthrough. It was to come, he decided, at Cambrai in northern France, where drier conditions would allow him to use a series of new tactics effectively – including the new wonder weapon, the tank. Eventually, in early November, Canadian soldiers took the ridge at Passchendaele. There had been no great breakthrough. The battle had mainly been an example of suffering and determination. It was not just the increased drunkenness, desertion and malingering that showed the damage to morale. An artillery signaller saw it in the eyes of the men shambling past his guns towards the horrors of the front line: 'No words of greeting passed as they slouched along; in sullen silence they filed past one by one to the sacrifice.'

To be fair to the military commanders, the battle at Cambrai that followed was a very different story, with greater expanses of ground taken in a much smaller conflict and in a fraction of the time. It showed that some form of breakthrough was possible, and was reported extravagantly by the _Daily Mail_ under the headline 'HAIG THROUGH THE HINDENBURG LINE'. Success was due to inventive new artillery and infantry tactics, but also to the deployment for the first time of massed tanks. Unfortunately, no one had much idea of how to capitalize on what the _Mail_ called this 'splendid success', and most of the ground captured was retaken by the Germans. The battle did not become the turning point in the war. But the impact of tanks caught the imagination of a people starved of good news. These mechanical messiahs were now talked up as war-winning weapons, a reputation they had failed to earn at the Somme. Science fiction made real promised a technological salvation. The government were quick to see some other uses for their new-found success.

Employing huge numbers of people to manufacture and detonate explosives (or rather, to fire bits of metal into the earth) was enormously expensive, and despite steep increases in taxation and greatly increased foreign borrowing, Britain had been virtually bankrupted by the cost of combat. Tanks now became an effective way of persuading the British people to lend their own money to the war effort. Within weeks of the fighting at Cambrai a tank had been driven into Trafalgar Square, to form the centrepiece of an advertisement for the sale of war bonds. As the band of the Coldstream Guards played patriotic tunes, cabinet ministers, chorus girls, dukes and duchesses, music-hall artistes and civic worthies clustered around the monster. As *The Times* reported, 'the much-loved Miss Madge Titheradge recited Alfred Noyes's "The Song of England" from the top of the tank.' Posters displayed near by showed German soldiers being crushed to death by British coins, while inside the tank sat two women selling bonds. At the edge of the crowd trinket-merchants set up stalls offering tank postcards, tank brooches and tank teapots. Later versions of the stunt were even more elaborate, with public squares turned into replicas of shattered Flanders villages and those willing to pledge particularly big sums offered the chance to send their donation in a canister strapped to a carrier pigeon. (They got to keep the canister as a souvenir.)

Soon, tanks were being deployed as the focal point of war-bond sales efforts all over the country, with 168 towns and cities competing to see who could raise the most money for the fighting. Children brought bags of halfpennies and farthings. In Birmingham a farmworker turned up with £75 in sovereigns and half-sovereigns that had been buried under his cottage floorboards for thirty years. An old man who brought £100 said it was all he could afford, but he would willingly have given more if he had it, in memory of his four sons, all of whom had given their lives.

Early in the war, the General Secretary of the National Union of Teachers, Sir James Yoxall, had explained to the schoolchildren of Britain that 'Germany is playing the sneak and the bully in the big

European school.' Germany had to be taught to 'play cricket', to play fair, to honour a 'scrap of paper', he said. A boy who behaved as Germany had done would be 'sent to Coventry by the whole school'. By 1917, in the foreshortened memories of children, the war seemed to have lasted an eternity. But it remained a distant menace – until, on 13 June that year, the practice of total war was made horribly plain.

It was lunchtime on a clear summer's day when pedestrians on the streets of the City of London looked up to see a fleet of four-teen big biplanes passing overhead. They looked, said someone afterwards, 'like so many huge silver dragonflies'. Bus conductors leaned off their platforms to gaze at the sky. On the pavements, men and women stood still and some began to cheer at what they assumed was a display of British airpower. Then, suddenly, bombs began to fall. The dragonflies were lumbering German Gotha bombers.

The country had suffered air attacks before – they had mainly come from the great hydrogen-filled airships made by the Zeppelin company. The Zepps were enormously sinister – 650 feet long, with a cabin slung below, and crewed by men who wore padded boots so as not to strike a spark that might turn the whole thing into an inferno. Everyone knew that the Zeppelin pilots preferred dark nights: for a couple of years now residents of eastern England had been keeping track of the phases of the moon to judge the likelihood of attack, and in cities where the Zeppelins had struck, blackouts were energetically enforced. When a raid came, police whistles blew, sirens sounded and searchlights tracked the skies. As they approached in the dark, the airships' propellers made what one survivor described as 'an odd, clunkety, clunkety noise . . . as if a tram with rusty wheels were travelling through the sky'.

But now it was broad daylight. And the aircraft which arrived that June day in 1917 were another proposition altogether – quicker, much more manoeuvrable than the lumbering Zeppelin balloons, and comparatively unaffected by the wind. This was not the first raid by Gotha bombers; from bases in occupied Belgium, the British capital was well within range, and previous attacks had done much to change perceptions of the war. When London's theatreland was hit, in a raid that took twenty lives, an outraged young officer on leave spoke for many when he exclaimed, 'It's no business to happen here,' as if a world war belonged only on the continent. This time, the raid dropped most of its bombs on the London docks and around Liverpool Street Station. But one of them fell upon a three-storey school in Upper North Street in Poplar, east London. It crashed straight through the building. On the top floor, a class of girls was having a singing lesson: one of them died instantly. On the floor below, the boys were being taught maths: one twelve-year-old was killed by flying rubble. Then the bomb broke through the floor into the basement, where there were fifty-four of the youngest children in the school. Here, it finally detonated. A soldier on leave was first into the room, and found it 'choked with struggling and screaming victims, many of them crying distractedly for their mothers. Little limbs had been blown from bodies and unrecognizable remains were littered among the debris of broken desks and forms.' Eighteen of the children had been killed and thirty horribly maimed. The Bishop of London told mourners at the mass funeral it was inconceivable that, after 2,000 years of Christianity, war was now being made against women and children.

All told that day 162 people were killed by German aircraft and over 400 wounded. They were all civilians: in this new and terrible warfare not only was there no distinction between combatant and non-combatant, talk of a 'front line' was increasingly meaningless. Three weeks later another wave of bombers struck, circling St Paul's in a V formation and dropping bombs that killed fifty Londoners. There were instant demands for punitive retaliation, with *John Bull* shrieking that 'the Huns deserve no more consideration than a mad dog or a venomous snake.' In the meantime, the blackout grew darker and the capital was ringed by anti-aircraft guns. Now, at the sound of warning whistles and sirens, people poured into cellars, shelters and Underground stations until Boy Scout buglers sounded the all-clear.

The bombing raids continued until May 1918, killing nearly a thousand Londoners and wounding almost three times that number. By comparison with the numbers of soldiers dying at the front, it was a small total. But casualty statistics were not the point. The impact of these raids was measured psychologically, in the distress they caused to those who wore no uniform, who had never seen and would never see those who were trying to kill them, and in the anxiety they provoked in men at the front, no longer sure that 'home' was necessarily a haven. The geographical self-confidence of centuries was shattered. Britain was no longer an island.

By June 1917, then, distinctions between civilian and military had become quaint anachronisms. But whether they were wearing uniform or not, all these people still had to eat. Finding a solution to this difficulty preoccupied the government throughout the year, and the solution they eventually chose marked a very significant social change.

At the start of 1917 German civilians were enduring what they called the 'turnip winter', because in many places turnips were all they had to eat. Exceptionally wet weather in the German autumn of 1916 had destroyed much of the potato crop, and fuel shortages disrupted distribution of whatever supplies were available. The British were rightly blamed for the ensuing hunger: after the German navy's retreat to port following the battle of Jutland, it had been comparatively easy for the British to mount an effective blockade of the short German coastline. Turnips made up most of the emergency food supplies that were distributed to try to keep the population alive, but the blockade brought on or aggravated thousands of cases of scurvy, rickets and tuberculosis, and at the end of the war Germany claimed that almost three-quarters of a million people had died as a result of it.

In February 1917, Germany reopened the campaign of unrestricted U-boat warfare which had been suspended after the sinking of the *Lusitania* two years earlier. All ships travelling to or from British ports were liable to be sunk on sight. The Kaiser thundered that his submarines would starve the British people 'until they, who have refused peace, will kneel and plead for it'. It was an extremely troubling prospect. Britain lived by trade, and the growth of imperial power had rendered the country unable to feed itself any longer. Before the war, four-fifths of the cereals it ate, over half the dairy produce consumed and almost all its sugar were imported. An ideological commitment to free trade had made the country more vulnerable to a blockade than either France or Germany, each of which was at least self-sufficient in sugar (indeed, before the war, German sugar beet had been copiously exported to Britain). By 1917 the British people were well used to 'making do' – indeed they had become accustomed to it since soon after the war began. Magazines offered patriotic recipes for 'war cake' or 'lentil loaf', which used no eggs, butter or milk, and only very small amounts of sugar: no one expected them to be prominent on the menus of fashionable teashops once peace returned. But making do was not enough, and appeals to self-restraint and better nature suffered from the same moral drawback as relying on volunteers to fill the army: they left the conscientious to carry the lackadaisical.

The obvious solution would have been to introduce universal rationing and see fair shares for all. Yet there was great political resistance to the idea – it was as unBritish as conscription, and the Asquith government had held out against it, as they had resisted conscription. It is rather hard to work out what was going through the minds of those who argued against rationing on the basis that it was bad for morale – can they really have believed that, without it, no one would notice there was a war going on? There were queues, queues and more queues for almost any sort of food. Fish came to be in such short supply that the Archbishop of Westminster granted Catholics special dispensation to eat cheap cuts of meat on fast days. Prices spiralled, with many foods doubling in cost and some, such as eggs, quadrupling. In December 1916 the government had appointed Lord Devonport, a very wealthy food retailer (he founded International Stores, 'the Greatest Grocers in the World'), as the country's first Food Controller. The title turned out to be something of a misnomer, for Lord Devonport did very little controlling and much exhorting – for instance, asking individuals to set an example by wearing a purple 'I Eat Less Bread' ribbon. But appeals for restraint were not enough. By April 1917, even those who could afford to eat in restaurants found that there was one day a week when meat was not available, and that lunch was limited to two courses.

The Board of Agriculture had already been given the power to requisition land or to replace inefficient farmers with prisoners of war and conscientious objectors who might grow more food. But this was also an area where women could make a significant further contribution. Since the early days of the war there had been women volunteers replacing men in the fields and forests, and despite initial resistance from some farmers to 'the lilac sunbonnet brigade', they had established themselves as an important part of the war economy. The menace of unrestricted submarine attack in 1917 was met with the formal creation of a Women's Land Army, complete with uniforms – a knee-length tunic, boots, puttees, breeches and slouch hat – and a roll of honour to commemorate those who died in farm accidents. They even had a marching song, which began, 'The men must take the swords, / And we must take the ploughs.'

It was emphatically *nothing* to do with lilac sunbonnets, said the President of the Board of Agriculture sternly, because 'there is no romance in it; it is prose . . . In all respects it is comparable to the work your men-folk are doing in the trenches at the front.' Commentators did their best to quieten worries about the damage that wearing breeches and tilling the soil might do to ideas of fragrant English womanhood, by emphasizing the healthiness of their lives. A reporter from the *Sheffield Daily Telegraph* reassured readers that 'an open air life has built them up into strong healthy-looking Amazons, a type for which England was renowned in the days of

Queen Elizabeth, when bright-cheeked and clear-eyed lasses were
bred on the land, lived on the land, and became mothers of the yeo-
men of England.' By July 1918 the Board of Agriculture reckoned
there were 113,000 of these Amazons deployed in the fields.

But crops take months to grow, and German submarines off the
Irish coast were now sending huge quantities of food to the bottom of the sea every day: in April 1917 alone the Germans sank
880,000 tons of merchant shipping carrying supplies to Britain. By
the end of the month, it was calculated that the country had
enough wheat to make bread for only six weeks. In May, the king
issued a Royal Proclamation, to be read out in churches across the
land for the following four Sundays. After much waffle (the word-
ing was based on a proclamation delivered by George III, over a
century earlier), it came to the point. The king requested his 'loving subjects' to reduce their intake of bread by at least a quarter.
There was a particular appeal to richer loving subjects: since they
could afford luxuries (tins of imported larks were said to be still
available occasionally in the shops), please would they eat more of
them, and leave bread to fill the stomachs of poor people?

Government propaganda consolidated the king's appeal, hec-
toring citizens to 'EAT SLOWLY, YOU WILL NEED LESS
FOOD' and advising that those who kept warm wouldn't need to
eat so much. Advertisements claimed that the accumulated weekly
total of discarded crusts did the work of twenty German submarines. 'Eat less bread and victory is secure' admonished a poster,
while leaflets advised citizens to 'look well at the loaf on your
breakfast table and treat it as if it were real gold because that British loaf is going to beat the German.' *The 'Win the War' Cook Book*
advised the cooks of the country that they were now in the front
line: 'The struggle is not only on land and sea; it is in *your* larder,
your kitchen, and *your* dining room.' The eating advice might have
come from a modern diet guide – you should leave a meal still feeling slightly hungry, eat as slowly as possible, masticate more, and
plan meals well in advance. The book was packed with recipes for
Swede Soup and Fried Mush (*sic*), interspersed with slogans like

'THE WOMAN WHO WASTES A CRUST WASTES A CARTRIDGE.' And anyone who threw rice at a wedding or fed a stray dog faced prosecution.

Though Britain possessed the most powerful navy in the world, the Kaiser's attempt to starve the British people nearly succeeded. The menace from vessels able to hide beneath the waves was so baffling to the Admiralty that at one point a psychic had been engaged to see if she could tell them where submarines were hiding. (She could not.) Another brainwave had been to train seagulls to land on enemy periscopes to give their position away, and a third to teach sea lions to seek U-boats out underwater. Eventually, despite the opposition of admirals who felt it beneath the dignity of the Royal Navy, Lloyd George pressed for the establishment of a convoy system, in which the merchant vessels that kept the country from starving were protected by destroyers fast enough to hunt down and eliminate any submarines which revealed themselves.

Survival also meant making much better use of what could be produced at home: less meat, more home-grown vegetables, especially potatoes. The dull and dutiful king, who had already given up drink for the duration, continued to set an example. Now he turned over the herbaceous borders at Buckingham Palace to turnips and cabbages (or had his gardeners do so) and donated the royal vegetables to a military hospital in a requisitioned office block in Waterloo. Other vegetable 'allotments' were being established everywhere – on waste ground, on golf courses and railway embankments, in parks and on tennis courts. Apostles of the Vacant Land Cultivation Society considered it the greatest change in land ownership for generations.* This too was an area in which women made a distinctive contribution, with crowds of spectators sometimes visiting the plots to cheer them on as they dug. An allotment holder in south London hymned them in 'Diana versus Mars', probably one of the worst poems of the war:

---

* It turned out to be a very temporary change: after the war developers clawed much of the land back and built all over it.

> Potatoes plump and carrots slender,
> Parsnips, succulent and tender,
> Stout cauliflowers, and portly cabbage.
> Gay Brussels sprouts and sombre spinach;
> Thus would England keep each day
> The German hunger-wolf at bay.

But it was not enough. There were industrial disputes all over the country, as workers complained of high prices, empty shelves and unfair distribution. Exhortations were all very well, but when poor people had spent their entire lives worrying about getting enough to eat, government restrictions on rice-throwing and the eating of buttered crumpets were apt to raise a hollow laugh. The Food Controller, Lord Devonport, was a self-made grocer: could his reluctance to introduce immediate restrictions have anything to do with the damage it might do to the profits the grocery trade made on the limited supplies which *were* available? It might be unBritish, but rationing's hour had come. The man whom Lloyd George appointed as the new Food Controller in June 1917, Lord Rhondda, was a Welsh coal magnate. He concluded that without proper rationing there was a real possibility of revolution in Britain. It would be introduced at the end of the year.

Sugar was first, to be followed by the rationing of meat and fats. Wives or mothers who happened to have a member of the family home on leave would still send him to stand in the grocer's or butcher's queue, because shopkeepers generally served men in uniform first, but the lines outside shops themselves were now shorter and much less anxious, for the principle of fair shares for all was widely accepted. This in turn led to prosecutions of citizens who abused the system. At the turn of the year came a case which attracted worldwide attention. 'MARIE CORELLI FINED FOR HOARDING SUGAR', reported the *New York Times* correspondent. A now largely forgotten novelist, Marie Corelli was said to have been the favourite author not only of the ageing Queen Victoria, but also of the middle-aged Edward VII and the

young George V – a sure sign of something or other, if not necessarily of literary merit. But royal patronage did nothing to protect
her after claims that railway porters had been seen delivering large
amounts of sugar to her house in Stratford-upon-Avon. A policeman reported that over the course of a month Miss Corelli's butler
had signed for deliveries of 179 pounds of the stuff. The writer's
imagination was undimmed and her defence indignant. She did
not deny that the quantities were larger than the ration allowance,
but claimed to be planning to make an abundance of jam, which
she intended to give away. Being 'interfered with' by the police
was an outrage. 'You are upsetting the country altogether with
your food orders and what-not,' she declared in court. 'Lloyd
George will be resigning tomorrow, and there will be a revolution
in England in less than a week.' Corelli was fined £50.

The revolution did not happen. But a good number of exemplary prosecutions did. And by a combination of rationing, naval
convoys and home-growing, Britain survived the Kaiser's attempt
to starve the country into submission. Instead, it was Germany
that experienced something close to revolution as a result of the
British naval blockade. In July 1917 King George followed up his
vegetable-growing by changing the name of the royal house from
the German 'House of Saxe-Coburg-Gotha' to the safely nonde-
script 'House of Windsor'.★

By late 1917 there really wasn't much to inspire confidence that the
war would be over any time soon. It was true that there had been
allied victories in the Middle East, where a predominantly Indian
force had captured Baghdad and where General Allenby had taken
Jerusalem just in time for the government to authorize a celebra-
tory peal of Christmas bells at Westminster Abbey – the first since

---

★ He had first had to establish precisely what his name *was*. The College of
Heralds was unsure – was it perhaps 'Wepper' or 'Wittin'? The king's private
secretary settled on 'Windsor' as a new name for the royal house, having discovered that at one time Edward III had been called 'Edward of Windsor'.

1914. Yet everyone knew that it was on the Western Front that the war as a whole would be won or lost. Passchendaele had been a most terrible bloodletting and the breakthrough at Cambrai had achieved little. The French army was exhausted and discontented. In Russia the newly installed Bolsheviks were now negotiating their own peace with Germany, taking the biggest army of all out of the alliance and freeing Berlin to redeploy the best part of a million soldiers elsewhere. Meanwhile, the ships bringing food to Britain were being sunk at a much faster rate than they could be replaced. Everyone was sick of the war.

There was, however, one particular cause for hope. The Kaiser's promise to torpedo the vessels of nations not directly involved in the war turned out to be a catastrophic misjudgement, for it was this that finally shifted the United States from neutrality to belligerence. This was precisely what British propaganda had been trying to achieve, but manipulating opinion in a nation whose very existence was built on a rejection of European empires had been very hard work. Even the killing of over a hundred American citizens on board the *Lusitania* in 1915 had not persuaded the country to abandon its declared neutrality, and when President Woodrow Wilson ran for re-election the following year he did so on the boast that he was the man who had kept America *out* of the war. Soon after being returned to the White House he produced a grand plan for world 'peace without victory', couched in platitudes about how 'only a peace between equals can last'. This naive ambition soon hit the buffers when it asked all parties to state their minimum terms. The allies' ambition was simple: they wanted the Germans to go home. The least that most of the German military and political class would accept was a neutering of Belgium and Poland, the surrender of French territory, the basis of a German empire in Africa, and a recognition of Austrian dominance in the Balkans. Unsurprisingly, Wilson's idea got nowhere. But when the Germans embarked upon unrestricted submarine warfare in February 1917, they achieved what British propaganda had failed to do for years and knocked the United States off the fence.

The U-boat campaign was a not very clever gamble by the Germans, and American opinion was outraged that US ships would everywhere be at the mercy of German submarines. 'If Germany wants war with the United States, let Germany have war with the United States,' roared the *New York World*. But the German Foreign Ministry took comfort from President Wilson's pieties about world peace, while the military in Berlin assured their political masters that the U-boat campaign would quickly finish Britain, so the war would be over before America could join it. The United States' neutrality was finally made untenable by something else, though: a telegram. Ever since the British had cut German telegraph cables in August 1914, military and diplomatic messages from Germany had had to be sent by wireless. Of course the messages were encrypted. But the codes were not beyond the team of code-breakers in Room 40 of the Admiralty. This unusual assortment of people – linguists, clergymen, bankers, mathematicians – under the command of the navy's Reginald 'Blinker' Hall (a man memorably described as looking like 'a demonic Mr Punch in uniform', with a twitch and a badly fitting set of false teeth which he clicked audibly when excited) had already played an outstanding role in the war effort. They had deciphered orders to the German fleet before Jutland, and intercepted instructions to the German vessel smuggling arms for the Easter Rising. Now they pulled off their biggest coup.

In January 1917, they decoded a message from Berlin to the German ambassador in Washington. After disclosing the plan for unlimited submarine warfare, it revealed that the German Foreign Minister, Arthur Zimmermann, was offering to form an alliance with Mexico and that Germany would support that country in attempts to recapture territory in Arizona, New Mexico and Texas which it had lost to the United States. On 1 March, American newspapers published the intercepted text, the British having spilled the beans to Washington. As anger grew in the United States, U-boats sank four American ships, and with them all German hope that the country might be kept out of the war any

longer. On 2 April the President addressed Congress, declaring the
German submarine campaign to be 'a warfare against mankind'.
Neutrality, he said, was no longer feasible. Dissenting voices who
detested the thought of joining forces with the old imperial power
were swamped by an overwhelming majority of legislators. On
6 April 1917 the President signed the declaration of war against
Germany.

There were plenty of Americans who were convinced that the
United States had entered the war on British misinformation,
which had consistently presented Germany as a menace to civilized values. 'I am one of the hundred and ten million suckers who
swallowed the hook of British official propaganda,' the radical
American writer Upton Sinclair remarked bitterly ten years later.
He blamed the subversion upon Gilbert Parker, a dandified popular novelist, Conservative MP and fervent imperialist whom no
one has heard of nowadays, but who had been in charge of British
propaganda in the United States. If Upton Sinclair is to be believed,
Parker should be credited as one of the creators of the military
superpower which came to dominate the world.

The commitment of the United States promised the victory which
had eluded Britain for the previous three years. But America could
not make any truly significant military contribution until the following year, and in the meantime Britain had to survive. That
meant facing down the growing numbers of people questioning
the management of the whole enterprise. A general sense of pulling together had quietened left-wingers in the trades union
movement, who felt that the confrontation was between imperial
dynasties and no business of the common man. But, as the cost of
living soared and the need for yet more men meant skilled workers
being conscripted, relations with employers soured. Five and a
half million days were lost to strikes in 1917 – 1.5 million of them
in May alone, despite a widespread fear that too much disruption
of industry endangered relatives and friends at the front. The king
himself was despatched by train around the country, to appeal for

the loyalty of disaffected workers. It was a gesture with tremendous impact: even 'Red' William Gallacher of the Clyde Workers' Committee admitted that the day the king appeared alone before an audience of workers in Glasgow, he became a royalist. But what really calmed the unrest were pay rises, tax concessions and the introduction of food rationing, which seemed to show that everybody was in it together.

More troubling for the war leadership was the discovery that among those people who had joined the fight by choice there were now some who had lost faith in it. Siegfried Sassoon, the handsome country gentleman who had volunteered as soon as the war began, was the most conspicuous of them. He was not one of the privileged few who indulged their consciences with disdainful letters to liberal periodicals. Nor was he a conscientious objector. Quite the opposite – his courage in battle had earned him the Military Cross and the nickname 'Mad Jack' among his men. 'It's no good being out here unless one takes the full amount of risks,' he confessed, death being merely the loss of a 'few years of ease and futility'. But when the 'Great Advance' on the Somme in 1916 turned out to be nothing of the kind, the naive convictions of a brave young man vanished. It was not that Sassoon lost faith in the aims of the war, but he was increasingly unhappy about the way it was being directed: the men with whom he shared a troop transport in February 1917 struck him as 'cabbages going to Covent Garden, or beasts driven to market . . . They have no worries because they have no future.' A spell in England recovering from a bullet wound to the shoulder deepened his disillusion. At house-parties of the literary hostess Lady Ottoline Morrell, he shared his anxieties with well-known and well-heeled opponents of the war, such as her lover Bertrand Russell. They encouraged him to make a public statement.

Getting the tone right would be difficult, for Sassoon believed that while most ordinary soldiers fervently hoped for the war to stop, most would say that 'the Boches had got to be beaten somehow.' Would it make the slightest difference for a solitary lieutenant to denounce the war, in the face of the moralistic rhetoric of Lloyd George's cabinet and the roaring of the Northcliffe newspapers? By June 1917 Siegfried Sassoon had found his words, and persuaded a sympathetic MP to read them out in the House of Commons the following month. The declaration was incendiary. 'The War is being deliberately prolonged by those who have the power to end it,' he said. What had begun as a defensive war had become one of 'aggression and conquest'. It could have been ended by negotiation. 'I have seen and endured the sufferings of the troops,' he said, 'and I can no longer be a party to prolong these sufferings for ends which I believe to be evil and unjust . . .'

It was a devastating indictment, from a young officer with impeccable credentials. The military response was more subtle than the court martial that might have occurred. Sassoon was ordered to attend a medical examination at his depot near Liverpool. He had already confided to his diary that he wished that decorated soldiers returning on leave would 'throw their medals in the faces of their masters' and demand to know why their womenfolk were excited at hearing they had shed German blood. Before he set off to be questioned by the medical hearing he went for a walk along the sand-dunes at Formby and took his own advice. After shaking his fists at the sky, he said, he tore the Military Cross ribbon from his tunic and threw it into the mouth of the Mersey. It lay limply on the water 'as though aware of its own futility' and eventually floated away.

The doctors' report on Sassoon described his conversation as disconnected and irrational and his manner as 'nervous and excitable'. 'He is suffering from a nervous breakdown and we do not consider him responsible for his actions,' they concluded. They sent him to a mental hospital.

12. Stiff Upper Lips

The wounded were given uniforms, even if they had no limbs to put in them.

Craiglockhart near Edinburgh was a run-down former spa hotel, or 'hydro', which had been requisitioned for the war effort. Instead of the Victorian guests who had once come to take the waters, this vast Italianate mansion was now filled with men whose minds had been damaged by war. Sassoon nicknamed the place 'Dottyville'.

If an evil scientist had set out to design an environment that would damage a man's mind as effectively as a high-explosive shell could destroy his body, he could not have done much better than a trench on the battlefield. The constant noise and danger were one thing. But what made the experience so particularly destructive mentally was that there was no escape: the trench that provided shelter was also a prison. Small wonder that men's minds broke under the stress and fear. The casualties of 'shell shock' stammered

and glared, shook and shambled. Sometimes they stuttered, sometimes they lost the power of speech almost completely. Sometimes
they walked with weird gaits, their legs flying wildly. Sometimes they
shuddered. Other times they were paralysed.

There was great official reluctance to recognize that these men
were ill. Generals worried that to do so would make fear of the
enemy respectable and very shortly entire military formations
would be presenting themselves as unfit for combat. One doctor
observed that 'The pressure of opinion in the battalion – the idea
stronger than fear – was eased by giving fear a respectable name.
When the social slur was removed . . . the resolve to stay with the
battalion had been weakened, the conscience was relaxed, the path
out of danger was made easy.' It was too subtle a wound for much
of the military to understand. In a post-war investigation by the
War Office, Lieutenant Colonel Viscount Gort VC, of the Grenadier Guards, asserted that shell shock was as infectious as measles
and could be suppressed or extinguished altogether with firm
handling. It was, he claimed, much less in evidence in the elite
regiments (like his own) than among the volunteers of Kitchener's
army, where many of the casualties were borderline mental cases
or 'Yahoos' anyway. Officers had to be taught 'man mastership' as
they were taught to master a horse. There may have been something in this. It was striking that some regiments with proud
battle-honours performed much better than others that did not
have them: it was as if some men could not countenance betraying
a history.

No one likes to lay themselves open to accusations of cowardice. Nonetheless, there are examples in war memoirs of men who
confessed that they had lost their nerve, yet rediscovered it when a
senior officer ordered them back into action. But for some – and
there was no easy way of predicting who they might be – the noise
and fear caused genuine mental collapse, and by late 1916 the army
had been forced to establish special wards in base hospitals to cope
with 'neurasthenia'. Here, the treatments were physical. Rigorous
exercise might cure sufferers. Massage and plenty of milk might

cure them. Strange diets might cure them. Electrical stimulation of muscles might do it. Some of these therapies even worked for a while. But at some point there was always a relapse. In 1930 there were over 30,000 shell-shock victims receiving disability pensions.

In late 1917, during Siegfried Sassoon's time at Craiglockhart, physical treatment was being pushed aside by the recognition that a mental illness required some form of mental treatment. The presiding spirit of the place was William Halse Rivers, a quiet, ascetic, rather shy man with a pronounced stammer. The son of a clergyman, he had combined a medical career with anthropology – he rather revelled in the hardship of field trips in the south Pacific. He was now commissioned as a captain in the Royal Army Medical Corps. Rivers noticed that there was a natural tendency among the men's visitors to avoid talking about the terrible experiences that had brought them there. Why dwell on something distressing? Better to engage the patient in sunny thoughts of family, of countryside, of pets and gossip. 'The advice which has usually been given to my patients', he found, 'is that they should endeavour to banish all thoughts of war from their minds.' In some hospitals men suffering from shell shock were simply forbidden to mention the war. It was well meant. But Rivers recognized that it was completely counter-productive to try to suppress traumatic experiences: the patient was never going to forget them. You had, instead, to talk about damaging events, not to the exclusion of happy subjects, but to accept them as part of life. He had divined a basic truth of psychiatric therapy, that 'what you resist, persists.' The significance of this recognition – which is still the basis of post-traumatic therapy – cannot be exaggerated. Sassoon may or may not have been suffering from shell shock. But he certainly found Rivers one of the most sympathetic men he had ever met.

For future generations the greatest legacy of Sassoon's time at Craiglockhart was the friendship he formed there with a fellow patient, Wilfred Owen, who was under the care of another therapist, Arthur Brock. Owen's shell shock had been brought on by intense combat, during which time he was blown up and spent three days trapped, alone, in the cellar of a house in the midst of the fighting. Brock believed in the therapeutic value of work, and encouraged Owen to take on the editorship of the hospital's six-penny magazine, *The Hydra*. The name was a pun on the building's former life as a 'hydro' and a reference to the many-headed mytho-logical serpent whose killing was the second of the trials of Hercules: just as the monster grew new heads when one was cut off, as soon as a patient finished his treatment at Craiglockhart he was replaced by another casualty from the front. The magazine was no great literary vehicle, being filled with what passed for humorous articles by men making light of their condition, and glowing endorsements for sports like golf and badminton. 'Many of us who came to the hydro slightly ill are now getting dangerously well,' Owen burbled in one of his editorials. Yet it was at Craiglockhart that Owen began the bitterest of all anti-war poems, 'Dulce et Decorum Est', and it was Sassoon who encouraged him to believe in his verse – even provid-ing the title of 'Anthem for Doomed Youth' ('What passing-bells for these who die as cattle / Only the monstrous anger of the guns'). As Owen's self-confidence grew, so too did his chances of being returned to the front as one of the cattle himself.

Sassoon's protest and Owen's poems were evidence of the limits to the human capacity to endure. They especially troubled the generals because their authors were members of an officer corps, upon whose courage and commitment the entire war rested. Courage – the decision not to run away from danger or, in the context of this new kind of warfare, simply to endure the utter helplessness of artillery bombardment – is, initially at least, an act of will. Fear – the natural reaction to menace – drove some men to acts of astonishing bravery, some to blasé indifference to risk, such as standing up while shells crashed around, and others to repeated heavy drinking. Did they drink because they were breaking, or break because they were drinking, one medical officer wondered?

Courage is will-power, whereof no man has an unlimited stock; and when in war it is used up, he is finished. A man's courage is his capital and he is always spending. The call on the bank may be only the daily drain of the front line or it may be a sudden draft which threatens to close the account. His will is perhaps almost destroyed by intensive shelling, by heavy bombing, or by a bloody battle, or it is gradually used up by monotony, by exposure, by the loss of the support of stauncher spirits on whom he has come to depend, by physical exhaustion, by a wrong attitude to danger, to casualties, to death itself.

The author of this analysis was Charles McMoran Wilson, a doctor who won a Military Cross at the battle of the Somme in 1916.* He was at odds with received wisdom. According to conventional thought, civilians who joined the army became increasingly battle-hardened by exposure to fighting and danger. Wilson's experiences led him to the conclusion that men gradually wore out, like an increasingly threadbare piece of clothing. If this calculation was correct, the military planners could no more presume upon infinite reserves of the 'offensive spirit' they so prized than they could upon the increasingly unprepossessing men being combed out from industries at home.

The greatest challenge was to find sufficient officers. At the start of the war there had been a corps of professional soldiers in this role. Let Winston Churchill's friend Adrian Carton de Wiart, VC, KBE, CB, CMG, DSO stand as an example. As he looked back on the greatest shedding of blood in history, de Wiart declared that 'frankly, I had enjoyed the war; it had given me bad moments, lots of good ones, plenty of excitement, and with everything found for us.' This is the authentic voice of a certain comic-book British officer – moustached, monocled, brave, thoughtless, for whom life's greatest pleasure was biffing the Germans. After being shot near Ypres, de Wiart recalled: 'My hand was a ghastly sight. Two of the fingers were hanging by a piece of skin, all the palm was shot away and most of the wrist . . . I asked the doctor to take

---

* His distinguished war record with the Royal Fusiliers was one of the reasons why Churchill chose him as his personal doctor in 1940.

my fingers off; he refused, so I pulled them off myself.' He was
badly wounded eight times all told, and won a Victoria Cross. It
was said that de Wiart literally felt no fear, and advanced into combat with no weapon but a walking stick, worried that if he had a
revolver he might shoot his own men.

Most British officers of the First World War weren't like this at
all, of course. For a start, this fearless Englishman was really half
Belgian and half Irish. Secondly, he was a professional soldier from
the old regular army – he had arrived in the trenches wearing a
black eyepatch, testament to the eye he had lost while fighting
with the Camel Corps against the 'Mad Mullah' of Somaliland in
1914. During the First World War he went on to rise to the rank of
brigadier general. But he belonged to that minority of young men
who had *chosen* to become a professional soldier. By the end of the
First World War those British army officers who were not dead
were more representative of the population as a whole than they
had been for centuries. And in the changing composition of the
officer class we can see the way in which the country itself was
altering. The young men who led the endless, fruitless attacks were
hardly more than boys, and some of them could calculate their life
expectancy in weeks. During the heaviest fighting on the Western
Front there were battalions which trudged back down the communication trenches with virtually all their junior officers missing.

The reason for this extraordinarily heavy casualty rate is that
they had been taught that an attack began with the platoon lieutenant clambering out of the trench and guiding his men from the
front, not prodding them forward from behind. With a lead of
two or three seconds, the cry was expected to be 'Come on!', not
'Go on!' German snipers very quickly learned that if they wanted
to have the greatest impact on the enemy, they should pick off the
figures in long tunics, Sam Browne belt and riding breeches (which
was why many subalterns chose to go over the top carrying rifles
and dressed as ordinary soldiers). Alfred Burrage, an engagingly
subversive writer of magazine romances, felt contempt for most
of his superiors in the army – he thought it 'a brain-wave on the

part of the lady' that one of the prostitutes in a Le Havre brothel used to wear a British captain's uniform for example. But even so, 'I, who was a private, and a bad one at that, freely own that it was the British subaltern who won the war.'

Ignorance may be sufficient explanation for the enthusiasm of some of the early volunteers, who reckoned the whole thing a rather jolly adventure. Soon after the despatch of the British Expeditionary Force, for example, a British civilian in grey flannels had been discovered driving around Flanders in a sports car on which he had mounted a rifle. He announced that he had attached himself to the army and had just shot a German – 'a walking one'. The young poet Julian Grenfell, who had even taken his gundogs with him to France, found the experience of crawling around in the territory between the trenches a lark. 'I have never felt so well, or so happy, or enjoyed anything so much,' he observed. Grenfell was a peculiar man, part sentimentalist, part brute, and to him – as to some others – the opportunity to shoot a German or two seemed a form of field sport. Infamously, in early October 1914 he recorded in his game diary '105 partridges' shot on a family estate. The next entry, written in the trenches and dated 16 November, reads '1 Pomeranian'. This is followed by 'November 17th: two Pomeranians'. To those with a good eye – the task appealed particularly to anyone who had ever stalked a deer – sniping held great attractions, and a number of officers took their own big-game rifles to the front, where they crawled and lay for hours watching through telescopic sights until they had learned the habits of the men opposite – when they stood to, when they ate and drank, where they relieved themselves. Then, one day, having grown familiar enough to recognize their faces and give them pet names, they drew a bead on their head or chest and shot them dead.

This combination of childishness and callousness can only be understood in the context of the education most of these young men had received. In May 1915 – the day after Grenfell died from a shrapnel wound to the head – *The Times* published his poem 'Into Battle', which became one of the most popular of the war:

> And life is Colour and Warmth and Light,
> And a striving evermore for these;
> And he is dead who will not fight;
> And who dies fighting has increase.

It is too archaic and too uncongenial to be the sort of verse that is set as a twenty-first-century school text. But at the time it struck a chord with a class who saw the war in the spirit of a crusade for civilization. Grenfell was far from the only poet who experienced the war as something cleansing and exhilarating, and – oddly – discovered pleasure in its terrible intensity. It was not that characters like Grenfell were immune to fear, for he admitted on another occasion to being 'petrified'. (And perhaps only those who have actually felt the terror of facing death can ever derive the exhilarating thrill that he expresses so heartily from just being alive.) But there was something more. To a certain sort of young man, the question of whether or not to join up and fight, and, when mounting an attack, whether or not to place oneself at greatest risk, was simply no choice at all.

These young men came overwhelmingly from the 'public' schools, which had been developed to offer the burgeoning middle class of Victorian England the opportunity to translate their sons into gentlemen. Famously, the schools were not primarily intellectual institutions, but were designed to instil attitudes of mind and patterns of behaviour. A minority of their pupils did manage to marry the schools' obsession with athleticism to intellectual achievement – Rupert Brooke had been a cricketer at Rugby, for example, Robert Graves a boxing champion at Charterhouse, Siegfried Sassoon a cricketer at Marlborough. The young men produced by these places did not, of course, all emerge in the physical form of Greek gods. But sport, cleaner air and better food had a measurable effect on their bodies. A public schoolboy officer was usually several inches taller than the poorer, less well-nourished men from the slums he was to lead into battle. It is also a fair generalization to say that the more distinguished products of these schools were not naturally subversive. In the emphasis on loyalty to the different houses in which they slept at school, obsession with sporting competition, anti-intellectualism and obedience to authority these schools cultivated a sense of duty, an awareness of hierarchy and a habit of command. At a time when British fee-paying schools present themselves as little more than exam-factories at the service of the rich, it is hard to appreciate how seriously they once took their social responsibilities. The sporting ethos was key: as the headmaster of Loretto, the oldest boarding school in Scotland, put it, schoolboy rugby produced 'a race of robust men, with active habits, brisk circulations, manly sympa-thies and exuberant spirits' ready to endure anything for Crown and country. They were a perfect nursery for the cadre needed to lead an army in combat. When the British Commander in Chief, Sir Douglas Haig, looked back at the end of the war, he decided that 'in the formation of character, which is the root of discipline, [the public schools] have no rivals.' At the outbreak of war over 150 of these institutions contained branches of the Officer Train-ing Corps, in which pupils spent one afternoon a week drilling and exercising. The OTCs had always been intended to provide a pool of potential officers should they be needed, and now they delivered them.

In the frantic rush to the colours between August 1914 and March the following year, 20,577 former members of school and university Officer Training Corps were commissioned. Thousands of others joined up as ordinary soldiers: some Territorial regi-ments, like the London Scottish (the 'Piccadilly Allsorts'), the Honourable Artillery Company and Queen Victoria's Rifles were well known for the number of gently born men in their ranks. In September 1914 the Royal Fusiliers founded no fewer than four public school battalions. Ten thousand of the recruits to the Artists' Rifles (nicknamed the 'Suicide Club') went on to be commissioned. There was such a rush to join up that that autumn, for the first time in 500 years, not a single boy from Winchester 'went up' to begin student life at Oxford.

The wise young man joining the army would follow the advice of Albert Trapman's *Straight Tips for 'Subs'*, published in 1915. He should only travel first class and acknowledge any other officer he bumped into with a polite 'Good morning'. While in theory all officers were equal in the mess, he must not invite anyone to have a drink with him, nor light up until he saw someone else smoking, should never mention a lady's name nor wear his sword. It was a sin to salute the bandmaster. He should never address a captain by his military rank alone, for only tradesmen did that. On the other hand, majors were always to be addressed as 'Major' or 'Sir'. Joining a regiment was evidently quite like being sent to another public school, albeit a particularly forbidding one. 'The Junior Subaltern (yourself!) is a blot on the earth until he justifies his existence.' The senior subaltern, meanwhile, was like a terrifying senior prefect; the captain above you, 'in loco parentis', was like a public school housemaster; and the colonel was to be treated as if he were the king while on parade, and off parade 'as you would treat a rich uncle from whom you have expectations'. When it came to their uniforms, these new young officers got away with what they could – bashing their caps into rakish shapes, having tailors alter the cut of their breeches, and choosing what they considered to be fetching shades of khaki from beige to dark green. They learned to ride, ready for the day they were promoted to the rank of captain or higher. They ambled down to the Army and Navy Stores in London, a posh co-operative created by late-Victorian military officers, where the Weapons Department could supply them with pistols and binoculars and everything from trench periscopes and ear-defenders to compasses, barometers and devices for slicing up barbed wire.* They couldn't wait to get to the front.

Great numbers paid for their privileged upbringing with their

---

* Before returning to France in 1916 Siegfried Sassoon borrowed his aunt's membership card for the store and emerged with a classic First World War basket of goods – 'a superb salmon, two bottles of old brandy, an automatic pistol, and two pairs of wire-cutters with rubber-covered handles'.

lives. Robert Graves, who had abandoned plans to study at Oxford in 1914 and joined the Royal Welch Fusiliers after hearing accounts of the atrocities in Belgium, claimed that the life expectancy of a junior officer in the trenches was a mere six weeks. About 37,500 officers were killed in the war, including, for example, well over a thousand from Eton, nearly 700 from Rugby and Cheltenham, 644 Harrovians, 457 boys from Malvern College and 447 from Uppingham. At the close of the war there was hardly a public school in the country that did not display a memorial to those who had gone straight from boyhood to grave. So what was it that so compelled them to offer up their lives in this way?

The business of leadership is essentially the manipulation of other people's emotions. To that end, the young officer had first to control his own feelings – and anyone who had been to public school had been hiding his emotions for years. A good officer could raise his men's spirits from gloom to good humour, a bad officer could count only on sullen acquiescence. This required the cultivation of trust and demanded that the officer develop self-confidence and a public readiness for self-sacrifice. In the face of danger, the natural human impulse is to flinch, cower and take shelter. But battle demanded the reverse – that infantrymen advanced into a storm of flying metal, and furthermore that they kept advancing as they saw their friends cut down, mutilated and screaming all around them. This was the reason for the subaltern's pretended insouciance, the walking sticks and cigarettes, pipes and hunting horns. It looked idiotic. But the whole thing was an exercise in defying normal human instinct.

These young men have frequently been considered figures of fun – upper-class numbskulls who marched their men into machine-gun fire and greeted fatal wounds with a light 'ouch', before shaking their arms in spasm and dying with a strangulated 'cheerio!' It is certainly true that those with the most privileged backgrounds often paid the heaviest physical price. And it is also true that some of them displayed remarkable stoicism. When the future Prime Minister Harold Macmillan, then a young lieutenant in the Grenadier Guards, was shot in the thigh after crawling out into no man's land to silence a machine gun, he lay in a shell hole for the best part of a day awaiting rescue, passing the time when he was not unconscious by reading Aeschylus in the original Greek. And what are we to make of the bravado in the face of near-certain death displayed by Household Cavalry officers as they advanced at Arras in 1917, singing, humming and whistling the 'Eton Boating Song'? This is behaviour so far beyond the compass of the twenty-first-century mind that it is much easier to snigger than to wonder. A more empathetic way of looking at them would be to recognize that, in the face of utter terror, the human soul seeks what comfort it can find. They were – literally – whistling to keep their spirits up.

In modern Britain, the war is best known to schoolchildren from the verses of poets like Wilfred Owen and Siegfried Sassoon. Their anti-establishment sentiments fit the mood of *our* times, but not of the boys who whistled while doing what they conceived to be their duty. It is useful to recall that Owen's public recognition did not come until well after the end of combat, when it did much to consolidate the assertion that the First World War was stupid, pointless and tragic. It is often forgotten that after their meeting at 'Dottyville' both Owen and Sassoon returned to the front, after which Owen too won a Military Cross for bravery. Owen even wrote a letter home to his 'dearest mother' telling her he had 'fought like an angel'. In his very last letter home – written as he sheltered with his men in the smoky basement of a forester's cottage, he told her he hoped 'you are as warm as I am, soothed in your room as I am here. I am certain you could not be visited by a band of friends half so fine as surround us here.'

Of course, what Lieutenant Owen was enjoying was not the war but the companionship of his platoon. In the short time available to them, the young officers, mostly unmarried and childless, assumed the role of parent, their immediate family being the few dozen men under their command. There must have been officers who were selfish, thoughtless and cowardly. But it is the better ones who strike the most resonant chord. The affection shown by the most impressive of these officers for their men expressed itself in numberless simple ways. One night, for example, Siegfried Sassoon found tea for five of his men who had arrived late in camp. 'Alone I did it,' he wrote in his diary. 'Without my help they would have had none. And I was proud of myself. It is these things, done for five soldiers, that make the war bearable.'

Sometimes the strength of devotion was so strong that the only adequate word for it is 'love'. As R. B. Talbot Kelly made the rounds of his men one evening, with heavy shellfire all around, he 'felt like a mother going round her children's bedrooms in a great thunderstorm, but in this case the thunderstorm was one of explosive and gas, and "mother" was many years younger than many of her "children". Metaphorically I tucked each detachment up in bed, told them they would be all right, and in due course returned to my own niche by the roadside.'

It would be sentimental to claim that these relationships were the start of lifelong friendships – when peace came, most of those serving couldn't wait to cast off their uniforms and return, if they could, to their previous lives. But something changed in British society once all classes had had to endure similar privations alongside one another. Like many of his privileged class, before 1914 Harold Macmillan had known virtually nothing of the personal lives of the sort of men he commanded. Being forced to share the same ghastly conditions created a bond between them that would never otherwise have existed. You can see it in Macmillan's reaction to the tedious task required of all junior officers of censoring his men's letters from the Western Front. As he was introduced to their anxieties and intimacies ('Mother . . . are you on the drink again? Uncle George writes that the children are in a shocking state'), he concluded that 'they have big hearts, these soldiers, and it is a very pathetic task to have to read all their letters home.' He formed a great affection for his men and later in life felt his constituency work one of the most rewarding aspects of being a politician, 'not so very different from the relations between a company officer and his men'.

Towards the end of 1917, worries about the endlessness of the war were growing – Siegfried Sassoon was not alone. H. G. Wells, who in 1914 had talked so chirpily about a 'war to end war', now wondered why 'the waste and killing' continued. The fault lay with the worn-out men in charge, who 'chaffer like happy imbeciles while civilization bleeds to death'. Then at the end of November 1917, a proper meat-eating member of the establishment publicly articulated the case for a negotiated end to the fighting. Henry Charles Keith Petty-Fitzmaurice, the fifth Marquess of Lansdowne, had been Governor General of Canada, Viceroy of India, Secretary of State for War and Foreign Secretary. He had supported the war in 1914, and had lost his youngest son in Flanders later that year. He now wrote a letter for publication in the *Daily Telegraph*. 'We are not going to lose this war,' he said, 'but its prolongation will spell ruin for the civilized world and an infinite addition to the load of human suffering, which already weighs upon it.' It was no sudden conversion. It had been a year since he circulated a similarly melancholy assessment to the cabinet, stressing the terrible losses to the officer corps. The overall supply of recruits for the army was running out, but in particular 'We are slowly but surely killing off the best of the male population of these islands.' It would be generations before the country recovered. And he took aim at the entire war leadership. 'The responsibility of those who needlessly prolong such a war is not less than that of those who needlessly provoke it.'

At the time, the Chief of the Imperial General Staff, Sir William Robertson (the first man to rise from private to field marshal), fired back what must rank as the rudest memo ever delivered to a cabinet. 'There are amongst us a certain number of cranks, cowards, and philosophers, some of whom are afraid of their own skins being hurt,' it began. Since then there had been a fourth –

and fruitless – 'summer offensive'. With publication of his letter in the *Telegraph*, Lansdowne was again monstered, this time by most of the press, as were the small number of people and organizations, such as the anti-war Union of Democratic Control, which supported him. Lord Northcliffe told the world the old boy had gone soft in the head, and in an editorial headlined 'Foolish and Mischievous' his *Times* heaped disdain: Lord Lansdowne had made himself the most popular man in central Europe, but all over Britain he would be met with 'universal anger and reprobation'. Lansdowne's own party leader, Andrew Bonar Law – who had lost two of his own sons that year – declared that it was 'nothing less than a national misfortune the letter should have been published'.

But Lansdowne's letter was *not* a surrender plan – he wanted to see 'a signal defeat' which would prevent future wars. He imagined an international organization to arbitrate in future disputes, and reassurances to Germany that the allies did not seek to crush the country or redraw the map of Europe. His plans were a great deal more sensible than the punitive terms eventually imposed upon Germany at the war's end, when the allies confused justice with humiliation. Instead of being taken seriously Lansdowne had been elbowed out of government when ministers saw his memo. There was no place in a war cabinet for a man who thought the country should be making peace.

But the problem Lansdowne had identified and now reiterated in his letter to the *Daily Telegraph* was real enough. The country *was* running short of men. In particular, it needed to find a new source of officers, for the public schools alone could not replace the vast number of young commanders being killed. So the War Office was forced to broaden its recruitment and seek out men who had joined as ordinary soldiers, but might now be made officers. Some of those now considered possible 'officer material' were quite unlike their elder mess-mates. When Duff Cooper, later the first Viscount Norwich, left the Foreign Office to join the Grenadier Guards in 1917, he was slightly put out to discover that among his fellow cadets were 'a shoemaker and window-dresser from Sheffield, and a bank clerk with a cockney accent'. These temporary officers – they were serving only for the period of the war – soon became known as 'temporary gentlemen'. The term sounds offensive. But there were some who rather revelled in it: they believed that being a 'temporary gentleman' marked you out from the pre-war regulars, who might have been familiar with how to manage the loyal toast or how to dress for Royal Ascot, but who knew next to nothing about the real world.

Not all attempts to persuade sergeants and corporals to apply for commissions were successful: officer training might take you out of the line for a few months, but at the end of it your life expectancy had been much reduced. Nonetheless, the old class divisions were bending. Before the war, perhaps 2 per cent of officers had served in the ranks. By 1918, it was reckoned that nearly 40 per cent of the officer corps came from lower- and middle-class backgrounds. Sir Douglas Haig boasted at the end of the war that in the new system of promotion on merit, he had found a taxi-driver, a schoolmaster and a lawyer commanding brigades; that 'the under-cook of a Cambridge College, a clerk to the Metropolitan Water Board, an insurance clerk, an architect's assistant, and a police inspector became efficient General Staff Officers', while 'a railway signalman, a coal miner, a market gardener and an assistant secretary to a haberdashers' company' had commanded battalions, and tailors, policemen and blacksmiths had led companies. The prevailing pre-war 'landed' tone of the officer class was succumbing to the cities and suburbs.

There was inevitably some anxiety about whether these new officers knew how to pass the port at dinner, or might eat their peas off their knives. But needs must, and help was readily at hand. A *Times* pamphlet, *The Making of an Officer* published in 1916, warned novices that they were not to spend their time 'motorcycling with females' or turning into 'a kinema creeper, bookworm or bar-loafer'. Some regiments held out against the influx longer than others, but the constant shedding of blood meant that almost a quarter of a million commissions were awarded in the course of the war.

Stuart Cloete, who went on to become a popular novelist, expressed the snobbish bewilderment of the traditional officer class when confronted by some of these new arrivals in the mess. He had joined the army straight from Lancing College. When he returned to his regiment after being seriously wounded in 1916, he discovered that most of his friends were dead, and the officers' mess was peopled by a different sort of person altogether. 'Many of them came from the lower middle-class and had no manners, including table manners, of any kind,' he primly recalled. 'I was profoundly shocked by what I saw and heard. Officers in public places with shop-girls on their knees. The way they talked . . . When my room mate, a captain, said, "I always wash me before I shave me," I felt the bottom of the barrel had been scraped for officer material.'

Machine guns made no distinction between those who ate their peas off their knives and those who didn't, as the British were being constantly reminded. In 1917 and 1918 the newspapers were full of casualty lists, curtains were drawn in industrial terraces, city pavements seethed with women in black dresses. And the wounded were everywhere, on the city streets, at the seaside, around the requisitioned country houses.

There was one particular type of wound that was especially distressing to look upon. Sentries raising their heads to look out into no man's land, men advancing into machine-gun bullets, an unlucky hit from a trench mortar or a fire in a ship or plane, trench or tank, above all the flying shrapnel from exploding artillery – there were multiple opportunities to acquire some of the worst wounds of all. The dead would later be memorialized. The disfigured, who had lost their noses, mouths or jaws, whose faces had perhaps been almost entirely blasted away, lived on as walking gargoyles. It is impossible to exaggerate the horror of many of these wounds. Quite apart from the physical consequences – a smashed face or missing jaw condemned a man to sucking his food through a straw for the rest of his life – there was the awful emotional cost. The wife or mother who had waited anxiously for your return blanched when she saw you. Your children might well flee in terror. Those twenty-first-century consumers whose vanity drives them to make plastic surgeons rich might care to reflect on the origins of the procedures they embark upon so casually.

For men who found themselves shipped back to Britain with their nose, jaw or forehead missing it was a rather more serious issue. Pilots and seamen had often been so badly burned that their faces had melted. There were casualties from the trenches with half their heads missing yet who somehow lived on. Records show that while about 41,000 men had limbs amputated, over 60,000 suffered head or eye injuries. A man without an arm is a man without an arm. A man without a face is man without an identity. Harold Gillies, the surgeon who did more than almost anyone else to have the treatment of these soldiers taken seriously, gave some indication of the gravity of these injuries when he described the casualties referred to him after the first day of the battle of the Somme as 'Men without half their faces; men burned and maimed to the condition of animals'. He had been warned beforehand that there would be extra casualties arriving from this first day of the big offensive, and expected perhaps 200. Two thousand arrived.

Harold Gillies was a remarkable man, who had rowed for Cambridge in the 1904 Boat Race, played golf for England, painted well and was a master of the delicately cast dry fly. When the war began, he had been working as a surgeon in London. The fighting had required the medical profession to learn fast how to save more lives, and there had been huge advances in battlefield first aid, antiseptics, anaesthesia and orthopaedic surgery. The key medical discovery, to which thousands owed their lives, was mundane – the recognition of the importance of 'wound excision', or the cutting away of all dead tissue and the extraction of debris, to prevent tetanus and gas gangrene. But in the heat of battle a wound to a face could be treated no differently from a wound to leg or arm or torso. Military surgeons who tried to patch up the injured did so by sewing the sides of a wound together, leaving a shorter or narrower limb. The man who had lost his nose remained without a nose, with his skin knitting into a horrible scar.

The men who survived these wounds lived with them for the rest of their lives. 'Hideous is the only word for these smashed faces,' one orderly thought. 'The socket with some twisted, moist slit, with a lash or two adhering feebly, which is all that is traceable of the forfeited eye; the skewed mouth which sometimes – in spite of brilliant dentistry contrivances – results from the loss of a segment of jaw.' There was little that could be done for some of the wounded: a nurse observed that 'it is not so hard to see a man die as to break the news to him that he will be blind and dumb for the rest of his life. [It] was something we had to do so often in that silent ward where only one in every ten patients could mumble a few words from the shattered jaws.' Depression was inevitable among the more gruesomely deformed. Nurses became accustomed to hearing men scream 'Kill me! Kill me!' On the wards where the serious cases were treated – known within the hospitals as 'chambers of horrors' – there were no mirrors and very, very few visitors. The one consolation for severely disfigured men was the thought that there was little chance they'd ever be returned to active service – the awful warning they presented to other soldiers was far too damaging to morale. Disfigured men who returned to civilian life in villages and towns across the land kept themselves hidden away: it was preferable to seeing the revulsion on the faces of those who caught sight of them. Becoming a cinema projectionist was the ideal job. The British respected their war dead, but they preferred to be unaware of this particular group of walking wounded.

Gillies determined to do what he could to repair the long-term damage. By late 1915 he had persuaded the army to let him establish his own specialist unit at a military hospital in Aldershot. It was gruelling work at the boundaries of medical science – operation after operation requiring endless stamina from both doctor and patient. But Gillies did not seem to know the meaning of the word 'impossible', and developed innovative technique after innovative technique. An admiring nurse described how 'He would set to work on some man who had had half his face literally blown to pieces with the skin left hanging in shreds, and the jaw-bones crushed to pulp that felt like sand under your fingers. And he would start slowly building up, grafting on a portion of bone taken from the patient's own rib here, padding over the torn flesh and muscles there, waiting until it healed sufficiently to have new skin grafted over it.' It was a slow and gradual process taking bones and cartilage from elsewhere in the body and grafting them on to the face. The process of creating a nose, for example, might take years, and at any stage infection could mean starting the whole thing again: antibiotics had not yet been developed. His patients came to feel a deep affection for the man who offered them the chance of readmission to the world, and the feeling was reciprocated: when a patient died, Gillies could be found weeping.

By the summer of 1917, a specialist hospital had been established in a former stately home at Sidcup in Kent, with over a thousand beds in huts in the grounds and private houses near by to accommodate the wounded men. Here, Gillies gathered together a team of surgeons from around the world. 'Always look a man straight in the face' was the advice given to new nurses at the clinic. 'Remember, he's watching you to see how you're going to react.' Civilians were weaker and less considerate: in the parks of Sidcup, benches for Gillies' patients were painted a distinct shade of blue, to warn local people of the horrific sights they might see if they chanced to look at the men sitting on them. Fifty miles away, in Burnham-on-Crouch, where there was a large convalescent home, people actually wrote to the matron, asking her to keep her patients indoors because the sight of damaged men was unendurable.

But how to decide which face to give a man chosen as suitable for surgery? One of Gillies' grateful patients recalled the surgeon breezing in on the day his nose was to be rebuilt and asking, 'Well, Paddy, your big day is here. What sort of nose do you think we ought to give you?' His patient replied, 'I'm not fussy, sir,' and they settled on a Roman nose to balance the man's round face. In other cases there were family photos to work from. And in a number of cases men who were less than confident about their pre-war looks presented pictures of other people altogether, Rupert Brooke, the pin-up of the age, being quite a popular choice. Surgery left angry scars on the face, and the swelling which followed might leave a man with something like an anteater's snout. Very few indeed were returned to their former appearance.

Those whose injuries were too dreadful to be repaired could be fitted instead with masks. In early 1916 Gillies had heard from a golfing friend that Henry Tonks, an assistant professor at the Slade School of Art, was spending the war as a lieutenant in the Royal Army Medical Corps. Gillies sought him out to make sketches of the disfigured men he was treating. He found a tall, beaky middle-aged man looking rather like 'the Duke of Wellington reduced to subaltern's rank'. Tonks in turn recommended a former pupil, Kathleen Scott (widow of the polar explorer Captain Robert Falcon Scott), to superintend the modelling of masks for the most badly damaged men. She was able to see beauty where most people shuddered, remarking of a drawing she had done that 'a young fellow with rather a classical face was exactly like a living damaged Greek head as his nose had been blown clean off.' Hers was very much a minority view.

Remaking these faces gave people who had no obvious military role a chance to play their part in the war. The sculptor Francis Derwent Wood, who was in his early forties and too old to join up when war broke out, had also managed to get into the Royal Army Medical Corps in 1915. Wood was accustomed to designing monuments to industrialists, generals and monarchs. Men in hospital wards from which mirrors were banned were almost the complete opposite. But now, in a section of the Third London General Hospital which the soldiers soon nicknamed the 'Tin Noses Shop', he began designing copper facemasks to cover the damage. After smothering the face in plaster of Paris to get a mould, Wood set about creating a metal mask, as near as possible to the photograph he had been given. Eyelashes and facial hair were made from slivers of metal foil, and spectacles, which anchored the device to the face, were soldered to the bridge of the mask's nose. For men who had lost their upper lip, a false moustache was hung below the metal nose. The mask was then enamelled in skin tones that might look vaguely natural. An orderly on one of the wards where the work was done claimed that the only difference friends of the wounded man would notice was that he had started wearing glasses and that 'he occasionally squints.' The final product, about the thickness of a visiting card, resembled the sort of thing that might be worn at a fancy-dress ball.

The masks were weird to look at and horrible to wear. They neither smiled nor scowled, and they did not age. They also got chipped. Francis Derwent Wood claimed that his masks enabled disfigured soldiers to regain their self-respect and self-reliance. But some soldiers left hospital with their masks and put them straight back in their boxes as soon as they were out of his sight.

By the age of ten, a schoolchild might have seen more damaged bodies than a twenty-first-century adult could ever expect to see. Before the First World War they might have caught an occasional glimpse of a maimed veteran of an imperial war tramping the roads or lining up for admission to the casual ward of a work-house. Now mangled bodies were a fact of life. And they told a very different story to the one the public had been shown in *The Battle of the Somme*.

13. At Last

Captured German guns become a playground in St James's.

In the spring of 1918, a member of parliament claimed to have discovered why the war was dragging on for so long. The whole thing was being sabotaged by hordes of sexual deviants.

Noel Pemberton Billing, a gangling, monocled self-publicist, drove around in a yellow Rolls-Royce, proclaiming his devotion to 'fast aircraft, fast speedboats, fast cars and fast women'. In December 1917, the newspaper he had founded, the *Imperialist*, claimed the Germans were corrupting the youth of Britain by introducing upstanding young British soldiers to the 'vices of the Cities of the Plain', in which 'Palestine taught nothing to Potsdam.' For it was a well-known fact that German subterfuge was controlled by degenerate homosexuals, or 'urnings'.*

---

* The term had apparently been coined by a German advocate of gay rights.

In the following edition, under the headline 'THE FIRST 47,000', Pemberton Billing claimed that enemy agents had traversed the country spreading practices 'which all decent men thought had perished in Sodom and Lesbia'. Sailors had been particularly targeted, but so had many others – 'Privy Councillors, wives of Cabinet Ministers, even Cabinet Ministers themselves, diplomats, poets, bankers, editors, newspaper proprietors, and members of His Majesty's Household'. The wives of senior public figures were a special risk, for 'in lesbian ecstasy the most sacred secrets of state were betrayed.'

The source for this lurid fantasy appears to have been a Captain Harold Spencer, who had been invalided out of military intelligence a couple of months earlier, on grounds of 'delusional insanity'. In February 1918 Pemberton Billing returned to the subject. Under the headline 'THE CULT OF THE CLITORIS', he disclosed that the exotic dancer Maud Allan was performing at an invitation-only production of Oscar Wilde's play *Salome*, public performances of which had been banned in Britain for several years. (Miss Allan had achieved some notoriety before the war with her interpretation of the title character in Wilde's play, since she performed the role wearing very little.) If the police were merely to get hold of the list of those who had applied for tickets, they could begin to break down the vast network of men and women who had been corrupted by filthy German urnings.

Then the discharged intelligence officer – recently appointed Pemberton Billing's assistant editor – published his belief that the voluptuous dancer was having an affair with Margot Asquith, wife of the former Prime Minister. The actress sued.

The libel case was a newspaperman's dream – an exotic dancer, enemy spies, sexual deviancy, compromised government ministers and a massive conspiracy to explain why the great patriotic efforts of British forces seemed to be achieving so little. Pemberton Billing opted to conduct his own defence. The public gallery was packed with wounded soldiers in their blue hospital uniforms. The judge chosen for the case, a Mr Justice Darling, was a Conservative party hack with a tiresome weakness for pompous legal jokes – there could hardly have been a judge in England less suited to preside over a case so pregnant with absurdity. The audience was particularly entertained when Pemberton Billing cross-examined a woman named Eileen Villiers-Stuart, who claimed she had been shown the Black Book of suspected enemy agents by a couple of army officers. Suddenly, Pemberton Billing banged the table in front of him, pointed at the judge and screamed, 'Is Mr Justice Darling's name in the book?'

'It is!' she shouted back confidently.

'Is Mrs Asquith's name in the book?' Pemberton Billing asked.

'It is,' she answered.

'Is *Mr* Asquith's name in the book?'

'It is.'

The overwhelmed judge attempted to order Villiers-Stuart from the witness box, but not before she had named other prominent politicians, including the German-speaking Lord Haldane, a long-standing target for conspiracists. With the court feverishly anticipating further sensation, Pemberton Billing called his next witness. This was Harold Spencer, the loopy former intelligence officer, whom he would soon sponsor to stand in a by-election as the 'Intern Them All' candidate. Spencer asserted that 'if a German agent is instructed to practise sodomy by his chief, he probably does,' whether he had a taste for the habit or not. Such agents were then assigned to loiter in the public bath-houses and pubs of England. He believed that a scandalous play like *Salome* could have an awful effect upon its audience, especially women, who were likely to be driven crazy by its sexual undercurrents, especially since, the court was told, 'an exaggerated clitoris' might even drive a woman to a bull elephant.

The elephant played no further part in court proceedings, although further witnesses of a similar level of credibility processed into the witness box. At last, Pemberton Billing delivered his final address to the jury. 'The Hidden Hand' was preventing proper management of the war, while sleazy theatrical productions like *Salome* depraved and corrupted the people. 'Do you think', he roared, 'I am going to keep quiet whilst nine men die in a minute to make a sodomite's holiday?' Billing was acquitted, leaving the court to thunderous cheers, with members of the crowd scattering flowers at his feet as he walked out of the Old Bailey down the street. Three months later, Eileen Villiers-Stuart was convicted of bigamy, and admitted that her evidence at the trial had been completely invented.

It was a very silly interlude whose only function had been to brighten the generally dour landscape. The story satisfied the British taste for salacious court cases – especially featuring people in high places with low appetites – and their readiness to think the worst of figures who presumed to consider themselves their betters. It also offered an answer, however ridiculous, to the important question being asked everywhere: why was the fighting going on for so long?

People all around were losing confidence in the management of the war. In December 1917 Lord Northcliffe had stopped short of publicly demanding the head of the commander of British forces on the Western Front, but he had called for 'the prompt removal of every blunderer on his staff'. When Haig's private secretary wrote to Northcliffe the next day, seeking a vote of confidence, the newspaper magnate replied that every household in the land had a memory of a dead man or the knowledge of one who was wounded or missing, and 'I doubt whether the Higher Command has any supporters whatever.' There was some consolation in knowing that Germany was in a terrible state and running out of men, as well as being short of food as a consequence of the Royal Navy's blockade. Britain, on the other hand, had survived the threat of starvation by U-boat. And there was now the prospect of massive reinforcement from the United States. But Haig was much less confident about the state of his own forces, which had been ground down by years of ceaseless combat. They were now facing an enemy that was negotiating a peace with Russia, a development which would soon enable it to transfer vast numbers of men from the Eastern to the Western Front.

In January 1918, the wealthy Conservative Lord Derby bet Lloyd George 100 cigars to 100 cigarettes that the fighting would be over within the year. Derby had been Lloyd George's co-conspirator in the putsch that had unseated Asquith and had been rewarded by replacing Lloyd George himself as War Secretary. But it cannot have been a very serious bet, more a triumph of hope over form. For it was clear from Lloyd George's actions that he saw no early end in sight. Like Northcliffe, he was disillusioned with the generals on the Western Front. His friend and patron, the wealthy newspaper proprietor Sir George Riddell, thought it significant that in September 1917 Lloyd George had 'been reading Macaulay's essay on Clive – perhaps the greatest of all generals not trained in a military school'. In 1914 there had been people who believed that the thing might be over by Christmas. Now, the Prime Minister feared that it would last until after Christmas 1918. Perhaps well after.

If, as Lloyd George believed, victory could be achieved only by prolonged pressure on the enemy – rather than by some ingenious new attack on the Western Front – priorities would have to change. The big challenge facing the country was to avoid starvation, protect itself from air raids and gather its strength. Such manpower as could be found would be needed in the shipyards and aircraft factories, in the navy and air force, instead of meeting the generals' constant demands for more soldiers. The conclusion of the cabinet committee wrestling with the problem of finding men was that 'the staying power of the Allies must be safeguarded until such time as the increase in the American forces restores the balance of superiority decisively in their favour.' Lloyd George had made as much as he could of General Allenby's capture of Jerusalem just before Christmas 1917, and hoped for more romantic-sounding victories from the expeditionary force fighting the Ottoman empire in the Middle East, but the grim reality was clear to everyone:

from now on all they could hope to do was hold the line on the Western Front, fight defensively and stick it out, either until help arrived or their enemies gave up. But how much longer could the British public keep faith with the war? When the Prime Minister went to speak to a trades union gathering, he concentrated on the nobility of the war aims, claiming that 'It is only the clearest, greatest and justest of causes that can justify the continuance for even one day of this unspeakable agony of the nations.' It was a characteristically passionate performance. But it had a slightly desperate edge to it.

The important thing was to endure. On Easter Sunday 1918 the Bishop of London took to the pulpit of St Paul's Cathedral to preach from the text 'Thanks be to God who giveth us the victory through Our Lord Jesus Christ.' Divine duty demanded another 30,000 women volunteers for work on the land. 'It is impossible', said the Bishop, 'that to the hand red with the blood of so many victims should be finally entrusted the domination of the world.' But in another sermon at the cathedral that day the Dean, William Inge, had acknowledged the burden of bereavement which lay on so many. His advice was not to parade loss, but to recognize that 'it is not of great moment whether God calls us in youth, in middle age or in old age.' More worldly figures recognized that the substantial numbers of American troops being shipped to Europe might also have something to do with the outcome.

With their arrival, though, came other moral concerns. In 1918, the editor of the American *Ladies' Home Journal*, on a visit to London sponsored by the British government, was appalled to discover that innocent young Americans were being openly solicited 'not only by prostitutes, but by scores of amateur girls' on the streets, in hotel lobbies, in bars and in restaurants. 'If the American woman knew what was going on here in the streets of London, there would be an outcry,' he wrote, begging the British government to stamp it out. It was a familiar anxiety. Pemberton Billing had warned of hordes of prostitutes on the continent, infected with venereal disease (by the Germans, of course), laying low the flower of the empire's manhood. When soldiers came home on leave from the front, with time on their hands and money in their pockets, there were inevitable consequences, and it was leading to a big health problem. Back in 1917, Sir Arthur Conan Doyle had written to *The Times* to warn readers of the squadrons of 'vile women' who 'prey upon and poison our soldiers in London', luring men to their rooms in 'harlot-haunted' parts of the capital, plying them with drink, and leaving them with a dose of disease. It appeared that American soldiers in London en route to the fighting were an especially vulnerable group.

Part of the reason for the spread of sexually transmitted diseases during the war had been the popularity of quack remedies. But it was not only personal embarrassment that made the promise of a discreetly obtained 'cure' so popular and lucrative. Apart from the financial penalties levied on a soldier deemed to have been admitted to hospital 'through his own fault', there was the rumour that conditions in the sections of base hospitals dedicated to treating such diseases were as bad as prison, and sometimes worse than life in the trenches. And public opinion at home would not countenance the provision of condoms: the answer was restraint. No wonder, then, that between August 1914 and November 1918 over 400,000 men were treated for VD.

At the time, no one knew precisely how widespread the disease actually was, but by 1918 it was claimed during a parliamentary debate that in England alone – ignoring the military hospitals in France – there might be the equivalent of a division of soldiers – about 15,000 men – suffering from syphilis or gonorrhoea. Some had evidently picked up the disease in continental brothels, but it was believed that about half of the infections had been caught while men were in Britain on leave or training. The Canadian-born Colonel Sir Hamar Greenwood, who had commanded a battalion on the Western Front, had already told parliament of numerous conversations he had had with the parents of young Canadian soldiers. 'We do not mind our boys dying on the field of battle for old England, but to think that we sent our sons to England to come back to us ruined in health, and a disgrace to us, to them, and to the country is something that the Home Country should never ask us to bear.' Part of the reason for the much higher level of infection among Canadian soldiers, over one-fifth of whom were said to have been infected in 1915, was that they were often paid five times more than British soldiers: the greatest protection for the Tommy was not so much the strength of his convictions as the thinness of his wallet.

In his letter to *The Times* Conan Doyle had worried about how Britain would explain to the colonies who offered their young men for the war why it was returning them with a sexually transmitted disease. Like many others, he did not see the men as exploiting women, but as defenceless victims: they were being assaulted by poisonous predators so intent on their prey that they would, in some instances, prise open the windows of buildings in which soldiers tried to shelter. He proposed that 'these women are the enemies of the country. They should be treated as such' and interned until six months after the end of the war. In March 1918, yet another regulation was incorporated into the Defence of the Realm Act, making it an offence for a woman suffering from VD to have sex with a soldier – even if the soldier in question was her husband, and even if he had given her the infection in the first place.

The US troops could hardly have arrived too soon. That spring, the Germans decided to launch a drastic offensive: one last heave before the economy at home collapsed, army morale imploded and reinforcements from the US gave the allies advantage of numbers. Between March and July 1918, Erich Ludendorff, probably Germany's most determined general, launched five great attacks to drive a wedge between the British and French armies, and to crush the British once and for all: he believed that, once the British had been defeated, the French would give up and sue for peace. It was the biggest artillery bombardment in the entire war and it very nearly succeeded.

The *Kaiserschlacht*, or Kaiser's battle, began at 4.40 on the morning of 21 March with an enormous bombardment by over 6,000 guns on the Somme battlefield in northern France. The shells fell as much on British headquarters and communication centres behind the front line as they did on the trenches. The plan was to destroy any possibility of counter-attack before the infantry arrived and was one of the techniques the Germans had developed to powerful effect while fighting the Russians on the Eastern Front. A British machine-gunner felt that 'the bowels of the earth had erupted, while beyond the ridge there was one long and continuous yellow flash. It was the suddenness of the thing that struck me most, there being no preliminary shelling but just one vast momentary upheaval.' The German guns fired well over a million shells in five hours. Five minutes after the bombardment stopped, at 9.40, thirty divisions of German soldiers poured out of the mist across 50 miles of front line. They were supported by another thirty divisions – the British were outnumbered three to one. In a single day the German forces took more ground than the allies had gained in twenty weeks in the same area. The retreat which followed was as bad a reverse as the British army suffered in the whole war – as bad, many felt, as any in its entire history.

But the Germans now became the victims of their own success, with the attacking soldiers soon far ahead of their supplies and blundering about in trenches and fortifications built by the allies. On 9 April they launched a second offensive further north, again intending to reach the Channel. This time much of the attack fell on a part of the allied line being held by exhausted and largely officerless Portuguese soldiers. Having suffered heavy losses, many of them ran away, obliging British forces alongside them to withdraw several miles. Britain now faced the real possibility of German troops on the shores of the Channel. On 11 April Haig issued the most famous order of the entire war. 'There is no course open to us but to fight it out. Every position must be held to the last man: there must be no retirement. With our backs to the wall and believing in the justice of our cause each one of us must fight on to the end. The safety of our homes and the Freedom of mankind alike depend upon the conduct of each one of us at this critical moment.'

It was a cliff-edge moment, which caused a deep shift in feeling at home. Before the German spring offensive began there had been strike and industrial dispute after strike and industrial dispute, as trades unions protested at increasingly frantic attempts to 'comb out' men for the front from what had previously been deemed (not least by the unions) occupations vital to the war effort. Now, staring defeat in the face, the number of strikes plummeted, men returned to work in the mines and factories, and production soared. Class and union solidarity was supplanted by patriotic solidarity. The previous November half a million days of work had been lost to strikes. In April 1918 the total dropped to 15,000. When the government appealed for people to work over the Easter-holiday weekend the response was, said Winston Churchill, now Minister of Munitions, 'excellent, and indeed almost embarrassing'.

At the front, after some frantic combat, and with the help of French reinforcements, the German attack was held back. The fighting in this great German offensive was as intense as any at either the Somme or Passchendaele, with the British suffering over a quarter of a million casualties, the French more than 100,000 and the Germans over 320,000 in under six weeks. But the Germans then followed up their offensive with further attacks designed to open the way to Paris. Again the assault began with an intense artillery bombardment, firing 2 million shells in just over four hours, and then sending in great waves of infantry. And again the Germans broke through, now to within 40 miles of Paris. As refugees streamed out of the city the British cabinet met to decide whether to evacuate the British Expeditionary Force altogether.

At the last minute, though, the German offensive faltered, partly because of an effective counter-attack by French and recently arrived American troops, and partly – as had happened in previous attacks – because the underfed German soldiers found the sight of food and drink in French towns and at British bases irresistible. Even elite infantry divisions paused to gorge themselves.

'Now we are already in the English back areas, or at least rest-areas, a land flowing with milk and honey,' a German lieutenant exclaimed after breaking through the front line.

> Marvellous people these, who will only equip themselves with the very best that the earth produces. Our men are hardly to be distinguished from English soldiers. Everyone wears at least a leather jerkin, a waterproof either short or long, English boots or some other beautiful thing. The horses are feasting on masses of oats and gorgeous food-cake. Cows, calves, and pigs find their way unobtrusively out of farmyards into the field-kitchen, and there is no doubt the army is looting with some zest.

There were German units now advancing with soldiers carrying chickens under their arms. Others drove cattle in front of them. When an Australian brigade counter-attacked near Amiens they found German soldiers 'drunk as owls' on the floor of a winery. They were dragged out by their feet and woke up imprisoned.

The German offensive won them ten times the amount of land taken by the allies in the whole of 1917. But it had cost them almost a million casualties. The Germans were spent.

The allies, on the other hand, were at last receiving vast reinforcements. As spring gave way to summer, American soldiers poured into Europe in ever larger numbers: at the end of March 1918 there had been fewer than 300,000 of them; by November that year, the figure would be nearly 2 million – a slightly bigger total than the new level of the British Expeditionary Force, which had itself been bolstered by the 350,000 more men 'combed out' and sent to France that spring. In the German army, by contrast, there were battalions of a notional thousand soldiers who could now muster only a couple of hundred gaunt, hungry, exhausted men in filthy uniforms. Crucially, the long transformation of the British economy into one devoted almost entirely to the war effort was all but complete. The French were manufacturing aircraft in great numbers – all told, the allies now had four times as many aircraft as the Germans possessed – enough to drown out the sound of the hundreds of tanks now being manoeuvred into position for a surprise counter-attack. British artillery was now also well supplied with shells, and was more accurate in its fire than its German counterpart. That summer, the allies fell on the Germans to devastating effect.

When British and empire forces struck at Amiens in early August, they achieved near-total surprise. Past experience had taught them how to integrate tanks and infantry in an attack: the tanks, over 500 of them, advanced en masse, with the infantry following directly behind. Nearly 2,000 aircraft supported the attack, shooting down enemy planes, providing intelligence and bombing German aerodromes. The artillery that supported them was not only more plentiful, it was much better employed. Scientific advances like 'flash spotting' (taking visual bearings) and 'sound ranging' (audible bearings) enabled gunners to locate the big German guns on the battlefield, and aerial reconnaissance had provided detailed maps – as a result, British artillerymen no longer had to fire lots of shells to get an accurate range by trial and error. German soldiers stumbled out of their trenches with their hands in the air, shouting 'Kamerad!' The German army's official history described it as the worst defeat of the war.

The week after the battle at Amiens the Kaiser summoned his senior generals to the little resort town of Spa in the Ardennes forest of Belgium. The town was best known to the outside world for its warm springs and the ornate hotels, promenades and casino for the entertainment of those who were visiting them. Here, in anticipation of victory in the spring offensive, the Kaiser had installed himself in an elaborate residence overlooking the German Supreme Headquarters, which was ensconced in the art deco splendour of the Hôtel Britannique. The assessment delivered here that August was bleak. After the Amiens disaster, Hindenburg and Ludendorff judged that Germany could not now win the war. To retain any dignity at all, the country would have to ask for an armistice. Yet it could make what was deemed an acceptable peace only by convincing the allies that it was still a mighty power. The decision was taken that, before trying to end the war, there would have to be another German victory on the battlefield. This was growing less likely by the day.

The allied advance rolled on. It was not a uniform picture, with German resistance much stronger in some areas than in others, and some of the allied soldiers getting so far ahead of their supply chain that they could not be fed properly. Yet the war was no longer a struggle between forces which were roughly equal – Germany was exhausted and enfeebled, the allies were bolstered and buoyant. There was no mistaking the relief that the tide seemed to have turned. The German army was not only taking heavy casualties, it was suffering from a serious absentee problem, and at home political dissent was spreading fast. The biggest obstacle in the way of the allied advance into Germany itself would be the line of massive fortifications running across northern France, nicknamed the 'Hindenburg Line', after the Germans' magnificently moustached veteran Field Marshal Paul von Hindenburg. This was a mass of deep trenches, concrete bunkers, barbed wire and machine-gun nests extending to a width of some 6,000 yards. It was intended to be impregnable: the fortifications even incorporated part of the Saint-Quentin canal, a 60-mile waterway running roughly south from Cambrai. At the end of September, employing their hard-learned expertise in industrial warfare, the allies attacked.

Initial assaults by American and Australian troops were fought off. But on 29 September the British unleashed a ferocious artillery bombardment on the section of the Hindenburg Line where the Germans had least expected an attack – the Saint-Quentin canal. In the space of twenty-four hours they fired almost a million shells. Here, in an audacious attack, men of the North Staffordshire Regiment seized a bridge across the canal moments before the Germans could detonate explosives to bring it down. Trench warfare was over: from now on, British and empire, French and American soldiers were on the attack, with the Germans fighting a series of rearguard actions as they retreated. At times they were falling back so fast that allied soldiers found it hard to keep up with them. At the end of September, facing catastrophe, the immensely stressed Ludendorff suffered some of sort of breakdown and decided that Germany must seek peace.

Workers in British factories did not know the thoughts of the German high command – and might not have believed any newspaper which claimed to know them anyway. What is strange is that the more successful the British army seemed to be on the battlefield, the less the industrial activists at home were inclined to stifle their discontent. In theory, strikes had been made illegal by the Defence of the Realm Act. In practice, there was nothing much the government could do when workers walked out. In the spring – when disaster seemed to loom – trades unionists had been willing to rein in their discontent. But July saw unrest in munitions factories and electrical companies. This was soon followed by strikes in coal mines, in cotton mills and on the railways. The Minister of Munitions, Winston Churchill, blamed militant 'pacifists and subversive elements of the labour world'. While there was opposition in some industries to government calls for manpower, in truth the reasons for unrest were often more domestic and mundane – anger at the rules being laid down about who worked where, and demands for better pay and working conditions and for bargaining rights.

Even the Metropolitan Police went on strike. That August a column of singing policemen tramped behind a piper through the centre of London, demanding a higher war bonus and formal recognition of their trade union. Although the *Morning Post* considered they should be treated like deserters in the army, the police had enlisted a good deal of sympathy. Noel Pemberton Billing advised them to get any agreement with the government in writing, because they were dealing with 'some of the biggest political crooks in history', and even Northcliffe's *Times* thought they were entitled to a fair hearing.

The police strike was a good-natured affair, and it did not last for long. A few soldiers were placed in Downing Street (striking policemen held their rifles for them as they clambered out of their lorries), and a machine-gun post was set up in the Foreign Office courtyard next door, but as talks with the government went on inside Number 10 a message was sent in to the Prime Minister that the Grenadier Guardsmen on duty had made it plain that they were not inclined to obey any order to clear the street. Outside, the policemen sang 'Keep the Home Fires Burning'. Inside Lloyd George gave in to almost all of the strikers' demands – on the grounds that 'This country was nearer to Bolshevism that day than at any time since.' He was panicking. But the fear of Bolshevism was everywhere: the Russian revolution of the previous year, in which hundreds of years of monarchy were overthrown, had shown what might happen.

But the German Supreme Command were more alarmed, for they could see the fate of their allies. In September 1918 Bulgaria threw in the towel. The country had been a key link between Germany and its ally, the Ottoman empire, uniting the power bloc that ran from the shores of the North Sea to the Persian Gulf. Bulgaria had conscripted some 900,000 men to fight alongside the Germans and had done much of the dirty work in crushing Serbia in 1915. By now, one-third of those conscripted had been killed or wounded. The soldiers' families were on the point of starvation. Their government signed an armistice with the allies, and the Bulgarian Tsar abdicated. Meanwhile, in the Middle East General Allenby's British, Indian and Australian forces, backed by T. E. Lawrence's Arab irregulars, achieved a stunning victory over Turkish forces and swept on to Beirut, Damascus and Aleppo. This forced the Ottoman empire to sue for peace: Mehmet VI would be the last sultan to rule Turkey. As for Austria-Hungary, many senior German officers had believed for years that their country was 'shackled to a corpse'. Now its dual monarchy and its great prison of nations were at the point of total disintegration.

The Kaiser liked to consider himself made of sterner stuff, but Germany was now exposed, weakened and increasingly riven with dissent. True, German forces were still on foreign soil, but the peace plan tabled by the American President in January, which required the withdrawal of German forces from most captured territory, looked ever more attractive to many members of the Kaiser's government. By November 1918, Germany had had enough.

Around seven in the morning of 8 November, six men walked through the Compiègne forest in northern France. They were led by a stocky, bespectacled figure in a long black coat. This was Matthias Erzberger, the leader of the Catholic party in the German parliament, who had been trying to persuade the government there to make peace since the middle of 1917. He had been chosen to lead a peace delegation to the allies in the hope that his known record of opposition to the war might induce them to be gentler on an almost beaten Germany. The hope was misplaced.

The delegation had crossed no man's land into a French sector of the front under a white flag the previous evening. Now they were taken to a line of railway carriages standing in a siding in the woods. This was the personal train of the French commander, Ferdinand Foch, equipped with an adapted restaurant car of the International Wagons-Lits Company. Here the German delegation would be brought face to face with some of the leaders of the men their forces had spent years trying to kill. The two teams confronted each other across a table.

It was Marshal Foch who spoke for the allied armies. Douglas Haig was not present – Britain's chief representative at the meeting was Admiral Rosslyn Wemyss, accompanied by two other senior naval officers. No other allied nations were represented. Marshal Foch, splendidly moustached, in a long coat and military kepi, and leaning on a stick, was stern. Why had the Germans come to see him? Erzberger said they wanted to hear the allied proposals for an armistice. Foch told him they had no such proposals: if the Germans wanted the fighting to stop, the conditions would be read out to them. Foch's chief of staff, Maxime Weygand, then did so: the Germans would withdraw from France and Belgium and hand over vast quantities of weapons and stores. The

allies would occupy the left bank of the Rhine – territory contested between France and Germany for centuries. The German
delegation blanched: the demands were about as severe as could be
imagined.

The key problem for Germany in accepting these terms lay at
home, where Bolshevism had taken root and a revolution was
gathering strength. In late October, admirals of the German navy
conspired to launch one final attack on the Royal Navy, in a sort
of *Götterdämmerung*. But large numbers of sailors simply refused to
put to sea. Soon, the communist red flag was flying over the naval
base at Kiel. The mutineers were followed by sailors in other bases
along the coast. On 9 November disaffected workers, sailors and
soldiers declared a republic in Berlin. The German delegation
begged Foch to allow their government to retain an army, so that
they could use it to put down the revolution. Foch refused.

The newly appointed Chancellor of Germany, Prince Maximilian
von Baden, had already written to President Wilson, thinking
America was more likely to be generous than nations like France
or Britain, which had been fighting for much longer, and inquir-
ing about a possible peace deal. Baden was well known as a
moderate figure, who had had the courage publicly to oppose the
unrestricted U-boat campaign. Now he had to make a decision
about what should happen to Kaiser Wilhelm II, in whose name
the war had been waged. Though command of the army had actually been in the hands of professionals like Hindenburg and
Ludendorff for years, everyone had seen the disastrous effects of
the Kaiser's bombastic ideas. The man still claimed to carry the
nation in his body and soul, but the politicians at Berlin were
deeply divided about whether the monarchy should be sacrificed
to save the country. More liberal figures felt that relieving him of
his burden was a small price to pay for the sake of peace. After all,
Germany was in the throes of what looked and felt very like a real
revolution, and, critically, the beaten-down army had lost faith in
the Kaiser: Ludendorff's successor, Wilhelm Groener, told the
Kaiser that his troops would not fight to keep him on the throne.

Seeing the terrible state of the country, Prince Max decided that the Kaiser would have to be jettisoned, and telephoned him to say that unless he abdicated Germany would be engulfed in civil war. Until the last moment, the man whose dreams of an imperial destiny for his people had sustained the whole catastrophe, maintained his refusal to countenance giving up. He was eventually worn down: he would agree to surrender the imperial German throne but would remain, he said, King of Prussia. Finally, even this figleaf had to be abandoned. On 10 November 1918, he took a train across the Dutch border and scuttled off into exile where he spent the next two decades waxing his moustache, ranting about the mistakes Germany had made and swearing that England was the home of the anti-Christ.*

The Kaiser's army was still in full retreat, pursued by allied soldiers, great numbers of whom were teenage conscripts. Both armies were exhausted, grimy shadows of their former selves. But morale was understandably high among the British, with the scent of victory in their noses: their greatest problem was still that they were advancing faster than they could be resupplied. As the generals deliberated, the German army was in headlong flight, slowing only to blow up bridges and wreck buildings, roads and railways. Significant numbers of German soldiers were simply vanishing from their units, hoping to make their way home without being caught by the military police. Throughout the night of 10 November Erzberger and his delegation haggled with Foch's team. By five on the morning of the 11th the terms of an armistice had been settled. It would come into force at eleven o'clock that morning, on the 1,568th day of the war.

Lieutenant R. G. Dixon of the Royal Garrison Artillery reflected on what it meant:

---

* In years to come, a belief would take hold in Germany that somehow the country had been betrayed by a governing elite, that the army had never really been defeated in the war. Erich Ludendorff was one of the most assiduous promoters of this idea, which the Nazis eagerly seized upon, arguing that if only they could have their way, Germany could be great again.

No more slaughter, no more maiming, no more mud and blood and no more killing and disembowelling of horses and mules – which was what I found most difficult to bear. No more of those hopeless dawns with the rain chilling the spirits, no more crouching in inadequate dug-outs scooped out of trench walls, no more dodging of snipers' bullets, no more of that terrible shell-fire. No more shovelling up bits of men's bodies and dumping them into sandbags; no more cries of 'Stretcher-bear-ERS!', and no more of those beastly gas-masks and the odious smell of pear-drops which was deadly to the lungs, and no more writing of those dreadfully difficult letters to the next-of-kin of the dead . . . The whole vast business of the war was finished. It was over.

Along the new front lines that evening, there occurred one of the great firework displays of history, as each side fired off the rockets they would now never need. After that, the oddest thing of all was the noise. For the first time in years, there was none.

At 11 a.m. on 11 November in London, firework flares normally used to warn of air attacks were fired into the sky. They sounded, said the *Manchester Guardian*, 'like a huge cockney chuckle of delight'. The Prime Minister appeared at the door of 10 Downing Street. He seemed overwhelmed by the occasion for a few moments, then declared, 'We have won a great victory and we are entitled to a bit of shouting.' Children were given the remainder of the day off school and excused homework for the rest of the week. The boy buglers who had run about the streets warning of air raids sounded endless all-clears. Tugboats on the rivers and trams on the streets tooted their horns. Legions of hawkers emerged from nowhere selling miniature Union flags. Lloyd George made another public appearance, this time at an upper window in Downing Street* accompanied by Bonar Law and Churchill. He hushed the crowd's cheering and told them they had been part of

* There was public access to Downing Street until a set of gates was installed during Margaret Thatcher's tenancy in 1989.

a victory unlike any ever seen. 'You have all had a share in it,' he said. 'Sons and daughters of the people have done it, and this is their hour for rejoicing.' A bus passed through central London marked 'Free to Berlin', but conductors everywhere had given up thought of collecting fares on any journeys. The House of Commons adjourned to give thanks at St Margaret's church. Crowds crammed Trafalgar Square, many of them singing 'Auld Lang Syne'. A group of Australian soldiers tore down hoardings that encouraged people to buy war bonds and started a bonfire at the foot of Nelson's Column. Groups of girls gathered in circles, dancing. Singing crowds swayed down the Strand and Whitehall. Even the dogs were swathed in red, white and blue.

It drizzled that evening, but the celebrating continued. Searchlights played across the sky, not searching for bombers or Zeppelins, but just for the hell of it. For the first time in years, the street lamps were illuminated. At theatres and on the streets people burst into 'God Save the King', 'Rule Britannia' or 'Land of Hope and Glory'. The minor writer Osbert Sitwell thought, 'The last occasion I had seen the London crowd was when it had cheered for its own death outside Buckingham Palace on the evening of the 4th of August 1914; most of the men who had composed it were now dead. Their heirs were dancing because life had been given back to them.'

A couple of weeks later a great victory parade was planned through London, to which Lloyd George invited Marshal Foch and the French and Italian Prime Ministers. When Haig discovered that instead of being at the head of the parade he was to be in the fifth carriage of the procession he could hardly contain his anger. He had put up with Lloyd George's conceit for years and endured all of his boasting and questionable decision-making, not least in having made Marshal Foch Commander in Chief of the allied forces while diverting much needed soldiers to sideshows in the Middle East and elsewhere. 'Now, the British Army has won the war in France in spite of LG and I have no intention of taking part in any triumphal ride with Foch and a pack of foreigners, merely to add to LG's importance and help him in his election campaign,' he told his diary. He noted that the parade was to finish with a reception at the French embassy, to which he had not been invited. Later he wrote to the king's private secretary about the 'impertinent message' he had received about the victory parade 'with a lot of foreigners'. On a Sunday, too. 'As you know,' he added, 'I hate ovations and nothing will induce me to receive a welcome (as C-in-C of the King's Forces in France) in combination with a pack of foreigners. The welcome must be purely British.' It may have been a *world* war. But there were limits.

14. After the Eleventh Hour

'Give us a job!'

It was over. Lieutenant Dixon had been crossing the Channel on leave when the news hit him. His boat had left the French coast while Britain was at war. As he approached Folkestone, the harbour exploded with siren toots from the vessels moored there, and cheering and waving from the quayside. His captain turned to him. 'Dickie,' he said, 'the bloody war's over! It's over!' As the lieutenant filled in the forms of disembarkation, a strange thought struck him, a counterpart to the horrible memories of dead and mutilated men, the incessant noise, fear and discomfort. He had a future to look forward to. It was not something he had thought about for years. He remarked to Captain Brown, a man of about forty, on the novelty of having a life to plan. The captain smiled and said, 'Yes. You've got a future now, Dickie. And so have I.

I wonder what we'll do with it, and what it will be like – because, you know, things are not going to be the same as they were.'

What *was* this new world to be like? Everyone would need to use their imagination. Britain itself had suffered little physical damage. But it had undergone a terrible trauma. Recreating a peaceable nation, dismantling the wartime economy, allowing men and women to resume the lives that the war had utterly disrupted would require determination, vision and courage. The essential choice was either to imagine a future or to try to reinvent a past. Dozens of wartime letters and diaries testify to a passionate desire in the darkest days of combat for the long summer of peace to resume, when the clock stood at ten to three and there was always honey still for tea. The fighting had gone on so long, had killed or maimed so many and had changed the country so much that it was very hard to see quite how the land of lost content could ever be rediscovered. The war had destroyed the map showing the way back. So the politicians' promises were of a new Britain, of 'homes fit for heroes' and of an end to the old assumptions about everyone knowing their place.

For a start, there was the question of what was to be done with the millions of men in uniform who couldn't wait to get out of it. Huge numbers of them were at bases in France for which there was quite obviously no longer any use. With the fighting finished, the men found themselves turning out for morning inspections, cleaning lots of kit and playing much football. Artillery units polished their guns and then polished them again. A private in the Royal Army Medical Corps found he was ordered one day to take a table out of an orderly room and carry it down the road to a barn. The next day he was ordered to carry it back. Many bases had weekly boxing competitions. In most places that December 1918, there were Christmas parties to be planned. Men were sent on leave, but then absurdly, they felt, had to take the boat back to the continent. Some units had horses to exercise, but as the weeks passed there were more and more veterinary examinations, after which all of the less impressive horses were sold to French and

Belgian horseflesh dealers, which distressed the men who had cared for them.★

The soldiers' frustration at the slow pace of approaching freedom was understandable. They had joined 'for the duration', and the war was now over: they had surely kept their side of the bargain? But the British government felt that troops were needed in Europe until the conclusion of peace treaties, and this would not come until the summer of 1919. Moreover the business of dismantling the military machine and demobilizing ('demobbing') the men in uniform had to be managed carefully. If they were all released at once, there would be mass unemployment and possible social unrest. So demobbing began not with the disbanding of entire units but with a policy of discharging men individually, in an order of precedence decreed by government: those who had a guaranteed job offer or who were judged vital to the business of reconstruction were discharged first, with preference given to married men and those who had seen combat. It soon became clear that this policy had a number of inbuilt flaws, not the least of them being that the men whose jobs were being held open for them were more likely to be those who had been swept into the army most recently: the employers of men who had been in uniform for a while had got used to their absence or found a substitute. And the whole process seemed to take for ever. There were some regiments in which men refused to obey orders

★ In some cavalry units, men were so attached to their horses that they sought them out at auctions afterwards. A Trooper Huggins in the Queen's Own Oxfordshire Hussars had a horse called Billy. Three months after returning to peacetime work on his farm Huggins borrowed money from his father and took the train to London where former war horses were being auctioned in Hyde Park. 'He found me! As I was looking round I heard a horse give a knicker, a soft neighing, and I turned round and there he was . . . We'd been right through the whole war together and all he'd got was a little bit of shrapnel on his nose once. I could go to any field he was in and call, "Come on, Billy," and he'd come galloping up to me. We had him for years, and he had a good life on the farm, did old Billy. He ended his days in clover.' (Trooper G. Huggins, D Squadron, Queen's Own Oxfordshire Hussars, quoted in Max Arthur, *We Will Remember Them: Voices from the Aftermath of the Great War* (London, 2009), p. 224.)

they disagreed with: here command became a question not of ordering but of cajoling or charming.

In early January 1919 thousands of soldiers began protests in the Channel ports from which they were supposed to be returning to their units in France after leave. The following day soldiers drove around the centre of London in lorries carrying placards which read 'We want civvie suits,' 'We won the war' and 'Promises are not pie crust.' (These were relatively genteel protests by comparison with Canadian soldiers at a camp on the north Wales coast, who in March 1919 became so sick of living in huts in the mud while they awaited transport home that they staged a full-scale riot in which five people were killed.) Winston Churchill – in his latest incarnation, as newly appointed War Secretary – set about tackling British soldiers' discontent by introducing a new demobilization policy, which operated on the simple principle that those who had been in the military longest got out the soonest. Within a year, a British army of almost 4 million had been reduced to fewer than a million. By 1922 it was down to 230,000.

The day after the Armistice was signed, Lloyd George had called an election. His campaign promised to punish the Kaiser, to force Germany to pay 'the whole cost of the war' and to make Britain a happier place. In one speech he reminded the people of Wolverhampton of how the Emperor Augustus had brought lasting peace to the Roman empire by settling soldiers on the land – he would do something similar in Britain, complete with training schemes to ensure that they could tell one vegetable from another. Knowing that an election was going to come sooner or later, in February 1918 his government had passed a law giving the vote to poorer men who had been required to risk their lives, but who would not have been enfranchised when the war began. The Act also allowed women to vote for the first time (although they had to be over thirty to do so). The election campaign was a very odd one indeed, since most prominent Conservatives sat in Lloyd George's coalition government, while many prominent Liberals opposed it. When Lloyd George and the Conservative leader Andrew Bonar

Law issued a letter of endorsement to candidates from both parties who supported the coalition, they effectively declared war on the Liberal party. Asquith sneered at these letters, which he compared to ration coupons, but their effect was telling – the great majority of those who received them were returned to parliament.

Lloyd George's most famous promise in this 'khaki election' was that he would build 'a country fit for heroes to live in', and although most soldiers seem not to have bothered to vote, the result was an overwhelming victory for the leaders of the wartime coalition government. Shortly before the election they put through a new Education Act, raising the school-leaving age from twelve to four-teen. In 1919 the first Ministry of Health was created. A Housing and Town Planning Act the same year promised half a million new homes within three years. But it did not reach even half that tar-get, because Lloyd George found it much easier to promise than to deliver. If only he had devoted to it the energy he had brought to the war effort and to selling off peerages and baronetcies through his swindler friend Maundy Gregory.

To many of the men discharged from the forces, Britain felt nothing like 'a land fit for heroes'. Those selected for demobiliza-tion got four weeks' leave, a railway warrant and ration book and some civilian clothes. They were allowed to keep their army over-coat, which, if they didn't need it, they could hand in at any railway station and be given £1 in exchange. After that they were on their own. There were said to be colonels running fruit-and-veg stalls, captains working as cabbies, gently born lieutenants labouring as porters. The damage done by war made matters worse: 'Old Eton-ian (twenty-seven) married and suffering from neurasthenia but in no way really incapacitated in need of outdoor work,' read one advertisement from a victim of shell shock in the personal column of *The Times* in 1919. 'Would be glad to accept post of head game-keeper at nominal salary.' In the post-war world their rank wasn't much use. Moreover, they were often up against younger men, many fresh from school or university. 'Do anything. Go any-where' was a familiar phrase in the personal columns. A subaltern pleaded for a £100 loan with the words: 'Five children. Wife seriously ill. No means. Urgent.' This could be the reality of life as a national hero.

The discharged officer only had to walk the streets to see the potential fate awaiting him, as former mess-mates struggled desperately to keep up appearances, the holes in their socks hidden by the increasingly thin leather of their old army boots. The celebrated ex-officer organ-grinder or match-seller told a common cautionary tale. After the war, a retired brigadier general claimed to have seen one of his particularly bloodthirsty captains standing on his head for the pennies that theatre queues might throw him.

There were over 720,000 men, however, and almost 200,000 more in the British empire, who would not be coming home. Their families were grieving: what they needed was a way to make some immediate sense of the loss.

In 1914 a couple of retired colonels had begun publishing *The Bond of Sacrifice*, a part-work which attempted to list all the officers who had died in the fighting, each entry illustrated with a photograph of a proud face staring out from under cap or bearskin, beret or tam-o'-shanter, many adorned with enormous imperial whiskers or clipped military moustaches and among them many a boy who looked too young to shave. Long before the carnage of the Somme, the two colonels had been overwhelmed by the scale of their task and the thing ceased publication. The use of the word 'sacrifice' in the title was clever, though. The politicians who had committed Britain to war had presented their decision as the dutiful honouring of obligations. At the end of the fighting, this idea that the dead had been 'sacrificed' was much the easiest way to come to terms with what had happened in keeping that pledge. Vellum registers and books of remembrance began to appear in churches, priories and cathedrals, with the endless names listed in black ink. By 1920 over 5,000 war memorials had been constructed across the land. More followed. They included church organs, sports fields, village halls, stained-glass windows, clock towers, memorial gates, sports pavilions and figures carved into chalk downland, but mostly they were crosses, statues or plaques set into walls. Hardly a corner of Britain had been untouched by the war, and out of the 16,000 villages in England there were perhaps only forty 'Thankful Villages' that did not need to try to remember men who had not returned. On the first anniversary of the Armistice came the first national two-minute silence, acclaimed by the Bishop of Ripon as an opportunity to appreciate that 'God really had a destiny for England and that with all our faults and short-comings, he had used us to fulfil that destiny in the world.' At the appointed hour, church bells tolled, artillery boomed, trains and buses stopped running, railway stations fell silent and schoolchil-dren and factory workers stood to attention. A shared silence transformed private grief into universal reflection.

The central focus for the first national commemoration was some-thing very strange – an empty tomb. It was the antithesis of war monuments celebrating victories or mausoleums holding the remains of a king or warrior or president. The Cenotaph in Whitehall had originally been a temporary construction designed by Edwin Luty-ens for 'Peace Day': the first anniversary of the signing of the Armistice. The memorial did not hold a body or praise a leader. It bore no statue or likeness. It did not shout or boast. It just carried the enigmatic inscription 'THE GLORIOUS DEAD'. This plain slab of stone also asserted the notion of sacrifice – an accessible enough idea for a population well versed in Bible stories. The French or the Belgians could look back on the war as one of national liberation: an invader had been driven out. For them, it had been a war of national survival, and the nation had survived. The British position was much more complicated. Some soldiers even emerged from the experience with a rather greater regard for their former enemies than for the people whose freedom they had fought to reassert.

The tone was reflected in the cemeteries established to hold the mortal remains of the men who never came home. Even a hundred years after the outbreak of the war, the plots of the Commonwealth War Graves Commission are still immaculately tended at the taxpayers' expense, to the tune of £60 million or so every year, and despite the clear absence of a saleable end-product it is hard to imagine many areas of public spending more immune to demands for cuts. The places are quite unlike most cemeteries in Britain, almost all of which have gradually grown in size over the years, and in which some graves are grander than others, some well tended, some overgrown or falling apart. In the war cemeteries, the dead lie beneath identical gravestones, regardless of rank or wealth, and carrying no word of how they met their end. Unlike the graves of his allies and enemies, a Commonwealth soldier's grave is adorned with a few extra details beyond his name – his rank, date of death, regimental insignia and, in some instances, a personal epitaph composed by the grieving family. Nonetheless, the contrast with the memorials on church and cathedral walls at home, acclaiming the heroic fates of those who died in colonial wars, could not be plainer. There you sense families trying to make sense of the fact that a son or father has perished in some distant adventure to advance Britain's imperial destiny. In the war graveyards sheer numbers presume to explain. And the dead lie in the twenty-first century as they lay throughout the twentieth – a visitor in 2030 will find them just as they were in 1930: age does not weary them, nor the years condemn. The government that once decreed the cost of rations and uniforms and allowances for soldiers also decreed their final resting place: in 1919 it set the maximum cost of headstones at £10, which made larger cemeteries more economical than small ones. In death they remain the mass-produced army they were in life.

Very soon after the end of the fighting, groups of tourists began visiting the places where these men had died. Between 1919 and 1921 at least thirty battlefield guidebooks were published in English, catering to those seeking, as *The Times* put it, to visit 'the ramparts where the civilisation of the world was defended'. Hotels were built to accommodate relatives anxious to see where their loved ones had fought and the lucky ones survived. In 1918, the soldier-poet 'Philip Johnstone' (a nom de plume) had foreseen how it might go:

> This is an unknown British officer,
> The tunic having lately rotted off.
> Please follow me – this way . . . the *path*, sir, *please*,
> The ground which was secured at great expense,
> The company keeps absolutely untouched,
> And in that dug-out (genuine) we provide
> Refreshments at reasonable rate.

Some of the early visitors were soldiers returning to the places where they had lived in squalor and terror – tourism as a form of catharsis. For mothers who had lost sons and found themselves unable to join in the bell-ringing, parties and celebrations to mark the end of the war, it perhaps gave a sense of quiet comfort to see where their son had breathed his last.

Others found solace in more bizarre ways. The war had brought such an upset to the natural order of things that there was a desperate hunger for reassurance about what had happened to children who had died before their parents. In private houses and at rented meeting halls across the land tables rose into the air, musical instruments played themselves and mediums went into trances or regurgitated something they called ectoplasm (generally a chewed rag which they claimed was charged with 'spiritual energy') as they passed on messages from the 'other side'. Between 1914 and 1919 the number of spiritualist organizations in Britain doubled.

A purported ability to communicate with the dead belonged firmly in the realm of Victorian table-knockers, clairvoyancy, telepathy, levitation, telekinesis and associated charlatanry. Yet otherwise-sensible people had been so distressed by their losses that they believed whatever emotional hucksters told them. Sir Arthur Conan Doyle, for example, may have created the great rationalist detective Sherlock Holmes, but he was a convinced believer. (Most notoriously, he told the world that some photographs which two sisters claimed to have taken at Cottingley Beck near Bradford showed genuine fairies.) When his son died from wounds suffered at the Somme, Conan Doyle became the 'St Paul of the New

Dispensation', offering 'a call of hope and of guidance to the human race at the time of its deepest affliction'. When it was suggested to him that he and his fellow believers were the victims of con-artists, he replied that 'when we receive a telegram from a brother in Australia we do not say: "It is strange that Tom should not communicate with me direct, but that the presence of that half-educated fellow in the telegraph office should be necessary." The medium is in truth a mere passive machine, clerk and telegraph in one. Nothing comes FROM him. Every message is THROUGH him.'

There is a perfectly sensible rebuttal to this absurd comparison, not the least part of which is that brother Tom is alive. But Conan Doyle was far from being the only intelligent person to have succumbed. The distinguished physicist and wireless pioneer Sir Oliver Lodge – the first Principal of Birmingham University – was another. His youngest son, Raymond, had joined the hordes of volunteers in 1914 and was killed by a piece of shrapnel near Ypres the following year. Sir Oliver took the inevitable War Office notification very hard indeed. Within days, this rational, practical-minded man had begun attending séances at which his dead son 'spoke' through a medium. Raymond told them he had many friends in what they called 'Summerland' and that he felt 'brighter and lighter and happier altogether'.

In 1916 Sir Oliver Lodge published *Raymond: or, Life and Death, with Examples of the Evidence for Survival of Memory and Affection after Death*. The book recounted numerous successful attempts to make contact with his son from beyond the grave. Raymond told his parents in these messages that he was well and happy, that he had not suffered when he died, that he had exactly the same features as before (apart from what sounds like some extra-terrestrial dentistry). He assured them that men who had been blown to pieces had been reconstituted on the other side. Raymond promised his mother that if she put a chair out for him, he would come and join the family for Christmas. In one exchange, Sir Oliver heard about accommodation in the spirit world: 'a house built of bricks and there are trees and flowers, and the ground is solid. And if you kneel down in the mud, apparently you get your clothes soiled.' A writer in the *Occult Review* informed bereaved parents that their sons were busy 'helping to form a Britain or Empire beyond the grave, a better Britain or Empire than exists now on the material plane'. In a nation full of families with missing sons, *Raymond* sold enormously well, going through a dozen editions between 1916 and 1919. In this and other accounts of life on the other side, everyone was always happy.

At least the Lodges had been formally told that their son was dead. At the end of the war there remained one especially vulnerable group of grieving relatives who had no such certainty. The decision that the bodies of the dead would be buried on or near the battlefields meant that most families had been denied the finality of attending a funeral. But the creation of war cemeteries – some of them enormous – in the places where British and empire troops had fought at least gave the bereaved a setting for their grief. They knew where their son was. But what of the 528,105 British and empire dead who had no known grave? There was something horribly corrosive about being told that your loved one was merely 'missing'. Death at least had a finality about it. But 'missing' was neither one thing nor another. It could keep a cruel uncertainty alive for weeks, months or even years. Where was he?

Often 'missing' signified that a soldier's body was unidentifiable or buried by the debris thrown up from a shell crater. But when a shell struck, there was frequently almost nothing left of a man at all: it was as if he had never existed. And so fiancées maintained engagements that could not end in marriage, and mothers clung to increasingly spectral hopes that one day Sam or George or Richard would knock at the door or push open the garden gate. Relatives and friends, understandably keen to give what comfort they could, mentioned cases of grieving parents who had received a letter out of the blue from a son who had got lost in the heat of battle, had been wounded or was being held as a prisoner. Nourishing a small glimmer of hope, anxious families wrote endless letters to the War Office, contacted organizations with links to Germany or fell prey to the perpetrators of séances. Throughout much of the war, officials of the Red Cross and the Order of St John interviewed uncountable numbers of soldiers travelling to and from the front in the hope of finding news of the missing. A year after the last definitive sighting of the disappeared man, the Red Cross sent families the judgement that he was now on the list of 'presumed dead': it was time to abandon hope.

The particular challenge of reconciling the unfortunate families of missing or unidentified men to their loss led in 1920 to an inspired idea. As with many an inspired idea, the notion of a tomb containing an unidentified corpse had many parents. A former army chaplain, David Railton, wrote to the Dean of Westminster recalling a rough wooden cross he had seen in early 1916 planted in the corner of a village garden on the Western Front. Written in pencil across it were the words 'An Unknown British Soldier'. Railton proposed exhuming an unidentified corpse and bringing it to England, to be buried among the kings, poets and prime ministers in Westminster Abbey. George V disliked the proposal, remarking that to stage a big official funeral two years after the war had ended might 'reopen the war wound which time is gradually healing'. But Lloyd George's instinct for public sentiment was more sophisticated and he talked the king round.

So, a few days before the second anniversary of the Armistice, soldiers exhumed the bodies of four unidentified comrades from separate battlefields on the Western Front.* They were taken to a makeshift morgue in northern France, where at midnight Brigadier General L. J. Wyatt, the officer commanding the remaining British troops in France, was blindfolded and asked to pick one out at random. The chosen body was then placed in a coffin built from an oak tree at Hampton Court Palace, draped in the heavily darned Union flag that had accompanied David Railton throughout the war (he had used it as an altar-cloth and funeral pall), and carried to Britain aboard a destroyer. At Dover a nineteen-gun salute was

---

* Records are very haphazard and some accounts talk of six bodies.

fired and a military band played as the coffin was disembarked. In London, on the morning of 11 November, it was placed aboard a gun carriage drawn by six black horses. Four admirals and four senior generals were among the military escort which accompanied the unidentified corpse to Whitehall, as guns boomed a field marshal's salute in Hyde Park. Shortly before eleven o'clock, the procession was joined by a firing party, marching with their rifles reversed. An enormous crowd, twenty or more deep, stopped its whispers and stood silent and bareheaded. Behind a phalanx of clergy, the coffin was taken towards Westminster Abbey, followed by the king and royal princes in military uniform, the Prime Minister and most of the cabinet. A guard of honour was made up of a hundred soldiers, sailors and airmen who had won the Victoria Cross. Inside Westminster Abbey, the pall-bearers included Field Marshal Lord Haig, Admiral of the Fleet Lord Beatty and the father of the Royal Air Force Lord Trenchard. Finally, the coffin was lowered into a hole dug in the floor of the Abbey and covered with the contents of a hundred sandbags filled with earth collected from the battlefields. The final hymn was a setting of Rudyard Kipling's 'Recessional', with its refrain 'Lest we forget, lest we forget'. The words had been written over twenty years earlier, as an injunction to remember the death of Christ at the height of the British empire. But Kipling's own son was among the missing, and many of those singing the final 'Lest we forget' that day in the Abbey had tears streaming down their faces. *The Times* called it 'the saddest, stateliest, most beautiful ceremony that London has ever seen'.

The corpse being buried could have been that of anyone – sniper or cook, hero or malingerer. That was the point, of course. The grave contained a body which anyone who had lost a son or husband could regard as theirs. Even four days after the interment there was still a 7-mile line of people waiting to lay flowers in commemoration, everything from ornate wreaths to single roses and tiny bunches of autumn leaves picked in gardens from Cornwall to Sutherland.

The Tomb of the Unknown Warrior gave a focus for mourning and provided an attempt at what would today be called 'closure'.

But what about the future? Would the population as a whole ever recover from the losses of wartime?

'I have come to tell you a terrible fact,' a senior mistress at Bournemouth High School for Girls had warned her pupils in 1917. What she then delivered was not a 'fact' at all. She went on: 'Only one out of ten of you girls can ever hope to marry. This is not a guess of mine. It is a statistical fact. Nearly all the men who might have married you have been killed. You will have to make your way in the world as best you can.' This alarming and wildly inaccurate claim is a very clear statement of one of the prevailing myths about the First World War: that of the Lost Generation. Because the deaths of over 720,000 British men raised immediate anxieties about how the country could ever make good the deficit. 'Who will give me my children?' lamented Vera Brittain at the end of her anguished poem 'The Superfluous Woman': her fiancé had been shot by a sniper at the end of 1915. She was not the only one to ask.

The whole of Europe was haunted by the spectre of the woman in black. An American journalist visiting Europe in 1918 reported frantic calls that 'civilisation is running short in the supply of men . . . in every house of government in the world, above all the debates on aeroplanes and submarines and shipping and shells, there is rising another demand. Fill the cradles! . . . In the defence of the state men bear arms. It is women who must bear the armies. Whole battalions of babies have been called for.' Self-appointed moralists also worried how all the hormonal energy of women without a partner would find an outlet. In a state of 'imaginary widowhood', the many women who were poised to reproduce but lacked the partners with whom to do so posed a threat to the social order, inciting adultery and promoting lesbianism. Lord Northcliffe talked of 'Britain's problem of two million superfluous women' and the *Daily Mail* proposed they be exported to Australia or

Canada. If they did not take themselves off, 'hordes of celibate women [would] go out into the world to earn a living, thereby driving *men* to emigrate.' By August 1921 the paper was suggesting that the human race was evolving into something like a hive of bees, with a small number of breeding females 'supported by the labour of an immense number of sterile female workers. Men will be utterly ousted.'

It was mostly hysteria. Of course the war changed the balance of the sexes – the 1911 census showed there had been slightly more women than men before it began (101 women for every 100 men), and in the 1920s the difference was bigger (113 women to 100 men). But most of the men who had worn uniform survived, and even when boyfriends or fiancés were killed, women might often find another. Vera Brittain overcame her grief and married a young professor, who 'gave her' the children she craved (who included the future Labour cabinet minister Shirley Williams). Some of the men who had gone to war returned from it mangled but with sufficient life in them at least to limp down the aisle. The fortunate ones had emerged completely unscathed and were now free to marry the young women from whom they had endured a protracted and worrisome separation. Some really did marry the women who had nursed them in army hospitals. The novelist Stuart Cloete claimed that he fell instantly in love with the first person he saw when he recovered consciousness while being treated for wounds in 1916 – a volunteer nurse in a pale-blue uniform, holding a glass jar full of thermometers. 'My nurse-wounded-soldier pattern was one with a thousand precedents,' he said, marked by male gratitude and female sympathy, 'a kind of almost incestuous maternal feeling for this man-baby.' He believed the possibility of imminent death had given these relationships an urgency absent in peacetime. 'It is the same force that makes desert plants flower, fruit and seed in such a frantic rush after a single shower of rain. If they are to survive, they must.'

With the end of the fighting, breeding began. In 1920 over 957,000 babies were born in England and Wales, a spectacular total which has not been equalled in any year since, even though the population of the two countries has grown massively. But apart from that single year, the pattern of births continued on much the same gentle decline as had been apparent before the war began. People had been worrying about the decline then, and they continued to worry about it now the war was over.

They had more cause for unease when Marie Stopes produced her revolutionary sex manual *Married Love*, written, she said, to save other women from the ignorance which had doomed her own marriage.* First published in 1918, this little maroon-bound book 'crashed into English society like a bombshell', as she put it. By 1925 it had been reprinted thirty-nine times and sold half a million copies. Marie Stopes opened her first birth-control clinic in 1921, under the slogan 'Joyous and deliberate motherhood – a sure light in our racial darkness'. Here she advised on rubber cervical caps and quinine pessaries. Not everyone shared the anxieties about the birth rate.

Peace also revealed the shallowness of the mass media's commitment to feminism. *The Times* was troubled in December 1918 by the fact that 'girls [leave] school knowing all about William the Conqueror, but very little about the method of preparing a first-class steak and kidney pudding.' The chairman of the Liquor Control Board, Viscount D'Abernon – an extremely rich financier whose extramarital affairs had earned him the nickname the 'Piccadilly Stallion' – believed, however, that female drunkenness had fallen by 73 per cent since 1914 as a result of 'occupation, steady wages, and an independent, self-supporting career', all of which had increased women's self-respect and confidence, and which was 'profoundly beneficial to the community'. Certainly, by the end of the war women's skirts and their hair were both shorter. Their breasts seemed smaller and their hips narrower. And the common

---

* She had married at the age of thirty-one. She later persuaded a divorce court that it was only when she had still not become pregnant several years later that she began intensive research in the literature of the British Museum and discovered that the relationship had never been consummated.

idea that marriage might never be an option did change how some lived their lives. One of those listening to the apocalyptic comments of the Bournemouth schoolmistress – that she would 'have to make your way in the world as best you can' – was Rosamund Essex. She never married – and nor, she said, did nine out of ten of her friends. She became instead a career woman, adopting a child as a single woman of thirty-nine and turning into a formidable editor of the *Church Times*. But such women were unusual, to judge from many of the newspaper advertisements that greeted peacetime. 'Back to Home and Duty' proclaimed the caption on an ad for Oatine face-cream. 'Now the war is won, many women and girls are leaving their work, their war jobs finished. They are naturally desirous of regaining their good complexions and soft white hands freely sacrificed to the National need.' But the cigarette-smoking, jazz-loving 'flapper' knew she could use face-cream whether she gave up work or not – and indeed that having a job of her own would be much more likely to allow her the decision.

Yet there remained the pressing issue of finding peacetime work for the nearly 4 million men in the army, the 400,000 in the navy and the nearly 300,000 in the air force. A private in the West Yorkshire Regiment returned home to try to pick up his old job and found a not unusual situation: 'The boss had got a couple of girls in. We had a chat and the manager said that the girls would have to leave because I wanted my job back, but he said that he would rather keep them on. I said we'd see about that.' Parliament saw about it. A Restoration of Pre-War Practices Act, eagerly supported by both the Labour party and most of the trades unions, gave men returning from the war priority over women. By May 1919, three-quarters of the formally unemployed were female. In 1921, the proportion of women listed as 'gainfully employed' was lower than it had been in 1911.

'The game-keeper, Mellors, is a curious kind of person,' says Lady Chatterley to her husband in D. H. Lawrence's most controversial novel, published ten years after the war ended. 'He might almost be a gentleman.' This is a very hard idea for her impotent, war-wounded, upper-class husband to believe. Perhaps, he thinks, Mellors had been an officer's servant during the war and picked up airs and graces above his station. He is wrong – despite his broad Derbyshire accent Mellors had been one of the great number of men promoted to officerdom from the ranks. For the assumptions so easily made about social class before the war were now everywhere under pressure. Pretentious restaurants and teashops at home continued to try to maintain clear Edwardian distinctions by displaying signs saying 'Officers Only'. But no longer could it be assumed even that all officers sounded or acted like members of the ruling class. When Alfred Burrage took his girlfriend out to dinner he found the restaurant packed with temporary gentlemen 'late of Little Buggington Grammar School, who had been "clurks" in civil life, and were now throwing their weight about on seven and sixpence a day and half salary'. Burrage had served throughout the war as a private and the sight disgusted him. But by 1918 it was reckoned that about four out of ten officers came from working- or lower-middle-class backgrounds. When the War Office examined the previous occupations of officers demobilized up to May 1920 it discovered that 266 of them had been warehousemen and porters, 638 had been fishermen and well over a thousand were former miners.

Wartime officer academies had done their best to give these young men a crash course in how to behave. But being both 'an officer and a gentleman' could no longer be assumed. When Lady Chatterley's husband thought about the position of the men who had risen from the ranks into the officer corps he concluded that 'it does them no good. They have to fall back into their old places when they get home again.' If only I could, many of them must have thought. The wise ones philosophically accepted that the war had been an unusual interlude, and that peacetime survival might demand a return to the clerking pool, or assisting on a haberdashery counter. Others found a reversion to their pre-war status very unattractive.

For the war had undermined all manner of apparent certainties. The higher death rates among officers meant that the upper classes had suffered the highest rate of loss, and even among survivors the tax rises necessary to fund the fighting had made pre-war lifestyles impossibly expensive. Rents paid by tenants had been capped by government. Ancient families, crippled by death duties, and now without sons to inherit, sold off their lands, often enabling tenant farmers to own land for the first time. By the end of 1919 over a million acres of English and Welsh land had gone under the hammer. It was a fatal blow to a pattern of semi-feudal power that had existed for centuries.

On the positive side, the war had often broken down class barriers in other ways. In just over four years, 5,704,426 men had served in the army. Shared experience of fear, pain, tedium, cold and wet had changed the way they saw the country to which they returned. As a political force, the aristocracy was finished. But privileged young men had had a most profound insight into the sort of men who were their fellow citizens. While some of those who survived raged inwardly, others – like the future Prime Minister Harold Macmillan – experienced a sense of guilt that they had lived when their friends had died. 'We certainly felt an obligation to make some decent use of the life that had been spared us,' he recalled: 'most of us were at a loss as to how to take up our lives again.' 'One-Nation' Conservatism had existed before the war (the term had been coined by Benjamin Disraeli in the middle of the nineteenth century) but had been displaced by enthusiasm for a more hard-nosed kind of capitalism. For men like Macmillan, the First World War helped them to rediscover it.*

In the aftermath of the war, class and politics began to align into a recognizably modern shape. The Bolshevik scare which so alarmed the political class all over Europe was never a reality in

---

* It was some of the middle class who now felt aggrieved, and in 1919 they even formed an organization – the Middle Class Union – to protest that the government was paying altogether too much attention to those further down the tree. It did not last long.

Britain. But the organization of labour during the fighting had led to a great increase in trades union membership, and the coming of peace meant that the industrial disputes which had raged across Britain before the war now resumed. There were more than twice as many strikers in Britain in 1919 as there were in Germany, where Bolshevism and revolution were a reality. In some areas, like Red Clydeside, these disputes had distinct political overtones, but in the great majority the British worker showed his usual preference for arguing about pay and conditions over political abstractions. Nevertheless, the split in the Liberal party created a perfect opportunity to consign the rump of liberalism to the margins of politics. When Lloyd George's government was discarded in 1922, it was the Conservatives who took power. In 1924, the Labour party would form its first, short-lived government. From now on, the battle would be between these two parties.

So what had it all done to Britain? Men who had fought together in the trenches – and women who had worked together in the factories – had first-hand experience of what 'the other half' was like: all may have waved flags, but now they had acquired a much deeper sense of what a nation really was. The efforts made and the risks taken by all classes meant that proper democracy in Britain could be denied no longer. Many of those who had survived their time in the forces emerged in much better health than they would have been in had they stayed living in industrial slums, and the idea of the state's responsibility for the health of its citizens could not easily be jettisoned. On the other hand, nearly three-quarters of a million men were dead. Half a million were seriously disabled, and a quarter of a million of them were amputees. Ten thousand men had been blinded. Sixty thousand were shell-shocked. There was not a family unacquainted with grief, not a corner of life unaffected. The British empire still existed – indeed, it grew slightly when the spoils of war were distributed at the peace treaty signed at Versailles. But it was a spent force and its days were numbered; and the harsh terms of the treaty are now often cited as one of the causes of the next world war that lay ahead. In the meantime, Britain had been bankrupted – the world's biggest creditor of 1914 now had massive debts.

Would Britain have gone to war in 1914 if its statesmen had appreciated what the effects would be? An actuarial assessment was as impossible in 1918 as it had been in 1914, because no one had any idea what the long-term consequences would be. Some of the people, doubtless, would have argued that consequences were not the issue: treaty obligations are solemn and binding, whatever the cost; others would – and did – object to war on principle. At the time, the country was a very long way from being a democracy, but public opinion – or what we knew of it – did not stop British participation in the Iraq War of 2003, so it is hard to believe that an anti-war mood on the streets would have counted for more in 1914.* (Besides, Britain was another country then, self-confident and accustomed to getting its way: the anti-war 'mood' was marginal.) Of course the whole thing was a bloody tragedy. But the question is not, would they have done things differently? It is, *at the time* what else could they have done at all?

Unlike France and Belgium, which had no choice, perhaps Britain might have stood aside and allowed Germany to build an empire on the continent. It would not have been dignified, or compassionate, and hardest of all it would have meant accepting a direct and powerful threat to British economic interests and security, but other countries – notably, of course, Germany – ignored treaties and appeals. Britain could have done so, too. The problem is that it would not have fitted with the British people's idea of who they were and what their country stood for. To follow such a course of action would have required them to hold a view of themselves that became possible only *after* the war. Even now, it is hard to imagine a British government making the case for doing nothing at all

* It is interesting, though, that Lord Lansdowne, the man who wanted to make peace with Germany in 1916 and again in 1917, was one of the very last representatives of the traditional ruling class, while it was more populist figures such as Lloyd George who wanted to continue to the last knock-down punch.

when a treaty guaranteeing a nation's integrity is violated, even if the commitment was entered into by people now long dead. If nothing else, the war ought to remain a warning to statesmen not to write cheques they themselves will not have to honour.

As for its consequences, it took a few years for the idea that the whole thing had been an almost unmitigated disaster to find common currency, but this notion has since become received wisdom. The retrospective narrative that supports it – the innocent conscripts, dullard generals and boneheaded battle plans – has become tiresomely familiar. Sometimes it reads as if the generals deliberately set out to murder their own men. Knowing, as we now do, how the outcome of the First World War contributed to the origins of the Second, and how it, in turn, made so much of the Cold War possible, it is unsurprising to find the Great War taught merely as 'pointless' sacrifice. But it is what happened *after* the war that is used to justify this adjective. The promises made by Lloyd George about a land fit for heroes were never delivered. The failure was not on the battlefield but at home.

It is precisely because it changed so much that we understand it so little. Before it began, the country had enjoyed half a century of being told that theirs was the greatest nation on earth. We have since had generation after generation of international decline. The men and women of the time were accustomed to going to church and being told how to behave, while we have had fifty years of being told we can make our own minds up about almost anything. The middle and upper classes of 1914 had been brought up on ideas of privilege and obligation, which made them respond to what they were convinced was the call of duty. Ordinary people, many of whom did not even have the vote, were accustomed to being bossed about and not listened to. Even the idea of 'sacrifice', which would have been entirely acceptable at the time, has been lost to us, discarded along with religious belief and replaced with the cost-benefit analysis which demands the inseparable adjective 'pointless'. As to why men volunteered to take part in such carnage, the short answer is they did not: the war they went off to fight in 1914 was nothing like the war of even one year later. As for the 'donkeys' in command, they were no better informed than anyone else, even if ignorance is no excuse. In the century since the war we have grown used to another kind of fighting, of tanks and aircraft and drones: we lack the means to imagine what they thought they were doing.

The war is the great punctuation point in modern British history, the moment when the British decided that what lay ahead of them would never be as grand as their past; the point at which they began to walk backwards into the future. There is a sense in which, like the desperate parents who could not believe their son was dead, the entire nation has been conducting a form of séance ever since.

Acknowledgements

All British military survivors of the Great War are now dead. But such an enormous event was bound to generate a great number of books, and literally thousands of them have been published. The most prolific sources, then, are libraries. I am very grateful to the staffs of the British Library, the London Library, the Bodleian Library, Cambridge University Library, the Liddle Collection at Leeds University, the National Army Museum, the Museum of London, the Imperial War Museum, the Library of Congress, the Smithsonian Archives of American Art and the Royal College of Surgeons.

I owe particular thanks to my clever and thoughtful editor, Will Hammond, who remained upbeat when I felt defeated by the sheer scale of the project, and to the formidable Ellie Smith, who oversaw production of the book, unfazed despite my late delivery of the manuscript. I was lucky enough to have the help once again of Peter James, the best copy-editor in England, and Douglas Matthews, the master of all indexers. Edward Madigan, research historian at the Commonwealth War Graves Commission, was kind enough to read the manuscript for accuracy. My partner, Elizabeth Clough, provided a final revision, clarified the time-line, howled at solecisms and helped with many otherwise awkward junctions. Any that remain are all my own work.

Most of all I thank Jillian Taylor, whose Stakhanovite capacity for research continues to amaze. I had no sooner asked a question than she had answered it. She is probably the perfect researcher – bright, resourceful, cheerful and indefatigable.

Notes

Introduction: The Cigar Box

2   'the only imaginative': Quoted in Peter Vansittart, *Voices from the Great War* (London, 1981), p. 86

2   In truth, the scheme: For a full-length and persuasive version of this argument see Peter Hart's *Gallipoli* (London, 2011)

5   How many other families: Adrian Gregory calculates that in 1919 approximately 4.5 million people, 10 per cent of the population, had lost close relatives in the war. See Adrian Gregory, *The Last Great War: British Society and the First World War* (Cambridge, 2008), p. 253

7   'like a picnic': Julian Grenfell, letters of 11 October 1914 and 3 November 1914, in Nicholas Mosley, *Julian Grenfell: His Life and the Times of his Death, 1888–1915* (London, 1976), pp. 236, 241

9   'the distance between': David Lloyd George, *War Memoirs*, vol. II (London, 1936), p. 2040

1. Tears and Cheers

14   'Doom! Doom! Doom!': David Lloyd George, *War Memoirs*, vol. I (London, 1933), p. 77

15   'The lamps are going out': Viscount Grey of Fallodon, *Twenty-Five Years, 1892–1916*, 2 vols. (London, 1925), vol. II, p. 20

16   'cricket, football and fishing': Memorandum by Sir Francis Bertie of conversation with Grey, 16 July 1914, PRO FO 800/161, cited in C. J. Lowe, *The Mirage of Power*, vol. III: *The Documents* (London, 1972), p. 488

17   'absolutely impossible that any State': Winston Churchill, *The World Crisis, 1911–1918* (London, 2007; first pub. 1923–31), p. 95

17   'about as bad as it can': H. H. Asquith, *Letters to Venetia Stanley*, ed. Michael and Eleanor Brock (Oxford, 1985), p. 123, letter 103, 24 July 1914

18 'Everything tends towards catastrophe': Martin Gilbert, *Churchill: A Life* (London, 1991), p. 268

18 'quite the stupidest people': Asquith, *Letters to Venetia Stanley*, pp. 125–6, letter 105, 26 July 1914

19 'natural and necessary enemies': The Earl of Stair, quoted in http://www.bodley.ox.ac.uk/dept/scwmss/projects/entente/entente.html

19 'there are no unpublished agreements': Grey to House of Commons, 11 June 1914, quoted in Niall Ferguson, *The Pity of War* (London, 1999), p. 79

19 'have created in France': PRO CAB 800/92, Grey memorandum, 20 February 1906, quoted in Ferguson, *The Pity of War*, pp. 63–4

20 At least one of the men: Lord Lansdowne to [Earl] Loreburn, 29 April 1919, quoted in Frank Winters, 'Exaggerating the Efficacy of Diplomacy: The Marquis of Lansdowne's "Peace Letter" of November 1917', *International History Review* 32 (2010), p. 28

21 To many educated Britons: See Richard Milton, *Best of Enemies: Britain and Germany – 100 Years of Truth and Lies* (Cambridge, 2007), pp. 12–13

22 'violently pro-French': Edward David (ed.), *Inside Asquith's Cabinet, from the Diaries of Charles Hobhouse* (London, 1977), p. 179

22 'two great communities': John Viscount Morley, *Memorandum on Resignation, August 1914* (London, 1928), pp. 19–20

23 'especial duty': Burns Diary, 27 July 1914, BL Add. MSS 46336

24 'very distraught': Asquith (quoting Edwin Montagu) to Venetia, in Asquith, *Letters to Venetia Stanley*, p. 161, letter 119, 9 August 1914

24 'England might have exerted': Morley, *Memorandum on Resignation*, p. 19

25 'diplomatic intervention': Belgian Grey Book [Diplomatic Correspondence Respecting the War], http://www.gwpda.org/papers/belgrey.html

25 'What can diplomatic': Sir Edward Grey, House of Commons, 3 August 1914, Hansard, Fifth Series, vol. 65, cols. 1809–32

26 'we are going to suffer': Ibid., col. 1823

26 'I am quite sure': Ibid., col. 1824

26 'the nations slithered': Lloyd George, *War Memoirs*, vol. I, p. 52

26 'we are now always surrounded': Asquith, *Letters to Venetia Stanley*, p. 150, letter 115, 4 August 1914

27 'a crazy man': Quoted in William Jannen Jr, *The Lions of July: Prelude to War, 1914* (London, 1996), pp. 360–61

27 'the poor Lichnowskys': Asquith, *Letters to Venetia Stanley*, p. 157, letter 116, 5 August 1914

28 'the great flood of luxury': David Lloyd George, *The Great War* (London, 1914), p. 14

29 'not an honest weapon': Archibald Hurd, quoted in Arthur Marder, *The Anatomy of British Sea Power: A History of British Naval Policy in the Pre-Dreadnought Era, 1880–1905* (London, 1964), pp. 358–9

29 'a hellish device': Asquith, *Letters to Venetia Stanley*, p. 158, letter 117, 6 August 1914

30 'I was treated like': Prince Lichnowsky, *My Mission to London, 1912–1914* (New York, 1918), p. 38

30 'not by the wiles': Ibid.

31 'take to the fields': 'Borough of Hove, Invasion Instructions to Inhabitants', in H. M. Waltrook, *Hove and the Great War* (Hove, Sussex, 1920), p. 85

31 'rendered useless': Quoted in E. S. Turner, *Dear Old Blighty* (London, 1980), p. 28

32 The headmaster of Malborough House: Vansittart, *Voices from the Great War*, p. xiii

32 'to my amazement': Bertrand Russell, *The Autobiography of Bertrand Russell: 1914–44*, vol. II (London, 1968), pp. 16–17

2. Contemptibly Small

35 'as a soldier': Kitchener to House of Lords, 25 August 1914, Hansard, Fifth Series, vol. 17, col. 501

36 That summer's day: Details given in Charles Carrington, *Soldier from the Wars Returning* (London, 1965), p. 45

36 'contemptible little army': Robin Neillands, *The Old Contemptibles: The British Expeditionary Force, 1914* (London, 2004), p. 2

38 'the best trained': *British Official History, 1914*, vol. I, pp. 10–11, quoted in ibid., p. 78

38 'in heavy guns': Ibid.

39 'All my thoughts': Field Marshal Viscount French of Ypres, *1914* (London, 1919), p. 11

40 'These glorious British soldiers': Ibid., p. 88

41 'I think you had better trust me': French to Kitchener, 31 August 1914, quoted in Richard Holmes, 'Sir John French and Lord Kitchener', in Brian Bond (ed.), *The First World War and British Military History* (Oxford, 1991), p. 120

41   'Paris will fall': Pease Diary, 31 August 1914, quoted in George Cassar, *The Tragedy of Sir John French* (London, 1985), p. 134

41   'put the fear of God into them': Asquith to Venetia Stanley, 1 September 1914, quoted in Cassar, *The Tragedy of Sir John French*, p. 134

42   'the one, Kitchener': General Victor Huguet [French liaison officer present at the meeting], *Britain and the War: A French Indictment* (London, 1928), p. 84

42   'French's troops': Quoted in George Cassar, *Kitchener's War: British Strategy from 1914 to 1916* (Washington, DC, 2004), p. 91

42   'Kitchener *knows nothing*': French to Churchill, 6 September 1914 (original emphasis), quoted in Holmes, 'Sir John French and Lord Kitchener', p. 121

43   'The stakes for which': French, *1914*, p. 216

43   'I thought the danger was past': Ibid.

43   'Every lover of art': Karl Baedeker, *Belgium and Holland, Including the Grand-Duchy of Luxembourg: Handbook for Travellers* (London, 1910), p. xi

44   'It is as if a plague': Diary of Lieutenant Colonel Wilfrid Smith, quoted in Michael Craster (ed.), *'Fifteen Rounds a Minute': The Grenadier Guards at War, August to December 1914* (Barnsley, 2012; first pub. 1976), pp. 111–12

45   'good dug-outs roofed': Diary of Major 'Ma' Jeffreys, 2 November 1914, quoted in Craster (ed.), *'Fifteen Rounds a Minute'*, pp. 127–8

45   'I think of him now': Lieutenant Colonel Wilfrid Smith, letter home, quoted in Craster (ed.), *'Fifteen Rounds a Minute'*, p. 140

46   'They are brave enough': Lieutenant Colonel Wilfrid Smith, quoted in Craster (ed.), *'Fifteen Rounds a Minute'*, p. 132

46   'what was as fine a Battalion': Quoted in H. C. Wylly, *The Green Howards in the Great War* (Richmond, Yorkshire, 1926), p. 50

46   'most of the men': J. F. Lucy, *There's a Devil in the Drum* (Eastbourne, 1992), p. 205

47   'They have broken us': Quoted in Nikolas Gardner, *Trial by Fire: Command and the British Expeditionary Force in 1914* (London, 2003), p. 218

47   'The line that stood': Quoted in Gary Sheffield, *The Chief: Douglas Haig and the British Army* (London, 2012), p. 92. Gary Sheffield is also the author of the comment that the German army came closer to defeating the BEF on 31 October 1914 than at any other time in the war

47   'The only men I have left': Quoted in Gardner, *Trial by Fire*, p. 218

48   'no more than one': French, *1914*, p. 237

49   The cost had been enormous: Statistics from Gardner, *Trial by Fire*, p. 227

49   'Ypres saw the supreme vindication': Quoted in Craster (ed.), *'Fifteen Rounds a Minute'*, p. 21

3. Willing for a Shilling

51 'to kill them not': Quoted in John Wolffe (ed.), *Religion in History: Conflict, Conversion and Coexistence* (Manchester, 2004), p. 61

53 'in old boots': Harry Cartmell, *For Remembrance: An Account of Some Fateful Years* (Preston, 1919), p. 33

54 'there can be no question': *Birmingham Daily Post*, 28 August 1914, Friday morning

54 'black-coated battalion': *Hull Daily Mail*, 1 September 1914, quoted in Peter Simkins, *Kitchener's Army: The Raising of the New Armies, 1914–16* (Manchester, 1988), p. 88

55 'wild and insubordinate': Asquith, *Letters to Venetia Stanley*, p. 298, letter 193, 30 October 1914

55 'How eager we were': Quoted in Cate Haste, *Keep the Home Fires Burning: Propaganda in the First World War* (London, 1977), p. 69

56 'If your young man neglects': Quoted in ibid., p. 57

58 'the Sphinx must': H. D. Davray, *Lord Kitchener: His Work and Prestige* (London, 1917), p. 34. 'They [the eyes] strike you . . . with a kind of clutching terror; you look at them, try to say something, look away, and then trying to speak, find your eyes returning to that dreadful gaze, and once more choke with silence' was the way Harold Begbie described them in *Lord Kitchener: Organizer of Victory* (Boston and New York, 1915), p. 99

59 'you cannot naturalize': Julian Symons, *Horatio Bottomley* (London, 2001; first pub. 1955), p. 141

59 'we, the British Empire': Quoted in Gary Messinger, *British Propaganda and the State in the First World War* (Manchester, 1992), p. 208

60 'It will be Hell': Letter to Stanley Spencer, 31 July 1914, in Geoffrey Keynes (ed.), *The Letters of Rupert Brooke* (London, 1968), p. 601

60 'a rotten trade': Letter to Lady Eileen Wellesley, 15–17 August 1914, in Keynes (ed.), *The Letters of Rupert Brooke*, p. 608

60 'more English': Nigel Jones, *Rupert Brooke: Life, Death and Myth* (London, 1999), pp. 375, 379

61 'You are doing [it]': Quoted in Matthew Hollis, *Now All Roads Lead to France: The Last Years of Edward Thomas* (London, 2011), p. 241

62 'dearest Mother and Dad': Quoted in John Lewis-Stempel, *Six Weeks: The Short and Gallant Life of the British Officer in the First World War* (London, 2010), p. 190

62 'more true, more thrilling': 'Death of Mr Rupert Brooke – Sunstroke at Lemnos', *The Times*, 26 April 1915

63 'If he's not a spy': Quoted in James Fox, '"Traitor Painters": Artists and Espionage in the First World War, 1914–18', *British Art Journal* 9 (2009), p. 65

64 'over five thousand': William Le Queux, *Spies of the Kaiser* (London, 1909), p. x

65 'a patriotic Englishman': Ibid., p. xi

65 'various little foreign restaurants': Willam Le Queux, Preface to *The German Spy System from Within* (London, 1915), p. 8

66 'Howling women': Quoted in Jannen, *The Lions of July*, p. 361

66 '66,000 trained German soldiers': Quoted in Panikos Panayi, *The Enemy in our Midst: Germans in Britain during the First World War* (New York and Oxford, 1991), pp. 36–7

67 'predilection for Germany': Quoted in ibid., p. 185

67 '2,000 Germans': Quoted in Vansittart, *Voices from the Great War*, p. 22

68 'Extirpation': Quoted in Panayi, *The Enemy in our Midst*, p. 203

68 'I have had just judges': Sir Basil Thomson, *The Scene Changes* (London, 1939), p. 233

68 'He never flinched': Ibid., p. 234

4. Learning to Hate

72 'unofficial armistices': II Corps Document G.507, quoted in Malcolm Brown and Shirley Seaton, *Christmas Truce: The Western Front December 1914* (London, 2001; first pub. 1984), p. 36

73 'special vigilance': Ibid., p. 55

73 'They sang "Silent Night"': Private Albert Moren [2/Queen's], interview for *Peace in No Man's Land*, BBC TV, 1981

73 'We are Fred Karno's army': II Corps Document G.507, quoted in Brown and Seaton, *Christmas Truce*, pp. 57–8

74 'It was just the sort of day': Second Lieutenant Bruce Bairnsfather [1/ Royal Warwickshire], *Bullets and Billets* (London, 1916), p. 32

77 'Most people agree': Miss G. M. West, quoted in Joyce Marlow, *The Virago Book of Women and the Great War, 1914–18* (London, 1998), p. 65

77 'How are your Belgian': Turner, *Dear Old Blighty*, p. 83

77 'unanswerable': Quoted in J. Lee Thompson, *Politicians, the Press & Propaganda: Lord Northcliffe & the Great War, 1914–1919* (Kent, Ohio, 1999), p. 37

78 'alarmingly like': Christopher Harvie, 'Bryce, James, Viscount Bryce (1838–1922)', *Oxford Dictionary of National Biography* (Oxford, 2004)

79 'no such children': Bryce Papers, quoted in Trevor Wilson, 'Lord Bryce's Investigation into Alleged German Atrocities in Belgium, 1914–15', *Journal of Contemporary History* 14 (1979), pp. 373–4

79 'A hair-dresser was murdered': *Bryce Report into German Atrocities in Belgium, 12 May 1915*, http://www.firstworldwar.com/source/brycereport.htm

79 'These disclosures will not': Ibid.

80 'Our homes are in danger': Will Crooks, *The British Workman Defends his Home*, quoted in Nicoletta Gullace, 'Sexual Violence and Family Honour: British Propaganda and International Law during the First World War', *American Historical Review* 102 (1997), p. 726

80 'same savagery and unbridled lust': Le Queux, Preface to *The German Spy System from Within*, p. 8

81 'like an invisible hand': Quoted in Diana Preston, *Wilful Murder: The Sinking of the Lusitania* (London, 2002), p. 189

82 'waving hands and arms': Quoted in ibid., p. 240

84 'I ain't no bloomin' 'Un': *Manx Quarterly*, no. 17, October 1916

84 'cannot stand the slightest opposition': Quoted in Panayi, *The Enemy in our Midst*, pp. 126–7

85 'People remembered the *Lusitania*': Captain Roland Bull [Queen's Westminster Rifles], letter, quoted in Brown and Seaton, *Christmas Truce*, p. 200

5. Drunken Swabs

86 'being as their [the German]': Private papers of John E. Attrill, Log of War, 1914–1916, IWM Documents 1364

88 'obvious balls': Private Papers of Surgeon Captain Leonard Alexander Moncrieff, IWM Documents 5610

88 'We had a splendid passage': Quoted in Mark Chirnside, *RMS Olympic, Titanic's Sister* (Stroud, 2005), p. 130

89 'whenever there is any doubt': Quoted in Haste, *Keep the Home Fires Burning*, p. 33

89 'undisguised contempt': Ibid.

90 'Kitchener cannot understand': Sir George Riddell Diary (quoting Smith), 25 August 1914, quoted in Thompson, *Politicians, the Press & Propaganda*, p. 28

90 the regional press: Michael Finn, 'Local Heroes: War News and the Construction of "Community" in Britain, 1914–18', *Historical Research* 83 (2010), pp. 520–38

91 'The British Expeditionary Force': Quoted in Haste, *Keep the Home Fires Burning*, p. 33

92 'I never saw such panic-stricken': Churchill to Northcliffe, 5 September 1914, quoted in Thompson, *Politicians, the Press & Propaganda*, p. 31

92 'the public can have no true': George Riddell, *Lord Riddell's War Diary 1914–1918* (London, 1933), p. 17

93 'We know that the advance': Quoted in Thompson, *Politicians, the Press & Propaganda*, p. 13

93 'few men in this world': Quoted in ibid., p. 19

96 'twopenny damn': Asquith to Venetia Stanley, in Asquith, *Letters to Venetia Stanley*, p. 562, letter 404, 22 April 1915

96 'not a word of truth': Quoted in Thompson, *Politicians, the Press & Propaganda*, p. 56

96 'a short and very vigorous': Northcliffe to French, 1 May 1915, Northcliffe Papers BL Add. MS 62159, quoted in Thompson, *Politicians, the Press & Propaganda*, pp. 56–7

96 'the want of an unlimited': *The Times*, 14 May 1915

97 'died in heaps': *The Times*, 19 May 1915

97 'it has never been pretended': *Daily Mail*, 21 May 1915

98 'find an occupation': 'I had to do this . . . if I was to avoid a public quarrel with him,' said Lloyd George. *The Political Diaries of C. P. Scott, 1911–1928*, quoted in Alice Marquis, 'Words as Weapons: Propaganda in Britain and Germany during the First World War', *Journal of Contemporary History* 13 (1978), pp. 479–80

98 rewarded him with a viscountcy: A. G. Gardner, quoted in D. George Boyce, 'Harmsworth, Alfred Charles William, Viscount Northcliffe (1865–1922)', *Oxford Dictionary of National Biography*

6. What Happened to Uncle Charlie

100 'I don't know what's': Quoted in Grey of Fallodon, *Twenty-Five Years*, vol. I, pp. 71–2

102 'my knowledge of': General Sir Ian Hamilton, *Gallipoli Diary*, 2 vols. (London, 1920), vol. I, p. 18

103 'Oh God! I've never been': Quoted in Alan Moorehead, *Gallipoli* (London, 1997; first pub. 1956), p. 92

103 'as though Sir Lancelot': L. A. Carlyon, *Gallipoli* (London, 2003), p. 130

104 'Our troops have done': General Hamilton, quoted in Hart, *Gallipoli*, p. 221

105 'what may be called "Yorkshire" ': General Staff War Diary, 11th Division, TNA WO 95/4297

106 'he will have to be watched': Hamilton, *Gallipoli Diary*, vol. I, p. 328

107 'a task to make angels weep': Sergeant A. L. G. Whyte, East Anglian FA, letter to Mr Hope, 4 December 1915, quoted in Mark Harrison, *The Medical War: British Military Medicine in the First World War* (Oxford, 2010), p. 192

107 'during the greater part': 7 August 1915, 35th Field Ambulance War Diary, Dardanelles 11th Division, 1 August 1915–30 August 1915, PRO WO 95/4298

108 'No energetic attacks': Quoted in Carlyon, *Gallipoli*, p. 423

108 'this is a young man's war': Hamilton, *Gallipoli Diary*, vol. II, p. 104

108 'he has to lie': Ibid., p. 161

108 'large reinforcements': General Sir Ian Hamilton to Kitchener, cable from MEF Headquarters, 17 August 1914, quoted in Hart, *Gallipoli*, pp. 365–6

109 'Great attack on the Dardanelles': *Daily Telegraph*, 27 April 1915

109 'as though the Carlton': Henry Nevison, *Last Changes, Last Chances* (London, 1928), p. 35

110 'the first Ottoman Turk': Ellis Ashmead-Bartlett, *Daily Telegraph*, 7 May 1915

110 'a masterpiece of organisation': Kitchener to the House of Lords, 18 May 1915, quoted in Jenny Macleod, *Reconsidering Gallipoli* (Manchester, 2004), pp. 120, 123

110 'There is no occasion': Archibald Hurd, 'The Naval Outlook in the Dardanelles', *Manchester Guardian*, 29 May 1915

111 'the most ghastly': Ashmead-Bartlett letter to Asquith [Ashmead-Bartlett retained a copy of the letter], 8 September 1915, Institute of Commonwealth Studies Library, London, Ashmead-Bartlett Papers, ICS 84/B/3/137

111 'You would refuse to believe': Gallipoli letter from Murdoch to Fisher, 23 September 1915, Murdoch Papers, National Library of Australia, MS 2823/2/1

111 'Sedition is talked': Ibid.

112 'a line possessing': General Monro, 'First Dispatch', *London Gazette*, 10 October 1916, quoted in Hart, *Gallipoli*, pp. 398–9

113 'It was not the Turkish Army': G. S. Patton Jr, *The Defense of Gallipoli* (Fort Shafter, Hawaii, 1936), p. 62

7. Mud

115 'being drowned': Papers of Major General C. H. Foulkes, from a 'very secret' report on gas casualties by Lieutenant Colonel Douglas, RAMC, quoted in Robert Harris and Jeremy Paxman, *A Higher Form of Killing* (London, 1982), p. 2

116 'When all is said and done': Siegfried Sassoon, *Memoirs of an Infantry Officer: The Memoirs of George Sherston* (London, 2013; first pub. 1930), p. 175.

117 'just like a boat': Lieutenant Alan Furse, 14 December 1915, quoted in Terry Carter, *Birmingham Pals: 14th, 15th & 16th (Service) Battalions of the Royal Warwickshire Regiment* (Barnsley, 1997), p. 111

117 'its butting impression was black': Edmund Blunden, *Undertones of War* (Oxford, 1956; first pub. London, 1928), p. 46

118 a new kind of fear: See Edward Madigan, ' "Sticking to a Hateful Task": Resilience, Humour, and British Understandings of Combatant Courage, 1914–1918', *War in History* 20 (2013), p. 88

118 'At length we reached': Private J. E. B. Fairclough, quoted in Carter, *Birmingham Pals*, p. 107

120 All in all, the trenches were a mighty labour: Henri Barbusse reckoned that the French front alone contained about 6,250 miles of trenches. Since the French held only just over half the front line, the British must have had about the same length. 'When we add the trenches of the Central Powers,' writes Paul Fussell, 'we arrive at a figure of about 25,000 miles, equal to a trench sufficient to circle the earth. Theoretically it would have been possible to walk from Belgium to Switzerland entirely below ground, but although the lines were "continuous", they were not entirely seamless: occasionally mere shell holes or fortified strong-points would serve as a connecting link' (Paul Fussell, *The Great War and Modern Memory* (Oxford, 2000; first pub. 1975), p. 44)

120 'Most of our time': Quoted in Jack Alexander, *McCrae's Battalion: The Story of the 16th Royal Scots* (Edinburgh, 2004), p. 129

121 'One can look for miles': Quoted in Alistair Horne, *Macmillan: The Official Biography* (London, 2008), p. 39

121 'Sometimes, jokingly': Cecil Lewis, *Sagittarius Rising* (London, 1936), p. 2

122 When a British commander: Brigadier F. P. Crozier, *The Men I Killed* (London, 1937), p. 96

122 'We have here beds': A. E. Wrench, diary, 11 March 1916, IWM 85/51/1, quoted in Alexander Watson, *Enduring the Great War: Combat, Morale and Collapse in the German and British Armies 1914–1918* (Cambridge, 2008), p. 23

125 'They crawl over you': Lance-Corporal Arthur Cook, quoted in Richard van Emden, *Tommy's Ark: Soldiers and their Animals in the Great War* (London, 2010), p. 167

126 'inhuman cries': Ardern Beaman, *The Squadroon*, quoted in James Hayward, *Myths and Legends of the First World War* (Stroud, 2002), pp. 102–3

127 'War is the normal occupation': Churchill to Siegfried Sassoon, September 1918, quoted in Siegfried Sassoon, *Siegfried's Journey* (London, 1982; first pub. 1945), p. 79

127 'profusion of old-fashioned': P. A. Brown, letter to mother, 8 October 1915, IWM 91/3/1, quoted in Watson, *Enduring the Great War*, pp. 23–4

127 'My daffodils': Quoted in Lewis-Stempel, *Six Weeks*, p. 93

127 'Will you please send': Captain Lionel Crouch, quoted in Emden, *Tommy's Ark*, p. 135

127 'The pansies': Second Lieutenant Alexander Gillespie, quoted in Emden, *Tommy's Ark*, p. 83

128 'ripping weather': Quoted in Emden, *Tommy's Ark*, p. 95

128 'They don't seem to care': Second Lieutenant James Foulis, quoted in ibid., p. 103

129 'the Corps Commander stood firm': Carrington, *Soldier from the Wars Returning*, p. 103

130 'could neither sing nor dance': P. B. Clayton, *Tales of Talbot House: Everyman's Club in Ypres 1915–1918* (London, 1920), p. 13

131 'why a judgement': Stuart Cloete, *A Victorian Son: An Autobiography, 1897–1922* (London, 1972), pp. 259–60

132 'what the infantryman in France knew': Blunden, *Undertones of War*, p. 149

133 'I spoke with caution': Lucy, *There's a Devil in the Drum*, p. 318

134 'I always feel': Lieutenant Christian Creswell Carver, letter home from France, 27 February 1917, quoted in Laurence Housman (ed.), *War Letters of Fallen Englishmen* (Philadelphia, 2002; first pub. 1930), p. 68

134 'the England for which': John Masefield, *St George and the Dragon* (London, 1918), pp. 4–7

135 'Men will not': Crozier, *The Men I Killed*, p. 68

135 'exemplary punishment': Cathryn Corns and John Hughes-Wilson, *Blindfold and Alone: British Military Executions in the Great War* (London, 2001), p. 125

136 'As they bound him': John Bickersteth (ed.), *The Bickersteth Diaries 1914–1918* (London, 1995), p. 225.

137 'Who would not die': Quoted in James Morris, *Pax Britannica: The Climax of an Empire* (London, 1968), p. 118

137 'I rejoice that war': Quoted in Lewis-Stempel, *Six Weeks*, p. 222

138 'When you have seen a shell': H. W. Yoxall, letter to mother, 5 February 1917, IWM P.317 Con Shelf

139 'was one thing to make jokes': Carrington, *Soldier from the Wars Returning*, p. 224

139 'We looked at each other': Cloete, *A Victorian Son*, p. 252

139 'A Corporal and six men': Carrington, *Soldier from the Wars Returning*, p. 98

140 'recognized as so far superior': Humphrey Carpenter, *J. R. R. Tolkien: A Biography* (New York, 2000; first pub. London, 1977), p. 89

8. *The Hand that Rocks the Cradle Wrecks the World*

142 'men who drink': Quoted in Christopher Martin, *English Life in the First World War* (London, 1974), p. 48

142 'Treating', or buying drinks: Turner, *Dear Old Blighty*, p. 86

143 'nice girls' from 'dreary manless suburbs': Lord Northcliffe, *At the War* (London, 1916), p. 31

143 The young feminist writer: The presence of such large numbers of women in the workforce persuaded even apparently die-hard enemies of votes for women, like Herbert Asquith, that when the war ended, it would be time to allow them to vote

144 'I'd never known': Quoted in Martin, *English Life in the First World War*, p. 63

144 'Tell the boys': Quoted in David Mitchell, *Women on the Warpath* (London, 1966), p. 267

144 'By George it's a glorious barrage': Quoted in Turner, *Dear Old Blighty*, p. 159

145 'should produce the stock': *Eugenics Review* 9 (1917), pp. 92–6, quoted in Richard Solway, 'Eugenics and Pronatalism in Wartime Britain', in Richard Wall and Jay Winter (eds.), *The Upheaval of War: Family, Work and Welfare in Europe, 1914–1918* (Cambridge, 1988), p. 374

145 that still left nearly 2 million: David Boulton, *Objection Overruled* (London, 1967), p. 79

146 'The idea that they have': Quoted in Will Ellsworth-Jones, *We Will Not Fight: The Untold Story of World War One's Conscientious Objectors* (London, 2008), p. 38

146 'you will be mightily sorry': Quoted in Boulton, *Objection Overruled*, p. 80

146 '*The Huns* are fighting': Arthur Kitson, *The Great Pacifist Conspiracy* (Stamford, 1918), pp. 22–4

147 genuine atrocities: See John Horne and Alan Kramer, *German Atrocities, 1914: A History of Denial* (New Haven and London, 2001)

147 'this will settle the matter': Quoted in Nicoletta Gullace, *'The Blood of our Sons': Men, Women and the Renegotiation of British Citizenship during the Great War* (New York, 2004), p. 107

147 'The genuine conscript': *Nation*, 17 July 1915, quoted in Gullace, *'The Blood of our Sons'*, pp. 105–6

148 'the gross injustice': Quoted in Gullace, *'The Blood of our Sons'*, p. 105

148 'servile state': Beatrice Webb, *The Diaries of Beatrice Webb*, ed. Norman and Jeanne MacKenzie, vol. III (London, 1984), p. 244, 2 January 1916

149 'Does anyone really suppose': Quoted in Caroline Moorehead, *Troublesome People: Enemies of War, 1916–1986* (London, 1987), pp. 4, 5

149 'The maxim that': Cartmell, *For Remembrance*, pp. 46–7

150 'Greek? You don't mean': John Graham, *Conscience and Conscription: A History 1916–1919* (London, 1922), p. 71

151 a course of hair restoration: Quoted in Adrian Gregory, 'Military Service Tribunals: Civil Society in Action, 1916–18', in Jose Harris (ed.), *Civil Society in British History: Ideas, Identities, Institutions* (Oxford, 2005), p. 180

151 'Ladies must have hats': Turner, *Dear Old Blighty*, p. 170

152 'You have never seen him yet': Cartmell, *For Remembrance*, pp. 84–5

153 'A man who conscientiously': Quoted in Ellsworth-Jones, *We Will Not Fight*, p. 61

153 'to kill Germans': Quoted in ibid., p. 42. There were plenty of big noises in the Church of England willing to speak up for killing Germans. The Bishop of Carlisle said the war was being fought on behalf of 'truth, justice and right-eousness', while the Bishop of Durham referred to the 'holiness of patriotism'

153 'I should try and interpose': Michael Holroyd, *Lytton Strachey: A Critical Biography*, quoted in John Sutherland, 'Introduction', Lytton Strachey, *Eminent Victorians* (Oxford, 2003; first pub. 1920), p. ix.

154 religious or ethical grounds: Precise numbers are impossible to calibrate, because in 1921 the Ministry of Health ordered the destruction of almost all the tribunal records. The historian Adrian Gregory writes that 'In 1917, the well-informed American journalist Arthur Gleason . . . claimed that only 2 per cent of appeals were based on grounds of conscience' (Gregory, 'Military Service Tribunals', in Harris (ed.), *Civil Society in British History*,

p. 178). Gregory also points out that the Bristol tribunal alone heard more cases than the authoritative estimate given for the total number of conscientious objectors in the entire country – conscience was a much smaller factor than the mythology suggests

154 'a deliberate and rank blasphemer': Turner, *Dear Old Blighty*, p. 175

154 'Earnest of face': Quoted in Boulton, *Objection Overruled*, p. 121

155 'Thank God from the bottom of my heart': Corder Catchpool, *On Two Fronts: Letters of a Conscientious Objector* (London, 1940; first pub. 1918), p. 48

155 'three maggots': Quoted in Ellsworth-Jones, *We Will Not Fight*, p. 93

156 'their conduct is exemplary': Quoted in ibid., p. 94

156 'we women will tolerate no such cry': Quoted in Robert Graves, *Goodbye to All That* (London, 1960; first pub. 1929), pp. 189–90

157 'Lady, *fiancé* killed': Advertisement quoted by Vera Brittain in a letter to Roland Leighton, in Mark Bostridge and Alan Bishop (eds.), *Letters from a Lost Generation: First World War Letters of Vera Brittain and Four Friends* (London, 2008), p. 164

158 'On Sunday I walk out': Quoted in Trevor Wilson, *The Myriad Faces of War: Britain and the Great War, 1914–1918* (London, 2010; first pub. 1986), p. 706

158 'Don't let your excitement': Quoted in George Robb, *British Culture and the First World War* (Basingstoke, 2002), p. 51

159 'my presence in the streets': Edith Smith, handwritten report of 1917, IWM, EMP.43/20

159 'two or three huge Australians': Freya Stark, quoted in Marlow, *The Virago Book of Women and the Great War*, p. 176

159 'kicked my shins': Cloete, *A Victorian Son*, pp. 273–4

160 'a serious social evil': 'Cocaine Hawking in the West End', *The Times*, 12 May 1916

160 'I found myself leading': Carrington, *Soldier from the Wars Returning*, p. 168

160 'We were not monks': R. Graham Dixon, 'The Wheels of Darkness', IWM 92/36/1, quoted in Joanna Bourke, *Dismembering the Male: Men's Bodies, Britain and the Great War* (London, 1996), p. 156

161 'Men and women do not "love"': Lewis, *Sagittarius Rising*, p. 191

162 'there were well over a hundred': George Coppard, *With a Machine Gun to Cambrai: The Tale of a Young Tommy in Kitchener's Army* (London, 1969), pp. 56–7

162 'seen up to twenty men': Max Arthur, *Forgotten Voices of the Great War* (London, 2002), p. 93

162 400,000 cases of VD: Bourke, *Dismembering the Male*, p. 161

163 men suffering from venereal disease: 'Checking of Venereal Disease' memorandum, 26 August 1918, PRO WO 32/4745

9. Lost at Sea

165 'a jackdaw or a magpie': Royal Commission on the Rebellion in Ireland, Minutes of Evidence, 1916, quoted in Charles Townshend, *Easter 1916: The Irish Rebellion* (London, 2005), pp. 24–5

166 'They have no sense of honour': Quoted in Townshend, *Easter 1916*, pp. 105–6

167 'the Countess took unfair advantage': Elizabeth Bowen, *The Shelbourne: A Centre in Dublin Life for More than a Century*, quoted in Townshend, Easter 1916, p. 167

167 'simply *swilled* brandy': Lady Cynthia Asquith, *Diaries 1915–1918*, quoted in Townshend, *Easter 1916*, p. 187

168 'practically crushed': Michael Foy and Brian Barton, *The Easter Rising* (Stroud, 2011), p. 286

169 'regardless of expense': Townshend, *Easter 1916*, p. 298

173 'abnormally agitated': Sir George Arthur, quoted in Donald McCormick, *The Mystery of Lord Kitchener's Death* (London, 1959), p. 11

174 'K.'s position at present is untenable': Wigram to Robertson, December 1915, quoted in Keith Neilson, 'Kitchener, Horatio Herbert, Earl Kitchener of Khartoum (1850–1916)', *Oxford Dictionary of National Biography*

174 'absolutely lacking in brains': The loyal Colonel Sykes' summary of the charges against Kitchener: House of Commons, 31 May 1916, Hansard, Fifth Series, vol. 82, cols. 2813–14

174 'iron grasp': Ivor Herbert, House of Commons, 31 May 1916, ibid., cols. 2789–90

175 'Do play the game': Colonel Norton Griffiths, House of Commons, 31 May 1916, ibid., col. 2819

176 'as though an express train crashed': Stoker Alfred Read, quoted in McCormick, *The Mystery of Lord Kitchener's Death*, p. 30

177 'Now we've lost the war': Guy Chapman, *A Passionate Prodigality*, quoted in Stephen Heathorn, '"A Great Grey Dawn for the Empire": Great War Conspiracy Theory, the British State and the "Kitchener Film" (1921–1926)', *War and Society* 26 (2007), p. 54

177 'drown'd in waters': G. G. Napier, *Kitchener Drowned* (n.p., 1930)

178 'the sneaky, slimy Hun': Quoted in Panayi, *The Enemy in our Midst*, p. 171

178 'to a noble English family': *The Message: Lord Kitchener Lives*, Received by Ala Mana, vol. I (Vancouver, 1922), pp. 20–25

179 'Now we can at last': McCormick, *The Mystery of Lord Kitchener's Death*, p. 78

10. The Great European Cup Final

180 'preparations were never so thorough': Douglas Haig, *War Diaries and Letters 1914–1918*, ed. Gary Sheffield and John Bourne (London, 2006), pp. 194–5

181 'Everybody at home': Sassoon, *Memoirs of an Infantry Officer*, p. 36

183 nor was his football idea entirely stupid: Nor was it original – there had been similar incidents elsewhere on the Western Front

183 had outlined his notion: See Lieutenant Colonel Alfred Irwin, in Arthur, *Forgotten Voices of the Great War*, p. 154

183 'Even on his knees': Quoted in Alexander, *McCrae's Battalion*, p. 162

183 'It was . . . an amazing spectacle': M. Gerster, *Die Schwaben an der Ancre*, quoted in Churchill, *The World Crisis*, p. 659

185 'wearing out': Quoted in Ferguson, *The Pity of War*, pp. 292–3

185 'the wounded were in wonderful good spirits': Haig, *War Diaries and Letters*, pp. 197–8

185 'the battle is developing slowly': Ibid., p. 201

186 'the British troops are capable': Ibid., p. 207

186 'The very attitudes of the dead': Quoted in Hayward, *Myths and Legends of the First World War*, p. 151. To be fair to Beach Thomas, he was subsequently deeply embarrassed by his despatches

186 'I hated seeing': Haig, *War Diaries and Letters*, pp. 200–201

187 'Herald the deeds': Quoted in Martin, *English Life in the First World*, p. 75

187 'It's Jim': 'Northern Section', *The Screen: The Cinema Managers' Journal*, 7 (14 October 1916)

187 'It reminded me of': Frances Stevenson, diary entry for Friday 4 August 1916, in *Lloyd George: A Diary by Frances Stevenson*, ed. A. J. P. Taylor (London, 1971), p. 112.

188 'For all the public know': Asquith to Churchill, 5 September 1915, quoted in Cameron Hazlehurst, *Politicians at War: A Prologue to the Triumph of Lloyd George* (London, 1971), p. 147

190 'And all the time': Lieutenant Geoffrey Malins, official cameraman at Martinpuich, September 1916

190 'blind creatures': *Daily Mail*, 14 September 1916

190 'Haig tried his forty tanks': Carrington, *Soldier from the Wars Returning*, p. 124

191 'there is not one of us': John Jolliffe, 'Asquith, Raymond (1878–1916)', *Oxford Dictionary of National Biography*

191 'I can honestly say': Asquith to Sylvia Henley, 20 September 1916, quoted in George Cassar, *Asquith as War Leader* (London, 1994), p. 197

191 '*shattered his nerve*': Lloyd George, *War Memoirs*, vol. I, p. 603

192 'My dear wife and children': Quoted in Richard van Emden, *The Soldier's War: The Great War through Veterans' Eyes* (London, 2009), pp. 187–8

193 'Day and night': Lieutenant Alan Furse, quoted in Carter, *Birmingham Pals*, p. 171

193 'strewn with bodies': Carrington, *Soldier from the Wars Returning*, p. 121

195 'were an extra visit': Cloete, *A Victorian Son*, p. 248

196 'his mane of white hair': Carrington, *Soldier from the Wars Returning*, p. 216

197 'his eyes wet with tears': Asquith to Venetia Stanley, 29 March 1915, quoted in Cassar, *Asquith as War Leader*, p. 83

197 'content to preside': Austen Chamberlain to his wife, 26 April 1916, quoted in Cassar, *Asquith as War Leader*, p. 210

198 'Northcliffe frankly wants a smash': Lloyd George to Asquith, 4 December 1916, quoted in Roy Jenkins, *Asquith* (London, 1978), p. 448

198 'supreme need': Lloyd George to Asquith, 5 December 1916, quoted in Jenkins, p. 448

198 'In the end': Quoted in Jenkins, *Asquith*, p. 460

198 'I am glad you are reading': Quoted in ibid., p. 461

198 'You did': J. M. McEwen, 'The Press and the Fall of Asquith', *Historical Journal* 21 (1978), p. 863

11. *Upsetting the Country Altogether*

201 'into a digester': 'Germans and their Dead: Science and the Barbarian Spirit', *The Times*, 17 April 1917

202 'my brilliant colleague': Frederic William Wile, 'Why I Believe the Germans are Ghouls', *War Illustrated*, 19 May 1917

204 'There! That's avenged': Corporal T. Newell, 171 Tunnelling Coy, Royal

Engineers, quoted in Lyn Macdonald, *They Called it Passchendaele: The Story of the Third Battle of Ypres and of the Men Who Fought in It* (London, 1993; first pub. 1978), p. 43

206 'sobbing moans of agony': Edwin Campion Vaughan, *Some Desperate Glory: The Diary of a Young Officer* (Barnsley, 2010; first pub. 1981), p. 228

206 'Dante would never': Papers of Lieutenant Colonel C. E. L. Lyne, 4 November 1917, IWM, quoted in Robin Prior and Trevor Wilson, *Passchendaele: The Untold Story* (London, 2002), p. 178

207 'No words of greeting': Aubrey Wade, *The War of the Guns* (London, 1936), p. 58

207 'HAIG THROUGH THE': *Daily Mail*, 23 November 1917

208 'the much-loved Miss Madge': *The Times*, 28 November 1917, quoted in Patrick Wright, *Tank: The Progress of a Monstrous War Machine* (London, 2000), p. 85

208 'Germany is playing the sneak': James Yoxall, *Why Britain Went to War*, quoted in Martin, *English Life in the First World War*, p. 97

209 'an odd, clunkety': Quoted in Martin, *English Life in the First World War*, p. 28

210 'It's no business': Quoted in ibid., p. 30

210 'choked with struggling': Quoted in ibid., p. 91

210 'the Huns deserve no more': Quoted in ibid.

212 'until they, who have refused peace': Quoted in Turner, *Dear Old Blighty*, p. 229

213 'there is no romance in it': Rowland Prothero, President of the Board of Agriculture, speaking at a women's war rally in London, quoted in Elaine Weiss, *Fruits of Victory: The Women's Land Army of America in the Great War* (Washington, DC, 2008), p. 12

213 'an open air life': 'Women's Land Army', *Sheffield Daily Telegraph*, 15 May 1918

214 'By July 1918 the Board of Agriculture': Carol Twinch, *Women on the Land: Their Story during Two World Wars* (Cambridge, 1990), p. 18

214 'look well at the loaf': Quoted in Martin, *English Life in the First World War*, p. 102

214 'The struggle is not only': *The 'Win the War' Cook Book* (London, 1918), inside cover

216 'Potatoes plump': Quoted in Gerald Butcher, *Allotments for All* (London, 1918), p. 26

216 'MARIE CORELLI FINED': *New York Times*, 3 January 1918

217 'You are upsetting the country': 'Miss Marie Corelli's Food Supply', *The Times*, 3 January 1918, p. 3

218 'peace without victory': President Wilson, 'Peace without Victory' speech, 22 January 1917, quoted in Mario DiNunzio (ed.), *Woodrow Wilson: Essential Writings and Speeches of the Scholar-President* (New York, 2006), p. 399

219 'If Germany wants war': Quoted in Thomas Boghardt, *The Zimmermann Telegram: Intelligence, Diplomacy and America's Entry into World War I* (Annapolis, Md, 2012), p. 161

219 'a demonic Mr Punch': Quoted in ibid., p. 83

220 'a warfare against mankind': President Wilson, 'Peace without Victory' speech, 22 January 1917, quoted in DiNunzio (ed.), *Woodrow Wilson*, p. 399

220 'I am one of the hundred': Quoted in Messinger, *British Propaganda and the State*, p. 68

221 'It's no good being out here unless': Siegfried Sassoon, *Diaries, 1915–1918*, ed. Rupert Hart-Davis (London, 1983), pp. 50–51, 31 March 1916

221 'few years of ease': Ibid., p. 74, 7 June 1916

221 'cabbages going to Covent Garden': Ibid., p. 132, 15 February 1917

221 'the Boches had got to be beaten': Siegfried Sassoon, *Siegfried's Journey, 1916–1920* (London, 1982; first pub. 1945), pp. 53–4

222 'The War is being deliberately prolonged': Sassoon, *Diaries, 1915–1918*, pp. 173–4, 15 June 1917 [final draft of the Statement]

222 'throw their medals': Ibid., p. 175, 19 June 1917

222 'as though aware': Sassoon, *Memoirs of an Infantry Officer*, p. 241

222 'nervous and excitable': Quoted in Max Egremont, *Siegfried Sassoon: A Biography* (London, 2005), p. 156

12. *Stiff Upper Lips*

224 'The pressure of opinion': Quoted in Vansittart, *Voices from the Great War*, p. 215

224 'man mastership': Lord Gort, quoted in Anthony Richards, *Report of the War Office Committee of Enquiry into 'Shell-Shock'* (London, 2004; first pub. 1922), p. 50

224 war memoirs of men who confessed: For example Lieutenant C. J. Arthur of the Royal West Kent Regiment, who admitted to going to pieces, but

'luckily the colonel . . . talked to me very severely and made me pull myself together. It was an effort, but, thank God, I succeeded' (quoted in Lewis-Stempel, *Six Weeks*, p. 293)

225 'The advice which has usually': W. H. R. Rivers, *Instinct and the Unconscious* (Cambridge, 1920), p. 187

226 'Many of us who came': Quoted in A. M. Crossman, 'The Hydra, Captain A. J. Brock and the Treatment of Shell Shock in Edinburgh', *Journal of the Royal College of Physicians of Edinburgh* 33 (2003), p. 12

226 Courage – the decision not to run away: Madigan, ' "Sticking to a Hateful Task" ', p. 88

226 'Courage is will-power': Lord Moran, *The Anatomy of Courage: The Classic WWI Account of the Psychological Effects of War* (London, 2007; first pub. 1945), p. xxii

227 'frankly, I had enjoyed the war': Adrian Carton de Wiart, *Happy Odyssey* (London, 1950), p. 89

227 'My hand was a ghastly': Ibid., p. 64

229 'I, who was a private': A. M. Burrage [writing as 'Ex-Private X'], *War is War* (Uckfield, 2009; first pub. 1930), p. 71

229 'I have never felt so well': Lady Desborough [E. A. P. Grenfell], *Pages from a Family Journal, 1888–1915* (privately printed, Eton, 1916), pp. 479–80

231 'a race of robust men': H. H. Almond, quoted in Tony Collins, *A Social History of English Rugby Union* (Abingdon, 2009), p. 49

231 'in the formation of character': J. H. Boraston (ed.), *Sir Douglas Haig's Despatches, December 1915–April 1919* (London, 1919), 21 March 1919

232 follow the advice of: Albert Henry Trapman, *Straight Tips for 'Subs': Hints on Commissions, Allowances, etc.* (London, 1915), p. 26

232 'The Junior Subaltern': Ibid., p. 20

234 'dearest mother': Wilfred Owen to Susan Owen, 31 October 1918, in Wilfred Owen, *Collected Letters*, ed. Harold Owen and John Bell (London, 1967), p. 591

235 'Alone I did it': Sassoon, *Diaries, 1915–1918*, p. 261

235 'felt like a mother': R. B. Talbot Kelly, *A Subaltern's Odyssey: Memoirs of the Great War 1915–1917* (London, 1980), p. 159

235 'Mother . . . are you': Letter to Helen Macmillan, 30 August 1915, quoted in Alistair Horne, *Macmillan: The Official Biography* (London, 2008), p. 36

236 'not so very different': Horne, *Macmillan*, p. 36

236 'the waste and killing': H. G. Wells, 'A Reasonable Man's Peace', reprinted as a pamphlet by a free-trade organization, which distributed over 200,000

copies. H. G. Wells, *In the Fourth Year: Anticipations of a World Peace* (London, 1918), pp. 32–3

236 'We are not going to lose': Lord Lansdowne, *Daily Telegraph*, 29 November 1917

236 'We are slowly but surely': Lansdowne Memorandum, 16 November 1916, quoted in Lloyd George, *War Memoirs*, vol. I, p. 517

236 'There are amongst us': Robertson Memorandum, 24 November 1916, quoted in Winters, 'Exaggerating the Efficacy of Diplomacy', p. 32

237 'the anti-war Union of Democratic Control': The Union had been founded in 1914 by Liberal and Labour politicians opposed to the war. Despite constant denunciations in the right-wing press for being 'pro-German', at its height it had 300,000 members, including figures like Bertrand Russell, Ottoline Morrell and Ramsay MacDonald, as well as numerous prominent Quakers

237 'nothing less than': *Gleanings and Memoranda*, vol. XLVIII, quoted in R. J. Q. Adams, *Bonar Law* (London, 1999), p. 263

238 'a shoemaker and window-dresser': Duff Cooper, *Old Men Forget* (London, 1935), p. 66

238 'the under-cook of a Cambridge college': Boraston (ed.), *Sir Douglas Haig's Despatches*, 21 March 1919

239 'Many of them came from': Cloete, *A Victorian Son*, p. 267

240 'Men without half their faces': Gillies quoted in Suzannah Biernoff, 'Flesh Poems: Henry Tonks and the Art of Surgery', *Visual Culture in Britain* 11 (2010), p. 30

241 'Hideous is the only word': Ward Muir, *The Happy Hospital* (London, 1918), pp. 143–4

241 'it is not so hard': 'Blackie' (Sister Catherine Black), *King's Nurse – Beggar's Nurse* (London, 1939), pp. 86–7

242 'He would set to work': Ibid., p. 86

242 'Always look a man': Anonymous, quoted in Lyn Macdonald, *The Roses of No Man's Land* (London, 1993; first pub. 1980), p. 154

243 'Well, Paddy, your big day is here': Horace Sewell, letter to Reginald Pound, 17 March 1963, quoted in Reginald Pound, *Gillies, Surgeon Extraordinary* (London, 1964), p. 58

243 'the Duke of Wellington': The comment is attributed to an unnamed 'London hostess' by Reginald Pound in *Gillies, Surgeon Extraordinary*, p. 30

243 'a young fellow with rather a classical face': Letter, H. Tonks to D. S.

McColl, 1916, quoted in Sarah Crellin, 'Hollow Men: Francis Derwent Wood's Masks and Memorials, 1915–1925', *Sculpture Journal* 6 (2001), p. 81

244 'he occasionally squints': Muir, *The Happy Hospital*, p. 152

244 regain their self-respect: Francis Derwent Wood, 'Masks for Facial Wounds', *Lancet* 189 (1917), p. 949

13. *At Last*

246 'THE FIRST 47,000': *Imperialist*, 26 January 1918

246 The libel case: Hayward, *Myths and Legends of the First World War*, p. 176

248 'the prompt removal': *The Times*, 12 December 1917

248 'I doubt whether the Higher Command': Quoted in Reginald Pound and Geoffrey Harmsworth, *Northcliffe* (London, 1957), p. 598

249 'been reading Macaulay's essay': Diary entry, 14 September 1917, in Riddell, *Lord Riddell's War Diary 1914–1918*, pp. 272–3

249 'the staying power of the Allies': Report of the Cabinet Committee on Manpower, 9 January 1918, quoted in David French, *The Strategy of the Lloyd George Coalition, 1916–1918* (Oxford, 1995), p. 185

250 'It is only the clearest': 'Speech to the Trade Unions, 5 January 1918', quoted in Lloyd George, *War Memoirs*, vol. II, p. 1510

250 'It is impossible': 'Easter Sermons', *The Times*, 1 April 1918, p. 8

250 'If the American woman knew': 'London Street Women. An American Editor's Indictment', *The Times*, 24 September 1918

251 'vile women': 'Soldiers in London. Letter to the Editor of *The Times*', *The Times*, 6 February 1917

251 'We do not mind': Hansard, Fifth Series, vol. 92, col. 2117, 23 April 1917

252 'these women are the enemies': *The Times*, 10 and 17 February 1917

253 'the bowels of the earth': Quoted in David Stevenson, *1914–1918: The History of the First World War* (London, 2005), p. 408

253 'There is no course open': David Stevenson, *With our Backs to the Wall: Victory and Defeat in 1918* (London, 2011), p. 73

254 'excellent, and indeed': Quoted in Gerard DeGroot, *Blighty: British Society in the Era of the Great War* (London, 1996), p. 120

255 'Now we are already': Rudolf Binding, *A Fatalist at War*, trans. Ian Morrow (London, 1929), p. 208

255 'drunk as owls': Captain F. C. Russell, Australian Imperial Force, quoted in Lyn Macdonald, *1914–1918: Voices and Images of the Great War* (London, 1991), p. 273

258 'pacifists and subversive elements': Quoted in Brock Millman, *Managing Domestic Dissent in First World War Britain* (London, 2000), p. 258

258 'some of the biggest': *The Times*, 31 August 1918

259 'This country was nearer to Bolshevism': Quoted in Gerald W. Reynolds and Anthony Judge, *The Night the Police Went on Strike* (London, 1968), p. 5

263 'No more slaughter': Lieutenant R. G. Dixon, 'The Wheels of Darkness', IWM 92/36/1

263 'like a huge cockney chuckle': *Manchester Guardian*, 12 November 1918

263 'We have won a great victory': *The Times*, 12 November 1918

264 'You have all had a share': Ibid.

264 'The last occasion': Osbert Sitwell, *Laughter in the Next Room* (London, 1977), pp. 3–4

264 'Now, the British Army has won': Haig, *War Diaries and Letters*, p. 489, 30 November 1918

265 'impertinent message': Letter to Sir Clive Wigram, 1 December 1918, in ibid., p. 490

14. After the Eleventh Hour

266 'Dickie . . . the bloody war's over!': Lieutenant Richard Dixon, Royal Garrison Artillery, quoted in Max Arthur, *We Will Remember Them: Voices from the Aftermath of the Great War* (London, 2009), pp. 51, 52

269 'We want civvie suits': Charles Loch Mowat, *Britain between the Wars, 1918–1940* (London, 1955), p. 22

269 'the whole cost': Quoted in ibid., p. 4

270 'Old Etonian': Quoted in Denis Winter, *Death's Men: Soldiers of the Great War* (London, 1979), p. 242

271 'Five children': Quoted in ibid.

271 a retired brigadier general claimed: Crozier, *The Men I Killed*, p. 72

272 'God really had a destiny': Quoted in ibid., p. 34

273 to the tune of £60 million: This £60 million total is divided between the UK, Australia, New Zealand, India, South Africa and Canada according to

the number of dead from each country. The UK therefore makes by far the largest contribution

273 'the ramparts where': *The Times*, 6 September 1919

274 'This is an unknown British officer': Philip Johnstone, 'High Wood', first published in the *Nation*, quoted in Marcus Clapham (ed.), *The Wordsworth Book of First World War Poetry* (Ware, 1995), p. 42

274 number of spiritualist organizations: 'In 1914, there were 145 societies affiliated to the Spiritualists' National Union (S.N.U.; founded in 1901); by 1919 there were 309.' Jenny Hazelgrove, *Spiritualism and British Society between the Wars* (Manchester, 2000), p. 14

274 'St Paul of the New Dispensation': Arthur Conan Doyle, *The New Revelation* (London, 1918), pp. 49–50

275 'when we receive a telegram': Arthur Conan Doyle, *The Vital Message* (London, 1919), p. 42

275 'brighter and lighter': Oliver Lodge, *Raymond: or, Life and Death, with Examples of the Evidence for Survival of Memory and Affection after Death* (London, 1916), pp. 98–9

275 'a house built of bricks': L.L. [Lionel Lodge] sitting with Mrs Leonard, 17 November 1915, quoted in ibid., pp. 183–4

276 'helping to form a Britain': Eustace Miles, 'Britain beyond the Grave', *Occult Review* XXIII, quoted in Jay Winter, *Sites of Memory, Sites of Mourning: The Great War in European Cultural History* (Cambridge, 1995), p. 62

277 'reopen the war wound': Harold Nicolson, *King George the Fifth: His Life and Reign* (London, 1952), p. 343

278 'the saddest, stateliest': *The Times*, 12 November 1920

279 'I have come to tell you': Recalled in Rosamund Essex, *Woman in a Man's World* (London, 1977), p. 5

279 'civilisation is running short': Mabel Potter Daggett, *Women Wanted: The Story Written in Blood Red Letters on the Horizon of the Great World War* (London, 1918), pp. 308–10

279 'Britain's problem': As Billie Melman points out in *Women and the Popular Imagination in the Twenties: Flappers and Nymphs* (London, 1988), p. 19, one year earlier the figure had been a mere million

280 'hordes of celibate women': 'A Million Women Too Many, 1920 Husband Hunt', 5 February 1920, quoted in ibid., p. 18

280 'supported by the labour': *Daily Mail*, 8 August 1921

280 'My nurse-wounded-soldier': Cloete, *A Victorian Son*, p. 257

280 'It is the same force': Ibid., pp. 257–8

281 'girls [leave] school': *The Times*, 2 December 1918

281 'occupation, steady wages': 'Sobriety among Women', *The War Worker* 8, quoted in Angela Woollacott, *On Her their Lives Depend: Munitions Workers in the Great War* (Berkeley, 1994), p. 127

282 'Now the war is won': Quoted in Robb, *British Culture and the First World War*, p. 63

282 'The boss had got a couple of girls': Private Walter Hare, 15th Battalion West Yorkshire Regiment, quoted in Arthur, *We Will Remember Them*, p. 134

282 'The game-keeper, Mellors': D. H. Lawrence, *Lady Chatterley's Lover* (London, 2007; first pub. 1928), pp. 57–8

283 'late of little Buggington Grammar': 'Ex-Private X' [pseud. Alfred Burrage], *War is War*, p. 217

283 'it does them no good': Lawrence, *Lady Chatterley's Lover*, pp. 57–8

284 'We certainly felt an obligation': Harold Macmillan, *The Winds of Change* (London, 1966), p. 98

Bibliography

Newspapers and Periodicals

Birmingham Daily Post
Daily Express
Daily Mail
Daily Mirror
Daily Telegraph
Evening Standard
Ex-Service Man
Exeter and Plymouth Gazette
Imperialist
John Bull
Lancet
Manchester Guardian
Manx Quarterly

New York Times
Observer
Punch
Scotsman
Screen
Spectator
Sphere
The Times
Wipers Times
War Illustrated
Western Daily Press
Western Times

Archives

Liddle Collection, University of Leeds
NA WO 33
NA WO 95
Private Papers, IWM

Books and Articles

Adams, R. J. Q., *Arms and the Wizard: Lloyd George and the Ministry of Munitions, 1915–1916* (London, 1978)
——, *Bonar Law* (London, 1999)
—— and Philip P. Poirier, *The Conscription Controversy in Great Britain, 1900–1918* (Basingstoke and London, 1987)

Adcock, Arthur St John, *For Remembrance: Soldier Poets Who Have Fallen in the War* (Uckfield, 2002; first pub. 1918)

Alexander, Jack, *McCrae's Battalion: The Story of the 16th Royal Scots* (Edinburgh, 2004)

Andrew, C. M., *Secret Service: The Making of the British Intelligence Community* (London, 1985)

Arthur, Max, *Forgotten Voices of the Great War* (London, 2002)

——, *We Will Remember Them: Voices from the Aftermath of the Great War* (London, 2009)

Ashmead-Bartlett, Ellis, *The Uncensored Dardanelles* (London, 1928)

Ashplant, Timothy G., Graham Dawson and Michael Roper, 'The Politics of War Memory and Commemoration: Contexts, Structures and Dynamics', *Routledge Studies in Memory and Narrative* 7 (2000)

Ashton, N. J., 'Hanging the Kaiser: Anglo-Dutch Relations and the Fate of Wilhelm II, 1918–1920', *Diplomacy and Statecraft* 11 (2000)

Ashworth, Tony, *Trench Warfare 1914–1918: The Live and Let Live System* (London, 1980)

Asprey, R., *The German High Command at War: Hindenburg and Ludendorff and the First World War* (London, 1994)

Asquith, H. H., *Letters to Venetia Stanley*, ed. Michael and Eleanor Brock (Oxford, 1985)

——, *Memories and Reflections*, 2 vols. (London, 1928)

Atkinson, Diane, *Elsie and Mairi Go to War: Two Extraordinary Women on the Western Front* (London, 2010)

Audouin-Rouzeau, Stéphane, *Men at War, 1914–1918: National Sentiment and Trench Journalism in France during the First World War* (Oxford, 1992)

—— and Annette Becker, *1914–1918: Understanding the Great War* (London, 2002)

Aulich, James and John Hewitt, *Seduction or Instruction? First World War Posters in Britain and Europe* (Manchester, 2007)

Babington, Anthony, *For the Sake of Example: Capital Courts-Martial 1914–1920* (London, 1993)

——, *Shell-Shock: A History of the Changing Attitudes towards War Neurosis* (London, 1997)

Baedeker, Karl, *Belgium and Holland, Including the Grand-Duchy of Luxembourg: Handbook for Travellers* (London, 1910)

Bairnsfather, Second Lieutenant Bruce [1/Royal Warwickshire], *Bullets and Billets* (London, 1916)

Baker, Peter Shaw, *Animal War Heroes* (London, 1933)

Balderston, T., 'War Finance and Inflation in Britain and Germany, 1914–1918', *Economic History Review* 42 (1989)

Bamji, Andrew, 'Sir Harold Gillies: Surgical Pioneer', *Trauma* 8 (2006)

Bar-Yosef, Eitan, 'The Last Crusade? British Propaganda and the Palestine Campaign 1917–1918', *Journal of Contemporary History* 36 (2001)

Barham, Peter, *Forgotten Lunatics of the Great War* (New Haven, 2004)

Barker, Ralph, *A Brief History of the Royal Flying Corps in World War I* (London, 2002)

Barnett, Correlli, *The Swordbearers: Supreme Command in the First World War* (London, 2000)

Barrett, Michèle, *Casualty Figures: How Five Men Survived the First World War* (London, 2007)

Bartlett, J. and Ellis, K. M., 'Remembering the Dead in Northop: First World War Memorial in a Welsh Parish', *Journal of Contemporary History* 34 (1999)

Barton, Peter, *The Somme* (London, 2006)

Beatty, Jack, *The Lost History of 1914: How the Great War Was Not Inevitable* (London, 2012)

Becker, Annette, *War and Faith: The Religious Imagination in France, 1914–1930* (Oxford, 1998)

Beckett, Ian F. W., 'Going to War: Southampton and Military Embarkation', in Miles Taylor (ed.), *Southampton: Gateway to the British Empire* (London, 2007)

——, *The Great War* (Harlow, 2001)

——, *The Making of the First World War* (Padstow, 2012)

——, *Ypres: The First Battle, 1914* (Harlow, 2006)

Beesly, P., *Room 40: British Naval Intelligence, 1914–18* (London, 1982)

Begbie, Harold, *Lord Kitchener: Organizer of Victory* (Boston and New York, 1915)

Bell, J. F., *Everyman at War: Sixty Personal Narratives of the War*, ed. C. B. Purdom (London, 1930)

Ben-Moshe, Tuvia, 'Churchill's Strategic Conception during the First World War', *Journal of Strategic Studies* 12 (1989)

Bennett, J. D. C., 'Medical Advances Consequent to the Great War 1914–1918', *Journal of the Royal Society of Medicine* 83 (1990)

Berghoff, Hartmut and Robert von Friedeburg, 'Reconstructing or Re-shaping Pre-War Britain?', in Hartmut Berghoff and Robert von Friedeburg (eds.), *Change and Inertia: Britain under the Impact of the Great War* (Bodenheim, 1998)

Best, Nicholas, *The Greatest Day in History: How the First World War Really Ended* (London, 2008)

Bickersteth, John (ed.), *The Bickersteth Diaries 1914–1918* (London, 1995)

Bidwell, Shelford and Dominick Graham, *Fire Power: The British Army Weapons and Theories of War, 1904–1945* (Barnsley, 2004; first pub. 1982)

Biernoff, Suzannah, 'Flesh Poems: Henry Tonks and the Art of Surgery', *Visual Culture in Britain* 11 (2010)

———, 'The Rhetoric of Disfigurement in First World War Britain', *Social History of Medicine* (2011)

Bilton, David, *The Trench: The Full Story of the 1st Hull Pals* (Barnsley, 2002)

Binding, Rudolf, *A Fatalist at War*, trans. Ian Morrow (London, 1929)

Bird, Will, *Ghosts Have Warm Hands: A Memoir of the Great War 1916–1919* (Nepean, Ont., 1997)

Birnbaum, K. E., *Peace Moves and U-Boat Warfare: A Study of Imperial Germany's Policy towards the United States, April 18 1916–January 9 1917* (Uppsala, 1958)

'Blackie' [Catherine Black], *King's Nurse – Beggar's Nurse* (London, 1939)

Blewett, Neal, 'The Franchise in the United Kingdom', *Past & Present* 32 (1965)

Blunden, Edmund, *Undertones of War* (Oxford, 1956; first pub. London, 1928)

Blythe, Ronald, *The Age of Illusions: England in the Twenties and Thirties, 1919–1940* (London, 1963)

Bogacz, Ted, 'War Neurosis and Cultural Change in England, 1914–22: The World of the War Office Committee of Enquiry into "Shell Shock"', *Journal of Contemporary History* 24 (1989)

Boghardt, Thomas, *The Zimmermann Telegram: Intelligence, Diplomacy and America's Entry into World War I* (Annapolis, Md, 2012)

Bond, Brian (ed.), *The First World War and British Military History* (Oxford, 1991)

——— and Nigel Cave (eds.), *Haig: A Reappraisal 70 Years On* (Barnsley, 1999)

Booth, Allyson, *Postcards from the Trenches: Negotiating the Space between Modernism and the First World War* (Oxford, 1996)

Boraston, J. H. (ed.), *Sir Douglas Haig's Despatches, December 1915–April 1919* (London, 1919)

Borg, Alan, *War Memorials: From Antiquity to the Present* (London, 1991)

Bostridge, Mark and Alan Bishop (eds.), *Letters from a Lost Generation: First World War Letters of Vera Brittain and Four Friends* (London, 2008)

Boswell, Jonathan S. and Bruce R. Johns, 'Patriots or Profiteers? British Businessmen and the First World War', *Journal of European Economic History* 11 (1992)

Boulton, David, *Objection Overruled* (London, 1967)

Bourke, Joanna, *Dismembering the Male: Men's Bodies, Britain and the Great War* (London, 1996)

———, 'Effeminacy, Ethnicity and the End of Trauma: The Sufferings of "Shell-Shocked" Men in Great Britain and Ireland, 1914–39', *Journal of Contemporary History* 35 (2000)

———, 'Heroes and Hoaxes: The Unknown Warrior, Kitchener and "Missing Men" in the 1920s', *War and Society* 13 (1995)

——, *An Intimate History of Killing: Face-to-Face Killing in Twentieth-Century Warfare* (London, 1999)

—— (ed.), *The Misfit Soldier: Edward Casey's War Story, 1914–1918* (Cork, 1999)

Bourne, J. M., *Britain and the Great War, 1914–1918* (London, 1989)

Bowley, A. L., *Prices and Wages in the United Kingdom, 1914–1920* (Oxford, 1921)

Brandt, Susanne, 'The Memory Makers: Museums and Exhibitions of the First World War', *History and Memory* 6 (1994)

Braybon, Gail, *Women Workers in the First World War: The British Experience* (London, 1981)

Briar, Celia, *Working for Women? Gendered Work and Welfare Policies in Twentieth Century Britain* (London, 1997)

Brittain, Vera, *Testament of Youth: An Autobiographical Study of the Years 1900–1925* (London, 1978)

Brown, I. M., *British Logistics on the Western Front, 1914–1919* (London, 1998)

Brown, Malcolm, 'The Christmas Truce 1914: The British Story', in Marc Ferro, Malcolm Brown, Remy Cazals and Olaf Mueller (eds.), *Meetings in No Man's Land: Christmas 1914 and Fraternization in the Great War* (London, 2007)

——, *The Imperial War Museum Book of 1918: Year of Victory* (London, 1998)

——, *Tommy Goes to War* (Stroud, 1999)

—— and Shirley Seaton, *Christmas Truce: The Western Front December 1914* (London, 2001; first pub. 1984)

Brown, William, *Psychology and Psychotherapy* (London, 1921)

Brownrigg, Douglas, *Indiscretions of the Naval Censor* (London, 1920)

Bruntz, G. G., *Allied Propaganda and the Collapse of the German Empire in 1918* (Stanford, 1938)

Bryant, Mark, 'Poster Boy: Alfred Leete', *History Today* 59 (2007)

Burrage, A. M. [writing as Ex-Private X], *War is War* (Uckfield, 2009; first pub. London, 1930)

Butcher, Gerald, *Allotments for All* (London, 1918)

Butterworth, Hugh Montagu, *Blood & Iron: Letters from the Western Front*, ed. Jon Cooksey (Barnsley, 2011)

Campbell, Christy, *Band of Brigands: The Extraordinary Story of the First Men in Tanks* (London, 2008)

Campbell, N. J. M., *Jutland: An Analysis of the Fighting* (Annapolis, Md, 1986)

Cannadine, David, 'War and Death, Grief and Mourning in Modern Britain', in Joachim Whaley (ed.), *Mirrors of Mortality: Studies in the Social History of Death* (London, 1981)

Carew, Tim, *Wipers* (London, 1974)

Carlyon, L. A., *Gallipoli* (London, 2003)

Carpenter, Humphrey, *J. R. R. Tolkien: A Biography* (New York, 2000; first pub. London, 1977)

Carr, William, *A Time to Leave the Ploughshares: A Gunner Remembers* (London, 1985)

Carrington, Charles, *Soldier from the Wars Returning* (London, 1965)

——, *A Subaltern's War, being a Memoir of the Great War from the Point of View of a Romantic Young Man* (London, 1929)

Carter, Terry, *Birmingham Pals: 14th, 15th & 16th (Service) Battalions of the Royal Warwickshire Regiment* (Barnsley, 1997)

Cartmell, Harry, *For Remembrance: An Account of Some Fateful Years* (Preston, 1919)

Carton de Wiart, Adrian, *Happy Odyssey* (London, 1950)

Cassar, George, *Asquith as War Leader* (London, 1994)

——, *The French and the Dardanelles: A Study of Failure in the Conduct of War* (London, 1971)

——, *Kitchener's War: British Strategy from 1914 to 1916* (Washington, DC, 2004)

——, *The Tragedy of Sir John French* (London, 1985)

Catchpool, Corder, *On Two Fronts: Letters of a Conscientious Objector* (London, 1940; first pub. 1918)

Cavaghan, Michael, *The Story of the Unknown Warrior* (Wigan, 2003)

Cawood, Ian and David McKinnon-Bell, *The First World War: Questions and Analysis in History* (London, 2001)

Ceadel, Martin, *Pacifism in Britain, 1914–1945: The Defining of a Faith* (Oxford, 1980)

Cecil, Hugh and Peter H. Liddle (eds.), *Facing Armageddon: The First World War Experience* (Barnsley, 2003; first pub. 1996)

Chapman, Guy, *A Passionate Prodigality* (Southampton, 1985; first pub. 1933)

Chickering, Roger, *Imperial Germany and the Great War, 1914–1918* (Cambridge, 1998)

—— and Stig Förster (eds.), *Great War, Total War: Combat and Mobilization on the Western Front, 1914–1918* (Cambridge, 2000)

Childs, D. J., *A Peripheral Weapon? The Production and Employment of British Tanks in the First World War* (London, 1999)

Chirnside, Mark, *RMS Olympic, Titanic's Sister* (Stroud, 2005)

Chisholm, Anne and Michael Davie, *Beaverbrook: A Life* (London, 1993)

Churchill, Winston, *The World Crisis, 1911–1918* (London, 2007, first pub. 1923–31)

Clapham, Marcus (ed.), *The Wordsworth Book of First World War Poetry* (Ware, 1995)

Clark, Alan, *The Donkeys* (London, 1991; first pub. 1961)

Clark, Andrew, *Echoes of the Great War*, ed. James Munson (Oxford, 1985)

Clark, Christopher, *Kaiser Wilhelm II* (Harlow, 2000)

——, *The Sleepwalkers: How Europe Went to War in 1914* (London, 2012)

Clarke, Peter, *Hope and Glory: Britain 1900–2000* (London, 1997)

Clarke, Tom, *My Northcliffe Diary* (London, 1931)

Clayton, P. B., *Tales of Talbot House: Everyman's Club in Ypres 1915–1918* (London, 1920)

Clifford, Colin, *The Asquiths* (London, 2002)

Cloete, Stuart, *A Victorian Son: An Autobiography, 1897–1922* (London, 1972)

C.N. [H. C. McNeile], *The Making of an Officer* (London, 1916)

Cocroft, Wayne, 'First World War Explosives Manufacture: The British Experience', in Roy Macleod and Jeffrey Allan Johnson (eds.), *Frontline and Factory: Comparative Perspectives on the Chemical Industry at War, 1914–1924* (Dordrecht, 2006)

Coffman, E. M., *The War to End All Wars: The American Military Experience in World War I* (Lexington, Ky, 1998)

Cohen, Deborah, *The War Came Home: Disabled Veterans in Britain and Germany, 1914–1939* (Berkeley, 2001)

Collier, Price, *England and the English from an American Point of View* (London, 1912)

Collingham, Lizzie, *The Taste of War: World War Two and the Battle for Food* (London, 2012)

Collins, Tony, 'English Rugby Union and the First World War', *Historical Journal* 45 (2002)

——, *A Social History of English Rugby Union* (Abingdon, 2009)

Colls, Robert, *Identity of England* (Oxford, 2002)

Connelly, Mark, *The Great War, Memory and Ritual: Commemoration in the City and East London, 1916–1939* (London, 2002)

——, *Steady the Buffs! A Regiment, a Region, and the Great War* (Oxford, 2006)

Cooper, Duff, *Old Men Forget* (London, 1935)

Coppard, George, *With a Machine Gun to Cambrai: The Tale of a Young Tommy in Kitchener's Army* (London, 1969)

Corns, Cathryn and John Hughes-Wilson, *Blindfold and Alone: British Military Executions in the Great War* (London, 2001)

Corrigan, Gordon, *Mud, Blood and Poppycock: Britain and the First World War* (London, 2003)

Cox, David, ' "Trying to Get a Good One": Bigamy Offences in England and Wales, 1850–1950', *Plymouth Law and Criminal Justice Review* 1 (2012)

Cox, Pamela, *Gender, Justice and Welfare: Bad Girls in Britain, 1900–1950* (Basingstoke, 2002)

Craster, Michael (ed.), *'Fifteen Rounds a Minute': The Grenadiers at War, August to December 1914* (Barnsley, 2012; first pub. 1976)

Crellin, Sarah, 'Hollow Men: Francis Derwent Wood's Masks and Memorials, 1915–1925', *Sculpture Journal* 6 (2001)

Crossman, A. M., 'The Hydra, Captain A. J. Brock and the Treatment of Shell Shock in Edinburgh', *Journal of the Royal College of Physicians of Edinburgh* 33 (2003)

Crozier, Brigadier General F. P., *A Brass Hat in No Man's Land* (London, 1930)
——, *The Men I Killed* (London, 1937)
Cruttwell, C. R. M. F., *A History of the Great War, 1914–1918* (London, 1982)
Culleton, Claire, *Working-Class Culture, Women, and Britain, 1914–1921* (Basingstoke, 2000)
Daggett, Mabel Potter, *Women Wanted: The Story Written in Blood Red Letters on the Horizon of the Great World War* (London, 1918)
Dakers, Caroline, *The Countryside at War 1914–18* (London, 1987)
Dallas, Gloden and Douglas Gill, *The Unknown Army: Mutinies in the British Army in World War I* (London, 1985)
Dallas, Gregor, *1918: War and Peace* (London, 2002)
Dangerfield, George, *The Strange Death of Liberal England* (London, 1935)
Das, Santanu, *Touch and Intimacy in First World War Literature* (Cambridge, 2005)
David, Edward (ed.), *Inside Asquith's Cabinet, from the Diaries of Charles Hobhouse* (London, 1977)
Davies, Frank and Graham Maddocks, *Bloody Red Tabs: General Officer Casualties of the Great War, 1914–1918* (London, 1995)
Davray, H. D., *Lord Kitchener: His Work and Prestige* (London, 1917)
DeGroot, Gerard, *Blighty: British Society in the Era of the Great War* (London, 1996)
——, *Douglas Haig 1861–1928* (London, 1988)
Desborough, Lady [E. A. P. Grenfell], *Pages from a Family Journal, 1888–1915* (privately printed, Eton, 1916)
Dewey, P. E., 'Food Production and Policy in the United Kingdom, 1914–1918', *Transactions of the Royal Historical Society* 30 (1980)
DiNunzio, Mario (ed.), *Woodrow Wilson: Essential Writings and Speeches of the Scholar-President* (New York, 2006)
Doyle, Arthur Conan, *The New Revelation* (London, 1918)
——, *The Vital Message* (London, 1919)
Doyle, Peter, *The British Soldier of the First World War* (Oxford, 2008)
—— and Julian Walker, *Trench Talk: Words of the First World War* (Stroud, 2012)
Dunn, J. C., *The War the Infantry Knew 1914–1919* (London, 1987; first pub. 1938)
Dunsterville, Lionel, *Stalky's Reminiscences* (London, 1928)
Egerton, G. W., *Great Britain and the Creation of the League of Nations: Strategy, Politics, and International Organization, 1914–1919* (Chapel Hill, NC, 1978)
Egremont, Max, *Siegfried Sassoon: A Biography* (London, 2005)
Ekins, Ashley and Elizabeth Stewart (eds.), *War Wounds: Medicine and the Trauma of Conflict* (Wollombi, NSW, 2011)
Eksteins, Modris, *The Rites of Spring: The Great War and the Birth of the Modern Age* (London, 1989)

Ellinwood, D. C. and S. D. Pradham (eds.), *India and World War I* (New Delhi, 1978)

Ellis, John, *Eye-Deep in Hell* (London, 2002)

Ellsworth-Jones, Will, *We Will Not Fight: The Untold Story of World War One's Conscientious Objectors* (London, 2008)

Elsey, Ena, 'Disabled Ex-Servicemen's Experiences of Rehabilitation and Employment after the First World War', *Oral History* 25 (1997)

Emden, Richard van, *Boy Soldiers of the Great War* (London, 2012)

——, *Fallen Soldiers and their Families in the Great War* (London, 2011)

——, *The Soldier's War: The Great War through Veterans' Eyes* (London, 2009)

——, *Tommy's Ark: Soldiers and their Animals in the Great War* (London, 2010)

—— and Steve Humphries, *All Quiet on the Home Front: An Oral History of Life in Britain during the First World War* (London, 2003)

Essex, Rosamund, *Woman in a Man's World* (London, 1977)

Ewing, A. W., *The Man of Room 40: The Life of Sir Alfred Ewing* (London, 1940; first pub. 1939)

Farrar, Martin, *News from the Front: War Correspondents on the Western Front 1914–1918* (Stroud, 1998)

Feilding, Dorothie, *Lady under Fire on the Western Front: The Great War Letters of Lady Dorothie Feilding*, ed. Andrew and Nicola Hallam (Barnsley, 2010)

Felstead, Sidney Theodore, *German Spies at Bay: Being an Actual Record of the German Espionage in Great Britain during the Years 1914–1918* (London, 1920)

Feo, Katherine, 'Invisibility: Memory, Masks and Masculinities in the Great War', *Journal of Design History* 20 (2007)

Ferguson, Niall, *The Pity of War* (London, 1999)

Ferris, J. (ed.), *The British Army and Signals Intelligence during the First World War* (Stroud, 1992)

Finn, Michael, 'Local Heroes: War News and the Construction of "Community" in Britain, 1914–18', *Historical Research* 83 (2010)

Fitzherbert, Margaret, *The Man Who Was Greenmantle: A Biography of Aubrey Herbert* (Oxford, 1985)

Fletcher, David (ed.), *Tanks and Trenches: First Hand Accounts of Tank Warfare in the First World War* (Stroud, 2009)

Flynn, George, *Conscription and Democracy: The Draft in France, Great Britain and the United States* (Westport, Conn., 2002)

Foden, Giles, *Mimi and Toutou Go Forth: The Bizarre Battle of Lake Tanganyika* (London, 2005)

Foley, Michael, *Hard as Nails: The Sportsmen's Battalion of World War One* (Stroud, 2007)

Fong, Giordan, 'The Movement of German Divisions to the Western Front, Winter 1917–1918', *War in History* 7 (2000)

Ford, Ford Madox, *Parade's End* (London, 1992; first pub. 1924–8)

Fort, Adrian, *Archibald Wavell: The Life and Times of an Imperial Servant* (London, 2009)

Fox, James, '"Traitor Painters": Artists and Espionage in the First World War, 1914–18', *British Art Journal* 9 (2009)

Foy, Michael and Brian Barton, *The Easter Rising* (Stroud, 2011)

Fraser, Peter, 'The British "Shells Scandal" of 1915', *Canadian Journal of History* 18 (1983)

French, David, 'The Meaning of Attrition, 1914–1916', *English Historical Review* 103 (1988)

——, 'The Military Background to the "Shell Crisis" of May 1915', *Journal of Strategic Studies* 2 (1979)

——, 'The Origins of the Dardanelles Campaign Reconsidered', *History* 68 (1983)

——, 'Spy Fever in Britain, 1900–1915', *Historical Journal* 21 (1978)

——, *The Strategy of the Lloyd George Coalition, 1916–1918* (Oxford, 1995)

French of Ypres, Field Marshal Viscount, *1914* (London, 1919)

Fridenson, P. (ed.), *The French Home Front, 1914–1918* (Oxford, 1992)

Fuller, J. G., *Troop Morale and Popular Culture in the British and Dominion Armies, 1914–1918* (Oxford, 1990)

Fussell, Paul, *The Great War and Modern Memory* (Oxford, 2000; first pub. 1975)

Gabriel, R. A. and K. S. Metz, *A History of Military Medicine*, 2 vols. (London, 1992)

Gardner, Nikolas, *Trial by Fire: Command and the British Expeditionary Force in 1914* (London, 2003)

Gassert, Imogen, 'In a Foreign Field: What Soldiers in the Trenches Liked to Read', *Times Literary Supplement*, 10 May 2002

Geppert, Alexander, 'Divine Sex, Happy Marriage, Regenerated Nation: Marie Stopes's Marital Manual *Married Love* and the Making of a Best-Seller, 1918–1955', *Journal of the History of Sexuality* 8 (1988)

Giangrande, Paul, 'The History of Blood Transfusion', *British Journal of Haematology* 110 (2000)

Gilbert, B. B., 'Pacifist to Interventionist: David Lloyd George in 1911 and 1914. Was Belgium an Issue?', *Historical Journal* 28 (1985)

Gilbert, Martin, *The Challenge of War: Winston S. Churchill, 1914–1916* (London, 1990; first pub. 1971)

——, *Churchill: A Life* (London, 1991)

Gill, Douglas and Gloden Dallas, 'Mutiny at Etaples Base in 1917', *Past & Present* 69 (1975)

Gillies, Harold and D. Ralph Millard, *The Principles and Art of Plastic Surgery*, 2 vols. (London, 1957)

Gilmour, David, *The Long Recessional: The Imperial Life of Rudyard Kipling* (London, 2002)

Ginzburg, Carlo, '"Your Country Needs You": A Case Study in Political Iconography', *History Workshop Journal* 52 (2001)

Girouard, Mark, *The Return to Camelot: Chivalry and the English Gentleman* (London, 1981)

Gladden, Norman, *Ypres, 1917: A Personal Account* (London, 1977)

Glover, Jon and Jon Silkin (eds.), *The Penguin Book of First World War Prose* (Harmondsworth, 1990)

Goebel, Stefan, 'Beyond Discourse? Bodies and Memories of Two World Wars', *Journal of Contemporary History* 22 (2007)

Goodall, Felicity, *We Will Not Go to War: Conscientious Objection during the World Wars* (Stroud, 2011)

Gordon, A., *The Rules of the Game: Jutland and British Naval Command* (London, 1996)

Graham, John, *Conscience and Conscription: A History 1916–1919* (London, 1922)

Graham, Stephen, *A Private in the Guards* (London, 1919)

Graubard, Stephen Richards, 'Demobilization in Great Britain Following the First World War', *Journal of Modern History* 19 (1947)

Graves, Robert, *Goodbye to All That* (London, 1960; first pub. 1929)

—— and Alan Hodge, *The Long Week-End: The Living Story of the Twenties and Thirties* (London, 1971; first pub. 1940)

Grayzel, Susan, 'The Enemy Within: The Problem of British Women's Sexuality during the First World War', in Nicole Dombrowski (ed.), *Women and War in the Twentieth Century: Enlisted with or without Consent* (Abingdon, 1999)

——, 'Nostalgia, Gender and the Countryside: Placing the "Land Girl" in First World War Britain', *Rural History* (1999)

——, *Women and the First World War* (Harlow, 2002)

——, *Women's Identities at War: Gender, Motherhood, and Politics in Britain and France during the First World War* (Chapel Hill, NC, 1999)

Greenwell, Graham H., *An Infant in Arms* (London, 1972)

Gregory, Adrian, 'British "War Enthusiasm" in 1914', in Gail Braybon (ed.), *Evidence, History and the Great War: Historians and the Impact of 1914–18* (Oxford, 2003)

——, 'A Clash of Cultures: The British Press and the Opening of the Great War', in Troy R. E. Paddock (ed.), *A Call to Arms: Propaganda, Public Opinion, and Newspapers in the Great War* (London, 2004)

——, *The Last Great War: British Society and the First World War* (Cambridge, 2008)

——, 'Military Service Tribunals: Civil Society in Action, 1916–1918', in Jose Harris (ed.), *Civil Society in British History: Ideas, Identities, Institutions* (Oxford, 2005)

——, *The Silence of Memory: Armistice Day, 1919–1946* (Oxford, 1994)

Grey of Fallodon, Viscount, *The Charm of Birds* (London, 2001; first pub. 1927)

——, *Twenty-Five Years, 1892–1916*, 2 vols. (London, 1925)

Griffith, Paddy, *Battle Tactics of the Western Front: The British Army's Art of Attack, 1916–18* (London, 1994)

—— (ed.), *British Fighting Methods in the Great War* (London, 1996)

Grigg, John, *Lloyd George: War Leader* (London, 2001)

Grinnell-Milne, Duncan, *Wind in the Wires* (London, 1957; first pub. 1933)

Grundy, Jim, ' "Lloyd George's Beer" or When It Was Illegal to Buy your Round', *Western Front Association* (11 December 2010)

Gudmundsson, B. I., *Stormtroop Tactics: Innovation in the German Army, 1914–1918* (London, 1989)

Gullace, Nicoletta, *'The Blood of our Sons': Men, Women and the Regeneration of British Citizenship during the Great War* (New York, 2004)

——, 'Sexual Violence and Family Honour: British Propaganda and International Law during the First World War', *American Historical Review* 102 (1997)

——, 'White Feathers and Wounded Men: Female Patriotism and the Memory of the Great War', *Journal of British Studies* 36 (1997)

Haber, L. F., *The Poisonous Cloud: Chemical Warfare in the First World War* (Oxford, 1986)

Haig, Douglas, *War Diaries and Letters 1914–1918*, ed. Gary Sheffield and John Bourne (London, 2006)

Hallifax, Stuart, ' "Over by Christmas": British Popular Opinion and the Short War in 1914', *First World War Studies* 1 (2010)

Halpern, P. G., *A Naval History of World War I* (London, 1994)

Hamilton, General Sir Ian, *Gallipoli Diary*, 2 vols. (London, 1920)

Hamilton, R. F. and H. H. Herwig (eds.), *The Origins of World War I* (Cambridge, 2003)

Hammond, J. L., *C. P. Scott of the Manchester Guardian* (London, 1934)

Hampton, Mark, *The Vision of the Press in Britain, 1850–1950* (Chicago, 2004)

Hardy, Dennis and Colin Ward, *Arcadia for All: The Legacy of a Makeshift Landscape* (London, 1984)

Harris, J. P. and Niall Barr, *Amiens to the Armistice: The BEF in the Hundred Days' Campaign, 8 August–11 November 1918* (London, 1998)

Harris, Robert and Jeremy Paxman, *A Higher Form of Killing* (London, 1982)

Harris, Ruth Elwin, *Billie: The Nevill Letters: 1914–1916* (Uckfield, 1991)

Harrison, Mark, 'The British Army and the Problem of Venereal Disease in France and Egypt during the First World War', *Medical Journal* 39 (1995)

——, *The Medical War: British Military Medicine in the First World War* (Oxford, 2010)

Hart, Peter, *1918: A Very British Victory* (London, 2009)

——, *Gallipoli* (London, 2011)

Hartcup, G., *The War of Invention: Scientific Developments, 1914–18* (London, 1988)

Haste, Cate, *Keep the Home Fires Burning: Propaganda in the First World War* (London, 1977)

Hayward, James, *Myths and Legends of the First World War* (Stroud, 2002)

Hazelgrove, Jenny, *Spiritualism and British Society between the Wars* (Manchester, 2000)

Hazlehurst, Cameron, *Politicians at War: A Prologue to the Triumph of Lloyd George* (London, 1971)

Heathorn, Stephen, ' "A Great Grey Dawn for the Empire": Great War Conspiracy Theory, the British State and the "Kitchener Film" (1921–1926)', *War and Society* 26 (2007)

Henniker, A. M., *Transportation on the Western Front, 1914–1918* (London, 1937)

Hermon, Lieutenant Colonel E. W., *For Love and Courage: Letters Home from the Western Front 1914–1917*, ed. Anne Nason (London, 2009)

Herrmann, D. G., *The Arming of Europe and the Making of the First World War* (Princeton, 1996)

Hessen, Robert, *Steel Titan: The Life of Charles M. Schwab* (Oxford, 1975)

Hiley, Nicholas, 'Counter-Espionage and Security in Great Britain during the First World War', *English Historical Review* 101 (1986)

——, ' "Kitchener Wants You" and "Daddy, What Did YOU Do in the Great War?": The Myth of British Recruiting Posters', *Imperial War Museum Review* 11 (1997)

History of the Great War Based on Official Documents, 29 vols. (London, 1923–49)

Hochschild, Adam, *To End All Wars: A Story of Loyalty and Rebellion, 1914–1918* (London, 2011)

Holden, Katherine, *The Shadow of Marriage: Singleness in England 1914–60* (Manchester, 2007)

Hollingham, Richard, *Blood and Guts: A History of Surgery* (London, 2008)

Hollis, Matthew, *Now All Roads Lead to France: The Last Years of Edward Thomas* (London, 2011)

Holmes, Richard, *Acts of War: The Behaviour of Men in Battle* (London, 2004; first pub. 1985)

——, *The Little Field Marshal: Sir John French* (London, 1981)

——, 'Sir John French and Lord Kitchener', in Brian Bond (ed.), *The First World War and British Military History* (Oxford, 1991)

——, *Tommy: The British Soldier on the Western Front* (London, 2011)

——, *The Western Front* (London, 1999)

Homberger, Eric, 'The Story of the Cenotaph', *Times Literary Supplement*, 12 November 1976

Hopkin, Dlian, 'Domestic Censorship in the First World War', *Journal of Contemporary History* 5 (1970)

Horn, Martin, *Britain, France, and the Financing of the First World War* (Montreal, 2002)

——, 'The Concept of Total War: National Effort and Taxation in Britain and France during the First World War', *War and Society* 18 (2000)

Horne, Alistair, *Macmillan: The Official Biography* (London, 2008)

——, *The Price of Glory: Verdun, 1916* (London, 1978)

Horne, John (ed.), *State, Society and Mobilization in Europe during the First World War* (Cambridge, 1997)

—— and Alan Kramer, *German Atrocities, 1914: A History of Denial* (New Haven and London, 2001)

——, 'German "Atrocities" and Franco-German Opinion, 1914: The Evidence of German Soldiers' Diaries', *Journal of Modern History* 66 (1994)

Hough, Richard, *The Great War at Sea* (London, 1983)

Housman, Laurence (ed.), *War Letters of Fallen Englishmen* (Philadelphia, 2002; first pub. London, 1930)

Howkins, Alun, *The Death of Rural England: A Social History of the Countryside since 1900* (London, 2003)

Huguet, General Victor, *Britain and the War: A French Indictment* (London, 1928)

Hurst, Sidney C., *The Silent Cities: An Illustrated Guide to the War Cemeteries and Memorials to the 'Missing' in France and Flanders, 1914–1918* (Uckfield, 2002; first pub. 1929)

Husbands, Geoffrey Ratcliff, *Joffrey's War: A Sherwood Forester in the Great War* (Nottingham, 2011)

Hutt, C. W., *The Future of the Disabled Soldier* (London, 1917)

Hynes, Samuel, *A War Imagined: The First World War and English Culture* (London, 1990)

Jalland, Patricia, *Death in the Victorian Family* (Oxford, 1996)

James, Lawrence, *Aristocrats: Power, Grace and Decadence: Britain's Great Ruling Classes from 1066 to the Present* (New York, 2009)

James, Pearl (ed.), *Picture This: World War I Posters and Visual Culture* (Lincoln, Neb., 2009)

Jannen Jr, William, *The Lions of July: Prelude to War, 1914* (London, 1996)

Jeffery, Keith, *Ireland and the Great War* (Cambridge, 2000)

Jellicoe, John Rushworth, *The Grand Fleet, 1914–16: Its Creation, Development and Work by Viscount Jellicoe of Scapa* (London, 1919)

Jenkins, Roy, *Asquith* (London, 1978)

Johnson, Claudia, 'Austen Cults and Cultures', in Edward Copeland and Juliet McMaster (eds.), *The Cambridge Companion to Jane Austen* (Cambridge, 1997)

Jones, Edgar, 'Doctors and Trauma in World War One: The Response of the British Military Psychiatrists', in Peter Gray and Kendrick Oliver (eds.), *The Memory of Catastrophe* (Manchester, 2004)

——, 'The Psychology of Killing: The Combat Experience of British Soldiers during the First World War', *Journal of Contemporary History* 41 (2006)

Jones, Max, *The Last Great Quest: Captain Scott's Antarctic Sacrifice* (Oxford, 2003)

Jones, Nigel, *Rupert Brooke: Life, Death and Myth* (London, 1999)

Jünger, Ernst, *Storm of Steel* (London, 2003)

Keegan, John, *The Face of Battle: A Study of Agincourt, Waterloo, and the Somme* (London, 1991)

——, *The First World War* (London, 1998)

Kelly, Andrew, *Cinema and the Great War* (London, 1997)

Kelly, Patrick, *Tirpitz and the Imperial German Navy* (Bloomington, Ind., 2011)

Kelly, R. B. Talbot, *A Subaltern's Odyssey: Memoirs of the Great War 1915–1917* (London, 1980)

Kenyon, David, *Horsemen in No Man's Land: British Cavalry and Trench Warfare 1914–1918* (Barnsley, 2011)

Kernot, Charles Frederic, *British Public Schools War Memorials* (Uckfield, 2001; first pub. 1927)

Keynes, Geoffrey, *The Gates of Memory* (Oxford, 1981)

—— (ed.), *The Letters of Rupert Brooke* (London, 1968)

King, Alex, Memorials of the Great War in Britain: The Symbolism and Politics of Remembrance (Oxford, 1998)

Kitson, Arthur, *The Great Pacifist Conspiracy* (Stamford, 1918)

Knocker, Elsie, *Flanders and Other Fields: Memoirs of the Baroness de T'Serclaes* (London, 1964)

Korte, Barbara and Anne-Marie Einhaus, *The Penguin Book of First World War Stories* (London, 2007)

Koven, Seth, 'Remembering and Dismemberment: Crippled Children, Wounded Soldiers and the Great War in Great Britain', *American Historical Review* 99 (1994)

Kumar, Krishan, *The Making of English National Identity* (Cambridge, 2003)

Lawrence, D. H., *Lady Chatterley's Lover* (London, 2007; first pub. 1928)

Lederer, Susan, *Flesh and Blood: Organ Transplantation and Blood Transfusion in Twentieth-Century America* (Oxford, 2008)

Leed, E. J., *No Man's Land: Combat and Identity in World War I* (Cambridge, 1979)

Lees-Milne, James, *Diaries, 1942–1954* (London, 2006)

Leese, Peter, 'Problems Returning Home: The British Psychological Casualties of the Great War', *Historical Journal* 40 (1997)

——, *Shell Shock: Traumatic Neurosis and the British Soldiers of the First World War* (New York, 2002)

Le Queux, William, *German Atrocities: A Record of Shameless Deeds* (London, 1914)

——, *German Spies in England: An Exposure* (London, 1915)

——, *The German Spy System from Within* (London, 1915)

——, *Spies of the Kaiser* (London, 1909)

Levine, Joshua, *Fighter Heroes of WWI* (London, 2009)

Lewis, Cecil, *Sagittarius Rising* (London, 1936)

Lewis-Stempel, John, *Six Weeks: The Short and Gallant Life of the British Officer in the First World War* (London, 2010)

Lichnowsky, Prince, *My Mission to London, 1912–1914* (New York, 1918)

Liddle, P. H., *Men of Gallipoli: The Dardanelles and Gallipoli Experience, August 1914 to January 1916* (London, 1976).

—— (ed.), *Passchendaele in Perspective: The Third Battle of Ypres* (London, 1997)

Lloyd, David Wharton, *Battlefield Tourism: Pilgrimage and the Commemoration of the Great War in Britain, Australia and Canada, 1919–1939* (Oxford, 1998)

Lloyd, Nick, *Hundred Days: The End of the Great War* (London, 2013)

——, *Loos 1915* (Stroud, 2008)

Lloyd George, David, *The Great War* (London 1914)

——, *War Memoirs*, 2 vols. (London, 1933–6)

Lodge, Oliver, *Raymond: or, Life and Death, with Examples of the Evidence for Survival of Memory and Affection after Death* (London, 1916)

Loez, André, 'Tears in the Trenches: A History of Emotions and the Experience of War', in Jenny Macleod and Pierre Purseigle (eds.), *Uncovered Fields: Perspectives in First World War Studies* (Leiden, 2004)

Longworth, Philip, *The Unending Vigil: A History of the Commonwealth War Graves Commission* (London, 1985)

Lowe, C. J., *The Mirage of Power*, vol. III: *The Documents* (London, 1972)

Lowry, Bullitt, *Armistice 1918* (Kent, Ohio, 1996)

Lubin, David, 'Masks, Mutilation and Modernity: Anna Coleman Ladd and the First World War', *Archives of American Art Journal* 47 (2008)

Lubow, Robert, *The War Animals: The Training and Use of Animals as Weapons of War* (New York, 1977)

Lucy, J. F., *There's a Devil in the Drum* (Eastbourne, 1992)

Macaulay, George, *Grey of Fallodon, Being the Life of Sir Edward Grey Afterwards Viscount Grey of Fallodon* (London, 1937)

McCartney, Helen, *Citizen Soldiers: The Liverpool Territorials in the First World War* (Cambridge, 2005)

McCormick, Donald, *The Mystery of Lord Kitchener's Death* (London, 1959)

MacDonagh, Michael, *In London during the Great War: The Diary of a Journalist* (London, 1935)

Macdonald, Lyn, *1914: The Days of Hope* (London, 1989)

——, *1914–1918: Voices and Images of the Great War* (London, 1991)

——, *1915: The Death of Innocence* (London, 1997)

——, *The Roses of No Man's Land* (London, 1993; first pub. 1980)

——, *Somme* (London, 1993; first pub. 1983)

——, *They Called It Passchendaele: The Story of the Third Battle of Ypres and of the Men Who Fought in It* (London, 1993; first pub. 1978)

——, *To the Last Man: Spring 1918* (London, 1998)

Macdonald, Scot, *Propaganda and Information Warfare in the Twenty-First Century* (Abingdon, 2007)

McEwen, John, '"Brass-Hats" and the British Press during the First World War', *Canadian Journal of History* 18 (1983)

——, 'The National Press during the First World War: Ownership and Circulation', *Journal of Contemporary History* 17 (1982)

——, 'The Press and the Fall of Asquith', *Historical Journal* 21 (1978)

McIntyre, Colin, *Monuments of War* (London, 1990)

Mackenzie, Compton, *Gallipoli Memories* (London, 1929)

MacKenzie, S. P., 'Morale and the Cause: The Campaign to Change the Outlook of Soldiers in the British Expeditionary Force, 1914–1918', *Canadian Journal of History* 15 (1990)

Macleod, Jenny, *Reconsidering Gallipoli* (Manchester, 2004)

McMeekin, Sean, *The Berlin–Baghdad Express* (London, 2011)

Macmillan, Harold, *The Winds of Change* (London, 1966)

MacMillan, Margaret, *Peacemakers* (London, 2001)

Madigan, Edward, *Faith under Fire: Anglican Army Chaplains and the Great War* (Basingstoke, 2011)

——, '"Sticking to a Hateful Task": Resilience, Humour, and British Understandings of Combatant Courage, 1914–1918', *War in History* 20 (2013)

Magnus, Philip, *Kitchener: Portrait of an Imperialist* (London, 1958)

Makepeace, Clare, 'Male Heterosexuality and Prostitution during the Great War', *Culture and Social History* 9 (2012)

Malvern, Sue, 'War, Memory and Museums: Art and Artefact in the Imperial War Museum', *History Workshop Journal* 49 (2000)

Manning, Frederic, *The Middle Parts of Fortune: Somme and Ancre, 1916* (London, 1929)

Marder, Arthur, *The Anatomy of British Sea Power: A History of British Naval Policy in the Pre-Dreadnought Era, 1880–1905* (London, 1964)

Marlow, Joyce (ed.), *The Virago Book of Women and the Great War, 1914–18* (London, 1998)

Marquis, Alice, 'Words as Weapons: Propaganda in Britain and Germany during the First World War', *Journal of Contemporary History* 13 (1978)

Marr, Andrew, *The Making of Modern Britain* (London, 2009)

Marrin, Albert, *The Last Crusade: The Church of England in the First World War* (Durham, 1974)

Martin, Christopher, *English Life in the First World War* (London, 1974)

Marwick, Arthur, *The Deluge: British Society and the First World War* (London, 1991)

Masefield, John, *St George and the Dragon* (London, 1918)

Massie, Robert, *Castles of Steel: Britain, Germany and the Winning of the Great War at Sea* (London, 2007)

Mellersh, H. E. L., *Schoolboy into War* (London, 1978)

Melman, Billie, *Women and the Popular Imagination in the Twenties: Flappers and Nymphs* (London, 1988)

The Message: Lord Kitchener Lives, Received by Ala Mana, vol. I (Vancouver, 1922)

Messenger, Charles, *Call-to-Arms: The British Army 1914–18* (London, 2006)

Messinger, Gary, *British Propaganda and the State in the First World War* (Manchester, 1992)

Miller, Geoffrey, *The Millstone: British Naval Policy in the Mediterranean, 1900–1914* (Hull, 1999)

Millett, Allan and Williamson Murray (eds.), *Military Effectiveness*, vol. I: *The First World War* (Cambridge, 2010)

Millman, Brock, *Managing Domestic Dissent in First World War Britain* (London, 2000)

Mills, Simon, *RMS Olympic: The Old Reliable* (Launceston, 1995)

Milton, Richard, *Best of Enemies: Britain and Germany – 100 Years of Truth and Lies* (Cambridge, 2007)

Mitchell, David, *Women on the Warpath* (London, 1966)

Mommsen, W. J., 'The Topos of Inevitable War in Germany in the Decade before 1914', in Volker R. Berghahn and Martin Kitchen (eds.), *Germany in the Age of Total War* (London, 1981)

Monger, David, *Patriotism and Propaganda in First World War Britain* (Liverpool, 2012)

Montell, Hugh, *A Chaplain's War: The Story of Noel Mellish VC, MC* (London, 2002)

Moorehead, Alan, *Gallipoli* (London, 1997; first pub. 1956)

Moorehead, Caroline, *Troublesome People: Enemies of War, 1916–1986* (London, 1987)

Moran, Herbert, *Viewless Winds: Being the Recollections and Digressions of an Australian Surgeon* (London, 1939)

Moran, Lord, *The Anatomy of Courage: The Classic WWI Account of the Psychological Effects of War* (London, 2007; first pub. 1945)

Morgan, Kenneth O. (ed.), *The Oxford History of Britain* (Oxford, 2010)

Morley, John Viscount, *Memorandum on Resignation, August 1914* (London, 1928)

Morris, James, *Pax Britannica: The Climax of an Empire* (London, 1968)

Morton, James, *Spies of the First World War: Under Cover for King and Kaiser* (Kew, 2010)

Moses, John A., 'The British and German Churches and the Perception of War, 1908–1914', *War and Society* 1 (1987)

Mosley, Nicholas, *Julian Grenfell: His Life and the Times of his Death, 1888–1915* (London, 1976)

Mosse, G. E., *Fallen Soldiers: Reshaping the Memory of the World Wars* (New York and Oxford, 1990)

Mowat, Charles Loch, *Britain between the Wars, 1918–1940* (London, 1955)

Muir, Ward, *The Happy Hospital* (London, 1918)

Murland, Jerry, *Aristocrats Go to War: Uncovering Zillebeke Cemetery* (London, 2010)

Murray, Nicholas, *The Red Wine of Sweet Youth: The Brave and Brief Lives of the War Poets* (London, 2011)

Napier, G. G., *Kitchener Drowned* (n.p., 1930)

Neal, Sarah, *Rural Identities: Ethnicity and Community in the Contemporary English Countryside* (Farnham, 2009)

Neander, Joachim and Randal Marlin, 'Media and Propaganda: The Northcliffe Press and the Corpse Factory Story of World War I', *Global Media Journal, Canadian Edition* 3 (2010)

Neillands, Robin, *The Great War Generals* (London, 1999)

——, *The Old Contemptibles: The British Expeditionary Force, 1914* (London, 2004)

Nelson, Robert L., ' "Ordinary Men" in the First World War? German Soldiers as Victims and Participants', *Journal of Contemporary History* 39 (2004)

Nevison, Henry, *Last Changes, Last Chances* (London, 1928)

Newton, Douglas, 'The Lansdowne "Peace Letter" of 1917 and the Prospect of Peace by Negotiation with Germany', *Australian Journal of Politics and History* 48 (2002)

Nichol, John and Tony Rennell, *Medic: Saving Lives from Dunkirk to Afghanistan* (London, 2010)

Nicholson, Juliet, *The Great Silence: Britain from the Shadow of the First World War to the Dawn of the Jazz Age* (London, 2009)

——, *The Perfect Summer: Dancing into Shadow in 1911* (London, 2006)

Nicholson, Virginia, *Singles Out: How Two Million British Women Survived without Men after the First World War* (Oxford, 2008)

Nicolson, Harold, *King George the Fifth: His Life and Reign* (London, 1952)

Northcliffe, Lord, *At the War* (London, 1916)

O'Connell, Robert, *Sacred Vessels: The Cult of the Battleship and the Rise of the U.S. Navy* (Oxford, 1991)

Oppenheim, Janet, *The Other World: Spiritualism and Psychical Research in England, 1850–1914* (Cambridge, 1985)

Orel, Harold, *Popular Fiction in England 1914–1918* (Hemel Hempstead, 1992)

Osborne, Eric, *The Battle of Heligoland Bight* (Indianapolis, 2006)

Osman, A. H., *Pigeons in the Great War: A Complete History of the Carrier-Pigeon Service during the Great War, 1914–1918* (London, 1928)

Overy, Richard, *The Morbid Age: Britain and the Crisis of Civilization, 1919–1939* (London, 2010)

Owen, Wilfred, *Wilfred Owen: Collected Letters*, ed. Harold Owen and John Bell (London, 1967)

Paddock, Troy R. E. (ed.), *A Call to Arms: Propaganda, Public Opinion, and Newspapers in the Great War* (London, 2004)

Panayi, Panikos, *The Enemy in our Midst: Germans in Britain during the First World War* (New York and Oxford, 1991)

Paris, Michael (ed.), *The First World War and Popular Cinema: 1914 to the Present* (Edinburgh, 1999)

Parker, David, *Hertfordshire Children in War and Peace: 1914–1939* (Hatfield, 2007)

Patton Jr, G. S., *The Defense of Gallipoli* (Fort Shafter, Hawaii, 1936)

Pegum, John, 'British Army Trench Journals and a Geography of Identity', in Mary Hammond and Shafquat Towheed (eds.), *Publishing in the First World War: Essays in Book History* (Basingstoke, 2007)

Pelis, Kim, 'Taking Credit: The Canadian Army Medical Corps and the British Conversion to Blood Transfusion in WWI', *Journal of the History of Medicine* 56 (2001)

Pennell, Catriona, ' "The Germans Have Landed": Invasion Fears in the South-East of England, August to December 1914', in Heather Jones, Jennifer O'Brien and Christopher Schmidt-Supprian (eds.), *Untold War: New Perspectives in First World War Studies* (Leiden, 2008)

——, *A Kingdom United: Popular Responses to the Outbreak of the First World War in Britain and Ireland* (Oxford, 2012)

Petter, Martin, ' "Temporary Gentlemen" in the Aftermath of the Great War: Rank, Status and the Ex-Officer Problem', *Historical Journal* 37 (1994)

Pinker, Steven, *The Better Angels of our Nature: The Decline of Violence in History and its Causes* (London, 2011)

Playne, Caroline, *Britain Holds On 1917, 1918* (London, 1933)

——, *Society at War 1914–1916* (London, 1931)

Plowman, Max, *A Subaltern on the Somme* (London, 1927)

Pollard, A. O., *Fire-Eater: The Memoirs of a V.C.* (London, 1932)

Pollock, John, *Kitchener: The Road to Omdurman and Saviour of the Nation* (London, 2001)

Porter, Patrick, 'Beyond Comfort: German and English Military Chaplains and the Memory of the Great War 1919–1929', *Journal of Religious History* 29 (2005)

——, 'New Jerusalems: Sacrifice and Redemption in the War Experience of English and German Military Chaplains', in Pierre Purseigle (ed.), *Warfare and Belligerence: Perspectives in First World War Studies* (Leiden, 2005)

Potter, Jane, *Boys in Khaki, Girls in Print: Women's Literary Responses to the Great War, 1914–1918* (Oxford, 2005)

Pound, Reginald, *Gillies, Surgeon Extraordinary* (London, 1964)

—— and Geoffrey Harmsworth, *Northcliffe* (London, 1957)

Powell, Anne, *Women in the War Zone: Hospital Service in the First World War* (Stroud, 2009)

Power, Frank, *The Kitchener Mystery* (London, 1926)

Pratt, E. A., *British Railways and the Great War*, 2 vols. (London, 1921)

Preston, Diana, *Wilful Murder: The Sinking of the Lusitania* (London, 2002)

Prete, Roy A., *Strategy and Command: The Anglo-French Coalition on the Western Front, 1914* (London, 2009)

Prior, Robin and Trevor Wilson, *Passchendaele: The Untold Story* (London, 2002)

Pugh, Martin, *The Making of Modern British Politics, 1867–1945* (Oxford, 2002)

Putkowski, Julian, *British Army Mutineers, 1914–1922* (London, 1998)

Read, Mike, *Forever England: The Life of Rupert Brooke* (London, 1997)

Reeves, Nicholas, *Official British Film Propaganda during the First World War* (London, 1986)

Reimann, Aribert, 'Popular Culture and the Reconstruction of British Identity', in Hartmut Berghoff and Robert von Friedeburg (eds.), *Change and Inertia: Britain under the Impact of the Great War* (Bodenheim, 1998)

Remarque, E. M., *All Quiet on the Western Front* (London, 1996; first pub. 1929)

Repington, Charles, *The Letters of Lieutenant-Colonel Charles à Court Repington*, ed. A. J. A. Morris (Stroud, 1999)

Reynolds, Gerald W. and Anthony Judge, *The Night the Police Went on Strike* (London, 1968)

Reznick, Geoffrey, *Healing the Nation: Soldiers and the Culture of Caregiving in Britain during the Great War* (Manchester, 2004)

Richards, Anthony, *Report of the War Office Committee of Enquiry into 'Shell-Shock'* (London, 2004; first pub. 1922)

Riddell, George, *Lord Riddell's War Diary 1914–1918* (London, 1933)

Rivers, W. H. R., *Instinct and the Unconscious* (Cambridge, 1920)

Robb, George, *British Culture and the First World War* (Basingstoke, 2002)

Rogerson, Sidney, *Twelve Days on the Somme: A Memoir of the Trenches, 1916* (London, 2006)

Root, Laura, '"Temporary Gentlemen" on the Western Front: Class-Consciousness and the British Army Officer, 1914–1918', *Osprey Journal of Ideas and Inquiry* 72 (2006)

Rothstein, Andrew, *The Soldiers' Strikes of 1919* (London, 1985)

Russell, Bertrand, *The Autobiography of Bertrand Russell: 1914–44*, vol. II (London, 1968)

Sassoon, Siegfried, *Diaries 1915–1918*, ed. Rupert Hart-Davis (London, 1983)

——, *Memoirs of an Infantry Officer: The Memoirs of George Sherston* (London, 2013; first pub. 1930)

——, *Siegfried's Journey, 1916–1920* (London, 1982; first pub. 1945)

Saunders, Nicholas, *Trench Art: Materialities and Memories of War* (Oxford, 2003)

Seipp, Adam, *The Ordeal of Peace: Demobilization and the Urban Experience in Britain and Germany, 1917–1921* (Farnham, 2009)

Sellers, Leonard, *Shot in the Tower: The Story of the Spies Executed in the Tower of London during the First World War* (London, 1997)

Seth, Ronald, *The Spy Who Wasn't Caught* (London, 1966)

Sheffield, Gary, *The Chief: Douglas Haig and the British Army* (London, 2012)

——, *Forgotten Victory: The First World War: Myths and Realities* (London, 2002)

——, *Leadership in the Trenches: Officer–Man Relations, Morale and Discipline in the British Army in the Era of the First World War* (Basingstoke, 1999)

—— (ed.), *War on the Western Front: In the Trenches of World War One* (Oxford, 2007)

——, *The Western Front Experience* (London, 2011)

—— and Dan Todman (eds.), *Command and Control on the Western Front: The British Army's Experience 1914–1918* (Staplehurst, 2004)

Shephard, Ben, *A War of Nerves* (London, 2000)

Simkins, Peter, 'The Four Armies 1914–1918', in David G. Chandler and Ian Beckett (eds.), *The Oxford History of the British Army* (Oxford, 2003)

——, *Kitchener's Army: The Raising of the New Armies, 1914–16* (Manchester, 1988)

——, Geoffrey Jukes and Michael Hickey, *The First World War: The War to End All Wars* (Oxford, 2003)

Simmonds, Percy, *For his Friends, Letters of 2nd Lt. P. G. Simmonds, Who Was Killed in Action on the Somme, July 1st, 1916* (Oxford, 1917)

Simpson, Keith, 'The British Soldier on the Western Front', in Peter Liddle (ed.), *Home Fires and Foreign Fields: British Social and Military Experience in the First World War* (London, 1985)

Sinclair, Upton (ed.), *The Cry for Justice: An Anthology of the Literature of Social Protest* (Philadephia, 1915)

Sitwell, Osbert, *Laughter in the Next Room* (London, 1977)

Smith, Carmen, *The Blue Cross at War, 1914–18 and 1939–45* (Burford, 1990)

Smith, Helen Zenna, *Not So Quiet . . . Stepdaughters of War* (London, 1930)

Smith, Leonard, *Between Mutiny and Obedience: The Case of the French Fifth Infantry Division during World War I* (Princeton, 1994)

——, *France and the Great War, 1914–1918* (Cambridge, 2002)

Solway, Richard, 'Eugenics and Pronatalism in Wartime Britain', in Richard Wall and Jay Winter (eds.), *The Upheaval of War: Family, Work and Welfare in Europe, 1914–1918* (Cambridge, 1988)

Spiers, E. M., *Haldane: An Army Reformer* (Edinburgh, 1980)

Stephenson, Andrew, 'Palimpsestic Promenades: Memorial Environments and the Urban Consumption of Space in Post-1918 London', in Julie Codell (ed.), *The Political Economy of Art: Making the Nation of Culture* (Cranbury, NJ, 2008)

Sterling, Christopher, *Military Communications: From Ancient Times to the 21st Century* (Santa Barbara, Calif., 2008)

Stevenson, David, *1914–1918: The History of the First World War* (London, 2005)

——, *Armaments and the Coming of War: Europe, 1904–1914* (Oxford, 1996)

——, *Cataclysm: The First World War as Political Tragedy* (New York, 2004)

——, *With our Backs to the Wall: Victory and Defeat in 1918* (London, 2011)

Stevenson, Frances, *Lloyd George: A Diary by Frances Stevenson*, ed. A. J. P. Taylor (London, 1971)

Stewart, Alexander, *A Very Unimportant Officer: Life and Death on the Somme and at Passchendaele* (London, 2009)

Stewart, Sheila, *Lifting the Latch: A Life on the Land, Based on the Life of Mont Abbott of Enstone, Oxfordshire* (Oxford, 1987)

Stibbe, Matthew, *German Anglophobia and the Great War, 1914–1918* (Cambridge, 2001)

Storey, Neil, *Women in the First World War* (Oxford, 2010)

Storrs, Ronald, *The Memoirs of Sir Ronald Storrs* (London, 1937)

Strachan, Hew, *The First World War* (New York, 2005)

——, *The First World War*, vol. I: *To Arms* (Oxford, 2003)

Strachey, Lytton, *Eminent Victorians* (Oxford, 2003; first pub. 1920)

Strong, Paul, *Artillery in the Great War* (Barnsley, 2011)

Summers, Anne, 'Militarism in Britain before the Great War', *History Workshop Journal* 2 (1976)

Sutherland, Katherine, *Jane Austen's Textual Lives: From Aeschylus to Bollywood* (Oxford, 2005)

Symons, Julian, *Horatio Bottomley* (London, 2001; first pub. 1955)

Taylor, A. J. P., *English History 1914–1945* (Oxford, 1965)

——, *The First World War: An Illustrated History* (London, 1963)

———, *The Troublemakers: Dissent over Foreign Policy, 1792–1939* (London, 1957)

Taylor, F. A. J., *The Bottom of the Barrel* (Bath, 1986)

Taylor, S. J., *The Great Outsiders: Northcliffe, Rothermere and the Daily Mail* (London, 1996)

Terraine, John, *The Smoke and the Fire* (London, 1981)

———, *To Win a War: 1918 the Year of Victory* (London, 2008; first pub. 1978)

Thane, Pat and Tanya Evans, *Sinners? Scroungers? Saints? Unmarried Motherhood in Twentieth-Century England* (Oxford, 2012)

Thom, Deborah, *Nice Girls and Rude Girls: Women Workers in World War I* (London, 2000)

Thomas, D. H., *The Guarantee of Belgian Independence and Neutrality in European Diplomacy, 1830s–1930s* (Kingston, RI, 1983)

Thomas, Edward, *The Last Sheaf* (London, 1928)

Thompson, J. Lee, *Politicians, the Press & Propaganda: Lord Northcliffe & the Great War, 1914–1919* (Kent, Ohio, 1999)

Thompson, Julian, *Imperial War Museum Book of the War at Sea, 1914–1918* (London, 2006)

Thomson, Sir Basil, *The Scene Changes* (London 1939)

Todman, Dan, *The Great War: Myth and Memory* (London, 2005)

Toland, Edward, *The Aftermath of Battle, with the Red Cross in France* (London, 1916)

Townshend, Charles, *Easter 1916: The Irish Rebellion* (London, 2005)

Trapman, Albert Henry, *Straight Tips for 'Subs': Hints on Commissions, Allowances, etc.* (London, 1915)

Travers, Tim, 'Command and Leadership Styles in the British Army: The 1915 Gallipoli Model', *Journal of Contemporary History* 29 (1994)

———, *How the War Was Won: Command and Technology in the British Army on the Western Front, 1917–1918* (London, 1992)

———, *The Killing Ground: The British Army, the Western Front, and the Emergence of Modern Warfare, 1900–1918* (London, 1987)

———, 'A Particular Style of Command: Haig and GHQ, 1916–1918', *Journal of Strategic Studies* 10 (1987)

Tuchman, Barbara, *The Guns of August* (New York, 1994; first pub. 1962)

———, *The Zimmermann Telegram* (New York, 1966)

Turner, E. S., *Dear Old Blighty* (London, 1980)

———, *Gallant Gentlemen: A Portrait of the British Officer 1600–1959* (London, 1956)

Turner, John (ed.), *Britain and the First World War* (London, 1980)

———, *British Politics and the Great War: Coalition and Conflict, 1915–1918* (New Haven and London, 1992)

Twinch, Carol, *Women on the Land: Their Story during Two World Wars* (Cambridge, 1990)

Vansittart, Peter, *Voices from the Great War* (London, 1981)

Vaughan, Edwin Campion, *Some Desperate Glory: The Diary of a Young Officer* (Barnsley, 2010; first pub. 1981)

Veitch, Colin, '"Play Up! Play Up! and Win the War!": Football, the Nation and the First World War 1914–1915', *Journal of Contemporary History* 20 (1985)

Verhey, Jeffrey, *The Spirit of 1914: Militarism, Myth, and Mobilization in Germany* (Cambridge, 2000)

Voeltz, Richard, '"Khaki Fever?" The Expansion of the British Girl Guides during the First World War', *Journal of Contemporary History* 27 (1992)

Voigt, F. A., *Combed Out* (London, 1929)

Wade, Aubrey, *The War of the Guns* (London, 1936)

Walbrook, H. M., *Hove and the Great War* (Hove, 1920)

Wall, Richard and Jay Winter (eds.), *The Upheaval of War: Family, Work and Welfare in Europe, 1914–1918* (Cambridge, 1988)

Warner, Philip, *The Battle of Loos* (Ware, 1976)

——, *Kitchener: The Man behind the Legend* (London, 2006)

Watson, Alexander, *Enduring the Great War: Combat, Morale and Collapse in the German and British Armies 1914–1918* (Cambridge, 2008)

—— and Patrick Porter, 'Bereaved and Aggrieved: Combat Motivation and the Ideology of Sacrifice in the First World War', *Historical Research* 83 (2010)

Watson, Frederick, *The Life of Sir Robert Jones* (London, 1934)

Watson, Janet, *Fighting Different Wars: Experience, Memory and the First World War in Britain* (Cambridge, 2004)

——, 'Khaki Girls, VADs, and Tommy's Sisters: Gender and Class in First World War Britain', *International History Review* 19 (1997)

Webb, Beatrice, *The Diaries of Beatrice Webb*, ed. Norman and Jeanne MacKenzie, 4 vols. (London, 2000)

Webb, Thomas E. F., '"Dottyville" – Craiglockhart War Hospital and Shell-Shock Treatment in the First World War', *Journal of the Royal Society of Medicine* 99 (2006)

Weintraub, Stanley, *A Stillness Heard around the World* (London, 1986)

Weiss, Elaine, *Fruits of Victory: The Women's Land Army of America in the Great War* (Washington, DC, 2008)

Wells, H. G., *In the Fourth Year: Anticipations of a World Peace* (London, 1918)

Wessely, Simon, 'Twentieth Century Theories on Combat Motivation and Breakdown', *Journal of Contemporary History* 41 (2006)

Wilkinson, Alan, *The Church of England and the First World War* (London, 1978)

Wilkinson, Roni, *Pals on the Somme 1916* (Barnsley, 2006)

Williamson, Henry, *The Wet Flanders Plain* (London, 1929)

Wilson, A. N., *After the Victorians: The Decline of Britain in the World* (London, 2005)

Wilson, H. H. (ed.), *The Great War* (London, 1914)

Wilson, Jean Moorcroft, *Isaac Rosenberg: The Making of a Great War Poet* (London, 2008)

Wilson, K. M., *The Cabinet Diary of J. A. Pease, 24 July–5 August 1914* (Leeds, 1983)

Wilson, Trevor, 'Britain's "Moral Commitment" to France in August 1914', *History* 64 (1979)

——, 'The Coupon and the British General Election of 1918', *Journal of Modern History* 36 (1964)

——, 'Lord Bryce's Investigation into Alleged German Atrocities in Belgium, 1914–15', *Journal of Contemporary History* 14 (1979)

——, *The Myriad Faces of War: Britain and the Great War, 1914–1918* (London, 2010; first pub. 1986)

—— (ed.), *The Political Diaries of C. P. Scott 1911–1928* (London, 1970)

The 'Win the War' Cook Book (London, 1918)

Winter, Denis, *Death's Men: Soldiers of the Great War* (London, 1979)

Winter, Jay (ed.), *The Experience of World War I* (London, 1988)

——, *The Great War and the British People* (Basingstoke, 1985)

——, *The Legacy of the Great War: Ninety Years On* (Columbia, 2009)

——, 'Nationalism, the Visual Arts and the Myth of War Enthusiasm in 1914', *History of European Ideas* 15 (1992)

——, 'Popular Culture in Wartime Britain', in Aviel Roshwald and Richard Stites (eds.), *European Culture in the Great War: The Arts, Entertainment and Propaganda, 1914–1918* (Cambridge, 1999)

——, *Remembering War: The Great War between Memory and History in the Twentieth Century* (New Haven, 2006)

——, 'Shell-Shock and the Cultural History of the Great War', *Journal of Contemporary History* 35 (2000)

——, *Sites of Memory, Sites of Mourning: The Great War in European Cultural History* (Cambridge, 1995)

—— and Antoine Prost, *The Great War in History: Debates and Controversies, 1914 to the Present* (Cambridge, 2005)

—— and Jean-Louis Robert, *Capital Cities at War: Paris, London, Berlin 1914–1919*, 2 vols. (New York, 2007)

Winters, Frank, 'Exaggerating the Efficacy of Diplomacy: The Marquis of Lansdowne's "Peace Letter" of November 1917', *International History Review* 32 (2010)

Wodehouse, P. G., *The Swoop! or, How Clarence Saved England* (London, 1908)

Wohl, Robert, *The Generation of 1914* (London, 1980)

Wolffe, John (ed.), *Religion in History: Conflict, Conversion and Coexistence* (Manchester, 2004)

Wood, Francis Derwent, 'Masks for Facial Wounds', *Lancet* 189 (1917)

Woodward, David, 'Did Lloyd George Starve the British Army of Men Prior to the German Offensive of 21 March 1918?', *Historical Journal* 27 (1984)

Woollacott, Angela, ' "Khaki Fever" and its Control: Gender, Class, Age and Sexual Morality on the British Homefront in the First World War', *Journal of Contemporary History* 29 (1994)

——, *On Her their Lives Depend: Munitions Workers in the Great War* (Berkeley, 1994)

Wright, Patrick, *Tank: The Progress of a Monstrous War Machine* (London, 2000)

Wylly, H. C., *The Green Howards in the Great War* (Richmond, Yorkshire, 1926)

Index

Ranks and titles are generally the highest mentioned in the text